Year	Period (in Japanese History)	
900	*Heian* (平安時代)	907 Tan[illegible]
		962 Holy Roman Empire established
		979 China united under Sung dynasty
1000		1066 William of Normandy invades England
		1096 First Crusade
1100		
1200	*Kamakura* (鎌倉時代)	1206 Genghis Khan unites Mongols
		1215 Magna Carta signed in England
1300		1260 Kublai Khan establishes Yuan dynasty in China
	Northern & Southern Courts (南北朝時代)	1339 Hundred Years' War between England and France
		1368 Ming dynasty in China
1400	*Muromachi* (室町時代)	1440 Johann Gutenberg's printing press
1500		1492 Columbus discovers America
	Warring States (戦国時代)	1517 Martin Luther starts Reformation in Germany
1600	*Azuchi-Momoyama* (安土・桃山時代)	1581 Netherlands become independent
	Edo (江戸時代)	1616 Manchus overrun China, establishing Ching dynasty in 1636
		1642 Puritan Revolution in England
1700		1688 Protestant "Glorious Revolution" in England
		1776 American independence
		1789 French Revolution
1800		1840 Opium War
		1861 American Civil War
1900	*Meiji* (明治)	1894 Sino-Japanese War
		1904 Russo-Japanese War
	Taishou (大正)	1914 World War I
	Shouwa (昭和)	1939 World War II
	Heisei (平成)	1991 Soviet Union is dissolved

Japanese Periods and Chronology of World History

Year	Period (in Japanese History)	Events
BC 300	*Joumon* (縄文時代)	4000 Mesopotamian civilization 3000 Indus and Hwang Ho civilizations 1500 Chinese Shang dynasty 1200 City-states emerge in Greece 334 Alexander the Great crosses the Dardanelles
0	*Yayoi* (弥生時代)	221 China united under the Ch'in dynasty 27 Roman Empire consolidated 4 Birth of Jesus Christ
AD 200		25 China united under Eastern Han dynasty 220 Three Kingdoms (Wei, Shu Han, Wu) period in China 226 Sassanids rule Persia
300 400 500	*Kofun* (古墳時代)	313 Constantine the Great embraces Christianity 375 Germanic migration 395 Roman Empire partitioned 439 Northern and Southern dynasties in China 486 Establishment of Frank kingdom 589 China united under Sui dynasty
600 700	*Asuka* (飛鳥時代)	610 Islam founded 618 Sui dynasty replaced by the Tang in China
	Nara (奈良時代)	755 Rebellions of An Lu-shan and Shih Ssu-ming in Tang China
800	*Heian* (平安時代)	800 Charlemagne crowned in Rome 862 Novgorod, predecessor of the Russian nation, founded

JAPAN

日本タテヨコ

Tatami are sturdy straw mats used for flooring in the typical Japanese home, comparable to Western carpeting. Made of a thick layer of bundled straw covered with a finely woven rush matting, tatami are meant to be walked on barefoot. Shoes and slippers alike are removed before entering a tatami room.

畳は、日本住宅の床上に敷くもので、欧米で言えばじゅうたんのようなものに当たる。わらで作った厚床の上にい草などで織った畳表を付けたもので、畳の上では靴、スリッパなしで歩く。

和英対訳 改訂第4版

AS IT IS

A BILINGUAL GUIDE
FOURTH EDITION

Gakken

JAPAN AS IT IS

Published by GAKKEN CO., LTD.
4-40-5, Kami-ikedai, Ota-ku, Tokyo 145-8502, Japan

Printed in Japan.

First published 1985
Second edition 1990
Third edition 1997
Fourth edition 2002

Printed in Japan

まえがき

この本は，外国の人に日本を紹介したいと思っている日本人や，日本に関心をもち日本をよく知りたいと考えている外国の人たちのためにつくった。特に日本語を学習する人には，日本についての幅広い知識が欠かせないので，大いに役に立つであろうと確信している。また，ビジネスで外国の人と付き合うときにも，日本をもっと知ってもらうことで好結果を期待できると思うので，ぜひプレゼントとして活用していただきたい。

初版，改訂第２版，改訂第３版とも幸い好評をもって迎えられ，世の中の激しい動きに対応するため，記述の変更や統計的数字を最新の数値に改め，ここに，第４版を発行する運びとなった。また，この版では英文中の日本語をすべてイタリック体で示すことにし，日本語の長音の表記に工夫を試みた。

本書は初版以来，①私たち日本人にはわかりきった日常的なことが，外国の人にはわからないことがあるので，それを解説する。②日本独特のものの見方や考え方を，できるだけその根源までさかのぼって解説する。③解説をわかりやすく客観的にするために，最新のデータを紹介し，また，可能な限り他国文化との比較を行う。④どこからでも読めるように，１項目１ページにする，を基本方針としている。

取り上げたテーマは，日本の政治・経済をはじめ，能・歌舞伎・相撲といった伝統文化はもちろん，日本人のものの考え方や行動のパターン，動物や植物のイメージといった分野にまで及ぶ。いわば，これは小型の日本百科事典であり，日本のことならなんでもこれ１冊でほぼ間に合うようになっている。

初版～第３版ともに，多くの読者から，励ましや，ご質問，ご叱正を頂戴した。この版についても最新・最良の内容を目指して努力をしたが，まだ不十分のところもあると思う。どのようなことでもご教示いただければ幸いである。

最後に，制作にあたっては，限られたスペースの中に必要な情報をできるだけ盛り込むという難しい執筆にあたられた方々や，その盛りだくさんの内容を日本のことを知らない人のために１ページの英文に翻訳するという至難の作業に取り組んでくださったF.ウレマン氏及びD.テルキ氏に心からお礼を申し上げる。

2002年１月
学習研究社・辞典編集部

This book was created for two major audiences: Japanese who want to explain Japan in English and English readers who want to know more about Japan. Among the latter, people studying Japanese should find it especially helpful because it provides a wide-ranging introduction to some of the many cultural and other informational aspects that underlie so much Japanese discourse. It is also a perfect gift for non-Japanese business people who know that understanding Japan better will help them in this very competitive market.

The first edition was written in 1985, the second in 1990 and the third in 1997. All were so well received that we have massively updated the time sensitive entries and produced a fourth edition. In this edition, we continue use of the romanization format that transliterates the *kana* phonetics that Japanese is written in. This emphasizes the elongation of vowel sounds—something that does not make a meaning difference in English but is crucial in Japanese—and gives you the information you would need to get the *kanji* on a Japanese-capable word-processing system. Yet even as the content has been updated, the basic premises have remained unchanged: (a) to elucidate the information and assumptions that most Japanese take for granted and to make them easily accessible to non-Japanese, (b) to explain distinctively Japanese customs and practices so that they can be not just accepted but understood, (c) to draw upon the latest statistics and international comparisons so that the explanations are objective and easy to understand, and (d) to make each entry complete in and of itself so that the reader can read them in order of interest with no loss of understanding.

Entries have been provided not only for the obvious areas of economics, politics, and such cultural themes as *nou* (noh), *kabuki*, and *sumou* (sumo) but also for Japanese thought and behavior patterns and the characteristics associated with various plants and animals. As a result, this is a very comprehensive introduction to Japan—almost a mini-encyclopedia—and it may well be the only all-around reference you need.

The earlier editions drew numerous comments, questions, and even corrections from readers, and this fourth edition is the better as a result. While every effort has been made to incorporate this feedback and to include the most useful information possible, we realize that different people will have different resources and perspectives, and we hope you will please feel free to contact us if you notice anything that needs mentioning.

Finally, we would like to thank the many authors who worked hard to pack so much information into so little space—as well as Fred Uleman and Dave Telke for producing translations that fit our space constraints and still remain informative for readers new to Japan and things Japanese.

この本で用いた
英文中のローマ字表記について

日本語の「アー」「イー」「ウー」「エー」「オー」の「ー」の音を含む語を英語としてアルファベットで表記する場合は，一般的には，Tokyo(東京)や Osaka(大阪)のようにその音を無視するか，あるいは noh(能)のようにhで表す方式が使われる。また，ふつうのローマ字表記では，この音を kōtsū(交通)や hōhō(方法)のように記号を付けて表記することが多い。

本書でも，第2版まではこのローマ字表記方式を採用していた。しかし，これらの表示方法では日本語を学習する外国の人には，この「ー」の部分が実際の発音上1拍になることや，かな文字の表記では「ああ」「いい」「うう」「えい，(ええ)」「おう，おお」となることはわかりにくい。(「ええ」は，外来語以外には日本語でほとんど使われない)

日本語学習者が英文を読み進むときに，文中に綴られている日本語を意識し，そのかな文字表記を知ることができることは重要であると思う。そうした問題を解決するために，この本では，英文中の日本語はすべてイタリック体で示し，上記の「ー」の部分をすべてかな文字の表記にあわせることにした。

例	「アー」	おかあさん(お母さん)	*okaasan*
	「イー」	おにいさん(お兄さん)	*oniisan*
	「ウー」	ふうしゅう(風習)	*fuushuu*
	「エー」	けいかく(計画)	*keikaku*
	「オー」	こうつう(交通)	*koutsuu*
	「オー」	おおきい(大きい)	*ookii*

なお，英文中における日本語をイタリック体にし，さらに「ー」の部分を *aa*, *ii*, *uu*, *ei*, *ou*, *oo* のようにしてかな文字表記にあわせるという方針で統一するため，地名・人名などの固有名詞にもすべてこのルールを適用した。しかし，ふつうの英語表記とは異なる *Toukyou*(東京), *Oosaka*(大阪), *juudou*(柔道)などの表記にとまどう読者もいることを考え，英語で一般的になっている語については，*Toukyou*(Tokyo)，*Oosaka*(Osaka)，*juudou*(judo)のように並記することにした。

ただし，本書に掲載してある地図では，その地名については，上記の方式ではなく一般的な英語表記を採用した。

A Note about the Romanization

As noted in the main text, Japanese is not normally written using the English alphabet. Instead, there are ideographic *kanji* characters and two phonetic *kana* scripts. However, these are commonly "romanized" for the convenience of people who do not read Japanese.

In romanizing, the problem is to find a method that both enables the beginner to approximate the Japanese sound and enables the more proficient student to learn something of the language through this very artificial medium. In doing the romanization for this book, we have stuck with most of the conventions. シ(pronounced "she") is written with an "*h*" as "*shi*" and not as "*si*." Likewise, チis "*chi*" and not "*ti*." And like the other systems, we have used the letters a, i, u, e, and o to represent the five vowel sounds. (With this, of course, comes the standard plea to please remember that Japanese vowel sounds are consistently the same. Thus "*a*" is always like the a in father, whether it is in ba, ta, sa, or anything else; "*i*" is always like the ey in key or the ee in bee; "*u*" is like the o of who; "*e*" like the e in bet; and "*o*" like the o in hope. If you see a "be," resist the temptation to give it an English pronunciation. "*Tobe*" (the imperative of the verb "to fly") is not the same as Shakespeare's "to be or not to be." Rather, it is more like "toe bay."

Quite aside from these sounds, Japanese is very different from English in that all syllables are the same sound length. Spoken Japanese is a very metronomic language. True, there is some syncopation with unvoiced beats when a consonant is repeated (e.g., *natta*) and the first occurrence is unvoiced in a kind of stammer effect that is not stammering, but the language is basically metronomic. Thus prolonging a vowel sound in a word—holding it or repeating it for two beats—makes the word sound like a different word.

Obasan (aunt) and *obaasan* (grandmother) are very different. In English, we lengthen syllables for clarity. Doing that in Japanese is counterproductive.

Because vowel length is so important in Japanese, and because it does not exist significantly in English, we have adopted a somewhat radical means of indicating vowel elongation in this text: we have transliterate the words exactly as they would be written in Japanese. Thus what the rest of the world knows as Tokyo has been given as *Toukyou* because these are doubled sounds in Japanese. (In some cases where a term is already established as English [e.g., judo and Tokyo], we also give the English version.) This is not prolonging the syllable. It is adding another syllable that has the vowel sound. In effect, we have dropped macrons—which most people tend to ignore—and been very intrusive in emphasizing vowel repetition. ("O" is a special case in that it is repeated either as "*oo*" or as "*ou*" depending upon the character used in the word.) In every case, we are transcribing what the *kana* would be—and this is also what you would input on a Japanese-capable word processor to get the desired *kanji*.

The only exception is on maps, where we have used the common English names.

Contents

N.B.

文中の＊印の項目は，各パートの最後にあるNotesのページに，解説あるいは写真・イラストがあることを示しています。
Asterisks in the text indicate words that are further explained in the notes at the end of each Part.

Editorial Staff

企画・制作
学研・辞典編集部

執筆協力(五十音順)

相川二元	Aikawa Tsugumoto	杉戸清樹	Sugito Seiju
青柳亮	Aoyagi Ryou	清野真智子	Seino Machiko
阿部実	Abe Minoru	高橋美幸	Takahashi Miyuki
池本薫	Ikemoto Kaoru	竹内二郎	Takeuchi Jirou
石井美穂子	Ishii Mihoko	田中省二	Tanaka Seiji
井尻千男	Ijiri Kazuo	千野境子	Chino Keiko
荻田守	Ogita Mamoru	中村洋一	Nakamura Youichi
奥西峻介	Okunishi Shunsuke	堀内克明	Horiuchi Katsuaki
木村利行	Kimura Toshiyuki	本多空次郎	Honda Sorajirou
佐草一優	Sakusa Kazumasa	松田瑞穂	Matsuda Mizuho
佐藤豊	Satou Yutaka	山崎千秋	Yamazaki Chiaki

翻訳
(株)ジャパン・リサーチ　Japan Research Inc.　テルキ デイブ　Dave Telke

デザイン
日下充典　Kusaka Mitsunori

イラスト
杵淵亮一　Kinebuchi Ryouichi
長岡慶八郎　Nagaoka Keihachirou

編集協力
石井紀子/遠藤由紀子/沖田真知子/椛沢洋一/長川恵/原田立/学研・調査資料室

写真・取材協力
学研・写真部/学研・調査資料室
原田勤(表紙カバー)/共同通信社(p.165花見)/慶応義塾大学考古学研究室(p.68縄文式尖底深鉢)/東京大学総合研究資料館(p.68弥生式壺形土器)/宮内庁(p.69聖徳太子及二王子像)/法隆寺(p.69釈迦三尊像,p.69金堂壁画,p.308金堂)/正倉院宝物(p.69鳥毛立女屛風)/平等院(p.70鳳凰堂)/神護寺(p.70源頼朝像)/東大寺(p.71金剛力士像)/鹿苑寺金閣(p.71)/長興寺(p.72織田信長像)/畠山記念館(p.72豊臣秀吉像)/毎日新聞社(p.166マージャン,p.310落語)/龍安寺(p.308方丈庭園)/伊勢神宮(p.308)/池坊家元池坊専永(p.310立華)/古流松藤会会長池田昌弘(p.310生花)/小原流家元小原豊雲(p.310盛花)/勅使河原和風会会頭勅使河原和風(p.310投入)/東京国立博物館(p.312埴輪)/吉徳コレクション(p.312嵯峨人形)/吉徳コレクション(p.312木目込人形)/斎藤良輔(p.312鳴子こけし)/全生庵(p.343円山応挙「幽霊」)

PART 1

日本と日本人
JAPAN AND THE JAPANESE

自然環境と国民性や文化のあり方とは，深くかかわりがある。日本の場合も，置かれた自然の条件から影響を大きく受けている。

***位置**

日本はアジア大陸の東岸沖に位置する島国である。6800以上の島のうち，主なものは北海道，本州，四国，九州，沖縄の５つ。海を隔てて北は樺太（サハリン）・シベリア，西は朝鮮半島・中国と隣接している。この位置は，大陸の政治的変動に巻き込まれることなく，大陸の文化を取り入れられる有利さをもっているため，日本は建国以来，固有の文化を残しながら，外来文化を摂取し，独自の融合文化を築いてくることができた。

国土と人口

全国土の４分の３が樹木に覆われた山地である。山は高くなく，本州中央部に標高2000～3000m級の，日本アルプスと総称される３つの山脈がそびえているほかは，2000mを超すのはわずかである。火山は著(いちじる)しく多く，主要なものだけで150を数える。大きな平野がないので，*河川(かせん)は短く急流を成している。日本列島は地殻変動帯に属しているため地震が多い。

面積は約38万㎢。イギリスの１倍半，アメリカのカリフォルニア州とほぼ同じである。人口はアメリカの約半分，１億2700万人。うち70％が関東南部から北九州に至る地域に住む。ベルギーやオランダのほうが人口密度は高いが，居住可能面積で見れば日本が上である。

気候

中緯度に位置して気候は温暖。中央部の東京の年平均気温は15.6℃である。列島の北端から南端まで3000㎞あるので温度差があり，年平均気温は６～22℃。雨は多く，年間降水量が4000㎜に達する地域もある。早春から夏の植物生育期，特に６月から７月の梅雨期にはよく雨が降る。夏と秋に年数回は襲来する台風も多量の雨をもたらす。

日本列島は規則正しく季節風の支配を受け，冬は寒帯気団が南下し，夏は熱帯気団が北上する。両気団に覆われる冬と夏は各数か月と長く，季節風交替の谷間にあたる春と秋は各２か月程度である。

冬は，北西季節風が吹いて雪が降り続く日本海側と，晴天が多く乾燥した太平洋側と対照的な天候分布になる。本州南部の夏は暑く，東南アジア並みかそれ以上で，典型的な照葉樹林帯の気候である。夏の３～４か月間，東南アジアなどと同じ気候ということは，日本の農耕文化の基層となったイモ・イネをはじめ，南方系の農作物が熱帯気団とともに北上した可能性があるということであり，この点が日本文化の基本的性格を南方型とする有力な根拠になっている。

Geography and Climate

In Japan as in any country, the nation's culture and national character have been largely molded by geography and climate.

Location*

Japan is an island nation off the east coast of Asia. Among its 6,800-plus islands, the five major ones are *Hokkaidou*, *Honshuu*, *Shikoku*, *Kyuushuu*, and *Okinawa*. Bordered across the seas on the north by *Karafuto* (Sakhalin) and Siberia and on the west by the Korean peninsula and China, Japan is far enough from Asia to have escaped involvement in continental upheavals and yet close enough to have benefited from continental culture. With unbroken cultural continuity, Japan has been able to adapt foreign influences into its own cultural development.

Land and Population

Japan is a mountainous land 75% covered by forests. Except for three ranges of mountains (collectively called the Japan Alps) 2-3,000 meters or more above sea level in central *Honshuu*, few of Japan's mountains exceed 2,000 meters. Many of the mountains are volcanic, and there are 150 important volcanoes. With few large plains, Japan's swiftly flowing rivers* tend to be short. Large-scale plate movements cause frequent earthquakes.

With about 380,000 square kilometers of land area, Japan is 50% larger than Great Britain or roughly the size of California, yet its population is over 127 million—half that of the United States. About 70% of the people live in the area from *Toukyou* (Tokyo) to *Kitakyuushuu*. Belgium and the Netherlands have higher overall population densities, but Japan has the highest population per arable land area.

Climate

Located in the middle latitudes, Japan has a generally mild climate. The average year-round temperature for centrally situated Tokyo is 15.6°C. However Japan runs north-south for 3,000km and average year-round temperatures vary greatly from 6°C to 22°C. Japan gets a considerable amount of rain, in some areas up to 4,000 mm per year. There is considerable rainfall from early spring throughout the summer growing season, particularly during the rainy season from mid-June to mid- July. Late summer and early autumn typhoons also bring heavy rains.

Japan has four distinct seasons, with the arctic air mass moving down from the north in winter, and the tropical air mass moving up from the south in summer. Winter and summer each last roughly four months, and spring and autumn each approximately two months.

Northwest winds in winter bring heavy snow to the Sea of Japan side of the archipelago, while on the leeward or Pacific side winter days are sunny and dry. Summers from southern *Honshuu* south are hot and jungle-like, comparable to, or even surpassing, Southeast Asia. Given the similarities in climate, it is possible to imagine that agriculture—including taro and rice, which form the basis of Japanese agriculture—was carried northward into Japan. This in turn provides a strong argument for saying that the underlying nature of Japanese culture follows the same mold as the cultures of Southeast Asia.

本州

国土の中では最大の231,045km²の面積をもつ。首都東京をはじめ，横浜・大阪・名古屋の4大都市があるほか，政治・文化・産業などあらゆる面で中心的役割を担っている。

島の中心部を北から南西にかけていくつもの山地が連なり，太平洋側は比較的温暖であり，日本海側は冬の積雪が多い。島の南側は多数の大都市があって，工業地帯を形成している。北部（東北地方）や中央部の北側（北陸地方）は，北海道と並ぶ重要な米の産地である。代表的貿易港である横浜・神戸，日本最高峰の富士山，日本最大の湖の琵琶湖も本州にある。

北海道

面積は本州に次ぐ83,451km²で，本州の北方にある。寒さが厳しく，夏も比較的涼しい。地形は雄大で，規模の大きい山地・火山・平野がある。平野では大型機械を使う農業や酪農が盛んで，山地は針葉樹の美林が多い。かつては漁業も盛んであったが，アメリカやロシアが200カイリ経済水域を設けて以来不振である。本州とは海底トンネルで結ばれている。

四国

面積18,783km²で，三方を本州南西部と九州に囲まれている。中央部に標高1000～2000mの山地があり，人口は海岸部に分散されて，山地の反対側との交通は不便である。瀬戸内海に面する北側は降水量が少なく，工業都市が連続する。太平洋に面する南側は温暖で降水量が多く，漁業や野菜の促成栽培が盛んである。本州との間に3ルートの架橋（かきょう）があり，最後の1つは1999年に完成した。

九州

面積42,154km²で，本州の南西にある。火山が多く，中央部に東西16km，南北24km，周囲120kmという世界最大のクレーターをもつ阿蘇山がある。気候は温暖で降水量が多く，南部は冬も暖かい。毎年8，9月にいくつもの台風が通過し，たびたび大きな被害を受ける。北部は工業都市が多く，南部は農業が主要な産業である。本州とは海底トンネルや橋で結ばれている。

沖縄

面積2,265km²で，東西約1000km，南北約400kmの海域に分布する大小の島々で形成されている。気候は温暖で，亜熱帯気候に覆われている。澄んだ海には珊瑚礁が発達しており，国内有数の観光地である。1945年から27年間，アメリカの直接統治下にあったが，72年に返還された。現在，在日米軍基地の約75%が配置されている。

The Main Islands

Honshuu

At 231,045km², this is the largest of Japan's many islands. It includes the four largest cities—the capital city, Tokyo, plus *Yokohama, Oosaka* (Osaka), and *Nagoya*—and is the political, cultural, and economic heart of Japan.

The mountain range running north-south down the island's spine separates *Honshuu* into a Pacific side and a Sea of Japan side. The Pacific side is generally mild, but the Sea of Japan side has heavy snow in winter. Southern *Honshuu* has many big cities and is heavily industrialized. The northern (*Touhoku*) and north-central (*Hokuriku*) areas are major rice growing regions. Japan's main international ports (*Yokohama* and *Koube*), the highest mountain (Mt *Fuji*), and the largest lake (*Biwa-ko*) are all on *Honshuu*.

Hokkaidou

This is the second-largest island—83,451km². It is fiercely cold in winter and cool even in summer. Yet it is very open land with impressive volcanoes and sweeping plains. Large-scale mechanized farming and dairy farming thrive on its broad expanses, and the hills are covered with beautiful conifers. Fishing used to be a major industry, but it has fallen into decline with the declaration of 200 nautical mile economic zones by the United States and Russia. *Hokkaidou* is linked to Honshuu by an underwater tunnel.

Shikoku

Only 18,783km² in area, *Shikoku* faces *Honshuu* and *Kyuushuu* to the north, east and west, and the Pacific Ocean to the south. In its center are mountains rising, 1,000～2,000 meters above sea level, and the population is scattered along the coastal lowlands with passage difficult from one side of the island to the other. The northern shore along the *Seto* Inland Sea gets very little rain and has a number of industrial towns. By contrast, the Pacific shore is warm with abundant rainfall, and is heavily into produce farming and fishing. Three bridge routes connect *Shikoku* to *Honshuu*, the last of them completed in 1999.

Kyuushuu

Kyuushuu lies southwest of *Honshuu*, with an area of 42,154km². It has numerous volcanoes, among them Mt *Aso*, which boasts the world's largest crater, measuring 16km east-west, 24km north-south, and 120km around. The climate is warm and rainfall abundant. Even winters are warm. Yet it suffers considerable typhoon damage every August and September. Northern *Kyuushuu* is mainly industrial while the south is agricultural. It is linked to *Honshuu* by underwater tunnels and bridges.

Okinawa

The islands of *Okinawa* are scattered over an area measuring about 1,000km east-west and 400km north-south, their total land area coming to 2,265km². The weather is warm and the climate semi-tropical. *Okinawa*'s clear waters have world-class coral reefs, and this is one of Japan's most popular tourist destinations. Occupied along with the rest of Japan in 1945, *Okinawa* was kept under American administration even after the Occupation ended in 1952 and did not revert to Japan until 1972. Yet even now, about 75% of U.S. military areas and facilities in Japan are in *Okinawa*.

日本の歴史の大きな特徴として，次の点を挙げることができる。
①原始の時代から現代まで，1万年の間，在来文化を一変するような他民族との大規模な融合がなく，独自の文化を守り続けていること
②その一方で，古くから外国の文化を熱心に取り入れて日本化し，文明の一流の水準に達していること

原始・古代（およそ1万年前～紀元後11世紀）

小国の乱立，国土の統一を経て，中国の制度に範をとった*律令（りつりょう）国家が成立する。しかし，次第にその矛盾が広がって地方政治が乱れ，武士団が成長していく。

• ***縄文（じょうもん）時代**　日本列島には洪積世の時代から人間が生活していたが，日本人種および日本語の原型が成立したと見られているのは，およそ1万年前から紀元前3世紀ごろまでの縄文期である。当時の人々は，数人から10人が1戸の竪穴（たてあな）住居に住み，生活を狩猟，漁労，採集に頼り，貧富・階級差のない社会を構成していたと言われていたが，青森県の三内丸山遺跡で長期的に営まれた大規模な集落が発掘され，イメージの転換がせまられている。

• ***弥生（やよい）時代**　紀元前3世紀ごろ，朝鮮から九州北部に稲作と金属器使用の技術が渡来した。稲作技術は，生産を増大し，貧富・身分の差を生み，農村共同体を政治集団化するなど，画期的な社会変化をもたらした。農耕に伴う信仰，儀礼，習俗なども広がり，日本文化の原型が形作られた。弥生時代は紀元後3世紀ごろまで続き，後期には東北地方にまで及んだ。

• ***古墳（こふん）時代**　紀元後4世紀半ばごろ，乱立していた小国が大和（やまと）政権によって統一された。統一の進展とともに，*前方後円墳によって代表される古墳が地方に広まった。この時代は中国から多くの知識，技術が流入した時代で，4世紀に大和政権は朝鮮半島へ進出して，大陸の高度な物質文化を輸入し，5世紀には朝鮮半島から渡来人が鉄器生産・製陶・機織り・金属工芸・土木などの諸技術を伝え，中国の文字である漢字の使用も始まった。6世紀に*儒教の摂取が本格的になり，仏教も伝来した。

7世紀に*聖徳太子が政治の刷新を図り，*大化の改新を契機に，天皇を中心とした中央集権国家の建設を目ざした。この場合も，中国の隋（ずい），唐を手本にしたが，このころから大陸文化の摂取にさらに積極的になり，9世紀末までに遣隋使，遣唐使を10数回も派遣することになる。

Japanese History (1)

Two characteristic features of Japanese history are (i) for over 10,000 years there have been no disrupting influxes of outside peoples, and (ii) an eagerness to borrow ideas and technologies from other cultures and adapt them for its own use.

Prehistory and Ancient History (c.8,000 BC to 11th century AD)
This period covers the early formation of tribes, their consolidation into scattered political entities, the establishment of a centralized government administered through the *ritsuryou** system adapted from China, and the gradual emergence of a powerful military caste.

- ***Joumon* Period*** (c.8,000 to c.300 BC) Humans have occupied the Japanese archipelago since the diluvial epoch, but the biological and linguistic roots of the modern Japanese are believed to have developed during the long period referred to as the *Joumon* period. *Joumon* people lived in pit houses with anywhere from a few to a dozen people per house. They hunted, fished and gathered food, and it was long thought that the society was classless and equalitarian with no stratification into ruler and ruled, rich and poor. However, a large *Joumon* village being excavated in *Sannai Maruyama* (*Aomori* prefecture) is revealing many new findings that do not fit the old theories.
- ***Yayoi* Period*** (c. 300 BC to c. 300 AD) Some time in the 3rd century BC, wet-paddy rice agriculture and metal-working technology were introduced into northern *Kyuushuu* from the Korean peninsula. The agrarian life which resulted marked a significant social change with the creation of classes and stratification by wealth and poverty within the political community. Agrarian values, ceremonies, and customs were developed and spread to form the rudiments of modern Japanese culture. By the 3rd century AD, *Yayoi* culture had extended as far as northeastern Japan.
- ***Kofun* Period*** (c.300-710) Around the middle of the 4th century, independent tribes scattered throughout Japan were consolidated under the *Yamato* clan. This shift toward a unified state is marked by the construction of large keyhole-shaped tomb mounds,* *kofun*, for the ruling elite. Knowledge and technology from China spread in this period. While the several forays which the *Yamato* mounted against the Korean peninsula were unsuccessful, they enhanced Japanese access to mainland amenities as 5th-century Korean immigrants introduced new techniques in iron making, potting, weaving, metal working, and civil engineering. Chinese writing was adopted in the 5th century, as were Confucian* and Buddhist teachings in the 6th century.

In the 7th century, Prince *Shoutoku*,* regent under Empress *Suiko*, further centralized the state and strengthened the imperial authority. His efforts were crystallized in the *Taika* Reforms* instituted by his successors in emulation of the (Chinese) Sui and Tang dynasties. Envoys were dispatched repeatedly to China well into the 9th century.

•奈良時代　710年に都を平城京(今の奈良市および近郊)に定めて律令(りつりょう)国家の隆盛期を迎えるが，農民の窮乏(きゅうぼう)，浮浪民の増加，*荘園(しょうえん)の拡大による*公地公民制の事実上の崩壊など，矛盾が出はじめる。この時代は国が仏教を厚く保護したため，仏教文化，とりわけ仏教美術が栄えた。日本最初の仏教文化である7世紀初めの*飛鳥(あすか)文化，人間的な若々しさに特色がある7世紀後半の*白鳳(はくほう)文化，唐の最盛期の文化の影響を受け，写実的で豊かな人間感情を示す8世紀中期の*天平(てんぴょう)文化などがそれである。

仏教美術と並ぶ，この時代の文化上の金字塔は『万葉集』である。『万葉集』は8世紀半ばまでの約400年間の，庶民から天皇に至る約4500首の歌を集めた歌集で，上代日本人の素朴な生活感情が率直に表現され，今でも多くの日本人に愛されている。このほか，現存する最古の歴史書『古事記』(712年)，最古の勅撰(ちょくせん)歴史書『日本書紀』(720年)，最古の漢詩集『懐風藻(かいふうそう)』(751年)などもこの時代の遺産である。

•平安時代　8世紀末に平安京(今の京都市)へ都を移し，律令体制の再建を図ったが，公地公民制が崩れて国家は財政難に陥った。894年を最後に遣唐使を中止したので，大陸文化の大量輸入も途絶えた。

10〜11世紀に*藤原氏が政権を独占し，荘園を経済的基盤として全盛を誇るが，地方政治の混乱によって治安が乱れ，武士団が成長していった。11世紀末に藤原氏に対抗して*院政が始まると，武士が中央政界に進出してくる。

平安時代は*国風文化を特色とする。9世紀にはまだ唐の影響を受けて，*密教と漢文学の弘仁・貞観文化が栄えたが，大陸との直接交流がなくなった10世紀以降になると，日本独特の貴族文化が生まれる。その代表が最初の勅撰和歌集『古今和歌集』(10世紀初め)，世界最古の長編小説『源氏物語』(11世紀初めごろ)，随筆『枕草子(まくらのそうし)』(1000年ごろ)などの文芸作品群である。これらの作品は，漢字から日本人が独自に作り出した「仮名(かな)」で書かれており，感性的な和語を書き表す「仮名」の発明があって初めて生まれたものである。「仮名」の出現により，女性の文学の世界への進出は目覚ましかった。

仏教は現世利益を図る密教とともに，10世紀後半から来世での幸福を説く*浄土教が流行した。建築・絵画・書・彫刻など，美術・工芸面でも国風化の傾向が著しかった。

• ***Nara* Period** (710-794) In 710 AD the capital was moved to *Heijoukyou* (present day *Nara* and environs) and the *ritsuryou* system flourished. But discrepancies gradually appeared with the increasing number of impoverished peasants and vagrants, and the effectual collapse of the *kouchi-koumin** concept brought on by the ever-expanding *shouen**.

Buddhist culture and art flourished under official patronage. The artistic and cultural legacy of the period goes from the early 7th century *Asuka* culture* through the vibrant *Hakuhou* culture* of the latter 7th century and culminates in the Tang-influenced humanistic *Tenpyou* culture* of the mid-8th century.

The *Man'youshuu* collection of about 4,500 verses by Japanese of all classes composed over a nearly 400-year span dates from this period. This eloquent record is still widely read and admired. Other important works are *Kojiki* (Record of Ancient Matters), written around 712 and the oldest Japanese history extant; 720's *Nihon Shoki* (Chronicle of Japan), the oldest known official history of Japan; and *Kaifuusou* (Fond Recollections of Poetry), the first (751) anthology of Chinese poetry by Japanese poets.

• ***Heian* Period** (794-1185) The capital was moved to *Heiankyou* (Kyoto) at the end of the 8th century and an attempt made to restore the *ritsuryou* system, but the impotence of the *kouchi-koumin* philosophy plunged the imperial government into financial difficulties. Missions to Tang China were stopped after 894 and the inflow of mainland culture dried up.

The *Fujiwara** family consolidated its grip on power in the 10th and 11th centuries, and the *shouen* became accepted as basic to the economy. The court's inability to control outlying regions led to widespread unrest and the emergence of a powerful warrior class. By the end of the 11th century, the *Fujiwara* regency had been thwarted by the *insei** system and the warrior class had become increasingly influential in central politics.

The *Heian* period is notable for its natively inspired art and culture.* In the 9th century, Tang influence was still strong, esoteric Buddhist sects* flourished, and *kanbun* writing in the Chinese style remained the leading form of literary expression. By the 10th century, however, a uniquely Japanese culture developed as shown by the first official anthology of *waka* poetry, the *Kokin Wakashuu* (Collection from Ancient and Modern Times) ; the *Tale of Genji*, recognized as the world's first novel; and the *Makura no Soushi* (Pillow Book), a collection of essays—all of which were written in the Japanese *kana* phonetic syllabary developed from Chinese characters or *kanji*. The invention of *kana* vastly facilitated the written expression of Japanese sensibilities and opened literature to women authors.

Going into the latter half of the *Heian* period, esoteric Buddhist sects introduced from China were joined by the natively inspired *Joudo* sect* and the trend toward native expression continued in the arts and literature.

中世(12～16世紀)
今までの支配者，王朝貴族に代わって新興の武士が政権を握り，封建制度を築き上げていく。

• 鎌倉時代　12世期末，*源頼朝(よりとも)が鎌倉に幕府を開いて武家政権が誕生した。それから1世紀半の間，東の鎌倉の武士は，西の京都の公家(くげ)と対立しながら，封建社会を形成していった。13世紀後半，モンゴル軍が2度にわたって九州北部に来襲したが，武士団の奮戦と大暴風雨のおかげでこれを退けた。しかし，これを契機に幕府の武士統制が困難となり，幕府は滅亡の道を歩むことになる。

文化面では，従来の公家文化を基礎に，動的，写実的で素朴な独特の武家文化が育っていった。宗教面では，*法然(ほうねん)・*親鸞(しんらん)・*日蓮などの名僧によって鎌倉仏教が生まれた。関東の武士には12世紀に宋から伝えられた禅宗が重んじられた。芸術にも新傾向が起こり，*鎌倉時代初期の彫刻は力強い写実性，豊かな人間味の表出で新風を巻き起こした。文学では武士の好みを反映して『平家物語』(原作は13世紀初め)のような軍記物語の傑作が出た。その他，随筆集『方丈記』(13世紀)，『徒然草(つれづれぐさ)』(14世紀)などが著された。

• 南北朝時代　後醍醐天皇は鎌倉幕府を滅亡させたが，足利尊氏(たかうじ)と対立し，京都の朝廷(北朝)と吉野(今の奈良県)の朝廷(南朝)が並立した。両朝の擁立を名目として，全国の貴族・武士は抗争を繰(く)り返した。また広範な民衆がこの動乱のために日本各地を移動し，東と西の異質な文化が融合した意味は大きい。

• 室町時代　14世紀後半，足利義満が京都の室町幕府を安定させてから2世紀余りの間に，政治・文化面とも，武家が公家を圧倒して優位に立った。室町幕府は諸国の有力な守護大名の力を集めて成立していたため，統制力が弱く，15世紀後半に入ると，全国各地に大名が群立する戦乱の世，いわゆる戦国時代となった。戦国大名はその地域の土地・人民を支配する強力な独立政権となり，武士が農民を支配する封建社会が成立する。経済面では明貿易など商業の進展が見られた。

文化面では，公家と武家の文化に禅宗の影響が加わった，14世紀末の金閣に代表される*北山文化，15世紀末の銀閣に代表される*東山文化が栄えた。能・狂言・連歌(れんが)など庶民も楽しめる文化が発達し，地方へも広まった。日本の伝統文化を代表する茶道・華道も，この時代に基礎が固まった。16世紀半ばに，南蛮人(ポルトガル人・スペイン人)が渡来して，鉄砲やキリスト教を伝えた。

Feudal Era (12th to 16th centuries)
This era saw the transfer of power from the imperial court to the newly ascendant military class and the building of a feudal system.

• ***Kamakura* Period** (1185-1333) Near the end of the 12th century, *Minamoto no Yoritomo** established a military government in *Kamakura.* Over the nearly 150 years of this period, the tug-of-war between the military in *Kamakura* and the court in *Kyouto* (Kyoto) fashioned feudal society. In the latter half of the 13th century, Mongol invasions twice threatened northern *Kyuushu* but were thwarted by sudden storms and stalwart defenses. Ironically, military rule became increasingly difficult in the ensuing years.

Culturally, *Zen* Buddhism had a wide following among the warrior class, and a new aesthetic of naturalism and simplicity developed within the conventional court culture. In religion, popular Buddhist sects emerged led by such outspoken monks as *Hounen,** *Shinran,** and *Nichiren.** Early *Kamakura* sculpture* is notable for its powerful realism and humanistic touches. Although military epics such as the *Heike Monogatari* (Tale of the *Heike*; early 13th century) dominated the period's literature, other notable works include the *Houjouki* (The Ten Foot Square Hut; 13th century) and the *Tsurezuregusa* (Essays in Idleness; 14th century).

• **Northern and Southern Courts** After finally overthrowing the *Kamakura* shogunate, Emperor *Godaigo* fell out with *Ashikaga Takauji*, the upshot being the establishment of a northern Dynasty in *Kyouto* and a Southern Dynasty in *Yoshino* (in what is now *Nara* prefecture). Nobility, warriors, and everyone else fought in the name of one court or the other, and this was an era of great flux and migration, the ultimate effect being to irrevocably mix the different regional cultures.

• ***Muromachi* Period** (1333-1573) Named after the district in *Kyouto* where *Ashikaga Yoshimitsu* consolidated his government in the late 14th century, this period is distinguished by the military's political and cultural preeminence. Yet the *Ashikaga* clan was too dependent upon the independent warlords' support to form a strong central government, and battles between competing warlords each with absolute authority over his own landholdings and subjects, were frequent by the latter half of the 15th century as this period developed into the *Sengoku jidai* (age of civil wars). Despite this, trade with Ming China flourished.

Zen Buddhism remained influential in both military and court circles. The two main artistic trends were the *Kitayama* culture* of the late 14th century, symbolized by the *Kinkaku* Gold Pavilion, and the *Higashiyama* culture* of the late 15th century symbolized by the *Ginkakuji* Silver Pavilion. *Nou* (Noh), *kyougen, renga* linked verse, and other popular arts evolved and spread, and the tea ceremony and flower arranging were founded. Portuguese and Spanish traders also contributed to Japanese culture in the mid-16th century with the introduction of firearms and Christianity.

近世（16世紀～19世紀半ば）

*将軍と*大名が土地・人民を統治し，経済的には農業生産に支えられる，いわゆる*幕藩体制が確立する。

・*安土（あづち）・桃山時代　戦国の戦乱が治まって全国の統一が完成し，*織田信長と*豊臣秀吉が政権を握った時代。国内の統一とともに海外との交渉も活発に展開して，豪華で壮大な桃山文化を生んだ。

・江戸時代　*徳川家康は，1603年に幕府を江戸(今の東京)に開き，以後260余年間，徳川氏が全国を支配する。幕府は天皇・公家（くげ）・寺社を厳しく統制し，幕藩体制を支える農民の支配に心を砕いた。17世紀前半，３代将軍家光のとき，鎖国によって幕藩体制の安定期を迎えるが，産業の発達，商品経済の発展に伴い，農民の自給自足の経営が崩れ，19世紀ごろから幕藩体制が揺らぎ始める。

庶民の文化がこの時代の特色。17世紀末から18世紀初めの元禄（げんろく）文化は，京都,*大坂などの上方地方を中心とする武士と町民の文化で,人形浄瑠璃（じょうるり）・歌舞伎・工芸などが盛んになった。特に町人文芸に優れ，小説の井原西鶴，俳諧（はいかい）の松尾芭蕉（ばしょう），人形浄瑠璃・歌舞伎の脚本作者近松門左衛門などが出た。19世紀初めの化政文化は舞台が江戸に移り，小説・歌舞伎・浮世絵・*文人画など多彩な町人文化が栄えた。

教育，学問も普及した。武士は幕藩体制維持の理論的根拠となる儒学，特に朱子学を学んだ。18世紀以降，日本の古典を研究する国学や*蘭学（らんがく）が発達した。多くの藩（大名の領地）で子弟教育用の藩校が設立され，民間では庶民の初等教育機関である*寺子屋が多くできた。

近代・現代（19世紀半ば～現代）

19世紀後半の開国を機に，日本は半世紀で近代国家に急成長する。

・*明治　欧米の先進諸国に追いつくために，政府は富国強兵，殖産興業，文明開化をモットーに，憲法の制定，国会の開設，不平等条約の改正など，近代化政策を次々に実行した。*日清戦争・*日露戦争の勝利を契機に，産業革命が進行し，資本主義が発達して，国際的地位も次第に上がった。明治の文化は，伝統文化と欧米文化が対立し，統合されていく方向で発達していった。

・*大正・*昭和　第一次世界大戦以降の日本は，*大正デモクラシーのような民衆勢力の台頭はあったものの，帝国主義的傾向を強め，昭和前期の1930年代から*十五年戦争に突入する。太平洋戦争の敗北を機に，日本は唯一の被爆国として，戦争を放棄し，自由で平和な文化国家の建設を目ざすようになった。

Japanese History (4)

Early Modern Era (16th to mid-19th centuries)
In this era the feudal lords* consolidated their control and a *bakuhan** administrative system was established with an agricultural economy.

• ***Azuchi-Momoyama* Period*** (1576-1600) Following decades of civil war, *Oda Nobunaga** and *Toyotomi Hideyoshi** held the reins of power, establishing relative peace and reviving overseas trade.

• ***Edo* Period** (1600-1867) Consolidating his position, *Tokugawa Ieyasu** made himself *shougun* and established his government in *Edo* in 1603. The shogunate kept the emperor, the nobility, and the religious institutions on a tight rein and strictly regulated the lives of the common people, mostly farmers, on whom the government ultimately rested. In the early 17th century, the third *shougun Iemitsu* closed the country to foreign commerce. While domestic commerce and industry flourished, agriculture fell upon hard times. By the 19th century, the *bakuhan* system was falling apart.

The *Edo* period had a vigorous popular culture. In the *Genroku* era the *Kyouto*(Kyoto)-*Oosaka*(Osaka)* area was a center of *joururi* puppet theater, *kabuki* and other arts. Literature soared to new heights with *Ihara Saikaku*'s fiction, *Bashou*'s poetry, and *Chikamatsu*'s drama. As the cultural focus shifted to *Edo* in the early 19th century, novels, *kabuki, ukiyo-e*, and *bunjinga** painting continued to prosper.

Advances were made in education and scholarship. As philosophical underpinning for the *bakuhan*, Confucianism and neo-Confucian teachings were major subjects of study for early-*Edo samurai. Kokugaku*, a nationalistic school of learning, and Dutch learning* grew in popularity after the 18th century. Many clans set up schools for *samurai* children, while townspeople sent their children to *terakoyu** schools.

Modern Era (late-19th century to the present)
• **Meiji*** (1868-1912) With the fall of the shogunate and the imperial restoration, the *Meiji* government ended Japan's seclusion and rushed to catch up with the industrialized West. Seeking to "enrich the country and strengthen the military," industry was promoted, Western culture was encouraged, a constitution was drawn up, a parliament was established, and the unequal treaties of the late *Edo* period were revised. Victories in the Sino-Japanese* and Russo-Japanese* wars gave Japan the opportunity to move forward with industrialization, develop a capitalistic economy and secure a position on the international scene. Culturally, this was a time for integrating traditional Japanese culture with the new imported Western culture.

• ***Taishou** and *Shouwa**** (1912 to the present) Despite a brief interlude of "*Taishou* democracy,"* Japan's imperialistic leanings intensified following the end of World War I, and in the early *Shouwa* period—the early 1930s—the nation embarked upon 15 disastrous years of war.* With the loss of World War II and the bombing of *Hiroshima* and *Nagasaki*, Japan renounced war and vowed to become a new nation of peace and freedom.

7 日本人の起源

日本人のルーツ探しは，明治以後，考古学・人類学・言語学など多方面から行われ，住居や神話の類似性からポリネシア系の南方(なんぽう)説，さまざまな文化の関連から中国南方説，古墳(こふん)や埋蔵品の馬具などから北方系の騎馬民族説，シベリアからの南下説などが言われてきた。第二次世界大戦後，特に近年になって，考古学的な発掘が進み，多数の人骨や石器，遺物が見つかり，さらに分子人類学，遺伝子研究など新しい学問分野が参入することによって，より客観的な研究とデータが整い，他民族，他人種との比較も容易になっている。

日本人の原型

現在の日本人の原型とされる人類は約１万8000年くらい前，日本にやってきたと見られている。この時代は，氷河期(ひょうがき)の最も寒かった時期に当たっており，海面が現在よりも140mほど下がっていたため，当時の食料であったマンモスを追って全地球的規模で民族移動が行われ，モンゴロイドが北米，南米にも渡った時期である。

日本周辺では間宮(まみや)，宗谷(そうや)，津軽(つがる)，対馬(つしま)の各海峡や黄海(こうかい)，琉球(りゅうきゅう)列島などが陸続きになり，このため北方からは，寒い気候に適応した，顔の凹凸が少ない，身長も低い新モンゴロイドが，南方からは，アジア大陸南部に広く住んでいた丸顔の古モンゴロイドが渡ってきた。この二つはやがて混交して，やや新モンゴロイドの特徴が濃く古モンゴロイドの特徴も合わせ持つ「原日本人」が生み出された。身体的な特徴は，丸顔で，背が低い，多毛性の人種である。

「原日本人」から現代日本人へ

「原日本人」は日本各地に住んでいたが，弥生(やよい)時代から古墳時代にかけて，朝鮮半島や中国大陸から，細面で背の高いより進んだ技術と文明をもった民族が西日本に移住してきて，「原日本人」に文化的な影響を与えるとともに，しだいに広く移り住み，「原日本人」とも混交していき，現代日本人が生み出されていった。ただ，その波及が，北日本と南西諸島に至るのが遅れたために，それらの地域には，日本人のプロトタイプのさまざまな特徴が残ることになったと見られている。

なお，現代の日本人を調べると，北には丸顔で背の低い人，南には細面で背の高い人が多いことがわかっている。

Origins of the Japanese People

Since *Meiji* times, archaeologists, anthropologists, and linguists have attempted to trace the origins of the Japanese people. Architecture and myths suggest a Polynesian origin, varied cultural characteristics point to southern China, tomb artifacts suggest a relationship to the mounted nomads of Korea and northern China, and other clues hint that the first Japanese made their way from Siberia across ancient land bridges. Human skeletons, stoneware, and other finds since the Second World War have supplied a wealth of data and facilitated scientific comparison with other peoples and races. This work has been supplemented by molecular anthropology, genetic research, and contributions from other new fields as well, but the results remain inconclusive.

The Japanese Prototype

The prototype of the modern Japanese is believed to have come to Japan about 18,000 years ago. This was the time of the last glacial period, when the world's oceans were 140 meters lower than they are now. Great migrations were being made all over the globe in pursuit of the mammoth and other sources of food. This was also when Mongoloid peoples migrated to North and South America.

Linked to the Asian continent by expanses of land bridging the Tatar, *Souya, Tsugaru*, and *Tsushima* straits and the Yellow Sea, and connected to the southern *Ryuukyuu* Islands, Japan was easily accessible to the migratory peoples. From the north came a new Mongoloid race, short and with relatively flat features adapted to hard northern climes, and from the south came the older Mongoloid race of round-faced people who populated much of the southern Asian continent. The intermixing of these two races resulted in the prototype Japanese distinguished primarily by new Mongoloid features but having old Mongoloid characteristics as well hairy, short of stature, and with a round face.

Modern Japanese

The commonly accepted hypothesis today is that prototype Japanese were fairly evenly distributed throughout Japan. From the *Yayoi* through the *Kofun* periods, tall, narrow-faced peoples representing more advanced Chinese and Korean civilizations immigrated to western Japan bringing their culture and technology with them. These immigrants were gradually assimilated into the indigenous stock, and the result was the modern Japanese. The intermingling of the tall immigrant peoples with the short indigenous Japanese took so long to spread, however, that examples of early prototype Japanese are still to be found in the northernmost and southwestern areas of Japan.

Interestingly, studies of modern Japanese racial characteristics have shown that people in the north tend to be short and round-faced while people in the south tend to be tall and narrow-faced.

照葉樹林文化地帯

日本の文化の根底となっている縄文(じょうもん)文化には，シベリアなどの北方(ほっぽう)文化の要素と，東南アジアなどの南方(なんぽう)文化の要素とが見られる。北方系の要素は近年発掘が進んでいる青森県の三内丸山遺跡の発掘品などから明らかになりつつあるが，シベリアなどにおける北方文化の実態解明が進んでいないため，今後の研究に待つところが多い。これに対して南方系の要素は，植物学者中尾佐助を中心とした植物生態学者，考古学者，文化人類学者らのグループが，東南アジアで広範囲なフィールドワークを行い，東南アジア文化とさまざまな共通性をもつことを実証した。この東南アジアに特有の文化を「照葉樹林文化」と言う。照葉樹というのは，カシ，クスノキ，ツバキ，サザンカといった常緑で，葉が厚く，表面が光り，深緑色をしている樹木で，東南アジアの熱帯雨林のすぐ北側，つまり中国の雲南省を中心に，西はヒマラヤからシッキム，南はミャンマー，ベトナム北部，東は中国南岸部から日本まで，この樹林が生い繁っている地帯を照葉樹林帯と呼んでいる。

共通の文化要素

この地帯は人種的にはモンゴロイドが住み，気候的にも似通っており，このため，共通した文化要素をもつに至ったものと思われる。早くから焼畑農耕が始まり，ヒエ，アワ，ソバ，大豆など，そして後には稲が栽培された。これらの雑穀類は，水にさらしたり，あく抜きをした上で粉にして煮て，*もちとして食べた。このため，焼畑農耕，穀類を粉にするためのうすやきねなどの道具，煮炊きするためのこしきなどの土器類の発達などが共通の文化となっている。

この地帯の特産品である*茶や*こんにゃく，*シソの飲食も特徴的であるし，大豆を原料とした納豆作りもこの地帯だけで行われている。食品以外では*漆(うるし)や蚕(かいこ)の飼育による絹の使用，*鵜(う)飼いによる漁業も，雲南からベトナム，中国南岸から日本まで，この地帯で広く見られるものである。

神話では，日本の『古事記』『日本書紀』に出てくる「天岩屋(あめのいわや)型」の日食神話，神の死体から何種類かの作物が生まれるという「死体化生型」の作物起源神話なども，共通するものである。信仰では，死者が山や丘の頂に帰り，死者の霊は山に眠るという「山上他界」の考え方も焼畑農耕民に広く分布している。男女が自分の思いを歌い合う「歌垣(うたがき)」の習俗，男が女の所に通う「妻問い婚」なども行われていた。

Sources of Japanese Culture

Shiny-leaf Culture

Japan's earliest civilization, the *Joumon* culture, shows signs of northern cultural influences from Siberia and southern influences from Southeast Asia. Northern influences are also showing up in the *Sannai Maruyama* site being excavated in *Aomori* prefecture, but much of this is still little-understood because the Northern civilization has yet to be elucidated. By contrast, there is a group of botanists, archaeologists, and cultural anthropologists, led by botanist *Nakao Sasuke*, who have done extensive field work in Southeast Asia and identified the characteristics common to the Southern culture. This group has named this common culture the shiny-leaf culture because it is characterized by its emergence in forests of evergreen trees with thick, dark green, and shiny leaves, such as *kashi* (oak), *kusunoki* (cinnamomum camphora), *tsubaki* (camellia japonica), and *sazanka* (camellia sasanqua). Located just north of Southeast Asia's tropical rain forests, this shiny-leaf forest belt spreads from China's Yunnan Province to the Himalayas and Sikkim in the west, Myanmar and northern Vietnam in the south, and the southern Chinese coast in the east.

Cultural Characteristics

The fact that the shiny-leaf forest belt's residents share a common climate and a Mongoloid racial heritage is believed to have given them a common culture as well. Agriculture started early in this region beginning with various types of millet, buckwheat, and soybeans and eventually extending to rice. These plants have to be processed before eating, and the soaking, grinding, and boiling needed to create the glutinous paste* eaten as a staple food are common processes throughout the region. These common experiences have also given rise to such common tools as mortars and pestles for grinding and earthenware pots for cooking.

Other characteristics common to this zone include the drinking of tea* and the cultivation and eating of *konnyaku** (Devil's tongue) and perilla.* *Nattou*, a fermented bean product made of soybeans, is found in various forms wherever the shiny-leaf culture's writ runs. Besides these common foods, the region is noted for its lacquer ware,* silk, and cormorant fishing.*

The myths of the region all include an eclipse myth, and stories of food plants sprouting from corpses abound. The region's scorched-earth farming societies share a belief that the dead return to hilltops and that their souls sleep within mountains. Although no longer practiced in some areas, other once-shared customs include the *utagaki* song festivals in which young boys and girls vied with each other in their songs, and the marriage custom of having the husband visit his wife regularly at her home instead of their living together.

内外の学者，研究者が挙げる日本文化の特性は多い。その中から代表的な4つを取り上げてみよう。

重層性

日本の文化は，系統の異なる文化が併存ないしは混在する重層文化である。例は周囲にいくらでもある。政治には新旧の制度が混在し，衣食住は和洋折衷であり，宗教は神仏をともに受け入れ，日常使う日本語の中には漢語が半分以上も含まれている，といったぐあいである。

重層文化が生まれた理由として，日本人は異質文化への好奇心が強いこと，在来文化を根こそぎ否定するような侵略を受けず，必要に応じて外来文化を取り入れる環境にあったこと，などが挙げられる。

均一性

日本の文化は，地域によって，宗教によって，あるいは人によって異なるということはなく，ほぼ均一，均質であると言うことができる。どこを切っても同じ断面が現れる「*金太郎あめ」というのがあるが，まさに日本の文化は金太郎あめと同じである。狭い国土に多数の人が住んでいることのほかに，日本人は長い間，生活の末端まで国家の統制を受けてきた経験から，個人よりも集団や国家を考える習性をもっていることが，文化の均一性を生んだ原因と見られる。

日本化

日本人は外来文化を日本化して，独自のものとしてしまう能力をもっている。平安時代に，漢字を日本化して仮名を作り出し，『源氏物語』などの傑作を生んだことは，日本の歴史(p.18)で見たとおりである。

鎌倉仏教は仏教が日本化された例である。6世紀に伝来した仏教は，鎌倉時代に法然(ほうねん)とその弟子親鸞(しんらん)が出て，外来宗教の域を脱し，日本の仏教となった。法然は専修(せんじゅ)念仏の教え，親鸞は悪人正機(しょうき)説といった，日本人に即した独特の教義を説いて宗教活動を展開したため，広く民衆の信仰を集めることができたのである。

現実的

日本人は現実的である。普遍的概念よりも個別的な事物を重んじる。仏教を現世利益的なものに変えたこともそうだし，江戸時代の幕藩体制の理論的根拠となった儒学も，理論面より応用面，実際面で優れていた。現代の科学でも，原理の追究より原理の応用・製品化の面で能力を発揮していることは周知のとおりである。

Characteristics of Japanese Culture

Japanese culture has many unique features, the following four being among the most characteristic.

Multi-layered

As shown in innumerable ways, Japanese culture is made up of many layers—old and new, foreign and native. Politics is a mixture of old and new customs. The three essentials of food, clothing, and shelter are blends of Japanese and Western elements. Japanese practice both Buddhist and *Shintou* rites, and more than half of the Japanese language is comprised of Chinese-derivative words.

Among the reasons for this multi-layered quality of Japanese culture are the curiosity Japanese people have for other cultures and the historic process of assimilation as Japanese welcomed foreign cultural elements without discarding indigenous customs and traditions.

Homogeneity

Varying little by region, religion, or person, Japanese culture is basically uniform throughout the country—like the *kintarou-ame** candy, which shows the same pattern no matter where it is cut. Not only does Japan have a large population on limited land, but the people have lived for centuries under centralized governments which regulated people's lives in minute detail. Primary importance has traditionally been placed on the group rather than on the individual, and this heritage accounts for much of Japanese society's uniformity.

Japanization

Japanese have been very adept at making foreign elements their own to create something that is uniquely Japanese. This trait goes back beyond the *Heian* period when Japanese *kana* script was created out of the more complex Chinese characters and was used to produce such great works as the *Tale of Genji*.

Kamakura Buddhism is another example of Japanization. Introduced to Japan in the 6th century, Buddhism did not spread until the appearance of *Hounen* and *Shinran*, respectively founders of the *Joudo* and *Joudo Shin* sects. *Hounen* taught that all that was needed to attain salvation was to recite the name of *Amida* Buddha, and *Shinran* , his disciple, elaborated on this by stressing that *Amida* Buddha had prepared the Pure Land precisely for the salvation of the wicked. These teachings, which stressed pure and simple faith over complicated rites and doctrines, appealed strongly to the common Japanese populace.

Pragmatism

The Japanese are very pragmatic, emphasizing specific circumstances more than universal truths. Indeed, it is this trait which made it possible to create Japan's this-worldly Buddhism and this is why the Confucian ethic of the *Edo*-period shogunate was far better in its practice than in its theory. Even in modern science, Japanese show more aptitude for applied science than for basic research.

10 日本人の自然観

自然との一体化

日本人にとって古来，自然はあくまで恵みを与えるもの，親しむべきものであり，決して人間と対立する厳しく，むごいものではなかった。これは日本が温帯の湿潤な地域にあって，自然環境が温和なものであったのに加え，縄文(じょうもん)時代以来の採集・漁労社会，それに次ぐ稲作を中心とした農耕社会にとって，自然は生育をもたらし，実りをもたらすものであったことによる。また，定着的な農耕社会である日本では，父祖代々がその自然とともに生き，やがて自然に帰っていき，自分自身もまたその道をたどる。それゆえ自然と自分を一体化し，自然の心をわが心として生きる感情が，日本人の哲学・思想・宗教などすべての精神活動の根本に流れている。

このような自然への親しみ，自然と我との一体化は，さらに，自然を楽しみ，現世を謳歌(おうか)する現実肯定の考え方を生み出していく。それはまた，「長いものには巻かれろ」の精神であり，太平洋戦争を「鬼畜米英」と言って戦い，敗れると何の抵抗もなくアメリカ文化に染まったのも，和の精神の底に流れるものもこれである。日本の宗教が現世利益をうたわなければ信者を集められないのも，また，日本人の現実肯定の表れであると言われている。

自然の観察と再現

他方，春夏秋冬の四季の微妙な変化が，農耕社会においては種まき，生育，収穫の兆候ともなるところから，自然の移ろいへの細かい観察が行われ，それは「松風の音を聞き，虫の音をめでる」といった自然への鋭敏な感覚をはぐくみ，それを基(もと)に，さまざまな芸術や生活習慣が生まれている。西洋絵画では17世紀に初めて独立した主題となった風景画も，日本では*山水画と呼ばれて鎌倉時代以来，つねに主要なテーマであった。文学においても，自然はいつも重要なテーマであり，特に和歌や俳句が，花鳥風月をうたい，俳句に*季語を詠(よ)み込むのも，その小世界に自然を取り入れようとする姿勢の表れである。

日本人の自然観は仏教の無常観によって増幅されたものだが，特に禅宗の思想と結び付いてからは，*幽玄・*わび・*さびの世界を生み出し，茶道や庭園，華道などにおいて，人工の極致として，ありのままの飾らない自然を再現するようになった。このような考え方は，芸術ばかりでなく武道でも行われ，後にスポーツ化した剣道・柔道・空手道などでも，その技量の奥義(おうぎ)は自然体，つまり，自然と一体となって，あるがままの力を発揮することであるとしている。

Japanese Concepts of Nature

Oneness with Nature

Nature has always been a familiar and friendly blessing to the Japanese, not a cruel foe, and this concept of nature is readily understandable in view of the Japanese islands' temperate climate and abundant rainfall. To the gathering and fishing peoples of the *Joumon* period, and the rice-cultivating farmers who followed, this environment was not only mild and non-threatening, but the source of all growth and fertility. The life cycles of the agricultural people of old Japan so closely followed the natural rhythm of the land that they were as one with nature, their very souls a part of the spirit of nature. This sense of oneness with nature underlies the Japanese ethos, its philosophy, thought, and religion, and it is part of the Japanese sensitivity to and enjoyment of nature.

The identification with nature has spawned a ready willingness to flow with the tide. The Japanese situational ethic—its resignation to the way things are and its emphasis on harmony at all cost—is well-illustrated by the Japanese openness to American culture after World War II, even though Japanese had vilified America and fought bravely against the United States during the war. Another aspect of this concern with their immediate situation is the lack of interest in religious promises of otherworldy rewards. They are more likely to be attracted by promises of immediate and this-worldly advantages.

Observation and Re-creation

The agricultural society's need to know when to plant, cultivate, and harvest its crops has sharpened the Japanese sensitivity to seasonal changes, heightening their awareness of the minutiae of nature—the wind in the pines and the singing of insects—and giving rise to a wide variety of arts and customs embodying this sensitivity. Landscapes did not become an accepted subject for Western painting until the 17th century, but in Japan they were already a major theme of the *sansui-ga** painting introduced from China in the *Kamakura* period. Nature has played a major part in Japanese literature as well, figuring prominently in seasonal references* in *waka* and *haiku* poetry, and in the custom of using seasonal introductions in correspondence and other writing.

The Buddhist concept of transience has been incorporated into the indigenous concept of nature as an extension of oneself. *Zen* teachings have given rise to the mysticism and rustic simplicity of *yuugen*,* *wabi*,* and *sabi** inherent in the tea ceremony, the Japanese garden, and flower arrangements. In all of these arts, the ultimate goal is to represent nature as it is. This extends even into the traditional martial arts such as *kendou*, *juudou* (judo), and *karate*, which teach that strength comes only when one is completely relaxed and as much at one with nature as possible.

複雑な多神教国

日本人の宗教心は，世界でも最も複雑なものであることは間違いない。よく言われるのが，「正月には神社に*初もうでに行き，春秋の*彼岸には寺に墓参りし，クリスマスにはケーキを食べ，プレゼントする」という年中行事や，「七五三で神社にお参りし，結婚式は教会で挙げ，葬式はお寺で」という通過儀礼における宗教の多様性である。

ふつう，多神教と言えば，一つの宗教が多数の神をもつことを指すが，日本の場合は，それぞれ体系化された多神教である仏教や神道があり，日本人の大部分はその両方の信徒で家には神棚も仏壇もあるうえ，時にはさらに，他の新宗教の信徒であることもありうる。加えて，*お稲荷(いなり)さん，*道祖神といったアニミズムやシャーマニズムに近い神にも抵抗なく手を合わせる。自動車を買えばおはらいをしてもらい，超近代的な工場のロボットに人名をつけて擬人化した扱いをするのなども，アニミズム的信仰の表れと言ってよさそうだ。これを裏付けるのは，文化庁が編さんしている『宗教年鑑』である。1997年版によれば，日本の宗教人口は２億776万人。総人口が約１億2000万人なので，日本人すべてがほぼ二つずつの宗教の信徒になっていることになる。

根底にある利益求心

このように，ある宗教に対する明確な信仰心はもたないが，心情として，あるいは基本的感覚として存在するのが日本人の宗教心と言えそうだ。その根本にあるのが，やはり日本人の自然観に基づく現実肯定の宗教的表現である，現世利益を求める心である。日本固有の民族信仰である神道はもともと豊作や部族社会の安全を祈る祈願神であり，インドで発生したときには自らの救いを得る宗教であった仏教も，日本伝来とともに祈禱(きとう)する宗教となった。こうして日本では，宗教は商売繁盛，家内安全，受験合格，安産に至るまで，多種多様な現世利益を祈る場となっている。「苦しいときの神頼み」「いわしの頭も信心から」のことわざが，日本人の宗教心の現世利益という特色を物語っている。

近年，若者の間に神秘主義，オカルティズムへの関心が高まった結果，1980年代から超能力や超自然主義を掲げた多くの小宗教集団（カルト）が生まれた。その一つであるオウム真理教が95年に東京の地下鉄で猛毒サリンによる大衆無差別テロを行った。オウム真理教が起こした別の刑事事件への牽制のためだったが，この事件は日本人の従来の宗教心に大きなマイナス要素として働き，宗教への警戒心が強まっている。

Japanese Religion

Overlapping Religions

Japanese beliefs are probably among the most complicated in the world because of the openness to all religions, as exemplified by the visits to *Shintou* shrines at New Year's,* trips to Buddhist temples in the spring and fall* to visit the family grave, and the modern custom of a cake and presents at Christmas. The *Shichi-go-san* celebration entails a trip to the local *Shintou* shrine, weddings may well be held in Christian chapels, and funerals are most often Buddhist.

Polytheism usually refers to a religion with many gods, but Japan doubles this by having many religions each of which may have many gods. It is not uncommon for a Japanese family to have both *Shintou* and Buddhist altars even though its members believe in yet a third faith. Many Japanese also feel a close affinity to *Inari*,* once an agrarian deity but now popular throughout Japan as an all-purpose god, and the *dousojin** on the edges of villages to protect villagers. The same person who has a *Shintou* priest perform purification rites for his new car may also work in an ultra-modern factory where he animistically gives the robots both nicknames and a measure of affection and respect. Statistics substantiate the evidence of Japanese culture's polytheistic quality. According to the Agency for Cultural Affairs' Religion Yearbook, Japan had a religious population of 207.76 million in 1997—nearly double the actual population of 120 million.

Here-and-now Orientation

While the Japanese tend to avoid identifying with any single religious doctrine, they do have an inherent reverence for all things, a reverence that stems from their strongly-rooted, nearly mystical affinity with nature and quest for this-worldly rewards. *Shintou*, Japan's indigenous religion, was originally a means of supplicating the gods for aid in agricultural endeavors and for protection at the tribal level. Buddhism, which started out preaching good works to attain salvation, was transformed in Japan to a religion of supplication. In Japan religion is a tool for petitioning for business profits, the safety of the household, success on school entrance exams, painless childbirth, and numerous other concrete rewards in the here and now. Common expressions such as *kurushii toki no kami danomi* (turning to religion in times of distress) and *iwashi no atama mo shinjin kara* (even the basest thing is sacred) further reveal the Japanese view of religion as a source of this-worldly benefits.

With young people more interested in mysticism and the occult, a number of small sects or cults have sprung up over the last decade or two preaching supernaturalism. It was one of these, Aum *Shinrikyou*, that engaged in random terrorism by releasing deadly sarin on the *Toukyou* (Tokyo) subways in 1995. This incident, supposedly intended to distract police investigating an earlier Aum crime, reaped general revulsion and has been devastating to the traditional Japanese indulgence toward religion.

よく働く日本人

日本人は非常によく働くという評価は，日本の経済発展とともに今では国際的にも定着している。ただ，そうした評価の裏に日本に対する羨望(せんぼう)と嫉妬(しっと)が潜んでいることは，例えば日本の経済活動に対して「エコノミック・アニマル」と称していることでもわかる。しかし，日本人からすると，欧米の評価にはどこか認識の誤りがあるようだ。

日本人にとって働くということは，必ずしも利益を求めることが第一義的な目的ではなく，働くという行為そのものに価値を見いだしているという説がある。評論家の*山本七平(しちへい)氏によれば，日本人の勤労というのは，すなわち仏教で言う成仏(じょうぶつ)するための修行であり，経済的利益は宗教的に動機づけられた，つまり，私欲のない労働の結果とされる。このような，結果として得られる利潤は是認(ぜにん)されると考えているというのである。現在の企業活動においても，この勤労に対する精神は生き続けており，それが，日本人が非常によく働くことの解答でもある。したがって，経済報酬は労働(時間)に対する対価であるという欧米的な勤労意識とは，その精神においてだいぶ異なることになる。この違いが，一方では契約社会に基づく企業経営を創出し，一方では独特のいわゆる日本的経営を生み出したと言う。

変わりつつある労働観

しかし，最近は仕事に対する考え方もだいぶ変化している。基本的に労働に対する価値を依然認めてはいるものの，意欲の点になるとかなり減少してきている。その背景としては，一つに労働の目的の喪失がある。低成長時代になり，いくら働いたからといって収入は増えない。高齢化により，ポスト不足で出世も期待できない状況で，具体的な目標が立てにくい。

また一方，経済的に一応豊かになるとともに，価値観の多様化が進み，特に若い世代に働くこと以外の価値を認める傾向が強くなりつつある。そして，OA化やロボット化などが進むにつれ，熟練技術が単純労働に取って代わられたり，労働時間の短縮，余暇の増大などにより，従来の勤労そのものの条件も変わってくる。このことは，しだいに労働観の変化をもたらすだろうし，それにつれて当然勤労意欲というのも変わると思われる。少なくとも，今までのような企業中心的な勤労意欲というのは確実に減退していくであろう。

The Japanese Work Ethic

Hard-working Japanese

As the Japanese economy has grown stronger, the Japanese people have come to be known worldwide as hard workers. However, this perception of Japan often includes negative elements, including the view that Japanese are simply "economic animals" pursuing profit above all else. Yet for their part, the Japanese feel that Western perceptions are distorted by their misunderstanding of a number of aspects of life in Japan.

To begin with, the zeal with which Japanese pursue their work is based not so much on the profit motive as it is on the value of work. The distinguished social commentator *Yamamoto Shichihei*,* for example, traces the Japanese work ethic to Japan's strong Buddhist tradition. As *Yamamoto* explains it, the act of working is subconsciously accepted as a spiritual discipline, and Buddhahood, not economic gain, is the prize to be gained through selfless devotion to one's work. Even today, this orientation lives on in Japanese companies, and this is a major reason why Japanese work so hard. As such, the Japanese work ethic differs radically from the modern European attitude that work is basically an exchange of labor (time) for money and that neither the work nor the act of working has any inherent value. This difference is also seen as a major cause of the differences between business management in the contractual West and what might be called Japanese style management.

Changing Attitudes

However, the Japanese work ethic has been undergoing significant change in recent years. While work is still held in high esteem, there has been considerable erosion on the motivation side. This is partly because the goals have become more elusive. In today's slow-growth climate, extra work is not always rewarded by a higher income, and the graying of the Japanese population is creating a shortage of upper-management posts.

In addition, as the Japanese have attained relative affluence, their values have become more individualized and many people—particularly young people—now place a greater emphasis on personal-interest activities outside of their work. As tomorrow's increasingly sophisticated office and factory automation technologies change work conditions and turn tasks that now require skilled expertise into routine jobs, there will likely be a significant shortening of the work week and the creation of more leisure time, gradually changing the way work is perceived. This will naturally have an impact on people's motivation. At the very least, there will be less of the company-oriented work ethic that has been so pervasive until now.

働きバチの暇つぶし

第二次世界大戦前の日本人は，祭りや湯治(とうじ)，芝居や寄席(よせ)などの地域社会に結び付いた伝統的な娯楽を楽しんでいた。だが，大戦後の生活文化のアメリカ化，農村から都市への移住，テレビの発達などが，伝統的娯楽を衰退させた。その中で，高度経済成長を支えた勤労者層は，「働きバチ」と呼ばれるように仕事一筋に生き，余暇(よか)時間を自己充実のためでなく，明日の仕事のための疲労回復やストレス解消のためと考えるようになった。娯楽もテレビを見てゴロ寝をするとか，盛り場で一杯飲むとか，同僚とマージャンをするなど，手軽で内容の乏しいものが一般的となった。中でも，日本独特の大衆娯楽*パチンコは，いつでも一人で遊べて，運がよければ景品稼ぎもできる，もっとも人気のある暇つぶし法だった。スポーツではゴルフが挙げられるが，これもあくまで仕事がらみが多かった。

娯楽観の変化

昭和40年代以後，日本人のレジャーに対する考え方は変化を見せ始め，余暇を仕事の余り時間とするのではなく，もっと積極的な意味で考えるようになった。

その一つが，成長率が大きく低下した昭和50年代前半に典型的だった生活向上型，あるいは自己投資型とでも呼ぶべき余暇利用法である。余暇を生活の資源として有効に使おうというもので，自分の教養を高めるための読書・学習や日曜大工のようなDIY（do-it-yourself）活動，スポーツでも健康づくりのためのジョギング，水泳など盛んに行われるようになった。そして，安定成長時代に入った昭和50年代後半からは，若い世代を中心に余暇そのものにより高度な楽しみを求める傾向が強くなり，バブル経済期にピークに達した。高級レストランで豪華な食事を楽しんだり，国内旅行よりも海外旅行に出かけるというぐあいに，楽しみには投資を惜しまないと考えるようになった。近年のバブル崩壊後は，自然志向のレジャーにも人気が集まるようになったが，一方では国内旅行よりも格安の海外旅行には依然として人気が集まっているなど，娯楽はいっそう多様化してきている。

なお，こうした娯楽観の変化とは関係がないが，パチンコは依然として人気が高く，また，近年老若を問わず圧倒的に人気があるのが，音楽だけ入ったテープやCDなどに合わせて歌う*カラオケである。もともとは盛り場のバーやスナックなどだけにあったカラオケセットだが，今では家庭にまで普及し，さらに世界に広まりつつある。

How the Drones Kill Time

Before the war, most Japanese recreations were such group or community activities as festivals, bathing in the hot springs, going to plays, or vaudeville. Yet the Americanization of Japanese life, the migration from farm to city, the advent of television, and other changes have not been kind to these traditions. At the same time, the working people who sustained Japan's rapid growth were so devoted to their jobs that they were characterized as "drones," and free time was seen not as a time of personal fulfillment but as a time to recharge for the next day's work. Thus recreation came to mean such readily accessible and relatively mindless pursuits as watching television, drinking with co-workers, and playing mahjong. Distinctively Japanese, *pachinko** was particularly popular, offering as it does the chance to enjoy yourself in solitude any time—and if you are lucky to take some winnings home. Golf was a popular sport, but most players were on the links for business reasons.

Changing Recreational Patterns

Japanese views of leisure started changing around the mid-1960s, and people have since come to see free time not as the interlude between work and work but as something to be used proactively.

One manifestation of this was the increasing number of people spending their free time on self-improvement or betterment in the late 1970s when the economy was doing badly. In this era, free time was a resource to be used - whether for do-it-yourself home carpentry, for educational reading or schooling, or for such fitness sports as jogging or swimming. As the economy steadied in the 1980s, Japanese recreation and leisure reached new heights—especially with young people—that peaked with the speculative "bubble." People dined out at expensive restaurants, traveled overseas as though it were domestic, and spent lavishly on enjoying themselves. With the bubble's collapse, people have gravitated toward more restrained and eco-type recreations. Yet at the same time, overseas travel remains very popular—often being cheaper than domestic travel—and leisure pursuits are more personalized than ever.

Unaffected by these changing trends, *pachinko* remains immensely popular. A new pastime that is popular with young and old alike is *karaoke**—sing-along tapes and CDs. It used to be that only bars and other drinking establishments had *karaoke* sets, but *karaoke* has now found its way into the home and is popular worldwide.

日本人の美意識の底には常に自然との一体感と，仏教の*諸行無常の考え方が流れている。しかし，時代の雰囲気によって，表現される美意識は異なる。

「もののあわれ」

日本人が中国文化の影響を消化し，独自の文化・精神を作り上げたのは平安時代とされている。この時代は「仏教が滅び，暗黒の世界になる」という「末法(まっぽう)の世」に当たるとされていたため，支配的だった美意識は「もののあわれ」である。あらゆる物事の中に，はかなさを見て，心に感動を生じるようすを言い，『源氏物語』をはじめとする文学の世界にもそれは色濃く反映されていた。

「わび」と「さび」

戦国の世が終わり，心の落ち着きを取り戻した時代に，力を得た町人がもった美意識である。「わび」は，茶道の中で生まれた美意識で，おごらず質素な中に，豊かさと静かな心を秘めたものである。*千利休をはじめ茶道の*宗匠たちは，一輪の野の花や日常雑器の中に美を見いだした。「さび」は松尾芭蕉(ばしょう)を中心とした俳句の世界で言われた美意識で，静かな孤高の心境を言う。「わび」も「さび」も禅の悟りの境地をバックボーンにもっている。

「いき」

江戸時代に町人が作り上げた美意識で，気のきいてセンスのよいことを言う。「いき」には「張り・あだ・あか抜け」の3条件があるとされ，張りとは自分の考えを貫く心，あだは下品にならないコケットリー，あか抜けは人生の表裏に通じた軽妙さと言える。

幕の内弁当の美意識

こうした伝統的な美意識を近代文明と調和させ，現代に花咲かせたものを「幕の内弁当の美意識」と言ったのが，*栄久庵憲司(えくあんけんじ)である。幕の内弁当には，ご飯と煮物・焼き物・漬物などさまざまなおかずが少しずつ彩りよく入っている。一つ一つの素材はごくありふれたものであるが，それらが全体としては調和のとれた美として，狭い弁当箱の中に美しくきっちり納まっている。「わび」「さび」そして「いき」の精神に立ち，見た目の美しさ，味という機能でも優れている。この幕の内弁当の美意識は，世界の市場で人気のあるコンパクトにパッケージされ，デザインも優れた家庭電器製品・オートバイ・自動車などの製品に生かされ，さらには日本がリードしている大規模集積回路の極微小の世界の根底にも存在していると言ってよい。

Japanese Aesthetics

While oneness with nature and the Buddhist feeling* that worldly display counts for nothing underlie the Japanese aesthetic, this has been expressed differently in different ages.

Pathos

It was in the *Heian* period that Chinese culture was adapted and Japanized into truly Japanese modes. Because this was seen as a degenerate era in which Buddhism declined and the forces of evil gained ascendancy, the dominant aesthetic of that age was one of pathos and insignificance. Every event was seen as inspiring for its transience and touching for its insignificance, and this ethic is perhaps most starkly depicted in the *Tale of Genji* and the other literature of the times.

Wabi* and *Sabi

When the raging civil wars ended and peace returned to people's hearts, it was the aesthetic of the newly powerful merchant class which prevailed. Born of the tea ceremony, *wabi* is an aesthetic of finding richness and serenity in simplicity. This was epitomized by the single wild flower and everyday plainness which decorated the tea houses of *Sen no Rikyuu** and other masters.* *Sabi* was a term for the beauty of such *haiku* as those by *Bashou*, and it speaks of a quiet grandeur enjoyed in solitude. Both *wabi* and *sabi* are closely linked to the *Zen* striving for enlightenment through nothingness.

Chic

Iki was the buzzword in the *Edo* period for the trendy fashionableness favored by the merchants. Generally, the three requirements for this chic *iki* were a persistence in being one's own person, a touch of class that refused to be vulgar, and a light lifestyle.

***Maku-no-uchi* Beauty**

Harmonized with modern civilization, this traditional sense of beauty finds expression today, says industrial designer *Ekuan Kenji*,* in the beauty of the *maku-no-uchi* boxed lunch. Here there are small portions of rice, pickled vegetables, grilled fish, and other foods—each quite ordinary in its own right—placed in harmonious arrangement to create a work of art in a small lacquered box. Embodying the principles of *wabi, sabi*, and *iki*, the lunch pleases both the eye and the palate. The same spirit which creates this elegantly compact *maku-no-uchi* boxed lunch also produces the home electronic appliances, automobiles, and other Japanese products that have proven so popular in the international marketplace—as well as the super-compact super-ICs where Japan commands a leading position. This is Japan's all-pervasive aesthetic of unostentatious functional beauty raised to its highest.

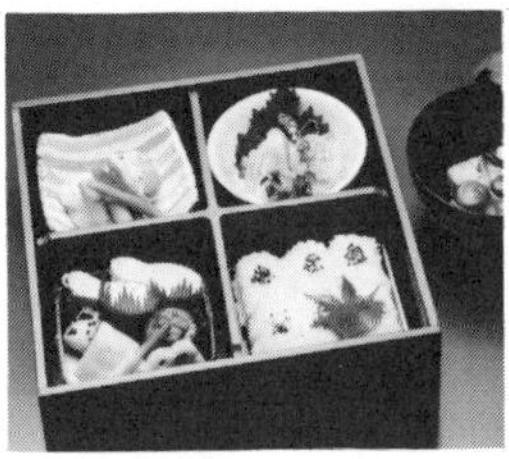

△幕の内弁当 ***(maku-no-uchi* boxed lunch)**

武士道

日本人の死生観に最も大きな影響を与えたのは仏教である。浄土宗は「厭離穢土・欣求浄土」と言って，汚れたこの世を離れ，*極楽浄土を求むべきだと唱えた。また禅宗の一派曹洞宗の日本における開祖道元は，その著『正法眼蔵』の中で，「生死を生死にまかす」として，生死の問題にとらわれることなく，死のときには生への執着を捨てて死に徹し，生のときには生に徹して一瞬一瞬に全力を尽くして生きることを教え，鎌倉時代以後，明日にも戦場に散るかもしれない武士たちの心の支えとなってきた。

江戸時代に入り，官僚化した武士に対する復古の動きとして，盛んに「武士道」が唱えられるようになる。江戸時代中期に九州佐賀藩の武士道の書『*葉隠』では，「武士道といふは，死ぬ事と見つけたり」と言ってのけている。ここでは禅宗のことばを一歩強めて，死に徹することが，完全なる生にもつながる，との考え方が示されている。

それを徹底したのが武士道における「切腹」で，腹という致死性の少ない部分を裂き，壮絶に死ぬことを演出して，自らの名と家名を活かし遺族への保障を得る。それが切腹という儀礼であり，また，制度でもあった。

*心中

心中も，江戸時代初めごろは，男女の愛情確認のための行為，例えば誓紙，断髪，入れ墨をすることを「心中立てる」「心中する」と言っていた。それが江戸時代半ばから二つとない生命をかけるようになったことから，「心中死」，または「心中情死」と呼ばれるようになり，歌舞伎や*浄瑠璃でもてはやされたこともあって，心中，すなわち情死心中となったものである。ここでも，死によって，愛情を全うしたのであり，「死によって活かす」という，日本固有の死生観が貫かれているのである。

自殺

日本は自殺が多いと言われるが，人口10万人当たりの自殺率は16.9人(1994年)，死亡者中の自殺者の割合は2.4%で，ロシアの37.9人，ハンガリーの35.9人などに比べると低く，世界の中位にある。

日本では「死によって活かす」自殺は，それ自体が潔い行為と見られ，罪悪視されることはない。これには仏教の厭世思想が果たした役割が大きく，自殺をタブーとするキリスト教文化圏の思想とはたいへん異なっている。

Bushidou

Buddhist concepts have had a major effect upon Japanese perceptions of life and death. The *Joudo* sect, one of the most popular Buddhist sects, for example, teaches that the world as we know it is tainted and that we must strive for rebirth in the *Joudo* Pure Land paradise.* In *Zen*, also, *Dougen*, founder of *Soutou Zen*, admonishes in his *Shoubou Genzou* (Treasury of the True Dharma Eye) that we should not question either life or death. Confronted with death, we should die readily, and while alive we should live every minute to the fullest. This concept of life and death was readily accepted in the *Kamakura* period and later by *samurai* who continually confronted death on the battlefield.

By the *Edo* period, the *samurai* were little more than bureaucrats, and *bushidou*, the way of the warrior with its ethics and guides for proper conduct, was stressed as part of the attempt to preserve the dignity of the warrior class. "*Bushidou* is a way of dying" is a famous saying from *Hagakure** (In the Shadow of Leaves), a book on *bushidou* written in the middle of the *Edo* period. *Hagakure* takes *Zen* teachings one step further by saying that being able to accept death is equivalent to living a full and complete life.

Seppuku, ritualistic suicide by disembowelment, was a means of protecting one's name and the honor of one's house through a dramatic and glorious death. In *bushidou, seppuku* was both a ritual and the epitome of ethical conduct.

Shinjuu*

In the early *Edo* period, expressions of love between a man and a woman, such as exchanging pledges, cutting one's hair, and tattooing, were referred to as *shinjuu*. Sometime in the latter half of the *Edo* period *shinjuu*, double love suicides, became prevalent and supplied ample story material for *kabuki* and *joururi*.* To the Japanese, death marked the culmination of the love between two people, and by this reasoning, *shinjuu* was a fulfillment of love.

Suicide

Although Japan is thought to have a high suicide rate, the actual (1994) figure is 16.9 suicides per 100,000 population. Suicide accounts for 2.4% of all deaths, ranking Japan in the medium range and well behind such countries as Russia (37.9) and Hungary (35.9).

One reason so many Japanese opt for suicide is that they see it as a means of fulfillment rather than a sinful act. This reflects Buddhist fatalism and is quite alien to Judeo-Christian admonishments against taking one's own life.

集団の重視

E.O.ライシャワーは『ザ・ジャパニーズ』の中で，日本人と欧米人とのいちばん顕著な違いを，日本人の集団重視に見ている。日本人といえどもこの見方は異論はないだろう。

確かに日本人の集団重視は過去，第二次世界大戦における玉砕や集団自決の悲劇，一億一心のスローガン，また今日，企業経営，サラリーマン社会などにおける集団の和の重視，果ては学校の生徒の制服に至るまで，広く深く根を張っている。「出る杭(くい)は打たれる」ということわざは日本人の処世術を端的に表しているし，集団に異を唱えたり，背を向けた者には「*村八分(はちぶ)」という処罰があった。例外はむろんあるが，日本の社会は個我の主張より，集団あっての個，個は集団にあって生かされると了解してきたと言える。

集団主義の形成

集団主義の成立は，日本の歴史的背景と無縁ではない。第一に，はるか弥生(やよい)時代に始まる稲作文化の影響がある。農村では今日もなお，田植えや稲刈り期には近隣どうしが助け合い，共同作業を行う習慣が一部に残っている。狩猟文化と異なり，そこでは集団作業と共同秩序とが必要であり，生活共同体なのである。儒教思想の影響も無視できない。忠孝を重んずるその道徳は江戸時代以降特に広まり，「家」制度にもつながった。家長は絶対の権限をもち，家族は「家」に従わねばならず，武士階級にあっては一朝事あれば御家(おいえ)断絶と，連帯責任を取らされた。

狭い国土に多くの人口ということも有力な一因だろう。朝晩の通勤電車の殺人的なラッシュは外国人のしばしば瞠目(どうもく)するところだが，当の日本人は甘受せざるを得ないし，そこから集団の調和という社会生活の知恵を身に付けるのである。住宅事情しかり。学校教育しかり。

集団主義の功罪

集団主義には当然ながらプラス，マイナスの両面がある。戦前の無批判な軍国主義化は後者であろうし，戦後の高度成長の原動力となったニッポン式経営は，たとえ一部にエコノミック・アニマルと批判を浴びても，全般的にはプラスの集団主義であり，外国から「日本に学べ」の声も出るわけである。しかし，当の日本ではこれとは逆に個性化，多様化への志向が年々強まっており，集団主義を日本人の永久不変の特性とする見方が見直される時代も来るかもしれない。

Groupism

Perceptions of the Group

Edwin O. Reischauer writes in his book, *The Japanese*, that Japanese groupism and Western individualism mark one of the most conspicuous differences between Japanese and Westerners. Very few Japanese would disagree.

In the past, Japanese group spirit was alarmingly evident in the gung-ho zeal of World War II, the mass suicides, and slogans such as *ichioku isshin* (a nation united) ; and today it is still broadly and deeply entrenched, not only in the blue-suit world of the office worker, but also in the school-uniform world of children. The pressure to conform is described by a Japanese saying that "The nail that sticks out gets pounded down", and the ultimate punishment of *murahachibu** ostracism that awaits non-conformists. It can generally be said that the group defines the individual in Japanese society, and the individual is only significant in so far as he or she represents the group.

Historical Roots

Japanese groupism's earliest traces can be found in the rice-farming civilization of the *Yayoi* period when rice cultivation required group effort. Even today, neighbors in many villages work together in planting and harvesting their crops. Unlike nomadic societies, agrarian cultures demand communal cooperation, discipline, and a sense of shared fate. Japanese groupism was also shaped by the nation's Confucian heritage. Confucian morality stressing filial piety became widespread in the *Edo* period as an integral part of the household system that made the household the basic unit of society. Under this system, the authority of the household head was absolute, all family members must obey the household, and all household members were collectively responsible for each other's actions, meaning that all could be punished for a serious offense by any.

Another fact that has helped shape Japanese groupism is that so many people live so close together. Foreign visitors stare in disbelief at the crowds that jam the commuter trains morning and evening, yet the Japanese put up with these conditions because they know that making the best of togetherness is the only choice.

Pros and Cons

Naturally, Japanese groupism has its positive and negative sides. On the negative side, it is reminiscent of the earlier blind obedience to military authority, but on the positive side group unity has contributed to the nation's phenomenal postwar economic growth, which, despite its "economic animal" aspects, continues to draw positive comment from people interested in learning from Japan. In recent years, however, Japanese have turned increasingly to individualism, and the idea of Japan as a monolithic group is coming up for reexamination.

「義理人情」という観念は，封建時代に確立し，重視された。しかし，現代においても芝居，映画，*演歌，浪曲などによく取り上げられ，日本人の共感を呼ぶテーマとなっている。

相克する義理と人情

義理人情は「義理」と「人情」という二つのことばを合わせたものである。義理とは，社会生活を営むうえでの他人に対する道徳的なルールである。つまり，親子・主従・師弟などの上下関係，友人・隣近所などの対等の関係において守らなければならない道義である。例えば，「人に恩をかけてもらったら，必ずそれに報いる」などで，それを踏みはずせば「義理を欠く」ことになる。これに対して，人情は，人間がだれでももっている自分や家族などへの愛情である。

　したがって，義理と人情はしばしば対立するものであり，日本では，人情よりも義理を重んじるべきだと考えられてきた。君主への義理から自分の子供を殺す，などは人情を抑えて義理を通した典型的な例である。義理人情は，この相克する二つのことばを並び用いることで，生きていくうえでのつらい感覚を，つまり「義理と人情の板挟(ばさ)み」に苦しむ様を表現している。

近松の作品に見る義理人情

江戸時代の文芸は義理人情を題材にしたものが多い。中でも近松門左衛門は心中物で，義理と人情の板挟みに苦しむ人間たちを描いて人気があった。近松の物語は，妻子がありながら*遊女に夢中になった商人が，商売を顧みずに破綻(はたん)し，その精算に遊女と心中する話である。登場人物がそれぞれの立場で義理と人情の板挟みになり，あれこれと悩み抜き，あれこれと行動し，あげくのはてに主人公とヒロインは心中するという悲劇に追い込まれていくようすが，人々の心を揺り動かしたのであろう。

現代の義理人情

近代的な契約精神に基づくビジネス社会に，封建時代のような義理人情は，もはや不必要なことは言うまでもないことであるが，日常の心配りとしての「義理を欠かないこと」は，なお求められることが多い。社会的な付き合いを重んじる人のことを「義理堅い人」と言って評価するし，中元・歳暮や冠婚葬祭に際しての贈答なども，義理が日本人の生活習慣に深く入り込んでいる例と言える。

Giri and Ninjou

The concepts of *giri* and *ninjou* were well established by the feudal period and remain important themes in the theater, film, *enka** songs, and *Naniwa-bushi* narrative ballads even today.

Conflict between *Giri* and *Ninjou*

Giri refers to the many social obligations which are needed for smooth relations in Japan's vertical society—between parent and child, master and servant, and teacher and disciple—and between equals such as friends and neighbors. As such, *giri* is the moral duty to fulfill obligations and repay favors received, and to fail to meet the requirements of *giri* is seen as a major moral shortcoming. In contrast, *ninjou* encompasses those all-too-human feelings and inclinations that we all share. *Giri* is what your mind tells you to do, and *ninjou* what your heart tells you to do.

It is only natural that *giri* and *ninjou* should come into conflict at times, and in Japan *giri* has most often taken precedence over *ninjou*. The classic case is that of the ancient warrior who had, in extreme cases, to kill his own child rather than betray his duty to his lord. Together, the combination of *giri* and *ninjou* (popularly represented by the run-on word *giri-ninjou*) symbolizes the anguish of being forced to choose between what your sense of duty tells you you have to do and what your emotions want you to do.

Chikamatsu's *Giri-ninjou* Plays

Many *Edo* period literary works focused on the eternal conflict between *giri* and *ninjou*, none more poignantly than the double-suicide plays of *Chikamatsu Monzaemon*. Thus the typical *Chikamatsu* play might be about a merchant who falls madly and passionately in love with a courtesan,* to the dismay of his family and the detriment of his business, until eventually, because they cannot bear to be apart and society will not let them be together, they commit suicide together. *Edo* audiences were greatly moved by these plays in which every actor battled with the dilemma of the *giri-ninjou* conflict, and which invariably culminated in tragic suicide as the only way out of the situation.

Giri and *Ninjou* Today

Although the contractual foundations of modern business practices have alleviated the intensity of some *giri-ninjou* conflicts, the concept of *giri* remains an important element in social relationships. A person who is careful to meet all *giri* obligations is greatly admired as *giri-gatai*; and such formal manifestations of social or business *giri* as the *chuugen* and *seibo* gifts in summer and winter remain, along with all of the many social obligations that go with marriages, births, funerals, and the other rites of passage of life, an integral part of the contemporary Japanese lifestyle.

まとまった休暇がめったにとれない多くの日本人にとって，大半の職場が休みになる正月は，一年の中でいちばんのんびりする期間である。日ごろ世話になっている知人，仕事の得意先への年始回りなど，まるきり仕事抜きというわけにもいかないが，それでも，こたつを囲んで*おとそを飲みながらテレビの正月番組を見たり，いつもは接触時間の少ない子供たちとも親子の対話をして過ごせる。

1月5日か7日ぐらいから仕事が始まるが，2月初めぐらいまでは付き合いを大事にする日本社会の慣例として，職場の同僚や知人との新年会に忙殺されて，正月気分がなかなか抜けない。その期間を過ぎると，今度は4月まで落ちつかない季節が続く。というのも，職場や学校などの新年度が始まるのが4月だからで，自分自身の職場での人事異動がどうなるか，転勤はないか，子供がいる場合は子供たちの進・入学，就職は大丈夫かと，何かと心配事が多くなる。

どうにか新しい生活のペースに慣れるのが5月ごろ。一息ついたところで，6月半ば過ぎから7月にかけて，夏のボーナスが支給される。住宅ローンを払ったり貯蓄に回した残りで，自分の欲しかったゴルフクラブなどを買い，妻や子供たちにも何か買ってやるのが，日ごろ，宮仕えの身のサラリーマンにとってはささやかな楽しみである。

7月下旬から約40日間，子供たちは学校が夏休みに入る。父親もその間に1週間ぐらいの夏休みをとるのが普通。日ごろ働きづめの父親としては家でゆっくりくつろぎたいところだが，旅行やドライブなどの家庭サービスでふだんの日より疲れてしまうか，逆に妻や子供たちだけ*里帰りや旅行に出し，父親は「にわかやもめ」で留守番というケースが多い。夏休みとは言えゆっくり憩えないのがつらいところだ。

気候が穏やかな秋は行楽シーズン。職場の運動会などに家族そろって参加して体を動かしたり，紅葉を求めてドライブやハイキングに行く家庭が多い。

12月に入ると，夫は28日の*仕事納めまで仕事に追われ，29日から年末の休みに入る。妻は大掃除や正月準備であわただしく過ごす。12月31日の大みそかには，家族そろって*年越しそばを食べながら，NHKの年末恒例番組「紅白歌合戦」などを見て，新年を迎える。

The Japanese Year

Largely unable to take any long vacations at other times of the year, most Japanese look forward to the New Year's holidays when most of the population is on vacation. Although not completely business-free, since it is a time for courtesy calls on the boss, good customers, and other people who have helped him during the year, this is a rare opportunity for the businessman to relax with his family, sitting around the *kotatsu*, sipping sweet *sake*,* watching the television specials, and talking leisurely with his children in a welcome change from the hectic pace of the rest of the year.

Work resumes about half a dozen days into January, yet the emphasis on congeniality means that the month is filled with new year's parties with friends and co-workers, and it is hard to get over the holiday spirit. Once these parties are over, a period of anxiety sets in from February to April. Because the business and school years start in April, people worry about personnel shifts and possible transfers at work and, if they have children, about whether or not the children will get into the school of their choice or find a good job after graduation.

It is not until May or so that people are able to settle down in the new year's routine. Soon afterward, in late June or early July, it is time for the summer bonus. This is a real treat for the beleaguered employee, enabling him to make another large payment on the mortgage, to put a little money aside for a rainy day, and perhaps even to buy that new set of golf clubs that he wanted, or to get something for the wife and kids.

Summer vacation for the children starts near the end of July and lasts about six weeks, and it is common for the man of the house to take a week off during this period. Although father would like to putter around the house and just do nothing for a change, the rest of the family wants to travel, and father often ends up more tired from vacation than from his normal work routine—that is, if he does not stay at home and bachelor while his wife takes the children to visit their grandparents.* It is a sad state of affairs when people cannot relax on their summer vacations.

The temperate fall is a season for enjoying outings. There are company field days with the whole family taking part in sports events, and many families go for hikes or drives in the country to see the autumn foliage.

Come December, and father wraps up the year's work* on the 28th and goes into vacation mode on the 29th. Mother, of course, is busy with the year-end cleaning and many preparations for the New Year's holidays. On New Year's eve, the whole family joins together in eating *toshikoshi-soba*,* watching NHK's *Kouhaku Uta-gassen* and other special programs, and welcoming in the new year.

人生80年。男は28.5歳，女は26.2歳で結婚し，結婚して２，３年の間に子供を１人か２人つくり，子供が成長して結婚するのが男女とも50代後半。60歳か65歳ぐらいで夫は仕事をやめ，その後は夫婦だけの老後を送る—というのが，現代の日本人のおおまかなライフスタイルである。

1950年代後半以降の高度経済成長時代には，諸外国から「エコノミック・アニマル」と評されたように，仕事に打ち込むためにはある程度，家庭を犠牲にしてもかまわないと考える「モーレツ型」がサラリーマンの主流だったが，現在では個人生活を大切にしたい(59.3%)，自分の趣味にあった暮らし方をしたい(72.8%)とする「マイホーム型」が多数を占めている(北越銀行「フレッシュマンの意識調査」1995年)。

子供中心の一生

その家庭での中心は，やはり子供である。３歳と５歳の男の子，３歳と７歳の女の子の祝いである11月15日の七五三のほかにも，毎年，３月３日の桃の節句には女の子の，５月５日の端午(たんご)の節句には男の子の，無事な成長を祈って祝う。６，７歳で子供が小学校に入学すると，今度は教育が親の最大の関心事になる。日本の教育は小学校６年間，中学校３年間が義務教育である。その上の高校への進学率は97%，大学へも二人に一人の割合で進学している。こういう高学歴社会を反映して，多くの親は子供を少しでもいい学校へ入れようと，小学生のころから塾通いをさせる。高校・大学の受験に失敗すると１，２年は予備校にも通わせる。教育費捻出(ねんしゅつ)は親にとっては頭の痛い問題だ。

子供が20歳になって成人式を終えると，一応，親の責任を果たしたことになるが，大学生は授業料も生活費も親がかり。結婚式の費用まで親に頼っている若者が少なくない現状だから，親が子供から解放されるのは，就職・結婚を経て，子供も自分の家庭をもったときということになろう。気がついてみると，夫は，もう定年が目の前。子供たちは自分の生活をエンジョイするばかりで，あまり親のことを顧みない。そのうち定年がやってくる。どこかで寂しさを感じながらも，ようやく夫婦二人して，趣味に生きたり，旅行を楽しんだりして余生を生きるというのが，日本人の一生の理想の姿である。ところが，近年，自らの一生を夫と子供のために犠牲にして来たと感じる初老の女性が，定年後の夫を見捨てて離婚し，自活の道を進むという風潮も出始めている。

The average Japanese life span is about 80 years. The average age at which people get married is 28.5 for men and 26.2 for women. In a few years, the typical Japanese couple has one or two children. By the time their children are out of the nest, Japanese parents are in their late 50s. With the husband generally retiring at 60-65, the elderly couple spends their remaining years enjoying life together.

During the rapid economic growth from the late 1950s through the early 1970s, when Japanese were referred to as economic animals, the typical employee devoted himself enthusiastically to his work, often at the expense of family life. Today, however, (according to a 1995 *Hokuetsu* Bank survey of young people just entering the work force), these people are more home-oriented, 59.3% saying their private lives take precedence and 72.8% saying they want to develop their own interests.

Focus on Children

The Japanese family revolves around its children. Ancient festivals to pray for the children's sound development are still celebrated today: *Shichi-go-san* (7-5-3) on November 15 for boys 3 and 5 and girls 3 and 7 years old, the Doll Festival on March 3 for girls, and Children's Day on May 5, traditionally a celebration for boys and now a national holiday for all children. Children start school at age 6-7, at which point education becomes a major concern for Japanese parents. The Japanese school system is divided into six years of elementary education, three of junior high school, three of high school, and four of university. Only the first nine years are compulsory, but 97% of Japanese junior high students go on to high school and half of the high-school graduates go on to college. In the highly educated Japanese society, parents work to get their children into as good a school as possible. Even as early as elementary school, children are sent to *juku* (cram schools) to prepare for their next-level entrance examinations, and those who do poorly the first time around on high-school or university entrance exams often spend a year or two boning up at special cram schools. All of this costs money, of course, and education is a major expense for the Japanese family.

While parents are not legally responsible for their children after they come of age at twenty, most parents continue to pay their children's living expenses and tuition through university, and many Japanese still expect their parents to defray wedding costs. Japanese parents find it difficult to get free of financial responsibility for their children until well after the children have finished their education, found jobs, gotten married, and settled down with their own children. Before they know it, father is near retirement and the children are too involved in their own lives to pay much attention to their parents. While post-retirement is an empty time for some people, the ideal is that husband and wife are finally free to pursue travel and other hobby interests together. Recently, however, some women have chosen this time to retire from their wife-and-mother roles, filing for divorce and moving out to spend these years doing all of the things they could not do before.

あいづちとうなずき

日本人は会話中にあいづちやうなずきを頻繁にする習慣があると言われる。「ハイ」とか「エーソウデスネ」とかのことばによるものも，頭や上体を前に倒す身ぶりだけのものも含めて，ある調査によれば日常会話の場合には数秒に1回の割合で観察されるほどである。しかし，すべてが「そのとおりだ」「了解した」という肯定の意味で行われているわけではなく，単に「ああ，そうですか」「そういうこともあるのですか」と相手の話を聞いているサインとして発しているだけの場合が多いことに注意すべきである。

こうした日本人と接して欧米人が「彼は確かにあのとき肯定した」と受け取ったとすれば，当の日本人によっては予想外のことである。逆に，こうしたあいづちやうなずきに慣れた日本人は，会話中に相手の話に何の反応も示してこない欧米人に不安感——この人は私の話を聞いてくれるのか？——を感じることになる。

婉曲(えんきょく)表現

日本人は自分の意見を確固としてもっていても，「私はこう考える」「私の意見はこうだ」という直接的な表現は避け，「こうなるのではないでしょうか」「こう考えたいのですがいかがでしょう」などといった婉曲な言い回しをするほうが適当で丁寧(ていねい)だと考える傾向が強い。相手に考慮や判断の余地を残してあることを言語表現のうえでもはっきりと言い，相手から返ってくる反応を取り込んで自分の主張を表現していこうとする姿勢の表れである。ともすれば，自分の意見をはっきりと言わない，主体性に欠けた言語行動と評価されることがあるが，むしろ，相手との協同作業で会話を進めていこうとする態度の表れであり，あいづちを頻繁にするという前述のことと共通している。

あいさつ

日本人はあいさつをよくすると言われる。確かに朝起きてから夜寝るまで，日常生活のさまざまな場面で決まって用いられる定型的なあいさつことばも豊富である。ただ，あいさつを交わすのは，何らかの意味で仲間うちと見なした相手にだけであって，例えば公園を散歩していて会った見知らぬ人，乗り物で同席しただけの人などにはよほどのことがないかぎりことばをかけることはまれである。彼らがその場では部外者・ヨソ者だからである。日本人が閉鎖的と評されるひとつの原因だろう。

Japanese Verbal Signals

Conversational Counterpoint

When two Japanese are talking, the listener not only listens but also nods along and voices various counterpoint phrases—much like counterpoint in music—to keep the rhythm of the conversation going. This custom of interspersing such interjections as *Hai* (yes) and *Ee, sou desu ne* (yes, quite right) was recently the subject of a statistical study which found that such interjections occur once every few seconds in the typical conversation. However, interjections do not necessarily express agreement with the speaker. People often use quasi-interrogative expressions such as *Aa, sou desu ka* (is that right?) and *Sou iu koto mo aru no desu ka* (can that be true?) to merely affirm that they are listening.

These "yes, I'm listening" interjections or nods can cause considerable confusion in cases where a non-Japanese speaker misconstrues them as signs of agreement. Conversely, a Japanese speaker can get confused and disconcerted when a non-Japanese listener fails to provide the appropriate counterpoint responses. Even though the listener is probably being very attentive, the Japanese speaker begins to wonder if the other person has not gone to sleep on him/her.

Indirect Expression

Even though the speaker might have a strong opinion about something, he will usually avoid such direct statements as "this is what I think" or "this is my opinion." Instead, the typical Japanese will use indirect phrases such as "don't you think so?" or "this is how it would seem to me, but what do you think?"—those roundabout, tentative phrases that are generally considered more appropriate for polite conversation. By using such indirect expressions, the speaker leaves room for the other side to disagree with the idea without having to disagree with the person—as well as leaving room for him/her to fine-tune his/her own statements to take account of the other side's opinions and avoid offense. While occasionally criticized as being wishy-washy, these efforts to soften statements of opinion—just like the responses mentioned above—all reflect the basic Japanese attitude that conversation should be a cooperative activity.

A Friendly Word

The Japanese are also fond of salutations and other civilities. From morning to night, the day is filled with a rich variety of pleasantries used for specific situations. However, as a general rule, these words are only spoken to friends and acquaintances, and most Japanese are not given to speaking to strangers in the park or on the train. Instead, such people are regarded as unknowns outside the ken of their concern, and this tendency to restrict sociability to people they already know is one reason why Japanese have acquired a reputation for being anti-social.

21 日本人のジェスチャー(1)

日本人の身ぶりやしぐさの中には，日本人に特有な，あるいは他国文化とその意味・用法が異なるものがある。

•おじぎ　日本人どうしのあいさつでは「おじぎ」をすることが基本である。立ったままの場合は，足をそろえて直立し，上体をかがめて頭を下げる。軽い会釈から，体を90度に折ってするおじぎまで，丁寧(ていねい)さの程度によって頭を下げる角度はさまざまである。畳の部屋では，必ず座ってあいさつする。「正座」の姿勢から身をかがめ，両手を前について頭を下げる。

日本人のあいさつでは体と体の接触はないのが普通で，握手の習慣は伝統的なものではない。日本人も握手をすることがあるが，日本人と外国人，立候補者と選挙民，タレントとファンなどの特殊な関係である場合が多い。

•座る　学校・会社など一般の生活ではすべていす式になっているが，家庭では日本人は伝統的には畳の上に直接座るか，座ぶとんを敷いて座る生活を続けてきた。最近では，一般家庭でも居間や食堂は洋間であることが多いので，畳の上に座らない若い世代も増えている。

畳の上での正しい座り方は「正座」で，両ひざをそろえて足を折り，かかとの上にしりを載せる。ふだんの生活で正座に慣れていないと，足がしびれてしまうつらい座り方である。楽な座り方には「あぐら」や「横座り」がある。「あぐら」は足を前で組んでしりを床に落とす。ズボンをはいた女性がまれに「あぐらをかく」こともあるが，これはむしろ例外で，「あぐら」は男性の座り方である。正座の足を少し横にくずした「横座り」は主に女性に見られる。

▽おじぎ(bowing)

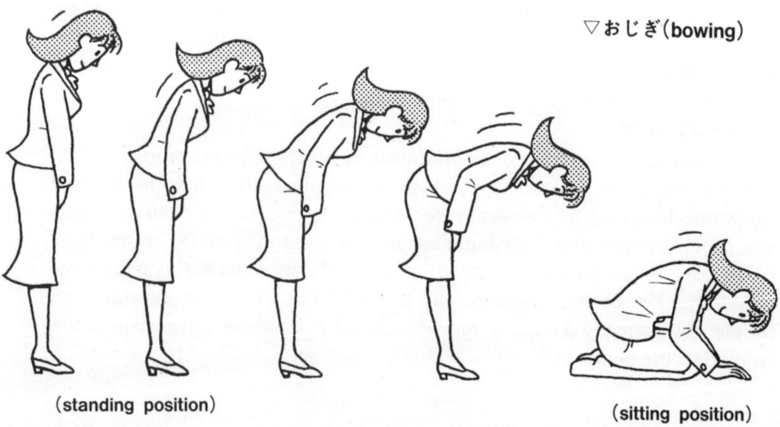

Japanese Gestures (1)

There are many gestures which are unique to Japan or which do not mean the same thing in Japan as they do elsewhere.

• **Bowing** Japanese greet each other by bowing. When bowing from a standing position, it is customary to stand at attention and bow from the waist. There are many levels of bowing, from a simple nod of the head to forming a 90-degree angle, depending on the degree of respect one wishes to convey. In a *tatami* room one always bows from a sitting position with feet tucked under the buttocks and both hands on the floor in front.

Japanese do not customarily touch each other in greeting, and shaking hands is not a traditional practice. When Japanese do shake hands it is usually with a foreigner or under special circumstances such as in the exchange of greetings between a politician and his supporters or a celebrity and his fans.

• **Sitting** While schools and companies furnished with desks and chairs are the norm today, the Japanese traditionally sat on *tatami*, either directly or on cushions, in their homes. However, many homes today are completely Western style with no *tatami* rooms, and an increasing number of young Japanese are unable to sit properly on *tatami*.

The proper method of sitting on *tatami* is to bend the knees 180 degrees, tuck your calves under your thighs, and sit on your heels. This can be a difficult posture to maintain if you are unaccustomed to it because the constant pressure is likely to make your feet go to sleep. Another, more comfortable way of sitting is to sit cross-legged, but this posture is usually reserved for men (although some women might sit this way when they are wearing slacks). Women would usually go from the formal to an informal sitting posture by shifting their feet to one side so that they are not actually sitting on them.

△正座
(proper method of sitting)

△あぐら
(sitting cross-legged)

△横座り
(feet to one side)

22 日本人のジェスチャー（2）

• マルとバツ　日本では，◯(マル)と×(バツ)のもつ意味は，明確である。◯は「正解」「合格」「勝つ」「OK」などのプラスのイメージを，×は「誤り」「不合格」「負け」「だめ」などのマイナスのイメージを表している。したがって，マルとバツの形状のものはすべてこれらの意味をもつと考えてよい。身ぶりとしては，親指とひとさし指で，あるいは時に両腕を頭上に回して「マル」を，両手のひとさし指，あるいは両腕を交差させて「バツ」を示す。

• 数の数え方　1～10まで片手だけで数える。1～5は，親指からひとさし指，中指と順に指を折っていく。6～10は反対に小指から順に折り曲げた指を開いていく。性別，年齢，その他にかかわりなく広く使われている。

相手に数を指し示すときには，手のひらを相手に向けて，指を軽く結んでひとさし指・中指・薬指・小指・親指の順で起こしていく。6～10は，残りの片方の手を使って同じ動作を加えていく。

• 手招き　手のひらを下に向けて軽く開き，手首から先を数回手前に動かす。性別，年齢にかかわらず使われるが，目上に対しては失礼になるので避けられる。

• 自分　「それは私です」「私？」という意味合いで，ひとさし指で自分の鼻を指す。

• 万歳　勝負に勝ったり，幸運を得たときに両手を挙げて喜ぶ動作。大勢で「万歳」と唱和して，幸運を願ったり，祝福の気持ちを表すことが多い。

△マル(OK)

△バツ(×)

△数の数え方
(counting)

△数の示し方
(indicating numbers)

Japanese Gestures (2)

• **Os and Xs** Circles and Xs have clearly defined symbolic meaning in Japan. The circle has such positive associations as correct, passing, winning, and OK. The X, on the other hand, stands for such negative things as mistake, failure, defeat, and rejection. These meanings are conveyed in all circumstances, whether written or as gestures. On a true/false test, true is O and false X. The circle is often formed with the thumb and forefinger or by holding the arms upraised with the fingers touching to make an O, and the X by crossing the forefingers of both hands or making a big X with the arms.

• **Counting** When counting on their fingers, Japanese use only one hand, starting with the fingers outspread and folding in the thumb, forefinger, middle finger, ring finger, and little finger for one through five; six through ten being the exact reverse as the little finger, ring finger, and so on are unfolded. This is the most commonly used method regardless of sex or age.

To indicate numbers to another person, it is customary to raise one hand with the palm outward and the appropriate number of fingers raised: starting with the forefinger for one and then adding, in order, the middle finger, the ring finger, the little finger, and finally the thumb. To count up to ten the fingers of the other hand are added in the same manner.

• **Beckoning** Japanese beckon with a waving motion with the palm down and the hand flapping up and down at the wrist. This gesture is used by Japanese of both sexes and all age groups, but it is considered impolite to beckon a superior this way.

• **Indicating Oneself** Japanese point to their noses with a forefinger to indicate themselves or to ask, "Who, me?"

• ***Banzai*** A shout made while raising both arms high to commemorate a victory or some other auspicious event. It is commonly done in unison by large groups to indicate felicitations toward a person or the success of some venture.

▽手招き(**beckoning**)

▽自分を示す
(**indicating oneself**)

▷万歳(***banzai***)

日本語は，日本人およびアメリカなどの日系移民によって使われており，使用人口のうえからでは，世界の言語の中で*上位に数えられるが，使用者および使用地域が限定されているため，今まで注目を集めることが少なかった。しかし，近年，国際社会における日本の地位の向上に伴い，日本語も国際語として学習されるようになってきた。

系統と歴史

日本語の系統についてはさまざまの説が提唱されているが，いまだに決着がついていない。文法上の類似点が多いため，朝鮮語(韓国語)，モンゴル語などのアルタイ諸語と関係づけようとする説がある。日本と共通の文化要素が見られる，中国南部からヒマラヤにまで及ぶ照葉樹林帯ないしその周辺の言語(例えばチベット語)の中に同じ系統の言語を求めようとする試みもある。ポリネシア語や*ドラビダ語と起源を同じくするという意見もある。

日本語の最古の記録は3世紀にさかのぼり，中国の歴史書の日本についての記事に引用された語彙(ごい)を最初とする。以来，日本語は漢字を借用して表記されてきたが，後に，漢字から発達した音節文字(仮名(かな))によっても表記されるようになった。現在，表意文字である漢字と表音文字である仮名を混用して表示するという正書法が使われているが，この正書法の複雑さが日本語の国際語化を妨げる一因となっている。

特徴

日本語は日本全国に通用するただ一つの言語であるが，地域，性，社会階層および職種によって顕著な方言差が認められる。特に，地域的方言差はそれぞれが方言で話し合えば，ほとんど意志の疎通を欠くことがあるほどであるが，東京方言を基礎としたいわゆる標準語が，教育およびマスコミの普及によって広く浸透している。日本語には，音声の長短が有意味である，高低アクセントがある，音節構造が単純であるなどという音声的特徴がある。音節の形式が単純であるから，同音異義語が多く，そのために，表意文字である漢字による表記が廃(すた)らないのである。

文化的影響が大きかったため，中国語からの借用が多く，中国語的単語は全語彙の60％以上だと言われる。近年，欧米の文物が導入されると欧米語，特に英語からの借用が顕著である。

その他，日本語の特徴としては，文法的機能が語幹と接辞の結合で表示される，いわゆる*膠着(こうちゃく)語であること，厳密な意味での人称代名詞という文法範疇(はんちゅう)が存在しない点などが指摘される。

The Japanese Language

Although the Japanese language is used by a large number of people,* including all of the Japanese in Japan and many Japanese immigrants overseas, its relatively isolated position has contributed to keeping it a minor international language. Nevertheless, Japan's increasing importance in the global community has sparked greater study of the Japanese language internationally.

Origins

There are many theories seeking to explain the origin of the Japanese language, none of which is uncontested. Citing the many grammatical similarities, some scholars have linked Japanese to Korean or to Mongolian and the other Altaic languages. Other scholars seek the language's origins in the ecologically and culturally similar societies from Southern China to the Himalayas. Yet others claim the language's origins are the same as the Polynesian or Dravidian languages.*

The oldest known record of Japanese dates back to the 3rd century, when a Chinese history book entry on Japan contained several Japanese words. Although Japanese has long used Chinese ideograms (*kanji*) for writing, it has also developed its own phonetic *kana* syllabaries based upon well-known ideograms. Today the ideograms and *kana* phonetics are used together in standard writing, and the complexity of this *kanji-kana* intermix is another factor keeping Japanese from becoming an international language.

Characteristics

Although it is the only language used in Japan, Japanese itself varies widely depending upon the speaker's regional identification, sex, social status, and occupation. Regional dialects are so strong as to sometimes impede communication among people from different areas, but these differences have diminished since the educational system and mass media adopted a "standard" Japanese based upon the *Toukyou* (Tokyo) dialect. The sound of Japanese is distinguished by short and extended vowel sounds with meaning-significant differences between them, pitch accents, and a simple consonant-vowel syllable structure. Yet the very simplicity of the sound structure means there are necessarily many homonyms, which is another reason for retaining the ideographic *kanji*.

Chinese has been a major influence upon Japanese culture and language, and over 60% of all Japanese words are drawn from Chinese. In recent years, however, the increasing access to Euro-American culture has meant a greater borrowing of words from Western languages, especially English.

Other features of Japanese are that it is an agglutinative language,* indicating grammatical structure by attaching markers to word stems, and that it has no personal pronouns per se.

3 種類の文字

現代の日本語は，基本的には，ひらがな，かたかな，漢字の 3 種類の文字で書き表される。もともと日本には固有の文字はなかった。奈良時代以前に中国から漢字が学び入れられて，日本語が漢字で書かれるようになり，さらに平安時代以降，漢字の字体をくずしたひらがなや，漢字の一部分を取り出したかたかなが用いられるようになって，現在のように 3 種類の文字が日本語に定着した。

ひらがな

ひらがなは，例えば「あ」が「安」,「い」が「以」など，それぞれ漢字のくずし字体から，日本で考案され定着した文字である。一文字ごとが，それぞれ日本語の発音上の単位である拍(音節)に対応した表音文字である。「゛」や「゜」などの補助記号もあって，濁音や半濁音を表すこともできる。もともとの日本語である和語(大和(やまと)ことば)を書き表すのに多く使うが，特に「が，から，けれども」などの助詞や「れる，られる，です，ます」などの助動詞はひらがなで書くのが普通である。また，一般的な文章は，ひらがなと漢字を混ぜて書くのが現代日本語では定着している。

かたかな

かたかなは，例えば「イ」が「伊」,「ロ」が「呂」などのように，同じ読みをもつ漢字の字形の一部分を取り出して，日本で考案され定着した。ひらがなと同様，表音文字である。現代では，西欧からの外来語(ホテル，ワイン，コンピューターなど)や，外国の地名・人名(イギリス，ソウル，シューベルトなど)，あるいは動物・植物の名前(ウサギ，カバ，バラ，バナナなど)を書き表すのにかたかなを用いるのが普通である。「ザーザー，ゴトゴト」などの擬音語，擬態語(オノマトペ)もかたかなで書くことが多い。

漢字

漢字は，もともと中国から取り入れた文字であるが，日本語を表記する文字として定着している。日本の地名や人名(特に姓)，あるいは中国から入った漢語などは漢字で書くのが普通であるほか,「国，町，海，山，花」「行く，住む，動く」などの和語を漢字で書くことも一般的である。変わった表記として「煙草(タバコ)，倶楽部(クラブ)」など西欧からの外来語に漢字を当てる例もある。

Japanese Writing

Three Scripts

Japanese writing today uses basically three scripts: *kanji*, *hiragana*, and *katakana*. Because ancient Japanese did not have a written language, *kanji* (lit. Han letters) were adopted and adapted from China before 500 AD and Japanese was written solely in *kanji*. Given the awkwardness of this system, sound-representing *hiragana* and *katakana* scripts were developed from *kanji* starting in the *Heian* period—*hiragana* from simplified writing of the *kanji* and *katakana* taking parts of the different *kanji*.

Hiragana

As mentioned, *hiragana* derives from simplified forms of the appropriate *kanji*. Thus あ[read:*a*] is a very simplified writing of 安[*an*] and い[*i*] a simplification of 以[*i*]. Each *hiragana* represents a single sound voiced for a single syllable. For some *hiragana* (and *katakana*), ゛ may be added to indicate voicing (k → g, s → z, etc.), or ゜ to change h into p. *Hiragana* is used primarily to write words or parts of words indigenous to Japanese—especially connectors such as *ga, kara* and *keredomo*, and word or sentence endings such as *-reru, -rareru, -masu*, and *-desu*. Most writing today is a mixture of *kanji* and *hiragana*.

Katakana

Katakana was created taking parts of *kanji*. Thus イ[*i*] comes from 伊[*i*] and ロ[*ro*] from 呂[*ro*]. In both *hiragana* and *katakana*, the simplification or part represented the *kanji* but the *kanji* was stripped of its meaning and used only to show the sound. Today, *katakana* is used primarily to write loan words from English and other non-*kanji* languages (e.g., ホテル[*hoteru*=hotel], ワイン[*wain*=wine], and コンピューター[*konpyuutaa*=computer]); foreign proper nouns (e.g., イギリス[*igirisu*=England], ソウル[*souru*=Seoul], and シューベルト[*shuuberuto*=Schubert]); and many plant and animal names (e.g., ウサギ[*usagi*=hare], カバ[*kaba*=hippopotamus], バラ[*bara*=rose], and バナナ[*banana*=banana]). *Katakana* is also widely used for onomatopoeia and other sound representations (e.g., ザーザー *zaazaa* [the sound of fast-running water] and ゴトゴト *gotogoto*[the sound of something simmering]).

Kanji

Imported from China, *kanji* are no longer thought of as an import but have become firmly established as the standard way to write much Japanese. Japanese proper nouns are usually written in *kanji*, the many terms that have come into the language from Chinese are still written in *kanji*, and there are numerous indigenous Japanese terms that are written in *kanji* given Japanese readings—including nouns (e.g., 国[*kuni*=country], 町[*machi*=town], 海[*umi*=sea], 山[*yama*=mountain], and 花[*hana*=flower]), verbs (e.g., 行く[*iku*=go], 住む[*sumu*=live], and 動く[*ugoku*=move]), and more. There are even some relatively recent terms from non-Chinese languages that are now sometimes written in *kanji* (e.g., 煙草[*tabako*=tobacco] and 倶楽部[*kurabu*=club]).

敬語とは

話したり書いたりするときには，その相手の人物や話題に登場する人物に対してうやまったり，へりくだったりする気配りがある。また，その場が改まった場であるか，ふだんの場であるかということについても気配りがある。これらは，日本人に限った気配りではないであろうが，日本語ではこうした気配りを敬語という特別のことばや言い回しによって表現するのが普通である。

同じ意味でも相手や場合で違った言い方

例えば，「だれかがどこかへ行く」という動作を表現するときでも，自分自身が目上の人の所に行く場合には「まいる・うかがう」などのへりくだった表現（謙譲語）を使うし，逆に目上の人がどこかに行く場合には「いらっしゃる・おいでになる」など敬った表現(尊敬語)を使う。また，親しい話し相手に気楽に話せる場では「行くよ・行くわ」が普通なのに対して，あまり親しくない相手の改まって話す場では「行きます・行くんです」などのていねいな表現を選ぶのが普通である。「ます，です」はていねい語と呼ばれる。

人の動作や状態，持ち物などにも敬語

上に挙げた「行く」の敬語は動作を表すことばの敬語だが，このほかにも「ご立派，おきれい」など人のようすや状態にも，また「お手紙，ご職業，お考え，ご家族」など人に属するものごと(持ち物)にも敬語の「お，ご」を付けて言う。

改まった言い方と普通の言い方

普通に敬語という場合には，上に挙げた尊敬語，謙譲語，ていねい語の3種類を指すが，話し相手や場所柄への気配りを表す表現はこれだけではない。例えば，「めし」と「ごはん」，「はら」と「おなか」など，同じ意味でもぞんざいな言い方と改まった言い方があって使い分けられる。また「始める」と「開始する」，「晴れ」と「晴天」，「すぐ」と「早速」などのように，ふだんの気楽な場面では和語を，改まった固い場面では漢語を，というような語の種類による使い分けもある。さらに，個々の単語にとどまらず，言い回しとしても，「ごめん・ごめんなさい・申し訳ございません」「うん，そうだよ・はい，さようでございます」「わかった・かしこまりました・承知いたしました」のように，同じ意味がさまざまな表現で使い分けられる。

What is *Keigo*?

In speaking and writing alike, Japanese expects the speaker or author to pay proper respect to the audience and to the individuals who might be referred to. There is also a certain formality expected in formal situations, and this compounds the emphasis on showing respect through language. While not unique to Japanese, the language used to show this respect is called *keigo*.

Different Ways to Say the Same Thing

Even the simple act of someone's going somewhere is expressed differently depending upon who is going where. If you yourself are going to see a higher-ranking person, the verbs for "go" are *mairu* and *ukagau*. (Because this is used to indicate your own lower status, they might be called "humblifics" as opposed to honorifics.) Should a higher-ranking person go somewhere, the honorific verbs would be *irassharu* and *oideninaru*. There are also levels of formality. If you are talking with close friends, "go" would easily be a casual *iku* with the masculine *yo* or the feminine *wa* markers added on. But in a more formal situation, even among equals, it would be *ikimasu* or *ikundesu*. In effect, the verbs in formal situations take the more polite *-desu* or *-masu* endings, making these what are called "*desu/masu*" situations.

More than Verbs

These same principles also apply to things and even attributes. A friend might be *kirei* (pretty), but the boss's daughter is *o-kirei* (pretty with the honorific "*o*" prefix). Likewise, you send a *tegami* (letter) but your professor sends an *o-tegami*. People in elevated positions have *go-shokugyou* (occupations), *o-kangae* (thoughts), and *go-kazoku* (families, with "*go*" being an alternative reading for the same honorific *kanji*).

Formal Expression and Everyday Expression

Keigo is usually understood to mean these three (honorifics, humblifics, and polite language), but there are also other ways to show respect for other people or places. For example, rice (and by extension, food) can be referred to as *meshi* or *gohan*, the stomach as *hara* or *onaka*, and more—the just-us-guys expression first and the mixed-company expression second in both examples. By the same token, using Chinese-origin terms is seen as more formal than indigenous Japanese terms, examples being *hajimeru* vs. *kaishi-suru* (both meaning "to start"), *hare* vs. *seiten* (clear skies), and *sugu* vs. *sassoku* (soon). It is not only words that have different levels of formality and deference. The same thing happens to entire phrases. For example, moving from informal to formal/deferential, "I'm sorry" can be *gomen*, *gomen-nasai*, or *moushiwake-gozaimasen*; "yes" *hai*, *sou desu*, and *sayoude-gozaimasu*; and "I understand" *wakatta*, *kashikomarimashita*, and *shouchi itashimashita*.

読み物，テレビ，演芸などでは繰り返し英雄が取り上げられる。それら日本人の好きな英雄を，3つのパターンに分けることができる。全国制覇の道半ばで倒れた失意の英雄，立身出世した英雄，そして，貴種流離譚(たん)に属する身分を隠して流浪する貴人である。これらは互いに重なり合って日本人好みの英雄を形作っていると言える。

源義経(よしつね)

失意の英雄の代表は源義経である。義経は，12世紀末に武家政治の時代を築いた源頼朝(よりとも)の弟で，頼朝とともに新しい時代を開いた。その後政治的陰謀に巻き込まれ，頼朝の許可なく軍事・警察組織の長である「判官」に任官し，頼朝と不和になり，失脚する。義経は頼朝に追われ，各地を流浪し，最後は東北地方で死ぬのだが，若い悲劇の英雄として伝説化している。さらに，義経には，北海道を経てシベリアに渡り，モンゴルに至ってチンギス・ハンになったという貴種流離譚の形の伝説まで生まれている。

このほか，群雄割拠(かっきょ)した戦国時代に全国制覇を目ざしながら倒れていった織田信長，*武田信玄，さらに，*明治維新の際，活躍しながら新時代を見ずに死んだ*坂本龍馬(りょうま)などもこのパターンと言ってよい。

豊臣秀吉・徳川家康

立身出世物語の典型は，戦国時代の天下統一を成し遂げた豊臣秀吉である。秀吉は足軽の子でありながら，織田信長の家来となり，さまざまな知恵と勇気で，ついに全国を統一する。秀吉に次ぎ天下を治めた徳川家康も，小大名の息子として12年間も人質となり苦労したが，後に天下を取った。徳川300年の治世を開いた人として，その言動が現代の経営者にもてはやされている。

水戸黄門

貴種流離譚でも源義経がその典型だが，このパターンの変形として，水戸黄門(徳川光圀(みつくに))がいる。徳川家康の孫に当たる大名で，名君と言われた。引退後，身分を隠して，二人の家来とともに全国を巡り歩いたとするフィクションで知られる。危機が近づくと，自分の身分を示す葵(あおい)の紋所を示して，悪をこらしめる。権力のもつ悪に対する庶民の批判であり，同時に庶民の権威志向のあらわれとも言われている。これらは，もしかして自分もそうした英雄となれるかもしれない，自分も英雄の子孫であったらよいのだが，という夢を庶民に与えるものであり，それゆえに，広く支持されてきたとも言えよう。

Popular Heroes

A study of the most popular historical heroes in Japanese literature, on television, and on the stage shows three types: the hero who fails while striving toward some noble ideal, the rags-to-riches hero, and the hero who abandons conventionality to become a lone crusader. Indeed, the Japanese hero is a composite of all three types.

Minamoto no Yoshitsune

The typical heroic failure is *Minamoto no Yoshitsune*. Younger brother of the late-12th-century warrior-statesman *Minamoto no Yoritomo*, *Yoshitsune* joined with *Yoritomo* to inaugurate a new era in Japanese history. However, he was later caught up in political intrigues and driven out when he incurred his brother's distrust by accepting appointment as imperial police commissioner without *Yoritomo*'s approval. Pursued by *Yoritomo, Yoshitsune* fled to the *Touhoku* region, where he died. Yet he remains a popular tragic hero, and stories later arose that he had escaped to Mongolia and reemerged as Genghis Khan.

Other heroes in failure are *Oda Nobunaga* and *Takeda Shingen*,* both of whom sought to unite the country and end its prolonged civil wars, and *Sakamoto Ryouma** who was an activist in the *Meiji* Restoration.*

Hideyoshi and Ieyasu

Toyotomi Hideyoshi's is a rags-to-riches story of his rise from humble birth to ruler of the entire country in the late-16th-century warring states period. Born to a low-ranking family, he became a retainer to *Oda Nobunaga* and quickly unified the country by dint of his bravery and intelligence. *Tokugawa Ieyasu*, who succeeded *Hideyoshi* as ruler of Japan, was born to a higher class but consequently spent 12 years in hostage captivity before gaining the freedom to make his bid for power. As the founder of the *Tokugawa* dynasty which ruled for over 250 years of peace, *Ieyasu* practiced a single-minded patience which continues to earn the respect of today's captains of industry.

Mito Koumon

The prototype crusader for justice, *Tokugawa Mitsukuni* (a.k.a. *Mito Koumon*) was a grandson of *Ieyasu* and a wise fief ruler. After retirement, the story goes, he and two faithful retainers dressed poorly and wandered the land seeking to right social wrongs. In the story, the dangers that they meet in trying to vanquish entrenched evil are often overcome by having *Mito Koumon* reveal his true identity at the crucial point and cow the evil doers into submission. Thus the story is at once a tale of the common man's fight against the abuse of authority and an invocation of authority to rectify such abuses.

These heroes' enduring popularity rests upon the common dream that anyone might himself be such a hero or the descendant of a hero.

日本人論の好きな日本人

日本人がいかに日本人論が好きか，それは書店に行けばたちまちにわかる。自分たちのことについて書かれた本がこれほど並ぶ現象が，およそ他のどの国で考えられようか。しかも，おかしなことに同国人よりも外国人の書いた日本人論のほうが，よりもてはやされるのである。

外国人の著した日本人論

外国人による戦後の代表的な日本人論をいくつか挙げると，第一にR.F.ベネディクトの『菊と刀』がある。「日本文化の型」と副題の付いた同書は，今や日本人論の古典と言える。E.O.ライシャワーの『ザ・ジャパニーズ』は駐日大使も務めた著者の日本研究の集大成で，記述は歴史，社会，政治，経済，あらゆる分野に及んでいる。E.F.ヴォーゲルの『ジャパンアズナンバーワン』は，そのタイトルが流行語になったほどジャーナリスティックな注目を浴びた。その背景には1980年代前半に醸成された日本大国論がある。

『誤解』はEC高官のE.ウィルキンソンが日欧関係に見る誤解と摩擦を直視，解決への道を探った労作。このほか，『孤立する大国ニッポン』(G.ダンプマン)，『縮み志向の日本人』(李御寧)，『ひよわな花・日本』(Z.ブレジンスキー)等々，日本人論はあらゆる国のあらゆる外国人によって書かれ，かなりは著者の国より先に日本で翻訳，出版されている。最大の読者は日本人だからである。

しかし，80年代末から米国で日本の経済力への脅威が叫ばれ，日本は特殊だとするリビジョニズムが起こった。フリードマンらが著した『来たるべき対日戦争』を皮切りに，ファローズ，ウォルフレンらが著書を発表，日本バッシングの理論づけとなっているところから，従来の日本人論とは異なるものとして，日本でも関心と警戒が高まっている。

日本人の著した日本人論

日本人の書いたものでは，70年に出版された『日本人とユダヤ人』(イザヤ・ベンダサン) がロングベストセラーで，日本人論ブームの先駆けであり，また『タテ社会の人間関係』(中根千枝)と『甘えの構造』(土居健郎)は，内外の評価も高い，日本人および日本社会研究の名著である。

日本人論が好きな理由

なぜ日本人は日本人論が好きなのだろうか。まず第一には，日本人がきわめて好奇心の強い民族であること，そして島国であるため外国からの影響に常に敏感であることが考えられる。さらに最近の日本人論の傾向からは，国際社会での日本の役割に，日本人が認識を深めつつあることもうかがえる。

The Japanese Identity Crisis

Any bookstore in Japan provides proof that Japanese love to ponder their national identity. What other people reads so much about itself? And strangely enough, the most popular of these books about the Japanese are those written not by Japanese but by foreign observers.

Foreign Works on Japan

There have been many important books of this genre since the war. Perhaps best known is Ruth F. Benedict's *The Chrysanthemum and the Sword*. This book, subtitled *Patterns of Japanese Culture*, is considered a classic. *The Japanese* by former U.S. Ambassador Edwin O. Reischauer is a scholarly collection of studies of Japanese history, society, politics, economics, and many other fields. Ezra Vogel's best-seller, *Japan As Number 1*, was so talked about in the popular press that the title became a buzzword in Japan. This book appeared at a time when discussions of things Japanese turned to the notion of Japan as a major world power.

Misunderstanding: Europe vs. Japan is a major work in which author Endymion Wilkinson takes a hard look at the fallacies and frictions that have plagued Japan-Europe relations and searches for solutions. Other popular books on Japan by foreign authors include *25mal Japan* by Gerhard Dambmann, *Smaller is Better* by O-Young Lee, *The Fragile Blossom* by Zbigniew Brzezinski, and a host of others by various authors of various nationalities. Many of these works were published in Japanese translation before being published in the author's own language, and Japan is clearly the world's best market for books on Japan.

In the late 1980s, a revisionist school arose that warned of the economic threat from Japan and branded Japan as standing outside the global community. Typical are George Friedman and Meredith Lebard (*The Coming War with Japan*), but the group also includes James Fallows, Karl van Wolferen, and others. Providing the theoretical rationalizations for Japan-bashing, these authors marked a significant departure from earlier observers, and their work is read with great interest and even alarm in Japan.

Books by Japanese Authors

There are, of course, many books by Japanese authors too. One is *The Japanese and the Jews* written under the pseudonym Isaiah Ben Dassan, a marathon best-seller that helped spark the books-on-Japan boom in the 1970s. Others are *Human Relations in a Vertical Society* by *Nakane Chie* and *Anatomy of Dependence* by *Doi Takeo*—both of which won international acclaim as scholarly sociological studies.

Reasons for the Fascination

Why do Japanese like so much to ponder their identity? Perhaps the most important reason is that Japanese are typically very curious. Other observers have argued that, as an island people, the Japanese are more sensitive to outside influences. Yet more recently, the current boom in books about the Japanese can also be seen as evidence that the Japanese are trying to come to terms with their role in the international community.

ウチとソト

日本を訪れた外国人が朝の通勤ラッシュを見て，まず驚くのは，「日本には，日本人ばかりがこんなに大勢いる」ということであるという。日本人と付き合うとき，複雑な多民族国家ではないことが，さまざまな人間関係や行動の基礎になっていることを忘れてはならない。

ほとんど千数百年も血縁集団を中心とした社会が維持されてきた結果，その社会やグループの中では，わざわざことばで言わなくてもしぐさ一つで理解し合えるものや，暗黙のうちに前提となっているようなことが多数存在する。それがわかり合えるのがウチ(内)の人間であり，わからない者はソト(外)の人間として，お客様扱いされるのである。

これは外国人に対しても同じで，日本の習慣や風俗を知らない人は，ガイジン(外人)として別格扱いで親切に扱われるが，日本社会に深くコミットする人は変なガイジンと呼ばれる。

間人主義

欧米で社会の基本は個人主義であるが，日本では“間人主義”であると言う人もいる。独立した人格である個人が作る社会ではなく，つねに社会の中で生活する一人として，人と人の間にいることを基本に置いた社会であると言うのである。ある人に意見を聞いても，「みんなはどう言っていますか」と聞き返されることもよくあることだ。

ホンネとタテマエということばも日本人の間ではよく使われる。ホンネというのは本音，つまり本当の声であり，タテマエは建前で，表向きの方針である。また，ホンネを個人の論理，タテマエを集団の論理としてとらえることもある。日本人は表向きの方針や集団の論理であるタテマエを優先するが，その奥に本当の声，個人の論理であるホンネが潜んでいることはよくある。

こうした，つねに他人や社会を気にしながら生きる日本人の生活の中には，yesでもnoでもない，中間的であいまいなことばがたいへん多い。「そのうちに」「いずれまた」「考えてみます」「検討してみます」などはいずれもyesでもnoでもない。ある時には上司や関係者の了承をあらかじめ得ておく「根回し」のための仮のyesであったり，ある時にははっきり断ると，相手を傷つけるのではないかとの配慮による婉曲(えんきょく)なnoであったりする。ただ，近年では国際的な商習慣を身に付けたビジネスマンも増えたので，yes，noをはっきりさせる方向には向かいつつある。

Getting Along with the Japanese

Us and Them

Foreign visitors who come to Japan and see the commuter-packed morning rush-hour trains are said to be amazed that there are so many Japanese in Japan. The fact that Japan does have such a high-density homogeneous population governs many of the social customs and personal mannerisms, making them different from the way people relate in more heterogeneous societies.

With virtually no major influx of immigrants over the last 1,000-plus years, Japanese society has developed numerous groups each with its own common consciousness and numerous tacit understandings that are reached or conveyed without a word being said. People who understand are insiders (us) and those who do not are outsiders (them) and treated as company.

The same is true of the reception accorded people from overseas: those who are not attuned to Japanese mores and customs are referred to as *gaijin* (literally "outsiders") and treated courteously as company, while those who have gotten inside Japanese society and learned the ropes are accepted and called *hen na gaijin* (outsiders who do not act like outsiders).

Emphasis on the Group

If the individual is the basic unit of Euro-American society, it is the group in Japan. This is not a society constituted by autonomous individuals, but one made up of people who are constantly interacting with society and constantly aware of this interaction. If you ask a Japanese what he thinks, he is very likely to answer by asking what everybody else thinks.

Two very commonly used words in Japanese are *honne* and *tatemae*. *Honne* is the true sound, or what a person really thinks, and *tatemae* is akin to the official position of the group he represents. Thus some people have characterized *honne* as the individual's voice and *tatemae* as the group's voice. Very often, a Japanese will give precedence to the official or group *tatemae* position, but that does not mean that he has entirely abandoned his personal *honne*.

Because individual Japanese are always conscious of what other people and the group are thinking, the lanuage has developed a large hedging vocabulary which is neither yes nor no. Among the most common are "I'll do what I can," "Let me get back to you on that later," "Let me sleep on it," and "I'll have to look into that." Sometimes these mean a tentative yes when someone is maneuvering behind the scenes to touch all the bases and line up support, and sometimes they are definite negatives phrased in a roundabout way to avoid hurting the other person's feelings. Recently, however, there are more and more businessmen with international experience who say yes and no loud and clear.

Notes

■1. Geography and Climate

location (位置) Japan's territorial rights today extend between the north latitudes of 45°31′and 20°25′and between the east longitudes of 153°59′and 122°56′.

rivers (河川) The *Shinano* River is the longest in Japan at only 367 kilometers.

●Main mountains, rivers, and lakes in Japan

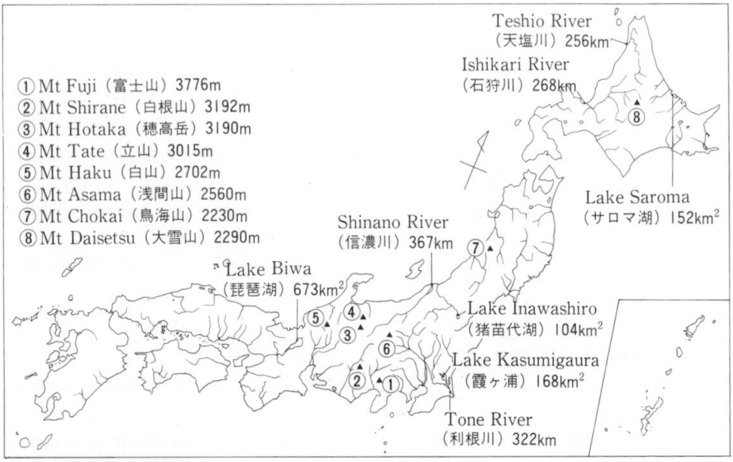

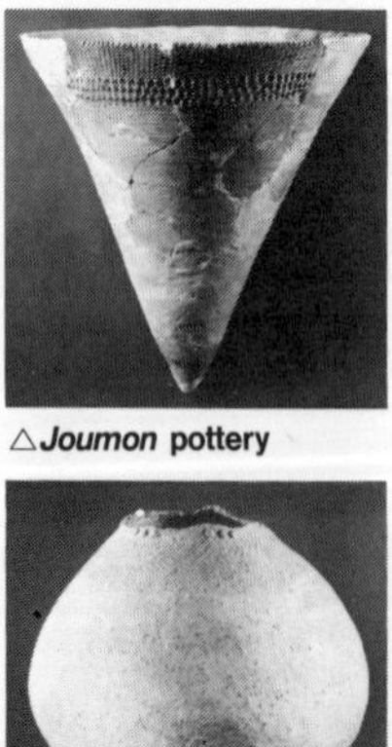

△*Joumon* pottery

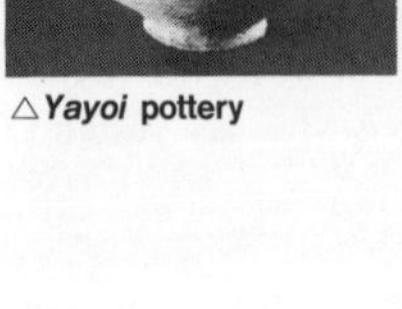

△*Yayoi* pottery

■3. Japanese History (1)

ritsuryou (律令) A code of laws and ethics evolved in China under the Sui and Tang dynasties and which was widely adopted by Japan and other East Asian countries. This code formed the basis for the early imperial governmental structure in ancient Japan.

***Joumon* period** (縄文時代) So named because of the *joumon* cord markings found on excavated earthenware from the New Stone Age period. *Joumon* pottery—probably used for food storage —is a gray, heavy, low-fired ware formed in a variety of shapes and richly decorated with impressed motifs.

***Yayoi* period** (弥生時代) Named after *Yayoi-chou* in *Toukyou* (Tokyo) where a wheel-thrown pottery of a style distinctive to this period was first discovered. A red ware fired at higher temperatures than the gray *Joumon* pottery of the preceding period, *Yayoi* pottery is usually very plain or decorated with only very simple motifs.

***Kofun* period** (古墳時代) The large mounded-earth tombs of this period indicate the emergence of powerful individuals with the ability to control significant groups of people.

keyhole-shaped tomb mounds (前方後円墳) Great tombs of the *Kofun* period shaped like old-fashioned key holes. The tombs of Emperors *Nintoku* and *Oujin* are of this type.

Confucian teachings (儒教) Confucianism offered a system of social organization, and, along with Buddhism, had a profound impact upon Japanese society and thought, forming the basis for feudal ethics.

Prince *Shoutoku* (聖徳太子) (574-622) The son of Emperor *Youmei*, Prince *Shoutoku* was a brilliant statesman who instituted the *kan'i juunikai* twelve cap ranking system and the Seventeen-article Constitution and sent Japan's first official emissaries to Sui China. A devout Buddhist, Prince *Shoutoku* sponsored the building of numerous Buddhist temples. His many achievements left a lasting mark on Japanese history.

***Taika* Reforms** (大化の改新) The *Taika* Reforms were instituted after a coup in 645 which laid the foundation for the establishment of the *ritsuryou* government.

△Keyhole-shaped tomb of Emperor *Nintoku*

△Prince *Shoutoku*

■4. Japanese History (2)

shouen (荘園) Landed estates belonging to the nobility and shrines and temples which formed the economic foundation of Japan in the medieval period. The last *shouen* was abolished during the time of *Toyotomi Hideyoshi*.

kouchi-koumin (公地公民制) The basic foundation for *ritsuryou* government, this was a concept in which all land and people were considered to be the property of the emperor. The right of private ownership and independence was not recognized.

***Asuka* culture** (飛鳥文化) A synthesis of *Kofun* period culture and the Chinese culture of the Northern and Southern dynasties period (439-589), this culture's artistic achievements are preserved in the temple architecture and sculptures of the *Houryuuji* and other temples of the period. Located in the southern part of the *Nara* plains, *Asuka* was the imperial capital for more than 100 years from the late 6th through the early 8th centuries until the capital was moved to *Heijoukyou* in 710.

△*Asuka* culture (The triad of the Budda *Shaka* with two attending bodhisattvas —*Houryuuji*)

△*Hakuhou* culture (The wall paintings—*Houryuuji*)

△*Tenpyou* culture (*Beauties beneath Trees*—*Shousouin* in *Nara*)

***Hakuhou* culture** (白鳳文化) A period of cultural flowering under the influence of early Tang culture. Represented by the sculptures of *Yakushiji* and the wall paintings—partially destroyed by fire in 1949—at *Houryuuji*.

***Tenpyou* culture** (天平文化) In architecture this cultural period is represented by *Toudaiji*, the *Shousouin*, and *Toushoudaiji*. Well-known *Tenpyou* paintings include *Yakushiji*'s *Kichijouten* portrait of a goddess of beauty and learning and the six-panel screen, *Beauties beneath Trees*, preserved in the *Shousouin*. Superb sculptures of the period are to be found in *Toudaiji*'s *hokkedou* (sutra repository) and *kaidan'in* (ordination hall).

Fujiwara (藤原氏) A powerful court family, the *Fujiwara* enjoyed wealth and prestige even greater than that of the imperial family at times. The *Fujiwara* attained their height of power under *Fujiwara no Michinaga* (966-1027), father of four empresses and grandfather of three emperors, and his son *Yorimichi* (992-1074).

insei (院政) A system of government in which retired emperors wielded the actual power, *insei* government was institutionalized by Emperor *Shirakawa* when he abdicated the throne in 1086. *Insei* continued as an occasional practice of the imperial court as late as 1840.

△**Native Japanese culture in the *Heian* period (*Byoudouin*'s Phoenix Hall)**

natively inspired art and culture (国風文化) The break with Tang China early in the *Heian* period provided an opportunity for a truly native Japanese culture to develop. The process of "Japanization" took place in nearly every area of aesthetics and intellectual activity. *Kana*, the syllabary characters evolved from Chinese characters, and *Joudo* Buddhism are just two examples of the uniquely Japanese achievements of the *Heian* period.

esoteric Buddhist sects (密教) Originating in India in the 7th and 8th centuries, esoteric Buddhism taught that the most sacred teachings of the Buddha should be kept secret. First introduced into Japan by *Kuukai* (774-835) and *Saichou* (767-822), the esoteric emphasis on chants and incantations appealed to the members of the imperial court and the esoteric Buddhist sects soon became the mainstream of Buddhism in Japan.

***Joudo* sect** (浄土教) The *Joudo* teachings of other-worldly salvation by such priests as *Kuuya* (903-972), *Genshin* (942-1017), *Hounen* (1133-1212), *Shinran* (1173-1262), and *Ippen* (1239-89) had broad appeal among nobility and commoners alike in an era plagued by constant wars, oppression, and natural disasters.

■5. Japanese History (3)

Minamoto no Yoritomo (源頼朝) (1147-99) A politically astute warrior, *Yoritomo* succeeded in establishing the supremacy of the warrior class in a single generation. He was cautious to a fault, however, suspicious of everyone around him including close relatives and vassals, and brought about the demise of his brother *Yoshitsune*, depriving himself of

△***Minamoto no Yoritomo***

an important and powerful ally in the process.

Hounen (法然) (1133-1212) Founder of the *Joudo* sect of Buddhism, *Hounen* taught that simply reciting the *nenbutsu* (*Namu Amida butsu*: I place my faith in the *Amida* Buddha) was enough to secure one's place in *Amida*'s Pure Land of the West paradise. His teachings had wide appeal, attracting adherents from the nobility, the warrior class, and the common people.

Shinran (親鸞) (1173-1262) A disciple of *Hounen* and founder of the *Joudo Shinshuu* sect of Buddhism, *Shinran* taught that all that was needed to attain salvation was to have faith. Like his master, he promulgated the recitation of the *nenbutsu*.

Nichiren (日蓮) (1222-82) Founder of the *Nichiren* sect of Buddhism. *Nichiren* believed that the true teachings of *Shakamuni* Buddha were to be found only in the Lotus Sutra (*Hokke-kyou*) and that one could be saved by reciting the *daimoku* (*Namu myou hourenge kyou*: I place my faith in the Lotus Sutra). His vigorous proselytizing and harsh denouncement of all other Buddhist sects antagonized the authorities and resulted in *Nichiren*'s repeated persecution. Still, *Nichiren* had great charismatic appeal especially for the lower-class *samurai* of the *Kantou* plains region.

△Early *Kamakura* sculpture (Statue of *Kongou Rikishi* in *Toudaiji* by *Unkei* and *Kaikei*)

early *Kamakura* sculpture (鎌倉時代初期の彫刻) The early *Kamakura* period is noted for its fine sculptures of Buddhist deities and revered monks. Among the most famous *Kamakura* sculptures are those by *Unkei* (?-1223), his son *Tankei* (1173-1256), and *Kaikei* (active in the early 13th century).

***Kitayama* culture** (北山文化) Named after the *Kitayama* district in *Kyouto* (Kyoto) where the 3rd *Ashikaga shougun, Yoshimitsu*, built the *Kinkaku* or Gold Pavilion in 1397. This culture is marked by the merging of court- and warrior-class aesthetics.

△*Kinkaku*

***Higashiyama* culture** (東山文化) In 1489, the 8th *Ashikaga shougun*, *Yoshimasa*, built a villa with a small temple, today referred to as the *Ginkakuji* or Silver Pavilion, in the *Higashiyama* district of *Kyouto* which epitomizes the culture of his time. Under the influence of *Zen*, *Higashiyama* culture prized simplicity, traditional elegance, and the austerity of *wabi*.

■6. Japanese History (4)

feudal lords (将軍・大名) *Shougun* is an abbreviation of *seii-tai-shougun* (barbarian-subduing generalissimo), a title first assumed by *Minamoto no Yoritomo* when he established his military government in *Kamakura*. *Daimyou* are landholding, semi-autonomous lords. Originally officials called *shugo-daimyou* appointed to administer the provinces, the *daimyou* had become powerful enough by the warring states period in the late 15th and early 16th centuries to compete for supremacy. In the *Edo* period (1600-1867) only lords with landholdings valued at 10,000 *koku* or more were classified as *daimyou*, a *koku* being equivalent to 180.39 liters of rice. There were approximately 270 *daimyou* in the middle of the *Edo* period.

bakuhan (幕藩体制) The name given to the government organization of the *Azuchi-Momoyama* (1573-1600) and *Edo* periods when Japan was governed by a *shougun* and *daimyou* with extensive landholdings called *han*.

***Azuchi-Momoyama* period** (安土・桃山時代) A period noted for its castles which functioned as *daimyou* residences and governmental headquarters as well as military defenses. *Azuchi* Castle built by *Oda Nobunaga* and *Oosaka* (Osaka) Castle built by his successor, *Toyotomi Hideyoshi*, had a grandeur worthy of their builders. The multi-storied donjon were the main features of the castles of this period. Castle rooms were lavishly decorated and furnished with gold-foil covered *fusuma* doors, walls, and folding screens. *Momoyama* is where *Hideyoshi* built his *Fushimi* Castle.

△*Oosaka* Castle

Oda Nobunaga (織田信長) (1534-82) An intrepid leader who laid the foundation for the unification of Japan in the 16th century. His hegemony nearly assured after numerous battles, *Nobunaga* built a sumptuous castle in *Azuchi* near Lake *Biwa*, but his conquests were brought to an abrupt end by his suicide at *Honnouji* in *Kyouto* (Kyoto) after a traitorous attack by one of his own vassals.

Toyotomi Hideyoshi (豊臣秀吉) (1536-98) See p. 63.

Tokugawa Ieyasu (徳川家康) (1542-1616) See p. 63.

Oosaka (大坂) The original characters used to write the name of the city of *Oosaka*. The present characters 大阪 have been in use since 1870.

△*Oda Nobunaga*

△*Toyotomi Hideyoshi*

△*Tokugawa Ieyasu*

bunjin-ga (文人画) A genre of Eastern painting, these are works painted by scholars, poets, and men of letters.

Dutch learning (蘭学) The study of Western learning through Dutch texts which began in the middle of the *Edo* period.

terakoya (寺子屋) The fundamentals of reading, writing, and arithmetic were taught at these schools generally established in *samurai* homes and in Buddhist temples and *Shintou* shrines.

Meiji, Taishou, Shouwa, Heisei (明治,大正,昭和,平成) After the fall of the *Tokugawa* shogunate and the beginning of Japan's modernization, era names have been changed at the beginning of each new emperor's reign. Historical periods prior to *Meiji*—are broadly referred to by the name of the seat of government, e.g. the *Nara* period, the *Heian* period, etc.

Sino-Japanese war (日清戦争) (1894-95) Fought over rights to Korea.

Russo-Japanese war (日露戦争) (1904-05) Japan won control over Manchuria and the Korean peninsula.

***Taishou* democracy** (大正デモクラシー) The democratic ideals and movements of the *Taishou* period in the early 20th century. It was during this period that many of the systems and philosophies of modern Japan were formed.

15 years of war (十五年戦争) The 15 years of war beginning with the Manchurian Incident of 1931 when Japanese forces embarked upon their invasion of northeastern China, and ending with the Pacific War, 1941-45, fought primarily between Japan and the United States.

■8. Sources of Japanese Culture

glutinous paste (もち) In Japan, pounded glutinous rice cakes are a special New Year's food also served on other happy occasions.

△Making rice cakes

tea (茶) The Japanese drink a variety of teas. *Sencha* and *bancha* are the most common types served in the home, while finely powdered *matcha* is reserved especially for the tea ceremony (see p. 255).

konnyaku (こんにゃく) A kind of tuber, *konnyaku* is processed into a tasteless gelatin-like food used by the Japanese in a variety of dishes.

perilla (シソ) Two types of this plant—green-leafed and purple-leafed—are used in Japan, primarily as a condiment and for pickling.

lacquer ware (漆) See p.269.

cormorant fishing (鵜飼い) Cormorant fishing in Japan can still be seen on the *Nagara* River in *Gifu* prefecture.

△Cormorant fishing on the *Nagara* River

■9. Characteristics of Japanese Culture

kintarou-ame (金太郎あめ) See picture.

△*Kintarou-ame*

■10. Japanese Concepts of Nature

sansui-ga (山水画) Monotone landscape painting was introduced from China near the end of the *Kamakura* period. The Buddhist monk *Sesshuu* (1420-1506) was a master of this genre and the creator of a powerful Japanese style.

seasonal references (季語) *Kigo* are terms relating to natural phenomena, animals, plants, customs, traditions, and rituals, and are employed in *haiku* to set a seasonal tone for the verse.

yuugen (幽玄) Originally meaning something too deeply hidden for human comprehension, this term gradually evolved into an aesthetic concept of mysterious and tranquil beauty.

wabi (わび) Stemming from the word *wabishi*, meaning lonely or sad, this is an aesthetic ideal of tranquility in the midst of poverty. An ambience of *wabi* is essential to the tea ceremony.

sabi (さび) A companion term to *wabi*, this concept was first established as an aesthetic principle in the poetry of *Matsuo Bashou* (1644-94). Like *wabi* it alludes to a sadness locked in one's heart and also has Buddhist connotations of selflessness and complete lack of desire.

△New Year's visits to *Shintou* shrine

■11. Japanese Religion

visits to *Shintou* shrines at New Year's (初もうで) Visits to shrines and temples to pray for the safety and good health of the family are customary at the beginning of the year. The *Meiji* Shrine in *Toukyou* (Tokyo), *Kawasaki Daishi* in *Kanagawa* prefecture, and *Naritasan Shinshouji* in *Chiba* prefecture each has more than three million visitors during the traditional three-day New Year's holiday.

△*Inari*

trips to Buddhist temples in the spring and fall (彼岸) *Higan* are Buddhist memorial services, and visits to family graves are the practice during this seven-day period observed twice a year around the spring and autumnal equinoxes. Literally meaning "the other shore," *higan*, or *o-higan*, refers to the attainment of enlightenment.

Inari (お稲荷さん) Formerly a god of cereals worshipped in *Fushimi* on the outskirts of *Kyouto* (Kyoto), *Inari* was later merged with the Buddhist guardian deity Dakini who was generally depicted riding a fox. This and the traditional reverence of the common people for the fox are probably behind *Inari*'s close association with the animal. Miniature *Inari* shrines marking sacred sites are common. They are distinguished by their smallness, bright red *torii*, and fox figure or figures. Deepfried bean curd, *abura-age*, is thought to be a favorite food of the fox.

△*Dousojin*

dousojin (道祖神) Stone markers meant to ward off evil spirits and catastrophes, *dousojin* are found along village boundaries, in mountain passes, and along country byways. Often these markers take on human form and bear inscriptions. Many *dousojin* are of an embracing man and woman and are revered as gods of marriage and fertility.

△*Pachinko*

■12. The Japanese Work Ethic

Yamamoto Shichihei (山本七平) (1921-91) Founder of the *Yamamoto Shoten* publishing company.

■13. Relaxing Japanese-style

karaoke (カラオケ) See p.245.

■14. Japanese Aesthetics

Buddhist feeling (諸行無常) A basic Buddhist tenet which teaches that all things of this world are transient and impermanent. Appealing strongly to Japanese sensibilities, this concept appears repeatedly in Japanese literature, songs, and dramas.

Sen no Rikyuu (千利休) (1522-91) Founder of the *Sen* school of tea. Considered the leading tea master of his time, *Rikyuu* perfected much of the philosophy of the tea ceremony.

masters (宗匠) *Soushou* are masters and often heads of schools of *waka* and *haiku* poetry, tea ceremony, flower arranging, and other traditional arts.

Ekuan Kenji (栄久庵憲司) (1929-) One of Japan's most renowned industrial designers.

■15. Views of Life and Death

***Joudo* Pure Land paradise** (極楽浄土) The Pure Land of the West paradise where *Amida*, bodhisattva savior, is believed to exist.

Hagakure (葉隠) A definitive work on *bushidou* written by *Yamamoto Jouchou* of the *Nabeshima han* in *Saga*, *Kyuushuu*, and completed in 1716.

shinjuu (心中) This term is also used in reference to multiple suicides such as of parent and child (*oyako shinjuu*) and families (*kazoku shinjuu*). The term *muri shinjuu* connotes a combination murder and suicide.

joururi (浄瑠璃) Narrative ballads chanted to *shamisen* accompaniment. There were originally several schools of *joururi*, *Kiyomoto-bushi*, *Tokiwazu-bushi*, and *Gidayuu-bushi*, among others, but *Gidayuu-bushi* is the most commonly performed *joururi* today

■16. Groupism

murahachibu (村八分) Ostracism was practiced in feudal Japan, but has been outlawed today.

■17. *Giri* and *Ninjou*

enka (演歌) Popular songs of human frailty and love with a distinctively Japanese melody.

courtesan (遊女) *Yuujo* is an old term no longer in use for prostitutes.

■18. The Japanese Year

sweet *sake* (おとそ) Originally an herbal *sake* thought to exorcise misfortunes and promote long life. *(O-)toso* is also the name given to *sake* served at New Year's.

visit their grandparents (里帰り) Originally *sato-gaeri* referred to a bride's first visit to her former home soon after marriage, but this term is commonly used today to refer to any brief visit to the home of one's birth.

wrap up the year's work (仕事納め) Originally the last day of work in the year for offices, today *shigoto-osame* refers to the last day of work for government ministries and agencies

△*O-toso* set

and for private corporations. It is customary to put in only half a day of work at *shigoto-osame*.

toshikoshi-soba (年越しそば) Noodles eaten on New Year's Eve, *toshikoshi-soba* is believed to be especially felicitous for a variety of reasons. One commonly accepted reason is that the long noodles will assure a long and prosperous life.

■23. The Japanese Language

large number of people (世界の言語の中で上位) In terms of the number of native speakers, Japanese ranks sixth after Chinese, English, Russian, Hindi, and Spanish.

Dravidian languages (ドラビダ語) The Dravidian languages, such as Tamil, are spoken in southern India and northeastern Sri Lanka.

agglutinative language (膠着語) In classical structural linguistics languages were classified typologically as agglutinative, isolative or inflective.

Typology, however, tends to isolate only one or two characteristics of a language in the interest of classification, and linguistic scholars today question its accuracy and meaningfulness.

■26. Popular Heroes

Takeda Shingen (武田信玄) (1521-73) A *daimyou* of the warring states period, *Takeda* opposed *Oda Nobunaga*. He died of an illness in the midst of battle.

Sakamoto Ryouma (坂本龍馬) (1835-67) A *samurai* from the *Tosa* domain, *Sakamoto* was a major proponent of imperial restoration. He was assassinated by a pro-shogunate *samurai*.

***Meiji* Restoration** (明治維新) Narrowly defined to refer to the 1868 coup d'etat that overthrew the *Tokugawa* shogunate, the *Meiji* Restoration more broadly marked Japan's opening to the West and the beginning of modern Japan's drive to industrialize.

PART・2

日本人の生活
JAPANESE DAILY LIFE

いくつかの指標から日本人の平均的な暮らしぶりを見ていくと，欧米並み，あるいはそれ以上に豊かな反面，非常に遅れている面もあることがわかる。

白書に見る暮らしぶり

恵まれている面から挙げていくと，２人以上世帯の１世帯当たりの平均年収は約673万円（2000年）とまずまずの金額となっている。殺人発生率は人口10万人に対して1.2人と先進国の中では最も低く，世界でも最も安全な国と言える。家電製品や車などの耐久消費財の普及率も高く，日本人は非常に豊かで便利な生活を享受している。しかし，一方で，恵まれていないのが住宅事情である。日本の都市は地価が高いため，都市部ではなかなかマイホームがもてず，１戸当たりの床面積も89.6m²と欧米に比べると狭い。下水道の普及率も全国平均で58%で，欧米の水準よりかなり低い。

日本人自身はそんな自分たちの暮らしをどう見ているのか。総理府が99年に行った「国民生活に関する世論調査」によると，現在の生活に対する満足度では「満足している」9.5%，「まあ満足している」54.2%，「不満だ」が10.4%であった。生活程度についても「中の上」が9.3%，「中の中」が56.2%で，日本人はおおむね自分たちの生活に満足しているという結果が出ている。こうした生活水準に対する満足度の向上のあかしとして，最近では物の豊かさよりも生きがいや人との交流などの心の豊かさを求める傾向が強まってきているという結果も出ている。

都市の暮らしと農村の暮らし

日本の都市には世界の大都市に劣らないほどの，あらゆる物やサービスがあふれている。都市生活者はレストランで気軽に世界の料理を楽しみ，数多いデパートで世界の一流品を買うことができる。こうした豊かで便利な都市の暮らしの中で，非常に深刻なのが住宅問題である。東京都の住宅地の平均地価は１m²当たり34万4900円（99年）で，近年は地価が下がっているとはいえ，マイホームをもつのはまだまだ難しい。

情報機関や交通機関の発達で，物やサービスについては農村と都会との較差はほとんどなくなってきている。農村生活者の悩みは若者たちが次々に都会へ出て行くことで，跡継ぎ不足，嫁不足といった現象が続いていることである。年寄り夫婦だけで田畑を守る家も増え，日本の農業を今後どうするかということも絡んで，社会問題化している。

Standard of Living

The statistics give a mixed picture of the Japanese standard of living. In some respects it is on a par with or even exceeds Western standards, and in other respects it lags behind.

Pluses and Minuses

Looking first at the areas where Japan leads, the average annual perhousehold (two persons or more) income was about ¥6.73 million in 2000. In addition, Japan is generally safe. The murder rate is 1.2 per 100,000 people, the lowest of any industrial country. Ownership of consumer electronics, automobiles, and other durables is widespread, and Japanese life is one of affluence and convenience. Housing, on the other hand, definitely lags behind. Land in Japanese cities is very expensive, so owning one's own home is quite difficult, and average floor space is 89.6m^2, quite small by European or American standards. Nationwide only 58% of the homes are connected to sewer systems, which is far below European or American standards.

What do the Japanese themselves think of their standard of living? In a 1999 survey by the Prime Minister's Office, 9.5% said they were satisfied, 54. 2% that they were more or less satisfied, and 10.4% that they were dissatisfied with their standard of living. Asked to characterize their standard of living, 9.3% said upper-middle and 56.2% middle-middle. Both sets of figures indicate that the Japanese are generally satisfied with their standard of living Further substantiating the idea people are generally satisfied, Japanese aspirations have recently shifted away from material possessions to such spiritually rewarding things as personal sense of worth and friendships.

Urban Life vs. Rural Life

Japanese cities offer a kaleidoscope of services and products at least the equal of those in any other major country. Urban Japanese can dine on gourmet food at world-class restaurants and purchase internationally.famous brand products at any one of the numerous department stores. Yet while urban life is affluent and convenient, housing is a major problem. Residential land in *Toukyou* (Tokyo) cost an average of ¥344,900/m^2 in 1999. Though land prices have gone in recent years, it is still quite difficult to own one's own home in *Toukyou* (Tokyo).

The rapid development of transportation and communication networks has nearly erased the disparity between urban and rural living standards. Nevertheless, Japanese farming villages are in trouble because increasing numbers of young people are deserting the family farm to migrate to the cities. There are fewer people left to farm the land, and the men that stay have difficulty finding brides. With more and more farming households made up of exclusively old people, there is widespread concern over Japanese agriculture's future.

*NHKが5年ごとに行っている「国民生活時間調査」の1995年のデータ(平日)によると，睡眠，食事，身の回りの用事などの，いわゆる生活必需時間に約10時間9分，仕事，学業，家事などに約8時間58分，その他余暇的な行事や移動などの時間に4時間26分，というのが，平均的な日本人の1日の生活時間である。

起床と就寝時間

70〜85年の同調査では，睡眠時間の国民平均は約8時間でほとんど変化がなかったが，90年は7時間39分，95年は7時間27分，2000年は7時間23分と減少が続いている。起床・就寝時刻について見ると，起床時刻はほとんど変化していないが，夜11時に起きている人の率は，平日で70年の24%，80年30%，90年39%，95年44%と就寝時刻は遅くなっている。日本人の生活が夜型化してきていて，宵っぱり型が増えているわけである。

食事の時間

日本人の食事時間は朝昼晩3食合わせても約1時間半と短く，食事のとり方も欧米とはだいぶ違っているようだ。朝食は午前7時から8時の間にとるのが普通だが，最近は朝食抜きの人も増えている。昼食は正午から1時間に集中しているのもきわめて日本的な特徴だ。日本ではサラリーマンが自宅へ帰って昼食をとるという習慣がないだけでなく，ほとんどの人が会社の社員食堂や，近くのレストランなどで手早く済ませる。オフィス街などにあるレストランでは順番待ちの行列ができるほど，この時間は混雑する。サラリーマン家庭では，父親は付き合いや息抜きなどで外で一杯やりながら夕食を済ませてしまうことも多く，家では母親と子供だけでとることも珍しくない。

通勤と通学時間

“高・遠・狭”という住宅事情を反映して，通勤・通学などの移動時間もバカにならず，首都圏では往復で平均1時間余りもかかる。日本のラッシュアワーは有名だが，通勤時間が朝7時から9時までに集中しているために，この間，各交通機関は超満員になる。

　全体的には，勤労者の仕事時間や主婦の家事時間は次第に減る傾向にあり，その分，レジャーや読書などの余暇的行動の時間が増えてきている。週休2日制の定着や家事の簡素化によって，自由時間を楽しむようになってきた現れと言える。

The Japanese Day

According to the latest (1995) in a long series of NHK* (Japan Broadcasting Corp.) surveys done every half-decade of how the Japanese spend their time, approximately 10:09 hours are spent on the "essentials" of eating, sleeping, and bodily hygiene, approximately 8:58 hours at work, at school, or in housework, and 4:26 hours in leisure activities or commuting.

Later Hours

Surveys from 1970 to 1985 showed that Japanese slept an average of about 8 hours a day. This figure was down to 7 hours 39 minutes in 1990, with a further decline to 7 hours 27 minutes in 1995, and 7 hours 23 minutes in 2000. People are still getting up about the same time they always did, but they are staying up later. In 1970, only 24% of the people were still up at 23:00 on an average weekday. In 1980, the figure was 30%; in 1990, 39%; and in 1995, 44%. Japanese are gradually becoming bleary-eyed night owls.

Meals

In sharp contrast to the more leisurely dining in the West, the average Japanese pattern is to spend little more than an hour and a half for all three meals—breakfast, lunch, and dinner—combined. Breakfast is usually between 7 and 8 a.m., but an increasing number of people have begun skipping breakfast. The custom of having everybody eat lunch from 12:00 noon to 1:00 p.m. is peculiarly Japanese. Not only do Japanese employees seldom go home for lunch, the fact that everybody has his or her lunch hour at the same time means company cafeterias and nearby restaurants are too crowded to allow anyone to eat leisurely. Long lines are a common sight at popular restaurants in downtown business districts. Since the Japanese businessman is usually late getting home, whether because he is eating out with business associates or because he is simply stopping off somewhere for a drink on the way home, mother and the children usually go ahead and eat without him.

Commuting

Expensive, distant, and small are the adjectives most commonly used to describe Japanese housing. Commuting to work or school can be quite time-consuming, taking more than an hour round-trip on average in urban centers. The well-known Japanese rush hour lasts from 7:00 to 9:00 a.m., during which time all forms of transportation are full to overflowing.

Nevertheless, the trend is toward less time spent at the office and on housework and more time spent on reading and other personal-interest activities. The two-day weekend is taking hold, and modern appliances have greatly simplified housework. More and more Japanese are enjoying more and more free time.

欧米先進諸国の例に漏れず，日本でも核家族化は時代の趨勢（すうせい）である。夫婦だけか，夫婦あるいは片親と未婚の子だけの核家族世帯は全世帯の6割にも達し，1940年までは5人台だった平均世帯人数も年々減少して，1998年には2.7人と3人を切るに至っている。夫婦に子供が一人か二人というのが，日本の一般的な家族構成と言えよう。

戦前・戦中の家族

親・子・孫と3世代が同居し，一家の主である夫が家父長として絶対的権威をもっていたのが，戦前の日本の平均的な家庭だった。妻を日本では「家内」とも言うように，一家の主婦は家にいて，夫や夫の両親である舅（しゅうと）・姑（しゅうとめ）に仕え，家事・育児一切を切り盛りした。戦中の食糧難時代には，出征した夫の留守を守って食糧の確保に奔走するなど，家のことでは夫に心配させないというのが，日本的家政学だった。

戦中・現在の家庭

こうした家庭のイメージも，戦後の核家族化に伴って，だいぶ変わってきている。かつては家風についても子供の教育・結婚についても主導権を握っていた“強い夫”像は後退し，現在では妻や子供の言い分にも耳を傾ける，ものわかりのいい夫が増えている。一方，妻の地位は「戦後，強くなったのは女性と靴下」ということばが一時はやったほど向上した。夫と同等の立場で自分の意見を言い，特に子供の教育については夫よりも強い決定権をもっているのが，現代の日本の妻たちである。妻の地位が向上した結果，顕在化してきたのが嫁・姑戦争である。嫁が自己主張をするようになったため，姑との摩擦が多くなり，夫は母親と妻の板挟みになって苦労する。

電気製品の普及で家事に時間がかからなくなり，子供が少なく育児に手のかかる期間も短くなった結果，家の中の仕事より生きがいを外に求めて働きに出る主婦も多く，今では主婦の二人に一人は働くに至っている。

しかし，戦後の主婦の地位を最も象徴的に物語っているのは，主婦が一家のさいふを握ったということだろう。欧米では一家の家計を預かるのは夫で，妻は必要な生活費だけを夫からもらうというのが一般的なようだが，戦後は妻が一家の大蔵大臣として夫の給料を管理し，生活のやりくりから貯蓄，財産運用，マイホーム建設資金づくりまでさい配するという家庭が増えている。

The Family

As in the West, the modern Japanese family is small. Some 60% of all Japanese households consist of couples only or a single parent and unmarried children. Back in 1940, the average family had five members. By 1998, it had dropped to 2.7. Thus the average Japanese family is mother, father, and one or two children.

Pre-1945 Situation

In prewar Japan, three generations (parents, children, and grandchildren) lived under the same roof. The father was head of the household, and his word was law. As one of the Japanese words for wife, *kanai* (lit. inside the home), implies, the prewar Japanese wife's place was in the home, serving her husband and her husband's parents, doing housework, and raising her children. During the war years when food was scarce, the Japanese housewife did everything she could to ensure that the family had enough to eat. She was expected to maintain the household while her husband was at the front, and she was not to burden her husband with the worries of keeping the family fed and intact.

Changes since the War

However, the Japanese family has changed considerably as the nuclear family has become the postwar norm. The father no longer has absolute authority in establishing family rules, governing his children's education, and granting permission for his children's marriages, and increasing numbers of fathers are listening to their wives and children. At the same time, the wife's role is also changing, as aptly illustrated by the once-popular phrase, "The two things that have gotten stronger since the war are women and stockings." The modern Japanese housewife has an equal say with her husband in family matters, and often more say when it comes to the children's education. One manifestation of this improved status for wives is the conflict which has erupted between wives and mothers-in-law. With the wife used to speaking out, there has been increasing friction with the traditional mother-in-law, and the hapless husband often finds himself caught in the middle.

With the time required for household work greatly diminished by modern electrical appliances, and with fewer children to raise, many Japanese housewives are finding fulfillment in work outside the home. Today, one of every two housewives has an outside job.

The most obvious proof of the wife's position is her grip on the family purse strings. In the West it is usually the husband who controls the family finances, giving his wife an allowance to do the shopping with. Yet in postwar Japan it is the wife who handles the money, making all of the major savings, investments, and even home financing decisions.

一家のさいふを握っている日本の主婦は，生活のやりくりを上手にするために，家計簿をつけていることが多い。こうした各家庭の家計簿を基にして総理府統計局が毎年発表している『家計調査報告』によると，1999年の勤労者世帯１か月の平均実収入は57万4676円，消費支出は34万6177円となっている。

かつては生活費の中で食料費の占める割合であるエンゲル係数か，衣食住などの基礎的支出の割合が消費生活を推し測るものさしだったが，“飽食の時代”にある現在の日本では，このものさしは通用しなくなってきている。具体的には，70年に32.2％だった勤労者世帯の１か月の食料費は80年27.8％，90年24.1％，99年22.5％と減少の一途をたどり，衣食住などの基本的支出の割合も同じく56.0％，49.7％，45.3％，43.6％と減少し，すでに50％を切っている。逆にその分増えているのが教養娯楽・教育・交際費などの選択的支出である。

増える教育費

選択的支出の中でも，高学歴社会を反映して，教育費のウエートが年々拡大しているのが最近の日本の家計の大きな特徴である。85年から99年までの消費支出と教育支出の年平均伸び率を比較した試算によると，消費支出が1.3％の伸びだったのに対して教育支出は2.9％といった伸び率だった。

これはあくまで平均の数字で，教育熱心な都市部や，大きい子供がいる世帯では，それだけ教育費支出の占める割合は高くなる。一例として，98年度に文部科学省が行った調査を挙げておくと，私立の中学生で１人当たり年間123万円，私立の高校生では101万円の教育費がかかっている。教育費を捻出(ねんしゅつ)するため，金融機関の教育ローンを利用している家庭も多い。

高い貯蓄率

日本人が貯蓄熱心な国民であることはよく知られている。総務省の貯蓄動向調査によると，2000年末の１世帯平均貯蓄現在高は1356万円で，前年より2.6％減，勤労者の貯蓄額は1250万円で，2.3％減であったが，欧米先進諸国と比べるときわだって高いほうである。日本人が貯蓄に熱心なのは豊かさの現れというより，年金の支給開始年齢が60歳から65歳へ後退したことなどによる老後への不安や，なかなかマイホームをもてない住宅事情のためと言えよう。

The Household Budget

It is generally the housewife who controls the family purse strings in Japan, and many women keep detailed records of the household accounts. According to an annual survey of household accounts by the Statistics Bureau of the Prime Minister's Office, average monthly household income for 1999 was ¥574,676, while average expenditures were ¥346,177.

Neither the Engel coefficient —used to measure the percentage of household expenditures spent on food—nor the percentage spent on the basic necessities of food, shelter, and clothing is an adequate indicator of the quality of consumer life in today's affluent Japan. Food accounted for 32.2% of the wage-earner household's monthly expenditures in 1970, but the ratio has decreased steadily since then, to 27.8% in 1980, 24.1% in 1990, and 22.5% in 1999. The same downward trend is evident in the food-shelter-and-clothing figure: 56.0% in 1970, 49.7% in 1980, 45.3% in 1990, and 43.7% in 1999. In contrast, there has been a marked increase in family spending on recreation, entertainment, and education.

The Growing Cost of Education

One recent and important feature of the Japanese household budget as regards nonessential expenditures is the yearly increase in education spending, reflecting Japanese society's emphasis on higher education. Figures comparing the average annual increase in consumer spending with education spending between 1985 and 1999 show that, while consumer spending increased at an average of 1.3%, education spending increased at an average of 2.9%.

These are only averages of course. In the highly education conscious larger cities, and in homes with older children, the portion spent on education is even greater still. To cite a survey conducted in 1998 by the Ministry of Education and Science by way of example, the cost for one student for one year at a private junior high school was ¥1.23 million, and for one year at a private high school was ¥1.01 million. Many families make use of education loans available from the financial community to pay for education expenses.

High Savings Rate

Japan has long been known as a country of fervent savers. According to a savings propensity survey conducted by the Prime Minister's Office, the average current savings balance per household at the end of 2000 was ¥13.56 million, down 2.6% from the previous year. This is quite high compared to other developed nations. The Japanese propensity to save, however, is attributed not so much to affluence as to (1) a feeling of uneasiness about old age, in part due to the raising of the age for welfare payments from 60 to 65, and (2) a housing situation in which it is difficult to own one's own home.

総務庁の1993年の「住宅統計調査報告」によると，日本の総住宅数は4588万で，総世帯数4116万世帯を大きく上回っている。日本人は，1世帯当たり1.1戸の住宅をもっていることになる。内訳を見ると，空き屋などを除いた居住住宅は4077万戸ある。そのうち，持ち家は2438万戸で59.8%，借家は1569万戸で38.5%となっている。建て方別では，一戸建てが2414万戸で59.2%，共同住宅が1427万戸となっており，5年前の前回調査に比べると，共同住宅の割合が4.5%増えている。

問題は住宅1戸当たりの面積で，日本の住宅は，かつて「ウサギ小屋」と評されたように，欧米に比べて一般に狭い。建設省の資料によると，日本の新築住宅の1戸当たり床面積は89.3㎡(93年)で，アメリカの162.0㎡(89年)には及ばないものの，フランスの105.5㎡(88年)やドイツの94.8㎡(91年)をやや下回っている。

大都会の住宅事情

日本の大都市圏の住宅事情は，“高・遠・狭”ということばで表現される。文字どおり，地価が高いために，市街地から遠く離れた郊外に，しかも狭い住まいしかもてないという意味である。例えば，東京圏で70㎡の新築マ*ンションを買う場合，80年代後半のバブル経済の時期には，勤労者世帯の年収の8.5倍も出さないと買えなかった。90年以降，バブルが崩壊して地価が下落したが，それでもまだ年収の6.4倍という高さである。96年現在も地価の低迷は続いているが，政府が目標としている年収の5倍以内という住宅価格は，まだ実現されていない。多くのサラリーマンは，少しでも地価の安い郊外に家をもたざるを得ないため，住まいと会社の間が遠くなって，片道1時間以上といった遠距離通勤を余儀なくされている。

変化する住まい観

従来の日本の住まいと言えば，木造に瓦*屋根，戸内をふ*すまや障*子で区切った，いわゆる日本家屋が主だったが，近年は鉄筋コンクリート造りのマンション志向派がしだいに増えてきている。これは，便利さ重視のライフスタイルを好む若い世代が増えてきたこと，本当は一戸建て志向ながら，地価が高くてなかなか一戸建てはもてない現状から，妥協住宅としてのマンションが見直されたことなども要因となっている。しかし，より根本的な理由は，家イコール家族という戦前の住まい観が，核家族化などによって変化し，若い世代を中心に，家は人が住む単なる器と考える人が増えたためだと思われる。

Housing

The 1993 housing survey shows 45,880,000 homes in Japan, which is far more than the 41,160,000 total households. If the figures are to be believed, the average Japanese household has 1.1 homes. Yet of this, 5,110,000 are unoccupied for one reason or another. Of the remaining 40,770,000, some 24,380,000 (59.8%) are owner-occupied and the other 15,690,000 (38.5%) are rental units. By type, 24,140,000 (59.2%) are single-family homes and the other 14,270,000 are multi-family units.

As such, the multi-family unit percentage is up 4.5 points over the 1988 figure. Looking at average floor space, Japanese homes generally have less floor space than Euro-American homes do and have been characterized as "rabbit hutches." According to the Ministry of Construction, average new-house floor area was 162.0m^2 in the United States, 94.8m^2 in Germany, 105.5m^2 in France, and only 89.3m^2 in Japan.

Urban Housing

Housing in Japan's principal metropolitan areas has been characterized as expensive, distant, and small. Because land is expensive, people have to live in the distant suburbs and, even then, can only afford a small house. Buying a 70m^2 new condominium* in the *Toukyou* (Tokyo) area during the "bubble" years of the late 1980s cost 8.5 times the average working household's annual income. Even after the bubble burst and prices came down, this was still 6.4 years' wages. While land prices are still coming down as of 1996, the government target that a 70m ^{2} condo should be within 5 years' wages has yet to be achieved. Going further and further out into the suburbs in search of affordable housing, the average company employee now finds one-way commutes of over an hour commonplace.

Changing Attitudes

While Japanese homes were formerly wooden buildings with tile roofs* and sliding-door partitions* inside, reinforced concrete condos have become much more popular of late. In part, this reflects the growing number of young households and their preference for convenience, but it is also because many people are opting for multi-family housing in lieu of the single-family homes they would prefer but cannot afford. Even more basic, however, is the changing concept of the home and family, from the prewar idea of many generations living together under a common roof to the contemporary view of the home as simply a place where the young nuclear family lives.

耐久消費財

経済的繁栄を象徴するように，日本の家庭には電気製品があふれている。昭和30年代(1955年〜64年)の家庭電化ブームのはしりに目標とされた洗濯機・冷蔵庫・掃除機などは，経済企画庁の調べによると，89年にすでにそれぞれ99.3%，98.6%，98.5%の普及率で，ほぼ全戸に１台ずつ行き渡っている。その後の目標となったのが“３C”，すなわちカラーテレビ・クーラー・車などの高級品だが，これらも98年の時点では99.2%，81.9%，83.1%と，日本の家庭では決してぜいたく品でなくなっていることを示している。全般に，同じ品物でもより機能性の高いものや普及途上にある高級品などで普及率の伸びが高くなっているのが特徴で，現在欧米でも人気を呼んでいるビデオは，81年に5.1%だった普及率が89年には63.7%，98年には76.8%と急速に広まりを見せている。日本人は，欧米並みかそれ以上の近代的な暮らし方をしていると言えよう。

日本的家具

その一方で日本人は，畳，布団，風呂，こたつといった日本の伝統的な家具類にも強い愛着をもっている。

- **畳**　畳は，日本住宅の床上に敷くもので，欧米で言えばじゅうたんのようなものに当たる。わらで作った厚床の上にい草などで織った畳表を付けたもので，一畳は約1.8×0.9m。畳の上では靴，スリッパなしで歩く。住まいの洋風化が進み，居間や子供部屋などは欧米流に板床かじゅうたん敷きにしていても，まだまだ畳敷きの和室も多い。
- ***布団**　欧米のベッドに当たる日本の寝具が布団で，畳んで*押し入れなどに入れておき，寝るときに畳の上に敷いて使う。折り畳みができるので，ベランダなどに干すと，新品のようにふっくらとして寝心地よくできるという良さが布団にはある。
- **風呂**　日本人の風呂好きは有名だが，欧米のシャワーと違って，日本では大きな湯船にたっぷり湯を張って，ゆっくりとつかる。
- ***こたつ**　こたつは冬季に下半身を暖めるための日本独特の生活家具である。炭火や電気などの熱源を四角い*櫓(やぐら)の中に置き，熱が逃げないようにその上に布団を掛けたものだが，こたつを囲んで家族が団らんするというのが，きわめて日本的な冬の光景になっている。

　こうした日本的家具に対する関心は欧米でも高まっているようで，日本旅館が外国人観光客に人気を呼んでいる。

Consumer Durables

The Japanese home is full of electrical appliances, symbols of the nation's prosperity. The main stars in the appliance boom of 1955-64 were the washing machine, refrigerator, and vacuum cleaner, and soon there was one of each in nearly every home (an Economic Planning Agency survey found that 99.3% of all Japanese homes had washing machines, 98.6% refrigerators, and 98.5% vacuum cleaners by 1989). Interest next shifted to the "three Cs", color television sets, air conditioners, and cars, and these have also achieved everyday status in the typical Japanese home (1998 diffusion rates being 99.2% for color TV sets, 81.9% for air conditioners, and 83.1% for cars). As a result, the demand is now for superior replacement models and wider ownership of other high-priced products. Popular in the United States and Europe as well as in Japan, video tape recorders, for example, have grown from 5.1% of all households in 1981 to 63.7% in 1989, and 76.8% in 1998. Overall, the Japanese lead very modern lives with a standard of living at least as high as that in the other industrial countries.

Japanese-style Home Furnishings

In seeming contrast to the demand for state-of-the-art consumer durables, the Japanese have a nearly equal passion for such traditional Japanese furnishings as *tatami*, *futon*, the Japanese bath, and the *kotatsu*.

• ***tatami*** *Tatami* are sturdy straw mats approximately 1.8×0.9m in size and used for flooring in the traditional Japanese home, comparable to Western carpeting. They are made of a thick layer of bundled straw covered with a woven rush covering, and shoes and slippers are removed before entering a *tatami* room. Nowadays Western trends in housing dictate carpeted floors for the living room and children's bedrooms, but many homes still have at least one room floored in *tatami*.

• ***futon*** Japanese-style bedding, or *futon*,* consists of thick quilts folded and put away in a closet* during the day, and laid out on the *tatami* at night. Light and easy to handle, *futon* are often aired to keep them fresh, soft, and comfortable.

• ***the Japanese bath*** The Japanese propensity for bathing is well known, and in contrast to the Western preference for a quick shower, the Japanese enjoy the luxury of a long soak in a deep tub full of clean, hot water.

• ***kotatsu*** The *kotatsu** is an original Japanese device used in the winter months. With charcoal or an electric heating unit placed under its four-legged frame and a *futon*-like quilt over it to hold in the heat, the *kotatsu* is a central piece of furniture in the winter as the whole family gathers around to talk and warm their feet under the quilt.

Indeed, the growing Western appreciation of Japanese-style furnishings may be one reason Japanese inns are so popular with visitors from overseas.

日本女性の着物姿はどの国へ行っても珍しがられるそうだが，日本国内においても，そうした事情はあまり変わらなくなってきている。女性に限らず現代の日本人は洋服が一般的で，着物を日常的に着るのはお茶，お花といった日本の伝統芸能のお師匠さんや落語家，力士などの特殊な職業の人に限られ，あとは，結婚式・成人式・正月などの儀式に着る装飾的なものになってしまっているためだ。したがって，自分で着物を着られる人も少なくなり，若い女性の中には“嫁入り修業”の一つとしているくらいである。

着物の変遷

洋服に対して在来の日本の衣服，つまり和服を総称して着物と言うが，一般的には羽織やコートを除いた，いわゆる長着(前でかき合わせて帯で締めるワンピーススタイルの現在の着物)を指すことが多い。長着の型が成立したのは奈良時代のことだが，平安時代のころまでは下着として着用されたものだった。その後，ズボンの袴(はかま)と合わせて着る表着となり，室町時代に男女とも袴が省略されて，今の着流しが一般的になった。江戸時代に入ると，着物は，特に男性の場合，封建社会の身分制と結び付き，さまざまな規制を受けるようになる。例えば，白無垢(しろむく)の肌着は大名でも嫡男だけにしか許されず，一般武士でも綸子(りんず)は着てはいけないことなどである。一般民衆は麻か木綿を常用した。しかし，町人の経済力が増すにつれて江戸時代末期から徐々に服装の自由化が進む。明治に入ると，皇族，軍人，官公吏，学生と順を追って洋服化が進み，一般にも普及した。

洋服の普及

男性の着物が身分制に縛られていたのに，女性の場合は，袖(そで)の長い振袖は娘の着るもので結婚すれば詰め袖という程度でそれほど厳しくなかったため，大正期ごろまでは着物生活が続いたが，女性も自我に目覚めだした昭和になって，急速に洋服が広まった。以来，男性の場合でさえ１世紀余りの短い日本人の洋服の歴史だが，現在では，若い女性が世界の一流デザイナーのプレタポルテを身に着けることが特別でないほど，すっかり洋服は定着している。その需要の高さから，ファッションショーの舞台も，パリ，ニューヨークから東京へ移りつつあると言われるほどで，森英恵，三宅一生，山本寛斎，高田賢三，山本耀司といった日本人デザイナーも，世界的に活躍するまでになった。

Western Clothing and the *Kimono*

A Japanese woman dressed in a *kimono** is becoming as rare a sight in Japan as it is overseas. Both Japanese men and women prefer Western clothing for their daily attire, and about the only people who wear Japanese-style clothing everyday are teachers of such traditional Japanese arts as the tea ceremony and flower arrangement, *rakugo* storytellers, and *sumou* wrestlers.* For most Japanese, the *kimono* is reserved for weddings, coming-of-age rites, the New Year's holidays, and other special occasions. Few can successfully dress themselves in the elaborate *kimono*, and many young ladies attend "*kimono* school" to learn this social grace before they get married.

The *Kimono's* Evolution

While *kimono* is a generic term for Japanese-style clothing, as opposed to Western-style, it more specifically refers to the long single garment overlapping in front and tied with a broad, stiff sash called an *obi**. The *kimono* traces its origins back to the *Nara* period, but it was simply an undergarment until the *Heian* period. Later it evolved into an outer garment worn by both men and women in combination with a *hakama** (long pantaloon-like skirt), and in the *Muromachi* period it finally reached its modern form without the *hakama*. In the hierarchical *Edo* period, the type and make of *kimono* was strictly regulated according to social rank, especially for men. For example, only the official heir to a fief lord could wear pure white underwear; ordinary *samurai* were forbidden to wear satin; and the common people could only wear flax and cotton. As the commercial class gained economic clout, the restrictions on dress were gradually relaxed toward the end of the *Edo* period. After the shogunate's downfall in the late 19th century, Western clothing spread to the imperial family, the military, the civil service bureaucracy, students, and finally to the general public.

Spread of Western Clothing

Whereas the *kimono* indicated rank for men, for women it generally symbolized marital status, unmarried lasses wearing colorful *furi-sode** *kimono* with long flowing sleeves, and changing to the more work-like *tsume-sode* after they married. *Kimono* continued to be worn as daily wear by women through the beginning of the 20th century until heightened consciousness sparked a change to Western dress after World War I.

It is only a little more than a century since the Japanese chose to adopt Western dress, but already young Japanese women wear leading designer fashions with ease. The fashion center of the world is shifting from Paris to New York to *Toukyou* (Tokyo), and Japanese designers such as *Hanae Mori, Issei Miyake, Kansai Yamamoto, Kenzou Takada,* and *Youji Yamamoto* are internationally recognized as among the best there are.

食生活と高度経済成長

戦後の日本，とりわけ，高度経済成長時代に入った1950年代後半以降に，日本人の生活は大きく変わった。それは，国民所得が大幅に増大したり，テレビ・洗濯機・冷蔵庫・炊飯器といった電化製品が普及したために，日本人の生活が非常に便利になると同時に，生活を楽しむゆとりができてきたからである。

当然，食生活においてもその影響が現れた。例えば食生活の考え方である。かつては「男子厨房に入るべからず」ということばがあった。これは，家庭内において料理を作るのは女性の役目で，男性がする仕事ではないという意味があるが，換言すると，男性が食事に興味を示すのは女々しいこととされていた。現在では，このことばは死語のようになり，男女を問わず，食事に関心をもつ人が多くなった。

また，台所の環境も一変した。以前は，家の間取りから見て条件の悪い位置に置かれることが多かったが，現在では，調理設備を整えるだけでなく，採光や通風など好条件の場所に配置したり，インテリアにも十分配慮している家庭が多い。

多様化する食生活

一日の食事回数は朝昼夕の 3 回で，最も重点が置かれているのは夕食である。戦前までは多くの家庭が日本料理中心で，米を主食に魚や野菜などの副食，それに*みそ汁と漬物という組み合わせが一般的であったが，戦後になって学校給食の影響でパン食が普及したり，肉類，卵，乳製品も多く取り入れられるようになった。

食事の内容は経済成長とともに多様化してきている。現在のほとんどの家庭では，日本料理だけでなく，洋食，中華とバラエティーに富んだ食事が食卓に並ぶ。それに，インスタントラーメンをはじめとする即席食品，半調理品，調理済み食品のようなひと手間かけるだけで食べられる食品が多く出回っている。

街に出れば，*すし，*てんぷら，*そば，*うどんなどの多くの日本料理とともに，中国料理やフランス料理やイタリア料理をはじめ，ドイツ，ロシア，インド，タイ，ベトナムなど世界各国の料理が楽しめるし，フライドチキンやハンバーガーなどのファーストフードもお好みしだいである。

さらに，一部では，健康食としての自然食品，ダイエット食，手作り料理が人気を博している傾向もある。とにかく現在の日本は飽食の時代にあると言う人もいるくらいなのである。

Recent Changes

Japanese lifestyles changed drastically in the decade of rapid economic growth which began in the late 1950s. As the nation's GNP soared, television sets, washing machines, refrigerators, and electric rice cookers proliferated, making life considerably more convenient and increasing leisure time.

These changes have naturally had an impact on the Japanese diet and attitudes toward food and eating. In the past, the kitchen was "off limits to men", a custom which not only indicated that cooking was women's work, but that even expressing an interest in food and cooking was somehow unseemly for a man. Today, this no longer holds true, and men and women alike are interested in what they eat and how it is prepared.

The kitchen has also changed. Whereas it was once given the worst location in the house, it is now often seen as one of the most important rooms, completely equipped and bright and airy.

Wide Choice

Three meals a day are the norm, with the evening meal usually the largest. Before World War II, everyone ate the traditional Japanese meal of rice supplemented by fresh fish and vegetables, *miso* soup,* and various pickles. After the war, however, bread became a mainstay of school lunches and this influenced dietary habits in society at large. People have also begun to eat more meat, eggs, and dairy products.

The Japanese diet has diversified as the nation has prospered. In the typical home today, Western and Chinese food is as likely to appear on the table as are more traditional Japanese foods. There has also been a phenomenal increase in instant foods such as instant *ramen*, semiprocessed and processed foods which require very little effort to prepare, and what can only be called junk food.

△Restaurant menu display

Eating out is common, and one can choose from a wide range of foods — Japanese foods such as *sushi,** *tenpura,** *soba,** and *udon,** as well as Chinese, French, Italian, German, Russian, Indian, Thai, Vietnamese, and many other international cuisines. Fast food chains serving fried chicken, hamburgers, and the like are also widespread.

Health-conscious Japanese are also accommodated by a variety of natural foods, diet foods, and restaurants specializing in home cooking. Japan is today a virtual paradise for gourmet and gourmand alike.

欧米型の食事と日本料理

近年，日本料理は栄養面からあらためて見直されてきている。特に外国ではダイエット食として注目され始め，理想的な食事の一つとして評価する人もいる。

確かに，欧米型の食事と日本料理とを比べてみた場合，欧米型の食事は肉類，乳製品などを中心とした高カロリー，高脂質であるのに対して，日本料理はてんぷらを別にすれば，油を使った料理が少なく，低カロリー，低脂質であり，かつ栄養のバランスもよい。

主食と副食

日本人の食生活には，伝統的に主食と副食という考えがある。主食は米で，普通は七部ないし精白についた*うるち米を水といっしょに炊いて常食にする。日本人の米食の歴史は古く，すでに弥生時代から食されているが，現在と同じようなご飯が登場するのは平安時代と言われている。

副食は，現在では肉類，乳製品，魚介類を問わず食卓にのぼるが，かつては日本列島が四方を海に囲まれているだけあって，魚介類が中心で，重要な動物性たんぱく源になっていた。魚介類の調理法は，焼く，煮る，蒸すなど多彩である。中でも「さしみ」はごく新鮮な魚介類を包丁さばきひとつで調理するもので，生で食べる日本独特の料理である。肉食も古くから行われていたが，仏教の普及によって禁忌されるようになり，どうしても魚介類に頼らざるをえなかった。

魚介類と並んで重要なのは，大豆加工食品である。これには，豆腐，*油揚げ，納豆などがあり，貴重な植物性たんぱく源として日本料理には欠かせない。そのほか野菜類もよく使われ，煮物，あえ物，酢の物，*おひたしなど野菜料理は豊富である。

調味料の王様しょうゆ

日本料理を語るとき，これらの主食や副食以上に忘れてならないのは，調味料のしょうゆ，みそである。特にしょうゆは調味料の王様と言ってよいくらい優れたもので，つけじょうゆ，かけじょうゆ，調味にとほとんどの料理に合う。日本料理がここまで発展したのも，このしょうゆという調味料に負うところが大きい。中国のしょうゆ，東南アジアの魚じょうゆもあることはあるが，これらと日本のしょうゆは味，香りとも全く異なる。みそはしょうゆほどではないが，みそ汁を始め，焼き物，あえ物などの調味料として重要である。

Western vs Traditional Diet

The traditional Japanese diet is gaining renewed acceptance both in Japan and overseas for its nutritional balance. Overseas, traditional Japanese foods are looked upon as ideal diet foods.

As many people have noticed, the meat- and dairy-product-based Western diet is much higher in calories and cholesterol than the Japanese diet which uses little oil or fats except for a few dishes such as tenpura, is low-calorie, yet is highly nutritious.

Staples and Side Dishes

The traditional Japanese meal consists primarily of rice as the staple supplemented by a number of side dishes. The rice is usually a non-glutinous rice,* partially or completely polished before being boiled. The Japanese have been rice-eaters since as far back as the *Yayoi* period, and rice as it is eaten today first appeared in the Japanese diet in the *Heian* period.

Although today meat and dairy products are just as common in Japan as fish, seafood has traditionally been an invaluable source of protein for this island nation. Side dishes of grilled, boiled, and steamed seafood are common, and *sashimi* (very fresh fish and shellfish eaten raw) is an especially popular and uniquely Japanese dish. While ancient Japanese also ate meat, the introduction of Buddhism and its injunctions against killing brought about a greater dependence on seafood as a source of protein nutrition.

△さしみ *(sashimi)*

Soybeans and soybean products are another important food in the Japanese diet. These include *toufu* (bean curd), *abura age** (deep fried *toufu*), and *nattou* (partially fermented soybeans), all of which are rich in vegetable protein. Numerous other vegetables are also eaten boiled, mixed with soybean paste or other flavorings, vinegared, or seasoned with soy sauce.*

Seasonings

Shouyu (soy sauce) and *miso* (soybean paste) are the primary flavorings used in Japanese cooking. *Shouyu* in particular is used in nearly all Japanese dishes, as a dip, as a sauce, and for seasoning, and it has played a major part in the development of Japanese cooking. Although other countries also have soy-based sauces, Japanese *shouyu* differs from its Chinese and Southeast Asian counterparts in both taste and fragrance. Although not used as much as *shouyu*, *miso* is a primary ingredient in soups, in flavoring fish or meat for grilling, and mixed with boiled vegetables as a flavoring.

五味五色五法の日本料理

日本料理には，家庭での日常の食事だけでなく，伝統的な行事食や宴席料理などがあり，依然として，現代の日本人の生活の中に生きている。諸外国ではすし，てんぷら，すき焼きなどが代表的な日本料理として知られているが，日本料理の特徴という点から言えば，むしろ，伝統的な行事食や宴席料理のほうがその色彩が濃い。

昔から，日本料理を「五味五色五法の料理」と言って，その特徴を表現する。「五味」とは，甘・酸・辛・苦・鹹（かん）（塩辛い）のことを，「五色」とは，白・黄・赤・青・黒のことを，「五法」とは生・煮る・焼く・揚げる・蒸すという料理法を指す。つまり，日本料理とはこれくらいデリケートな料理だということである。素材の持ち味を生かしながら，味・香り・色をだいじにし，春夏秋冬の季節感をも重視する。材料の旬（しゅん）（最もおいしい時季）にも気を配る。さらに，料理を盛り付ける器も，料理によってあるいは季節によって，色・形・材質について配慮するのである。

伝統的な日本料理

伝統的な日本料理に次のようなものがある。

- **＊本膳（ほんぜん）料理**　室町時代に武家の礼法とともに定められたもてなしの形式が基になった料理。現在では，冠婚葬祭などの儀礼的な料理としてわずかに残っているだけであるが，ほかの伝統的な日本料理の形式や作法上の基本になっている。
- **＊茶懐石（ちゃかいせき）**　茶の湯で茶を出す前に供する簡単な料理。懐石とは，温めた石を懐に抱いて腹を温めるのと同じくらいに，空腹をしのぐという意味である。懐石料理とも言う。
- **＊会席料理**　本膳料理よりもずっと形式ばらず，くつろいだ形の宴席料理。言うなれば日本のパーティー料理である。現在の日本料理店で供する宴席料理の多くがこれである。
- **＊精進（しょうじん）料理**　魚介類や肉類を用いずに，大豆加工品や野菜，海草などの植物性食品だけを使った料理。これには，仏教の禅宗に伝わる精進料理と，黄檗山万福寺（おうばくさんまんぷくじ）に伝わる普茶料理がある。
- **＊おせち料理**　正月の祝い料理で，五段重ねの漆塗りの＊重箱に各種の料理を詰めて出すもの。昔は，特別な行事の日に，神に供える料理のことを言っていた。

Traditional Japanese Dishes

The Three Fives

Japanese cuisine is rich in variety, encompassing everything from the simplest home-cooked meal to special meals for ceremonial occasions and fabulous banquets. Japanese dishes popular overseas include *sushi, tenpura*, and *sukiyaki*, but these have fewer traditional elements than do ceremonial and banquet menus.

The Japanese diet is commonly said to consist of five flavors, five colors, and five basic methods of preparation. These are the five flavors of sweet, sour, hot, bitter, and salty; the five colors of white, yellow, red, green, and black; and the five preparations of raw, boiled, grilled, deep-fried, and steamed. Japanese foods are prepared to retain as much of their natural flavor as possible, and great importance is placed on the delicacy of color, fragrance, and taste. The season of the year is also stressed, with foods being served at their peak season. Serving dishes as well play an important role; their color, shape, and material being carefully matched to the food and season.

Traditional Japanese Cooking

While there are far too many kinds of traditional Japanese cooking to list them all, some of the best-known are:

• ***Honzen-ryouri**** This formal banquet style was originally the method for presenting food to guests in the *samurai* homes of the feudal *Muromachi* period. *Honzen-ryouri* is served today only on such ritual and ceremonial occasions as weddings, funerals, and other formal occasions. Still, *honzen-ryouri* remains a basic influence in all traditional Japanese cooking styles and manners.

• ***Cha-kaiseki**** This is a simple lunch served to guests before serving tea. The characters for the term *kaiseki* refer to the warmed stones that Buddhist monks used to put next to their stomachs to ward off hunger, and connote a frugal meal. Today this tea-lunch style is commonly known as *kaiseki-ryouri*.

• ***Kaiseki-ryouri**** Written with different characters from *kaiseki* above, this informal banquet style than *honzen*, and may be thought of as the typical Japanese party menu. Much of the food served at modern Japanese-style restaurants is in the *kaiseki* or informal banquet mode.

• ***Shoujin-ryouri**** Abstaining entirely from the use of any meat or fish, *shoujin-ryouri* is an all-vegetarian diet of soybean products, vegetables, seaweed, and rice. The two best-known schools are the *shoujin-ryouri* of *Zen* Buddhism and the *fucha-ryouri* served at the *Zen Oubakusan Manpukuji.*

• ***O-sechi-ryouri**** This is the festive food eaten at New Year's, and it is often served in a five-layer set of lacquer boxes.* In olden times, *o-sechi-ryouri* was used to refer to the food prepared as offerings to the gods on special occasions.

旧厚生省の『人口動態統計』によると，1999年に結ばれたカップルは76万2028組で，前年より約２万2600組減り，人口1000人当たりの婚姻率も6.1と減っている。この婚姻率は，71年の10.5から減り続け，87年には5.7で統計開始以来最低を記録したが，90年代は5.9〜6.4の間を上下している。一方，離婚は25万0529組で，離婚率は2.00に達し，統計開始以来最高を記録した。この数字は，アメリカ（4.60）やスウェーデン（2.53）などの離婚先進国に比べれば低いものの，日本でも離婚が珍しくなくなったことを表している。これまでは夫婦になれば「ともに白髪の生えるまで」添い遂げるというのが，日本人の結婚観だったが，うまくいかなければ別れたほうがよいという欧米型の結婚観に，急速にかわりつつあると言える。

見合い結婚

結婚に際してきわめて日本的なものに「見合い」がある。見合いというのは，本人どうしの自由恋愛によって結ばれるのではなく，「仲人」と呼ばれる仲介者が結婚したいと思っている男女を紹介し，当人どうしが気に入れば結婚まで世話をするというしくみである。たいていの場合，適齢期の息子や娘をもった親が，当人のスナップ写真や「釣り書き」という結婚のための経歴書を添えて，仲人に相手探しを頼む。適当な相手が見つかったところで双方の親も同席して，顔合わせの見合いとなる。この見合いで趣味や家庭についての抱負などを語り合って，自分の結婚相手にふさわしいかどうかを判断するのである。戦後の民主化によって，恋愛結婚が増えている中でも，見合い結婚は相変わらず支持されていて，恋愛８割見合い２割という傾向は，ここ数年変わっていない。

ジミ婚・ハデ婚

ある銀行の96年の調査によると，結納，結婚式，披露宴，ハネムーン，新居などにかかる日本人の結婚総費用は平均794万2000円であった。その中で，ホテルで豪華*結婚式を挙げ，ハネムーンは海外へというハデ婚と呼ばれるカップルの結婚総費用は984万4000円であった。費用の掛け方には幅があるが，その費用を本人たちだけで賄うカップルは少なく，親の援助を受ける場合がほとんどである。親族などの意向を組み入れたこうした伝統的な結婚式を行うカップルがいる一方，従来の形式的な結婚式や披露宴は行わず，入籍だけといういわゆるジミ婚のカップルも徐々に増えてきている。

Marriage and Divorce

According to the former Ministry of Health and Welfare Population Dynamics Statistics, 752,028 couples were married in 1999, down approximately 22,600 from the previous year, lowering the marriage rate to 6.1 per 1000 population. After declining from 10.5 in 1971 to 5.7 in 1987 when it bottomed out, the marriage rate fluctuated between 5.9 and 6.4 per 1000 during the '90s. On the other side of the ledger, 1999 saw 250,529 divorces, putting the divorce rate at 2 per 1000, a new all time high for Japan. While still low in comparison to other developed nations such as the U.S. (4.60) and Sweden (2.53), this figure shows how not uncommon divorce has become in Japan. The Japanese ideal used to be that once joined in matrimony, husband and wife would stay together until death did them part. This is rapidly being replaced by a more Western view of marriage, where, if things don't work well, it's better to get a divorce.

Miai

Arranged marriages are very Japanese. The arranged marriage starts not with love between the young man and woman, but with an introduction by a go-between who thinks they would make a good couple. If they find they hit it off, the go-between sees them through to marriage. Often a young man's or woman's parents will take their child's picture and a brief personal sketch to a go-between and ask him/her to look for a suitable match. Once a suitable person has been found, the young people are introduced at a formal meeting (the *miai*) with their parents present. At the *miai*, they usually talk about their personal interests, the kind of families they want, and other generalities in an effort to see how compatible they are. Even with the rapid increase in non-arranged "love" marriages that accompanied postwar democratization, the *miai* system still has a strong following, and the pattern recently has been that 20% of the marriages are arranged marriages.

Lavish and Quiet Weddings

According to a survey done by one of the major banks in 1996, when everything is taken into account—including the dowry, the wedding,* the honeymoon, the costs of moving into a new apartment, and everything else — getting married costs an average of ¥7,942,000 in Japan. And for the people who have lavish wedding receptions at classy hotels and then honeymoon overseas, the average runs to ¥9,844,000. Very few of these couples foot the entire bill themselves, and most people rely upon financing from their parents. Yet just as these big weddings with all the trappings to please all the relatives garner the attention, the other end of the spectrum is represented by the growing number of people who forsake the traditional ceremonies and celebrations and simply notify city hall.

日本には国教と言えるような特定の宗教がないので，故人の宗教やその遺志などによって，葬儀・告別式の方法も仏式，神式，キリスト教式，無宗教式といろいろある。身内に不幸があった場合，遺族の代表として死亡から葬儀までの中心となる喪主と，喪主や遺族に代わって実務的な仕事を取りしきる世話人とを決めるまでの段取りはすべて共通だが，その後の葬儀・告別式のやり方はそれぞれの方式によってだいぶ違ってくる。ここでは最も一般的な仏式を中心に紹介しておく。

仏式の葬儀と告別式

キリスト教・新教の納棺式に当たるのが通夜で，死者を葬る前に家族・親(しん)戚(せき)・友人など，故人にゆかりの深い人々が夜通し棺の前で守る。祭壇は葬儀社に頼んで飾り付けるが，経験豊かで「○○式」と告げるだけで，その方式どおりに最後まで式次第の世話をしてくれるのが，日本の葬儀社の特徴である。次に僧侶を呼んで読経してもらい，死者の死後の名前である*戒名を付けてもらう。その後，参列者が*焼香し，軽い酒食をとりながら故人をしのぶのがしきたりになっている。昔は遺体を寝かせたまま通夜を行い，その後に納棺したが，最近は衛生的配慮から，通夜の前に納棺を行うようになった。

死者を弔う葬儀と，死者に会葬者が最後の別れを告げる告別式は引き続き行われるのが普通だが，場合によっては遺族や近親者だけで葬儀を行い，一般会葬者は告別式にだけ参列するとか，公葬にするためにすぐ葬儀が行えないようなときには，死後２，３日以内に，取りあえず近親者だけで密葬を行い，後日，正式の葬儀，告別式を行うこともある。キリスト教の献花の代わりに，仏式では祭壇で合掌し，焼香して死者に別れを告げる。告別式の後，火葬場に行き火葬，骨上げを済ませ，遺骨とともに帰宅して翌日，埋葬(納骨)をする。墓地が正式に決まらない場合や，遠くてすぐに行けないような場合には，寺院の納骨堂にいったん遺骨を預け，後日，埋葬することもある。

法要

キリスト教の場合，昇天記念日に礼拝や追悼ミサを行うように，仏式でも故人の死後，冥福(めいふく)を祈って読経する法要という行事がある。死後７日目の初七日，同様に四十九日，百か日。命日に行う一周忌，三回忌，七回忌などの年忌法要もある。盆や，春秋の彼岸にも墓参りをして，死者をしのび，供養する。

Funerals

Because there is no state religion in Japan, there are many different types of funeral services, including Buddhist, *Shintou*, Christian, and secular, depending upon the deceased's religion or last wishes. Most people handle the business of making funeral arrangements in much the same way—one family member is chosen as "chief mourner" and this person, sometimes with help from outside the family, makes the arrangements—but the services themselves vary widely from family to family. Nonetheless, Buddhist rites are the most common in Japan.

Buddhist Wakes and Funerals

Like many Christian and other funerals, Buddhist funerals include a wake at which family, relatives, and close friends mourn beside the coffin. Buddhist wakes begin with the preparation of the funeral altar by a professional mortician. Japanese undertakers have extensive experience with all manner of services, and one has only to specify the type to have everything taken care of from start to finish. Next, a Buddhist priest arrives to chant sutras and give the deceased a posthumous Buddhist name.* After the posthumous naming, it is customary for the people attending the wake to burn incense* before reminiscing about the deceased over a little food and drink. In the past, the body lay outside the coffin until the end of the wake, but it is now more common for the body to be encoffined before the wake.

Although the wake is usually followed directly by the funeral, in some cases the funeral is attended by close friends and family only and a separate memorial service is held for a wider group of mourners. At times, a small private funeral soon after the death may precede a large public funeral several days or even weeks later. Instead of presenting flowers as is done in Japanese Christian funerals, Buddhist mourners pray before the funeral altar, burn incense, and pay their last respects to the deceased. After this, the mourners proceed to the crematorium for the cremation rites, including placing the deceased's ashes into a cinerary urn, and the mourners take the urn home with them to keep until the burial rites the next day. If no cemetery has been selected yet, or if it is too far away to reach right away, the urn may be kept at a local temple's cinerarium until it can be properly buried.

Memorial Services

Just as Christians hold church services or memorial masses on the anniversary of a loved one's death, Buddhists also meet after the funeral to recite sutras and pray for the deceased's soul. In Japan, these services are held primarily on the seventh, forty-ninth, and one hundredth days following the death and on the first, second, and sixth anniversaries. In addition, people visit family graves during the summer *bon* season and the spring and autumn *higan* seasons to remember the dead and to leave offerings of flowers, food, and drink.

正月

日本人の1年の生活を区切る節目が，正月である。正月期間は，官庁も民間企業も学校も休みになって，国民こぞって新しい年の初めを祝う。正月は陰暦の第1月，つまり1月を指し，年頭に当たって家々の祖先の霊を迎えて，その年の実り豊かなことを祈願するのが本来の意味であった。しかし，一般的には1月1日から7日までの*松の内を言い，その意味も単に新年を祝うというものに変わってきている。

正月準備は前年の暮れに始まり，各家庭では大掃除をして家の内外を清め，祖先を迎える*門松を門前に立てたり，正月に食べる*雑煮用のもちやおせち料理を用意したりで，主婦はてんてこ舞いになる。俗に民族大移動と言われる大移動が始まるのもこのころで，故郷へ帰る人，旅行に出る人で各交通機関は連日大混雑となる。旧年最後の大晦日(12月31日)の夜には，翌年も細く長く生きられますようにと，そばを食べて年を越すのが習わしである。

明けて1月1日から3日までの三が日，あるいは門松を取る7日までの松の内の間に，新年のさまざまな行事が行われる。最も正月行事らしいのが，「初もうで」と「年始回り」で，たいていの人が近くの神社や寺に参拝して1年の無事を祈り，親戚(しんせき)や職場の上司など，日ごろ世話になっている人々の家へ新年のあいさつをして歩く。ふだんは洋服が多い日本女性が*髪を結い，着物で着飾って歩くのもこの正月期間である。書面で年始回りに代えるものとして発達した*年賀状も，正月には欠かせないもので，もらった年賀状の多寡がその人の社会的地位を物語るような一面もある。子供たちの中には凧(たこ)上げ，独楽(こま)回し，羽根つきなど昔からあった正月の遊びをして過ごす子もいる。正月の小遣いである「お年玉」をもらうのも，子供の大きな楽しみである。

盆

正月に次いで，日本の年中行事の大きなピークとなっているのが盆で，釈迦の16弟子の一人が，7月15日に，地獄に落ちて苦しむ亡母をねんごろに供養して救ったという仏教説話に基づいて，7月13日から15日(地方によっては1か月遅れ)までの間，仏壇に供物を供えて，祖先の霊を祭る。盆には，広場に大きな櫓(やぐら)を組み，近所中集まって，*笛や*太鼓に合わせてみんなで踊る*盆踊りが，各地で開かれる。

Shougatsu and Bon

Shougatsu

For the Japanese, *shougatsu* serves to punctuate life with an annual beginning and end. *Shougatsu* is a time when government offices, private companies, schools, and everyone else takes a few days off to celebrate the arrival of the new year. The Japanese word for January, *Ichigatsu* (first moon), reflects *shougatsu*'s original significance as the beginning of the lunar year, a time when families paid their respects to their ancestors and prayed for successful crops. Nowadays, however, the first week of January* is generally referred to as *shougatsu* and is celebrated as simply the start of the new year.

Come late December and Japanese homes are abuzz with activity as housewives clean the house and garden, set traditional pine ornaments called *kadomatsu** outside the front door to welcome ancestral spirits, and prepare holiday foods such as *o-sechi-ryouri, zouni,** and *mochi.* Just prior to the new year's arrival is the big urban exodus—a period of several days during which every transportation artery is clogged with people leaving the city to return to their ancestral village or to take a vacation trip. On New Year's Eve it is common to eat *soba* noodles to symbolize long lives and continuity across the years.

Many special events take place during the first week of the new year, and especially during the first three days. The two most typical are the first visit to a shrine or temple, where people gather to pray for good fortune during the year ahead, and the formal New Year's calls paid to relatives, company superiors, and anyone else to whom you have become indebted during the past year. It is also during this week that Japanese women, most of whom ordinarily wear Western clothing, take the trouble to put their hair up* and wear a traditional *kimono*. New Year's calls have to some extent been replaced by *nengajou** (New Year's cards), an indispensable part of *shougatsu* if only because receiving large numbers of *nengajou* is an indication of high social status. Some children spend *shougatsu* flying kites, spinning tops, playing Japanese battledore, and enjoying other traditional pastimes. Another treat for the children is *otoshidama*—small gifts of money from parents and relatives.

Bon

After *shougatsu*, the other big holiday of the year is *bon*, based on the Buddhist legend describing how, on the 15th day of the seventh month, one of Buddha's 16 disciples made a generous offering to save his mother from torment in hell. Today *bon* is observed between July 13 and 15 in *Toukyou* (Tokyo) (and one month later in most other parts of Japan) by placing offerings on the *butsudan* (small Buddhist altar) in the home, and by otherwise seeking to please the ancestral spirits. Communities all over Japan erect stages in the squares for musicians playing flutes,* and drums* to accompany everyone in special *bon-odori** dances.

いずれも子供の無事な成長を祝う，日本の年中行事である。

ひな祭り

ひな祭りは3月3日に行われる女の子の*節句で，正しくは「桃の節句」と言う。女の子が将来いい伴侶に恵まれて幸せな結婚ができますようにと，内裏(だいり)びな，三人官女，五人ばやしなどの*ひな人形を段飾りに飾り，白酒や紅白のあられで祝う。いつまでも飾っておくと縁が遅れるという言い伝えから，3月3日を過ぎたらすぐしまい込むのがしきたりとなっている。娘の嫁入り道具の一つとして，ひな人形一式をもたせる習わしも残っている。桃の節句が女の子の節句として広まったのは明治以降のことで，もともとは男女を問わず，子供たちが野外へ出て野遊びをする日であった。これに，桃の節句とは関係なく，平安時代の貴族の子女たちの間で楽しまれていたひな遊びとが江戸時代に結び付いて，しだいに女の子のお祝いになったと言われている。

端午(たんご)の節句

3月3日の桃の節句に対して，5月5日の端午の節句は男の子のお祝いである。この日はまた「こどもの日」として国民の祝日にもなっている。男の子のいる家庭では*よろい・*かぶとなどの*五月人形を飾り，屋外に*こいのぼりを立てて，菖蒲(しょうぶ)や*かしわもちで，その子の立身出世を祈る。この端午の節句も，古くは災厄を避けるために，菖蒲などの薬草や鳥獣を捕る薬猟(くすりがり)の日だった。菖蒲は尚武(しょうぶ)(武事を尊ぶこと)に通じることから，室町時代から，紙製のかぶとに菖蒲の花を飾るようになり，江戸時代になって，武者人形やこいのぼりが現れた。広く定着したのは，やはり明治に入ってからのことである。

七五三

七五三は，*数え年3歳と5歳の男児，3歳と7歳の女児に，晴着を着せて宮参りをする祝いで，11月15日に行われる。江戸時代の武家社会のしきたりが一般化したもので，当時，武家の子女は3歳で男女とも初めて髪を伸ばす「髪置きの儀」を行い，その後，男児は5歳になると初めて袴(はかま)を履く「袴着の儀」，女児は7歳で初めて，それまでのひもを解いて本式の帯を用いる「帯解きの儀」を行った。

どの祝いも，メーカーやデパートの商魂にあおられて，年々華美になってきており，こうした風潮に対する批判も一部にはあるが，子供たちの成長を祈る親心のほうが勝っていると言えよう。

*Hina Matsuri, Tango no Sekku,** and *Shichi-go-san* are all annual events celebrating children and praying for their sound development.

Hina Matsuri

Celebrated on March 3, *Hina Matsuri* (Doll Festival), formally known as *Momo no Sekku* (Peach Festival), is for girls. It is a time when girls pray for a good marriage, set out tiered platforms decorated with *hina-ningyou** (*hina* dolls usually including emperor and empress, three court ladies, and five musicians), and enjoy treats such as *shirozake* (sweet *sake* with rice malt) and red and white candies. Leaving the *hina* dolls out too long is said to delay marriage, and it is customary to put them away soon after March 3. Traditionally, the *hina* doll collection has been part of a new bride's dowry. *Momo no Sekku*'s popularization as *Hina Matsuri* occurred only since the *Meiji* period; earlier it had been a picnic festival for both boys and girls. The Doll Festival has its roots in the ceremonies and rituals involving dolls performed by the daughters of the *Heian* nobility, and it was only later, during the *Edo* period, that these dolls came back into fashion and gradually evolved into a Girl's Day tradition connected with *Momo no Sekku*.

Tango no Sekku

May 5 is a day for boys. Long the *Tango no Sekku*, it has been officially renamed Children's Day and made a national holiday. Families with sons buy armored* *samurai* dolls and miniature helmets,* hang out *koi-nobori*,* buy irises and *kashiwa-mochi,** and pray for their sons' success in life. *Tango no Sekku* used to be a day for hunting game and gathering medicinal herbs, such as iris leaves. *Shoubu* in Japanese, the iris has a homonym meaning "military spirit," from whence came the *Muromachi* custom of decorating paper helmets with iris leaves. *Samurai* dolls and *koi-nobori* first appeared in the *Edo* period, but it was not until the *Meiji* period that these customs became popular nationwide.

Shichi-go-san

Literally, 7-5-3, this celebration falls on November 15 and is a time for boys who have reached their third or fifth birthday* and girls who have reached their third or seventh to dress up and pay their respects at the local shrine. A popularization of various rituals observed by the *Edo*-period *samurai* class, *Shichi-go-san* originally included various rites of passage: boys and girls aged three were permitted to begin growing their hair long, boys aged five could start wearing *hakama* (a divided skirt worn by men), and girls aged seven were given an *obi* instead of rope to tie their *kimono*.

As doll manufactures, department stores, and other merchants vie for profits, these celebrations are becoming more lavish every year, and some people now say they should be abandoned or at least purged of this ostentation. Yet the festivities are likely to continue as outlets for parental affection and the desire to see their children succeed.

もともとは伝統的な祭りではないが，商魂たくましいデパートや商店街の巧みな客寄せ作戦に使われ，すっかりお祭り化した行事に，七夕とクリスマスがある。

七夕

七夕は奈良時代に中国から渡って来た星祭りの一つで，天の川を隔てて向かい合っている牽牛(けんぎゅう)星と織女(しょくじょ)星が，陰暦の7月7日に，年に一度の逢瀬(おうせ)を楽しむという「牽牛織女」の伝説に基づいている。この日，中国では織女星を祭って，女性が裁縫の上達を祈る風習があったことから，日本でも五色の*短冊(たんざく)に願い事を書き，色紙や折りづるなどといっしょに庭に飾った笹竹につるして，*習字や手芸などの上達を祈ることが行われるようになった。

織女星を日本では「棚機津女(たなばたつめ)」と言ったため，陰暦の7月7日と，その日に行われる行事を「七夕」と総称するようになったものだが，地方によっては太陽暦の7月7日や，一か月遅れの8月7日ごろに行うところもある。

いずれにしても七夕は，家庭や，子供を教育する，昔で言えば寺子屋のようなところで，こぢんまりと行われた夏の風物詩だった。それが，いつのころからか下火になり，その代わりに盛んになったのが，商店街の七夕である。大きな飾り玉や，人気者の人形などを軒並みにつるし，お祭りムードを盛り上げて客足を呼ぼうというわけである。宮城県仙台市や神奈川県平塚市の七夕はそのはでさで全国的に有名で，観光の目玉の一つにさえなっているほどである。

クリスマス

キリストの降誕を祝うクリスマスも，本来，キリスト教国でない日本では無縁のものだったが，これも，デパートなどが商戦の一環として宣伝に努めたため，今ではすっかり日本人に定着した行事となっている。さすがにクリスマス休暇はないが，イブには小さなツリーを飾り，みんなでケーキを食べたりプレゼントを贈ったりすることが，多くの家庭で行われる。各デパートでは，12月に入ると，大小さまざまのツリーを店内に飾り付け，このときが稼ぎ時とばかり，「クリスマス・ギフト・セール」と銘打って，華々しい客取り合戦を展開する。

2月14日のバレンタインデーも年ごとに盛んになっているが，その行事がもっている宗教的な意味合いとは全く無関係に行われているところが，いかにも特定の宗教がない日本らしい。

Tanabata and Christmas

Although not traditional festive occasions in Japan, *Tanabata* and Christmas have both recently been seized upon by department stores and other merchants and developed into major commercial attractions.

Tanabata

The *Tanabata* Festival came to Japan from China during the *Nara* period and is based on the folk legend of the Cowherd Star (Altair) and the Weaver Star (Vega), two lovers whose celestial paths cross but once a year—on the seventh day of the seventh month of the lunar calendar. In ancient China, *Tanabata* was a time when women prayed to the Weaver Star for sewing skills, and this custom was transformed in Japan into one in which prayers for academic proficiency and such cultural arts as *shuuji** are written on multicolored streamers of paper* attached to bamboo poles along with *origami* cranes and other decorations for display in the family garden.

The Japanese name *Tanabata*, written with the characters for "seven" and "evening," is a phonetic writing of *Tanabatatsume*—the Japanese pronunciation of the Chinese characters for "the Woman Weaver"—and reflects the timing of the festival on the seventh day of the seventh month. For most Japanese, this day is July 7 on the Julian calendar, although in some areas *Tanabata* is observed on August 7 in keeping with the older traditions.

In either case, *Tanabata* used to be a time when people gathered at home or at *terakoya* schools to enjoy a warm midsummer evening. This custom eventually yielded to the lavish, commercialized *Tanabata* Festivals held in shopping districts. Festival sponsors draw crowds of potential customers with parades of oversized prayer poles, dolls resembling popular singers and actors, and other displays conducive to a festive mood. The *Tanabata* Festivals held in *Sendai* and *Hiratsuka* have won national fame for their gaudiness and attract tourists from far and wide.

Christmas

The religious celebration of the birth of Jesus was observed by almost no one in this non-Christian nation until merchants saw it as a sales opportunity, but Christmas celebrations are now quite popular among Japanese. Christmas is not an official holiday in Japan, but most families observe the day by gathering on Christmas Eve to decorate a small Christmas tree, eat decorated cakes, and exchange presents. In early December, department stores begin decorating their floors with ornament-laden Christmas trees while vying to attract shoppers with advertisements for special Christmas sales.

St. Valentine's Day is another celebration that has become very popular in Japan in a form absolutely devoid of any religious connotations—a twist which is only natural in this secular nation.

16 日本の祭り

日本ほど祭りの多い国も珍しい。各地に根付いた伝統的な祭りから，近年，民間で始められた「*浴衣(ゆかた)祭り」や「温泉祭り」まで，多彩な祭りがあって，毎日，日本のどこかで祭りが行われていると言っても言いすぎではない。

もともと日本の祭りは，農耕儀礼に由来する農村の春の豊作祈願祭や秋の収穫祭が中心で，その後これに，悪霊，疫病を払うための都市の夏祭りが加わった。いずれも神々をもてなして，祭りの担い手である，その土地の居住者の繁栄と結束を願うものだったが，江戸時代以降，しだいに形骸(けいがい)化し，祭りは日々の暮らしに区切りをつける一種のレクリエーションとなった。昭和，とりわけ戦後に入ってからはその意味合いさえ薄れて，すっかり観光化した祭りも少なくない。数ある祭りの中から有名なものをいくつか紹介すると——

• **青森・*ねぶた祭り**　8月1日の夜から7日にかけて行われる青森の夏の風物詩。木や竹の骨組みに紙を張り，これに『*三国志』の英雄や*加藤清正のトラ退治などの勇壮な絵を書いて作った，縦横数メートルの灯籠(とうろう)が，何台も町々を練り歩き，最後にその灯籠を海に渡して祭りは終わる。「ねぶた流し」と言って，眠気を払って，祖先の霊を慰める盆を迎えるための祭りである。

• **東京・*三社(さんじゃ)祭り**　江戸の町に夏の到来を告げる浅草神社の例祭。5月17，18日に町内から数十体の*みこしが繰り出し，*びんざさらと呼ばれる古い楽器を鳴らしてにぎやかに踊る「びんざさら舞」という珍しい舞いが奉納される。下町情緒あふれる庶民の祭りだ。

• **京都・*祇園(ぎおん)祭り**　京都には，「賀茂の*競馬(くらべうま)」や「*葵(あおい)祭り」など，古都ならではのみやびやかな祭りが多いが，最も豪華なのが，7月1日から一か月間も行われる「祇園祭り」だ。なかでも15，16日の宵山は圧巻で，散在する鉾(ほこ)から祇園ばやしの鉦(しょう)の音が流れ，鉾町一帯は不夜城となる。

• **福岡・*博多どんたく**　5月3，4日に行われる民間の港祭り。*しゃもじを叩きながら歌う博多松ばやしや，仮装行列で，全市が一大歓楽境と化す。

こうした日本の代表的な祭りには，観光をかねた見物客が全国から集まり，数百万人の人出となる。外国人観光客も年々多くなっている。

Japan is a land of festivals. Not only are there numerous festivals based on age-old traditions, there are also many newer theme festivals such as *yukata** festivals, and hardly a day passes without some sort of festival somewhere.

Japanese festivals originally centered on agrarian rituals such as spring prayers for bountiful rice crops and autumn harvest celebrations. These were later joined by the urban summer festivals for driving away evil spirits and plagues. All of these festivals were intended to placate the gods and ensure the community's continuing solidarity and prosperity, and it was not until the *Edo* period that festivals began to be popularized as diversions from everyday life. In recent decades, and especially since the end of the war, festivals have grown even more devoid of meaning, and many now exist mainly as tourist attractions.

• ***Nebuta* Festival*** (*Aomori*) This celebration of summer takes place from the evening of August 1 through August 7. Enormous floats depicting famous warrior-heroes from ancient China* or famous Japanese *samurai* such as *Katou Kiyomasa** are lit from within so that they glow as they are paraded throughout the city and, at the end of the festival, set adrift on the sea. This closing ceremony, called *nebuta-nagashi*, symbolizes the dispelling of sleep in order to usher in the *bon* season when ancestral spirits are welcomed and entertained.

• ***Sanja Matsuri**** (*Toukyou* (Tokyo)) This festival began as a parade to herald the arrival of summer. Every May 17-18, scores of *mikoshi** are carried through the streets to *Asakusa* Shrine, accompanied by *binzasara** percussion instruments which set the beat for a wild dance called *Binzasara no Mai*. Held in the traditionally working-class *shitamachi* part of *Toukyou*, the *Sanja Matsuri* has a very plebeian mood.

• ***Gion* Festival*** (*Kyouto* (Kyoto)) *Kyouto*, the nation's capital for many centuries, hosts a large number of traditional festivals, among them the *Kamo no Kurabeuma** and the *Aoi Matsuri*,* but grandest of them all is the *Gion* Festival which begins on July 1 and lasts throughout the month. The highlight of the *Gion* Festival is on July 15 and 16, when floats with *gion-bayashi* musicians playing bells and other instruments light up the nighttime streets.

• ***Hakata Dontaku**** (*Fukuoka*) The *Hakata Dontaku* festival is held in *Fukuoka* on May 3 and 4 every year. Featuring singers beating rice paddles* as well as a procession of numerous people wearing colorful costumes, *Hakata Dontaku* makes the whole city of *Fukuoka* come alive with merriment.

These major festivals draw millions of participants and spectators from all over the country—and increasingly large numbers of non-Japanese tourists as well.

消費のしかた

日本では買い物は主婦のだいじな日課である。かつては，毎日夕方4時，5時ごろに近所のスーパーや肉屋，魚屋，八百屋に出かけて，その日の夕食分と翌日の朝食・昼食分ぐらいをこまめに買うということが一般的であった。日本では，魚，野菜類を多くとる食生活が長かったため，鮮度をとてもたいせつにしてきた。そうした習慣から，多少めんどうでも，なるべく新鮮なものを求めて，毎日買い物をしたのである。このような購買習慣は，既成市街地において依然として残っている。

しかし，モータリゼーションの進展などから，このような消費パターンには大きな変化が見られる。個人商店が減少する一方で，ディスカウントストア，ショッピングセンターという新業態による小売りが勢力を拡大している。また，郊外の割安な土地を活用して，大規模な駐車場を備えた大型ショッピングモールが各地に出現し，たくさんの客を集めている。その結果，駅前などの商店街に，閉店してシャッターを下ろしたままの店があちこちにある光景が，全国で見られるようになった。こうした流通業界の変化が，まとめ買いなど購入パターンの変化をいっそう促している。

通信販売も小売業全体を上回る伸び率を達成している。しかし，通信販売の低価格は，無店舗販売によるコストの低さを反映したものであったが，大手スーパーなどによる価格破壊の進行で，その利点は消えつつある。また，コンピューターネットワークが新しい通信販売の媒体として広がりつつあり，今後の動向が注目される。

消費傾向の変化

かつては衣食住が消費の中心だったが，今では衣食住以外の選択的支出が消費の過半数を占めており，この傾向は今後も増加するだろうと予想されている。経済企画庁では，2010年の消費生活を展望している。それによると，急速な高齢化，自由時間の増大，意識・価値観の変化などによって，医療サービス，ケア付き住宅，レジャー・旅行などの時間消費型消費，学習・交際費などの心の充足のための支出は，増大するだろうと予測している。また消費をめぐる環境としては，エネルギー・資源多消費型の見直し，自然環境の保全に配慮した節度ある生活スタイルへの転換が課題となっている。

The Japanese Market

Shopping Patterns

Shopping is an important part in the daily routine of the Japanese housewife. It used to be she would go to the local supermarket or fishmonger's, butcher's, greengrocer's, etc. every afternoon and buy just enough for dinner that day and next morning's breakfast. Because the Japanese diet was heavy on fish and vegetables, it was important that they be fresh. So even though it was sometimes a chore, she went shopping every day for fresh ingredients. In fact, this shopping pattern still persists where there are strong neighborhoods.

Yet consumer habits have changed radically with motorization. A decrease in the number of small, individually owned shops on the one hand has been accompanied by a great increase in retail enterprises in the form of discount stores and shopping centers. Shopping malls are also popping up at various locations, taking advantage of the cheaper land prices outside urban centers to create sprawling parking lots, and attracting hoards of customers. As a result, it is now common throughout Japan to see stores with shutters permanently closed dotting the shopping avenues typically surrounding train stations. These changes in the pattern of merchandise distribution are causing a shift in consumer patterns away from daily shopping to weekly shopping.

Mail-order sales also moved onto center stage, growing faster than the sector as a whole. Yet while mail-order had a price advantage because it did not have the same overhead, the big chains soon slashed their own prices to erode that advantage. At the same time, the BBSs and Internet have come to be a new and much-watched channel for mail-order.

Changes in Consumption Trends

It used to be that most spending was for the essentials of food, shelter, and clothing, but now the majority of consumer spending is on non-essential items, and this shift is expected to intensify. Looking ahead to an older population with more free time and greater diversity of values, the Economic Planning Agency outlook for consumer behavior in 2010 forecasts increased spending on health and medical care, full-care retirement homes, such time-intensive items as travel and recreation, and education and socializing for personal fulfillment. At the same time, people will have to outgrow today's energy- and resource-intensive consumer habits and develop more modest lifestyles appropriate to the need for environmental restoration.

18

贈答

日本人は贈り物が好きな国民だとよく言われる。結婚祝いや誕生祝いといった他の国にもある贈り物はもちろん，ちょっとした訪問にも手土産を持参して，敬意や好意を表すというのが，日本的な習慣になっている。かつてレーガン政権の国家安全保障担当補佐官だったR.アレン氏が，日本の出版社から取材の謝礼として，1000ドルの現金小切手と腕時計を受け取っていたことを申告し忘れて，辞任する騒ぎがあった。日本では，取材の際に若干の金品を贈ることは珍しくないが，アメリカでは，政府の高官，補佐官などは，いかなるプレゼントも黙って受け取ることは禁じられている。アレン事件は，そうした贈り物に対する日米の習慣の違いを象徴するものと言えるだろう。

中元・歳暮

さまざまな贈り物の中でもきわめて日本的なものが，中元，歳暮である。中元は暑中見舞いを兼ねて6，7月ごろに，歳暮は一年の感謝を込めて年末に，ともに，日ごろ世話になっている人たちに贈る季節の贈答で，ひところ近代的な合理主義者から，「虚礼廃止」といった批判があったにもかかわらず，個人どうしでも企業間でも，相変わらず盛んに行われている。デパートの商戦も年々激しくなり，最近では自宅やオフィスから電話で注文できる「ファクシミリ・オーダー」や，指定の日時に届く「アポイント便ギフト」など，新しいサービスで勝負するデパートが増えてきた。

その他の贈答

引っ越しそばも欧米にはない習慣で，引っ越し先の近所にそばを配りながら，自己紹介と「今後よろしく」というあいさつをして回る。しかし，近年ではそばの代わりにはがき，ハンカチ，*手ぬぐいとか菓子を配ることが多い。

そのほか子供の七五三，入学，進学，成人式，会社関係者の栄転祝い，病気の治癒を祝う快気祝いなど，実に多様な贈り物があり，家計を預かる主婦にとって，交際費捻出(ねんしゅつ)は頭の痛い問題になっている。また，一方，同じような品物が集まって，家庭で使われもせず山積みになっている頂き物を安く買い取り，それをまた安く売るという「贈答品買い取り業」もある。

一見，実に非合理的に見えるこうしたやり取りの中に，合理主義では割り切れない人間関係の機微を求める日本的贈答習慣のエッセンスがある。

Gift-giving

Japanese love to give gifts. While it is common in all countries to give gifts for birthdays, weddings, and other special occasions, in Japan people paying even a casual visit often bring a gift as a token of respect or affection for the host. Many years ago, Richard Allen, then President Reagan's National Security Advisor, had to resign because he had failed to report a $1,000 check and a watch given him by a Japanese publishing company in gratitude for his granting them an interview. In Japan, it is not at all unusual to give gifts to people who consent to interviews and otherwise provide information, but in the United States, government officials at all levels are required to report any gifts they may receive. As such, the Allen incident illustrates how much Japanese and American gift-giving customs differ.

Chuugen and *Seibo*

Best-known of Japan's many customary gifts are the *chuugen* and *seibo* gifts. The *chuugen* (mid-year) gift often serves in lieu of the greeting in the hot summer months to inquire after the health and well-being of friends and work associates, and the *seibo* (year-end) gift stems from the custom of giving someone a gift as a token of appreciation for everything s/he has done for you during the past year. Despite the efforts of modern-minded critics to do away with such "empty formalities," seasonal gifts are still regularly exchanged among individuals and companies. For their part, department stores are contriving ever-more ingenious ways of promoting gift-giving, including such new services as accepting gift orders by facsimile and delivering gifts at specified dates and times.

Other Gift-giving

Hikkoshi-soba (moving-in noodles) is another uniquely Japanese custom by which people who have just moved into a new neighborhood go from door to door handing out *soba* noodles as gifts to the new neighbors while at the same time introducing themselves and generally expressing the hope that they will become good neighbors. Today people often give small towels,* post cards, handkerchiefs or sweets instead of *soba*.

A large variety of gifts are given on a number of happy occasions: such personal milestones as the 7-5-3 festival, starting or graduating from school, becoming an adult, getting a promotion at work, and recovering from an illness; and it is a real headache for many housewives to find money in the household budget for all of these gifts. Responding to this situation, there are now used-gift companies that buy up piles of unopened and unwanted gifts at low prices and resell them at a discount.

Gift-giving, like many other typically Japanese customs, seems quite illogical on the surface, yet somehow it makes sense in the context of human relations which themselves defy logical explanation.

日本は世界一の新聞大国と言える。全国紙，地方紙122社が，毎日（朝・夕刊合わせて）推定約7200万部以上の新聞を発行している。ユネスコの統計によると，この部数は崩壊前の旧ソ連の約１億4000万部を除けば，アメリカの5700万部，中国の2800万部，イギリスの1900万部，フランスの1300万部を上回る数字である(94～96年)。普及率で見ても，日本は人口1000人当たり約580部で，ノルウェーの約610部についで高い。これはドイツの394部，イギリスの332部，アメリカの212部という普及率をしのぎ，新聞の大好きな国民であることを示している。

新聞の歴史と信頼度

日本には100年以上の歴史をもつ新聞社が少なくない。こうした新聞社は，日本が江戸時代から明治に突入したころに，自由民権運動という言論自由化の中から生まれたもので，新聞の掲げる論調は世論(オピニオン・リーダー)として高い社会的信用を得ている。「新聞は社会の*木鐸(ぼくたく)」ということばは，そうした新聞の信頼性を表したものであり，また信頼に足るものとしての役割を期待されてもいる。アメリカの調査では，新聞を信頼すべき情報源と思わない人や，テレビにより信頼を置く人が増えているようだが，日本では新聞の優位性はまだ失われていない。ただ，高い信用性ゆえに権力主義に陥りやすく，政治権力に抱き込まれやすい欠点をもっていることも否めない。日本の賢い読者たちは過去の経験からそれを学んでおり，購読紙を変更したり，数紙を併読したりして，新聞の権力主義に一種の牽制(けんせい)を働かせている面がある。そのため，各社の発行部数はつねに流動的である。

新聞の発行部数と現状

最大発行部数の新聞社は，1874年設立の読売新聞で，朝刊・夕刊合わせて毎日1455万部を発行している。これは１社としては世界最大の発行部数で，旧ソ連の『プラウダ』のような巨大新聞が大幅に部数を減らした現在，中国の『人民日報』(300万部）をもしのぎ，自由主義国の民営商業紙としては驚異的な数字である。アメリカ最大の発行部数は，『ウォール・ストリート・ジャーナル』の178万部，『ニューヨーク・タイムズ』の108万部。また，イギリスでは『ザ・サン』410万部，というところだが，日本には『読売新聞』以外にも『朝日新聞』1259万部，『毎日新聞』583万部，『産経新聞』『日本経済新聞』などの全国紙があり，これら五大紙が圧倒的に強いのが特徴である。日本の新聞流通の大きな特徴は，戸別配達制度をとっていることで，新聞の93％は家庭や職場に直接配達される。宅配サービスがこれほど普及している国は外国にはなく，日本の新聞普及率の高さを支える大きな要因にもなっている。

Newspapers

Japan has been called the most newspaper-reading country in the world. With 122 national and local newspaper companies issuing about 72 million newspapers a day (including morning and evening editions), circulation easily tops the U.S.'s 57 million, China's 28 million, the U.K.'s 19 million, and France's 13 million. Indeed, it is exceeded only by the former Soviet Union's 140 million (UNESCO data). On a per-capita basis, Japan has 580 newspapers per 1,000 people, topped only by Norway's 610 and well above Germany's 394, the U.K.'s 332, and the U.S.'s 212.

History and Credibility

There are a number of Japanese newspapers that go back well over 100 years. Established during the free-speech reforms effected by Japan's freedom and people's rights movement following the downfall of the feudal system and the rise of the *Meiji* government, these newspapers served as opinion leaders and gained the public trust. The newspapers were accepted as the nation's conscience*, and they were expected to repay the public trust by behaving honorably. While U.S. surveys have shown that people trust the news they get from television more than they do that from the newspapers, newspapers are still more-trusted in Japan. Yet because they are trusted, it is all the more dangerous when newspapers fall prey to authoritarianism or are manipulated for political purposes. Knowing this, and knowing how newspapers have sometimes served propaganda purposes, the wise reader changes newspapers frequently or reads several at the same time, with the result that circulation figures are in constant flux.

Circulation

The newspaper with the largest circulation today is the *Yomiuri Shimbun*, established in 1874. Morning and evening editions combined, it has a daily circulation of 14,550,000. This makes the *Yomiuri* the most widely read newspaper in the world, now that Pravda's circulation has fallen off sharply with the collapse of the Soviet Union, and easily surpasses the Chinese *People's Daily*'s 3,000,000. By comparison, the U.S. paper with the largest circulation is the *Wall Street Journal* at 1,780,000, and second largest is the *New York Times* at 1,080,000. In the U.K., the *Sun* has a circulation of 4,100,000. The only real contenders for the title of circulation leader are other Japanese newspapers: the *Asahi Shimbun* with a circulation of 12,590,000, and the *Mainichi Shimbun* with 5,830,000. These three newspapers are all distributed nation-wide, as are the *Sankei Shimbun* and the *Nihon Keizai Shimbun*. These five newspapers dominate Japanese newspaperdom. One of the features distinguishing Japanese newspaper circulation is that 93% are home-delivered (including delivery to offices), and only 7% are sold at newsstands. No other country matches this delivery rate, which is a big factor contributing to high circulation rates.

高い普及率と視聴率

日本でテレビ局が開設され，放送が開始されたのは1953年のことで，以来急速に各家庭にテレビが普及し，現在では普及率99%を超える。ほとんどはカラーテレビで，一家に２～３台のテレビをもつ家庭も増えており，視聴状況もたいへんよい。

NHKが調べた「国民生活時間調査」(2000年)によると，国民１人がテレビを観ている時間は１日平均３時間25分。高齢化社会を反映して，高い年齢層の視聴時間が増えている。

ラジオも普及率は高いが，聴取状況はそれほどよいとは言えない。かつては音楽メディアとして若者に人気があったが，今はその機能をＣＤやテープに奪われているためである。

世界有数の放送国

日本の放送は，受信料を財源として全国に同じプログラムを流している公共放送局(ＮＨＫ)と，広告収入に依存し地域に基盤を置くその他の民間放送局(民放)という併存体制をとっている。民放テレビ局は１県に２局，主要地区で３～５局あり，全国では約130のＶＨＦ局を数える。それらの多くがラジオ局をも併設していて，民放ラジオ局は全国で約100社ある。その他にＵＨＦ局もほぼ１県に１局の割合で作られつつあり，日本はその置局状況からして世界でも有数の放送国と言える。

多彩な番組

東京には，日本テレビ(読売新聞社系)，ＴＢＳテレビ(毎日新聞社系)，フジテレビ(産業経済新聞社系)，テレビ朝日(朝日新聞社系)，それにテレビ東京(日本経済新聞社系)のキー局があり，全国の地方テレビ局とネットを組み番組配信をしている。

このほかに，放送衛星を使うBSアナログ放送と通信衛星を使うCSデジタル放送があり，2000年12月からはBSデジタル放送も始まった。これらはNHKと民放とで合計10チャンネルあり，高画質高音質が売り物である。BSデジタル放送では，通信機能を使った双方向の番組作りやサービスが可能になり，一方的に観るだけだったテレビの役割が変わろうとしている。

ニューメディアとしての都市型CATV（ケーブルテレビ）も全国で約150施設もでき，受信契約数も100万世帯に達している。サービスの多様化，多チャンネル化時代に入って，どの放送局も放送番組の質の向上が求められている。

Radio and Television

Popularization

The first Japanese television station was established and started broadcasting in 1953. The new medium quickly caught on and people rushed to buy sets. Today, the diffusion ratio is over 99%, and most of them are color sets. Indeed, many homes have two or three sets as television is moving from a family medium to a personal medium.

A 2000 NHK report on how people spend their time found that an average of 3 hours 25 minutes per day is spent in television viewing. Higher age groups are spending more time watching TV, as expected in an aging population.

Most households also have radios, but they are not as popular. Formerly popular with young people as music media, radios have since yielded place to compact discs and music tapes.

Broadcasting Everywhere

Japanese broadcasting has both a national network (NHK) financed by subscription fees and providing the same programming nationwide, and commercial broadcasters who rely upon advertising revenues and service a limited area or region. There are two commercial television stations per prefecture and perhaps 3-5 in major areas, for a total of about 130 VHF stations nationwide. Most of the stations also operate radio stations, and there are about 100 commercial radio stations nationwide. In addition, work is also underway to establish roughly one UHF television station per prefecture, meaning that Japan joins the ranks of the world's leading broadcasting nations.

Richly Varied Programming

In *Toukyou* (Tokyo), viewers have a choice of NHK's general programming channel 1 and its educational channel 3, as well as the commercial channels 4 (*Nihon* Television, affiliated with *Yomiuri Shinbun*), 6 (*Toukyou* Broadcasting, with *Mainichi Shinbun*), 8 (*Fuji* Television, with *Sankei Shinbun*), 10 (Television *Asahi*, with *Asahi Shinbun*), and 12 (Television *Toukyou,* with *Nihon Keizai Shinbun).* These major networks all have ties to local or regional networks as well.

In addition to the above Japan has BS analogue, broadcast by broadcasting satellite, and CS digital, broadcast by communications satellite, and beginning in December 2000, BS digital. A total of 10 channels are available, including both NHK and commercial networks, and high image and sound quality are the big sales points. In the case of BS digital, the use of communications technology makes possible interactive programming and service. Heretofore a matter of unidirectional viewing, the very role of television is being redefined.

Urban style cable television as well is provided by about 150 instillations nationwide, with over one million households subscribing. Japan is entering a new multi-service, multi-channel era, with all stations striving to meet the demand for higher quality programs.

出版王国

出版統計の取り方は国によって異なるので，正確な比較は難しいが，日本が世界でも有数の出版王国であることはまちがいない。97年1年間に，日本では約6万2300点の新刊書籍が発行された。主な国の新刊書籍出版点数は中国7万点，イギリス10万1800点，ドイツ7万4200点，アメリカ6万2000点，フランス3万4800点などとなっている(95〜96年)。これらの国の言語がいずれも国際的に通用しうる言語であるのに対して，日本語はそうでないことを考え合わせると，日本の出版点数は非常に多い。小さな島国に1億2600万人も住んでいること，加えてその民度が高いことといった恵まれたマーケットがあることが，出版活動を盛んにしていると言える。

本好きな日本人

実際，日本人は本好きで，通勤，通学の電車の中で本や雑誌を読む光景が日常的に見られる。97年1年間の推定総発行部数を見ると，書籍は約15億7400万冊，雑誌は約52億2400万冊で，その総売上げ金額は約2兆5900億円にも達している。人口一人当たりにすると，1年間に本を12冊，雑誌を40冊読み，そのために一人当たり年間約2万円を支出していることになる。70年代までは雑誌より本の売上げ高のほうが高かったが，79年にそれが逆転してからは，“雑誌の時代”と言われる状況が続いている。若者を中心に，堅苦しいイメージの書籍よりも，手軽に安く読める雑誌のほうが好まれるようになったためである。出版社の数は約4300社に上り，社員が1000人を越す大手出版社から一人の零細出版社まで，企業規模の格差は非常に大きい。

巨大なコミック市場

日本の出版を語るうえで忘れてはならないのが，コミック本，コミック雑誌の巨大な市場である。日本では，年間約23億部のコミック(本・雑誌)が刊行され，これらは全販売部数の約39%を占めている。毎号100万部以上出ているコミック雑誌が10余誌もあり，発売部数トップの週刊コミック誌は毎号555万部(95年の推定)も出ている。これらのコミックは，子供だけでなく，20〜30歳代の成人も読む。しかし，電車の中でいい年をした大人がコミックを読んでいる姿には，眉をひそめる人も多い。日本のコミックは外国でも人気が高く，テレビ化・映画化権料を含め，出版社にとってコミックはドル箱になっている。

Publishers' Paradise

Although the different statistical methodologies make any exact international comparison impossible, Japan is clearly one of the world's major publishing powers. In 1997 alone, Japanese publishers put out about 62,300 new titles. Approximate figures for other leading countries are 70,000 for China, 101,800 for the U.K., 74,200 for Germany, 62,000 for the U.S., and 34,800 for France. This Japanese figure is all the more impressive in light of the fact that, unlike Chinese, English, French, and German, Japanese is not an international language. In a way, Japanese publishers are lucky to have a large (approx. 126 million), well-educated, and affluent population living in a relatively small area.

Book-loving Japanese

Japanese love to read, and it is not uncommon to see people reading books and magazines on the trains as they commute to and from school or work. Estimated publication figures for 1997 are about 1.574 billion books and 5.224 billion magazines, with total sales for both categories combined coming to about ¥2.59 trillion. On a per-capita basis, this is 12 books and 40 magazines for total spending of about ¥20,000. Until the late 1970s, books outsold magazines, but magazines took the lead in 1979 and have stayed on top ever since. Young people especially prefer the easily approachable magazines to books with their somewhat stuffy and straight-laced image. There are about 4,300 publishing companies—ranging all the way from giant companies employing over 1,000 people to small one-man outfits doing specialty work.

The *Manga* Market

Manga (comics)—both books and magazines—are a major player in this market. It is estimated that total *manga* circulation is about 2.3 billion per year (books and magazines combined), and this accounts for about 39% of all publishing. There are over 10 *manga* magazines that have monthly circulations of over a million, and estimates are that the best-selling weekly *manga* magazine is estimated to have sold 5.55 million every issue in 1995. Obviously, this is not kid stuff, and people in their 20s and 30s are also avid readers. Yet there are still many people who look askance at adults reading *manga* in the trains. Japanese *manga* are also popular overseas, and the royalties, television rights, and other income make *manga* a very lucrative business for many Japanese publishers.

車社会日本

日本は急速な車社会の時代を迎えている。日本の自家用乗用車保有台数は1965年に132万台であったものが，98年には4990万台と，約38倍になった。全国的には公共交通の発達しなかった地域に急速な車社会化が見られ，1世帯に1台以上という割合の県もある。

欧米では1920年代から自動車が普及し，道路も整備されていったが，日本で自動車が普及したのは戦後になってからである。しかし，その後の急成長ぶりは目覚ましい。特に，1950年代後半以降の高度経済成長時代に入ってから，貨物輸送が飛躍的に増大し，自動車工業の発達で性能のよい自動車が次々に生産されるようになり，鉄道の斜陽化もあって，自動車は陸上輸送の花形となった。

急ピッチで進む道路整備

車社会になるとともに，道路への依存度が大きくなるのは当然であるが，日本の道路はまだ十分とは言えない。道路の総延長は約115万kmであるが，舗装されているのは75%ほどである。しかし，道路整備は重要国策として取り組んでおり，舗装率は1945年にはわずか1.2%であったことから見ても着実に成果を上げてきていると言えよう。とりわけ，高速道路の建設はめざましく，急ピッチで進んでいて，現在は青森と鹿児島間のほとんどが結ばれている。

高速道路地図(Expressway Network)

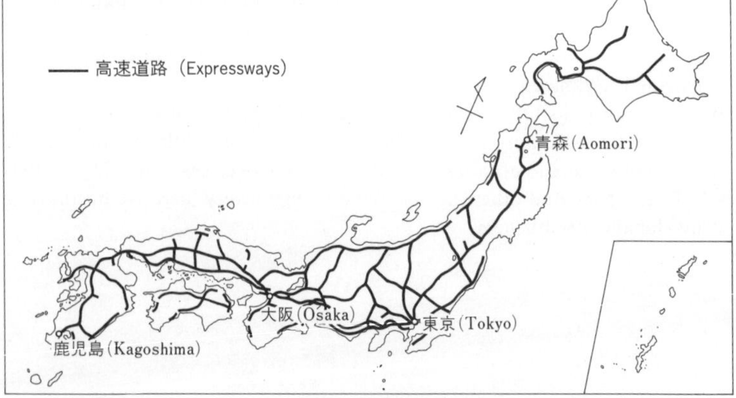

Roads

Automotive Japan

In a relatively short time Japan has become an automotive society. In 1965 there were 1.32 million passenger cars, but by 1998 this number had gone up more than 38-fold to 49.90 million. Regions with little public transportation have taken the lead in automobile ownership, and some prefectures average more than one car per household.

In the U.S. and Europe automobiles appeared on the roads in the 1920s, stimulating the construction of extensive highway networks. In Japan, the automobile did not come into common use until after the Second World War, but its dissemination was especially rapid in the years of fast-paced economic growth which began in the latter 1950s, when trucks became a major means of transporting goods. As a result, automobiles have come to dominate overland transport, the railroads slipping into decline as advances in automotive technology have led to more functional and more attractive vehicles.

Road Construction

The phenomenal increase in automobile transport has made Japan's roads more important than ever. The present road network is far from sufficient. There are approximately 1,150,000 kilometers of roads, and about 75% are paved. Road construction, paving, and maintenance are a primary concern for the national government, and, as evidenced by the fact that only 1.2% of all roads were paved in 1945, considerable progress has been made. A particularly strong effort has been made in expressway construction, and today most of the distance between *Aomori* and *Kagoshima* is linked by expressways.

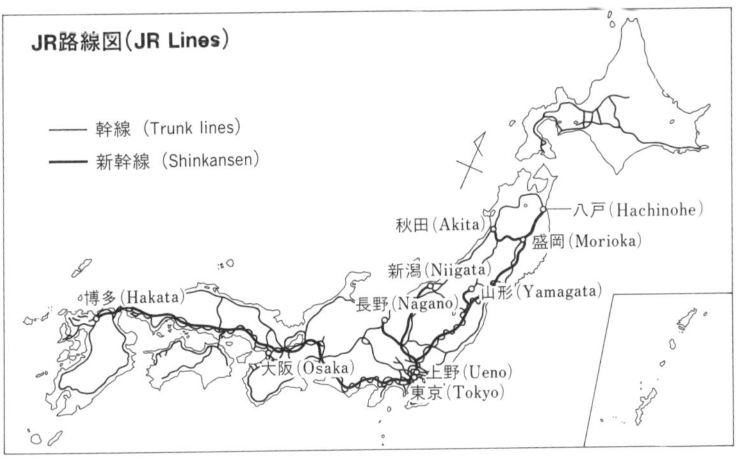

日本の鉄道網は，全国を結ぶJR線(旧国鉄)と，大都市に発達した私鉄・地下鉄網から成っており，日本各地を旅行するのにはJR線，大都市生活には私鉄・地下鉄が便利である。

現在，鉄道は２万7400kmを営業しているが，この大部分を占めていた旧国鉄は，旅客・貨物とも自動車や飛行機に圧迫され，新幹線と大都市の一部の路線を除いて，ほとんどの路線が赤字となり，これまでに累積した赤字額は16兆円にも上った。このため国鉄は1987年４月に６ブロックに分割され，それぞれ民営鉄道として再スタートを切った。したがって，日本の鉄道は一部公営を除きほとんどが民営となった。

新幹線

「夢の超特急」と呼ばれた新幹線は旧国鉄が開発したもので，64年10月，営業時速210kmで，東京－新大阪間を走り始めた。国鉄の安全技術をフルに駆使した新幹線は，以来日本の大動脈として成長し続けた。乗客の死傷事故は一度もなく，世界で最も安全な鉄道と言われている。現在の路線は，東京－新大阪間の東海道（552.6km）をはじめ，山陽（新大阪－博多間623.3km），東北(東京－八戸間631.9km)，上越(大宮－新潟間303.6km)，長野(高崎－長野間117.4km）に増えた。その後，在来線を利用するミニ新幹線（山形－福島，秋田－盛岡）も開業している。

各線とも，各駅停車の特急，限定停車の超特急の２種類の列車が走り，「こだま」「ひかり」「のぞみ」（東海道・山陽新幹線）など，それぞれ独特のニックネームがつけられている。

私鉄と地下鉄

私鉄は主に大都市と近郊都市を結び，また地下鉄は大都市内で縦横に発達している。私鉄は全国で6850km営業しており，運転本数も多く，都市住民の足となっている。

地下鉄は，戦前は東京と大阪にしかなかったが，現在はこのほかに名古屋，横浜，神戸，京都，札幌，福岡，仙台などの都市が加わり，営業キロ数は604kmに上っている。とりわけ，1927年に走り始めた首都東京の地下鉄は，公私営13路線が縦横に走り，１日729万人を運ぶ主要交通機関となっている。その営業キロ数は総延長で，249kmあり，ニューヨーク，ロンドン，パリ，モスクワに次いで世界第５位。

Rail Transport

Japan's rail system includes the JR network (the post-privatized Japanese National Railways or JNR) with lines nationwide and other private railways and subways in the major urban areas. The JR is especially convenient for travel to or in outlying areas, while the private lines and subways are important urban commuter links.

The JR, which has most of the 27,400km of track in Japan, has lost much of its passenger and freight custom to automobiles and airlines, and the only lines that are operating in the black are the *shinkansen* and certain urban lines. At the time it was privatized in April 1987, the JNR was ¥16 trillion in the red. With privatization, the system has started over again, being split up into six regional passenger companies and one freight company, and turned over to private management. As a result, there are few public-sector rail lines left in Japan.

Shinkansen

Since the start of service between *Toukyou* (Tokyo) and *Oosaka* (Osaka) in October 1964, the 210-kph *shinkansen* service has been one of Japan's main transportation arteries. It is arguably the world's safest rail line, without a single major accident in more than three decades of service. Today, *shinkansen* service has expanded to include not only the 552.6-km *Toukaidou* line between *Toukyou* and *Oosaka* but also the 623.3-km *Sanyou* line between *Oosaka* and *Hakata*, the 631.9-km *Touhoku* line between *Toukyou* and *Hachinohe*, the 303.6-km *Jouetsu* line between *Oomiya* and *Niigata*, and the 117.4-km *Nagano* line between *Takasaki* and *Nagano*. Then,"mini"*shinkansen* trains designed to run on the narrow gauge tracks of ordinary lines began service between *Yamagata* and *Fukushima* in 1992 and between *Akita* and *Morioka* in 1997.

Each line includes two types of trains—expresses that stop at every station and super-expresses that stop only at a few main stations. On the *Toukaidou* and *Sanyou* lines, for example, the ordinary express is called the *Kodama* (echo) and the super-express the *Hikari* (light) or, for newer models, the *Nozomi* (hope).

Other Private Lines and Subways

Numerous other private rail lines link Japan's cities to their suburban satellites, while subways provide inner-city transportation. There are 6,850km of private lines other than JR throughout the country, with trains running at frequent intervals.

Only *Toukyou* and *Oosaka* had subways before the war, but there are also subways in *Nagoya, Yokohama, Koube, Kyouto* (Kyoto), *Sapporo, Fukuoka* and *Sendai* now—604km of track in all. *Toukyou's* system, which went into operation in 1927, now has a total of 13 public and private lines carrying 7.29 million people a day. With 249km of subway track, *Toukyou* is fifth worldwide after New York, London, Paris, and Moscow.

治安優良大国日本

日本のように治安がよく，安心して市民生活の営める国はほかにないのではないだろうか。日本に来たことのある外国人や，海外に出たことのある日本人は，だれでもみなそう思うようだ。アメリカの都会のようにドアにいくつもの鍵(かぎ)をつけなくてもいいし，子供の誘拐を心配することもまずない。そして何より，日本の街は女性が夜でも一人歩きできる。これは日本の治安のよさを示すいちばんのバロメーターである。ニューヨークの地下鉄に深夜女性が乗ることなど考えられないが，日本の地下鉄では，深夜一人でも不安を感じることはない。それだけ安全なのである。

しかしながら，近年は，従来ほとんどなかった銃による犯罪や外国人の犯罪，少年犯罪，ネット犯罪なども増えつつあり，憂慮されている。

低い犯罪発生率と高い検挙率

日本の治安のよさは，犯罪に関する各国のデータにも明確に現れている。96年の統計では，人口10万人当たりの犯罪の発生率が最も多いのはイギリスの9745件で，次いでドイツ7869件，フランス6072件，アメリカ4616件と続き，日本は1608件と先進国の中では最も少ない。また人口10万人当たりの殺人発生率で見ても，アメリカ6.3人，フランス3.7人，ドイツ3.5人，イギリス2.7人に対し，日本は1.2人で最小である。一方検挙率を見ると，アメリカ21.3%，フランス28.7%，ドイツ52.3%，イギリス29.3%に対して，日本は38.2%で２番目に高い。検挙率が高いことが，日本では犯罪を抑制する要因にもなっている。

*交番・駐在所制度

犯罪の多発に悩んでいるアメリカなど諸外国の警察は，一時，治安のよさを守る日本の警察制度を盛んに研究していた。その結果，日本の治安のよさの秘密は，日本独特の「交番・駐在所制度」にあるのではないかと分析して，外国の警察の中には日本を参考にするところも出てきている。大組織である警察署の出先機関として街の角々に設けられているもので，そこを中心に警官が受け持ち区域を常にパトロールして回るシステムになっている。そこには周辺住民の調査票が備えてあり，つねに不審な動きがないかどうかを牽制している。また万が一事件が起きたときも，近くの交番からすぐに現場に駆けつけられるし，瞬時に警戒網を敷くこともできる。日本の警察の初動捜査の強みは，全国津々浦々に散在している交番・駐在所なくしては考えられないことである。

Public Order in Japan

A Safe Place to Live

Perhaps nowhere else in the world can city dwellers live as free from fear of crime as in Japan—that is the impression among foreigners who have lived in Japan and Japanese who have traveled abroad. Japanese urbanites do not have to multi-lock their doors or worry that their children may be kidnapped. In fact, Japan's streets are safe enough for women to walk alone at night—an impressive indication of public peace and order. While few women would even think of riding a New York subway alone at night, unescorted women routinely board Japanese subways late at night without a second thought.

Despite this, in recent years there has been a worrisome increase in crimes involving firearms, crimes committed by non-Japanese or by minors, as well as crimes involving the internet, etc.

Little Crime, Most Arrested

Japan's relative safety is illustrated by the crime statistics. According to 1998 statistics, the U.K. had 9,745 crimes per 100,000 population, Germany 7,869, France 6,072, America 4,616, and Japan 1,608—ranking Japan lowest among developed countries. The murder rate per 100,000 population was 6.3 in the United States, 3.7 in France, 3.5 in Germany, 2.7 in the U.K., and 1.2 in Japan. Again, Japan is the lowest. By contrast, arrest rates were 21.3% in the United States, 28.7% in France, 52.3% in Germany, 29.3% in the U.K., and 38.2% in Japan—placing the nation second from the top. This high arrest rate works as a crime deterrent in Japan.

*Koban** and *Chuuzaisho*

Looking for some solution to their high crime rates, U.S. law enforcement officials have studied the Japanese police system and concluded that one secret to Japan's good statistics is to be found in the *koban* (police box) and *chuuzaisho* (live-in police box), and this system has since been adopted in a number of other countries. In effect, these are neighborhood outposts linked to the central police stations. Located here and there in the community, they are base points from which police do their patrols. Each *koban* has a roster of neighborhood residents and keeps an eye out for suspicious behavior. And if there is an incident, someone can rush to the scene from a nearby *koban* and it is easy to set up surveillance. The *koban* are an essential element in enabling the Japanese police to respond quickly to any need.

工業をはじめ，さまざまな分野での近代化が進む中で，人の健康をむしばみ健全な生活を阻害する種々の公害問題が発生している。日本では，明治20年代の栃木県足尾銅山の鉱毒事件をきっかけに公害病が認知されるようになったが，公害問題が深刻化したのは，1960年代になってからである。

公害惨禍と反公害運動

1950年代に，熊本県水俣(みなまた)で有機合成化学工場廃液によって，住民が有機水銀中毒になるという水俣病が発生した。以後，富山県神通(じんづう)川流域でのカドミウム中毒・イタイイタイ病，三重県四日市(よっかいち)の工場排煙が原因で発生した四日市ぜんそく，新潟県阿賀野川流域の第二水俣病など，局所的な公害病が相次いだ。いずれの事件も裁判で被害者側が勝訴したため，企業や行政はそれぞれの立場から，公害防止のために積極的に取り組むようになった。さらに，環境浄化に取り組む市民運動や，環境に優しい生活を送るためのエコライフ運動も浸透し，日本の公害問題は急速に改善されつつある。

環境問題への対応

日本では1967年に，公害防止の観点から公害対策基本法が制定され，公害問題に関して企業・国・地方公共団体の責務の分担を明らかにし，悲惨な公害病の再発阻止の努力を進めてきた。しかし，現代の環境破壊は以前のような限局的な公害とは異なり，地方レベルから国家レベルへ，さらには地球規模の問題へと拡大しつつあり，この法律では対応できないことが多くなり，1993年に廃止され，新しく環境基本法が誕生した。この中で，環境基準は「人の健康を保護し生活環境を保全するうえで維持されることが望ましい基準」として，大気環境基準・水質環境基準・騒音環境基準・土壌環境基準を打ち出した。しかし，環境に関する基本理念や施策の枠組みを定めただけで，具体的な規制処置は示されているわけではない。

「いらないものは捨てる」から「使えるものは再利用」へ

2000年５月に循環型社会形成推進基本法が成立した。しかし日本では，年間5000万トンを超える一般廃棄物があり，その80％が焼却炉で焼かれているのが現状で，欧米に比べ立ち遅れが目立っている。家電製品のリサイクルの有料化も，ようやく動き出したに過ぎない。

焼却炉で発生するダイオキシンに対しても，対応が遅れた。1999年７月にダイオキシン類対策特別措置法が成立したが，基準値は欧米を下回るものだった。また，古いコンデンサーなどに含まれているPCB（ポリ塩化ビフェニール）の処理も急がれている。DDTやビスフェノールＡなど内分泌攪乱(かくらん)化学物質（環境ホルモン）として懸念されている物質が使用されたり，身の周りに残ったりしていることも，問題となっている。

Industrialization and other aspects of modernization have generated serious pollution, threatening the people's health and eroding the quality of life. This was first brought to Japan's attention by the pollution from the *Ashio* copper mines in *Tochigi* prefecture in the late 19th century, but it was not seen as a national problem until the 1960s.

Pollution Horrors and Anti-pollution Campaigns

In the 1950s, there was a serious outbreak of debilitating nervous deterioration among people who ate seafood contaminated with organic mercury discharged into *Minamata* Bay (*Kumamoto* prefecture) by a large chemical company. This was so dramatic that the affliction was named for the site—*Minamata* disease. This was followed by a rash of other pollution-related disasters including cadmium poisoning and *Itai-itai* disease in the *Jinzuu* River basin in *Toyama* prefecture, *Yokkaichi* asthma caused by toxic exhaust from industrial complexes in *Yokkaichi* in *Mie* prefecture, and *Minamata* II in the *Agano* River basin in *Niigata* prefecture. With the victims consistently winning their court cases, companies and government agencies involved have taken an active interest in pollution prevention. In addition, citizen campaigns have also arisen for environmental restoration and environmentally sound lifestyles, and the Japanese environment is becoming noticeably better.

Dealing With Environmental Problems

The Basic Law for Environmental Pollution Control was passed in 1967 to delineate the national government, business, and local governments' responsibilities in pollution prevention, and major progress was made under this law in rectifying the worst of the pollution. However, while localized pollution from clearly identifiable causes has been largely abated, pollution is today more widespread—being regional, national, and even global. Because the 1967 Basic Law was not equipped to deal with such pollution, it was replaced with the new Basic Environment Law in 1993. This law stipulates the air cleanliness, water purity, noise abatement, and soil standards that should be met to preserve human health and sound residential environments. Yet the law only stipulates the environmental goals and policy framework and does not provide specific regulatory mechanisms for their attainment.

From Throw Away to Reuse

The Basic Law for Promoting Creation of a Recycling Ethic was passed in May 2000. But with over 50 million metric tons of ordinary waste produced each year, and 80% of that being incinerated, Japan clearly lags behind the U.S. and Europe. The recycling of electric appliances into useable materials is only just getting underway.

Japan is also far behind in dealing with dioxin created by waste incinerators. A Special Measures Law for Dealing with Dioxin was passed in July 1999, but permissible standards are not as stringent as in the U.S. and Europe. How to deal with PCB (polychlorinated biphenyl) contained in condensers, etc. is another priority. Also a problem is the use and residue in the environment of such suspected environmental hormones as DDT and bisphenol A, which disrupt the endocrine system.

日本の社会保障は公的扶助(生活保護)，社会福祉(障害者・老人・児童福祉など)，社会保険(年金・健康保険・労働災害補償保険など)，公衆衛生および医療(伝染病予防・保健所・公害対策など)の4本柱から成っている。社会保障制度が確立されたのは第二次世界大戦以後で，当初は公的扶助や公衆衛生の比重が高かったが，1950年代後半以降の高度成長期には社会福祉が，そして高齢化社会を迎えた現代は社会保険，特に年金制度と医療保険・介護保険に力が注がれている。

財政支出に占める社会保障関係費も戦後一貫して伸び，2001年度には約17兆5600億円，予算の5分の1となっている。日本の社会保障費給付額が国民所得に占める割合は欧米先進国に比べまだ低いが，急速な高齢化に伴い，社会保障費が増大，財政悪化の一因となっている。

国民に浸透する医療保険

国民すべてがなんらかの健康保険に加入しており，よく発達している。健康保険にはサラリーマン，日雇，公務員などの被用者保険と，そうでない人のための国民健康保険があり，その加入比率は6対4である。被用者保険は雇用主(企業)が保険の掛け金を約半分負担するのに対し，国民健康保険は国が半分の掛け金を負担してくれるが，医療費給付の自己負担分は被用者保険が20%なのに国民健康保険は30%と差がある。

2000年4月からは介護保険制度が導入された。40歳以上の国民はすべての加入が義務付けられており，保険料は単純平均で1人1か月2500円。介護サービスを受けるには認定が必要で，原則として1割負担することから，「弱者切り捨て」との批判を受け，地方自治体が本人負担をカバーしているところが多い。

改革が急がれる年金制度

老齢年金(65歳以上）には，被雇用者の厚生年金(雇用主が半額負担）と，国の国民年金がある。すべての国民は満20歳になると，国民年金に加入することが決められている。しかし，高齢者人口の増加，少子化による若年層の減少，低金利政策による基金運用難が続き，年金財政が悪化している。日本の65歳以上の老年人口は，2015年には3188万人，総人口の25.2%を占めることが予想されることから，老後の年金制度の改革が急務となっている。

現在，アメリカの制度にならった確定拠出型年金（日本版401k）が導入された。この制度では，加入者が年金の運用先を指定し，その運用実績により給付額が変動することになる。

Social Welfare

The four pillars of social welfare in Japan are assistance for the indigent; care for the handicapped, elderly, and other disadvantaged; social security including pensions, health insurance, and worker's compensation; and public health care such as vaccinations, health centers, and environmental protection. Most of these policies were created after the war with the initial emphasis on assistance for the indigent and public health, but the rapid economic growth prompted greater concern for society's disadvantaged, and demographic trends have lent special urgency to the issue of social security for senior citizens.

Social welfare-related spending has increased steadily since the close of WW II to roughly ¥17.56 trillion in 2001, or a fifth of the government's budget. Even though welfare-related spendings comprise a smaller proportion of national income tax revenues in Japan than in North America and much of Europe, they are on the rise as the population grows rapidly older, and are a threat to fiscal policy flexibility.

Medical Insurance

All Japanese are covered by some form of health insurance. Health insurance is provided either by employees' insurance for employees and their families, or by national health insurance, the former covering 60% of the population, and the latter the remaining 40%. Employers pay about half the premium for employees' insurance and the government does the same for national health insurance. The greatest difference between the two is that the individual must pay 20% of actual medical costs under employee's insurance, but 30% under national health.

A long term care insurance system was introduced in April 2000. All persons over 40 years of age are required to join, and the cost averages out to ¥2500 a person per month. Authorization is required to receive long term nursing care services, and, as a rule, the individual must pay 10% of all costs. This system has come under criticism for "cutting off the weak", and in many cases municipalities bear these costs.

A National Pension System Badly in Need of Reform

The two types of old age pension plans available are employees' pension (employer paying one half the costs) and the national pension plan, in which everyone reaching the age of twenty is required to enroll. This system is running into increasingly serious financial trouble, however, because of the increasing number of old people, the decreasing number of younger people due to fewer children per family, and continuing difficulties in fund operation due to a low interest rate policy. With the number of elderly people over 65 expected to reach 31.88 million—25.2% of Japan's total population—by 2015, there is an urgent need for reform of the old age pension system.

Recently a defined contribution annuity plan was adopted, which is a Japanese version of the American 401k pension fund. Persons enrolling in this plan designate whether they want their money invested in high-risk, high-return stocks or low-risk, low-return bonds, and payments are made according to how well these investments do.

戦後，日本の教育制度は大きく変わった。それまでの６・５・３・３制に代わって小学校６年，中学校３年，高等学校３年，大学４年の，いわゆる６・3・3・4制が導入された。これに伴い，義務教育も６年から９年に延長され，男女共学も一般化した。今日の就学率100%，識字率100%という数字は日本が世界に誇るものである。高校は義務教育ではないが，進学率は97%に達し，特に都市部では事実上全員入学に近い。しかし，希望する高校へ行けるとはかぎらず，不本意な入学が増えるなどの弊害が出ている。
４年制大学は最古の*東京大学をはじめとする国立大学が99，東京都立大学など公立大学が72，さらに早稲田大学，慶應義塾大学など私立大学が478ある。進学率は短大を含めて49.1%となり，大衆化が著しい。

日本の大学

日本の大学の外国と比較しての最大の特色は，入学試験の厳しさだろう。かつて“四当五落”なる流行語が生まれたが，これは，「睡眠時間を５時間も取っては合格はおぼつかない。４時間で合格」という意味で言われたものだ。現在，国立大学の入試は全国一斉に行われる大学入試センター試験と，各大学が個別に行う試験との併用である。私立大でもセンター試験の活用が増え始めた。希望者の殺到する有名国公私立大学への門は依然狭い。学部では医学部の人気と難度が群を抜いている。希望大学へ入るための*浪人も一般的であり，予備校は教育産業として立派に成り立っている。

新しいタイプの大学として，1985年から放送大学が学生の受け入れを開始し，これまでに１万5000人を超える卒業生を出した。イギリスの放送大学にならって，ラジオ・テレビ放送と通信教育を組み合わせた教育を行うもので，運営費の約７割は国庫補助金という準国立大学である。また，実践的な職業教育や専門的な技術教育を行う専修学校の役割も高まっている。1999年度からは，専修学校の専門課程の修了者が大学に編入学することもできるようになった。

教育制度の改革

「教育の機会均等」「男女共学」などを掲げた戦後の教育は，めざましい量的拡大を遂げたが，知識偏重で画一的な教育に陥った。大量生産・高品質・高効率を必要とする産業界に役立つ人材の育成には貢献したが，思考力や判断力，創造力，学ぶ意欲の低下のほか，いじめ，校内暴力，登校拒否など病理的な状況を招いた。教育改革は政府の重要政策課題の一つで，完全学校週５日制のほか，中学校・高等学校を併設して６年間の一貫教育を行う公立学校の設置など，学制改革にも及んでいる。また，高齢化社会に対応した生涯教育の拡充も求められている。

The Japanese Education System

Japan's educational system underwent major reform after World War II. The old 6-5-3-3 system was changed to a 6-3-3-4 system (six years of elementary school, three each of middle and high school, and four of college). In addition, compulsory education was extended from six years to nine and most schools went coed. Japan boasts one of the world's best-educated populations, with 100% enrollment in compulsory grades and zero illiteracy. While not compulsory, high school enrollment is 97% nationwide and nearly 100% in the cities. This does not, however mean everyone is getting into the high school of his/her choice, and many people are settling for second- or third-best. At the university level, there are 99 national universities, of which the oldest is the University of *Toukyou*(Tokyo)*, 72 public universities, and 478 private universities. Some 49.1% of all high school graduates go on to college or junior college, making this very commonplace.

Japanese Universities

What most distinguishes Japanese universities from their foreign counterparts is the difficulty of their entrance examinations. A few years ago, the term *yontou-goraku*(four-pass, five-fail) came into vogue with its warning that anyone getting more than four hours of sleep a night will fail the university entrance exams. Today, the entrance exam process for the national universities has two parts: a standard exam given by the National Center for University Entrance Examinations which everyone takes on the same day, and the university-specific exam administered by each school. More and more private universities are also requiring this standard test. The competition to get into the elite universities is very stiff, and admission to medical school is especially prized. Because students who fail to get into the school of their choice commonly study full-time as *rounin** for a year or two until they pass the exam, cram schools have developed into a major industry.

A University of the Air was inaugurated in 1985. Patterned after the British Open University, it employs radio and television broadcasts together with correspondence courses. Approximately 70% of its operating costs come from a national treasury subsidy. Specialist schools offering practical job training or specialized technical training are also becoming increasingly important, and now it is possible for specialist school graduates to go on to a university.

Education Reform

Calling for equality of opportunity, coeducation, and other improvements, the postwar system made education available to the masses, yet it soon fell into the trap of academic quantification. While it contributed importantly to producing the kind of people industry needed to efficiently mass-produce quality products, the down side of this was that students were less able to think and judge for themselves, were less innovative, and had less thirst for knowledge. The darker side was also manifest in hazing, violence in the schools, and a rising drop out rate. Education reform is one of the government's major concerns and, besides shortening the school week to five days, includes such features as the creation of public schools which unite both junior high and high school levels to give an integrated six year education. Also needed are enhanced opportunities for continued learning throughout life fitted to the requirements of an aging population.

日本は高学歴社会で進学率が高いため，受験競争が厳しい。いい大学に入るためにはいい高校，いい高校に入るためにはいい中学へというぐあいにして，多くの子供たちは小学校の頃から受験勉強を意識した勉強中心の学校生活を余儀なくされる。学期は3学期制で，新学期は4月に始まる。平日の授業時間は，小学校高学年以上はだいたい6時限で，世界の中でも長いほうに属する。しかも日々の勉強は厳しく，宿題も付き物で，家での予習，復習が習慣づけられている。休みは夏休みが40日あまり，冬休みと春休みがそれぞれ2週間くらいで，休みのときにも宿題がある。2か月を越す長い夏休みがあり，ほかにもイースター，クリスマスと何かにつけて休暇が多く，宿題も少ない欧米とはたいへんな違いである。日本企業の海外進出で増えている帰国子女の中には，こうした学校教育の違いになじめず，カルチャー・ショックを受けて不登校になる者もあり，一部で深刻な問題となっている。

多彩な学校行事

受験重視の一方では，バラエティーに富んだ学校行事も少なくない。春や秋に行われる遠足，修学旅行は生徒たちの楽しみの一つである。前者は日帰りで動物園や名所旧跡などに行くことで，社会科の課外授業の一環として行われる。修学旅行は小，中，高校の最終学年のときに，文字どおり修学の意味で行われる。日数は1週間前後で，行き先は古都・京都を中心とする関西や九州，北海道，東京などが多い。最近は中国・アメリカなど海外に行く学校も増えている。

このほか体育の成果を競う運動会，劇や合唱，演奏を披露する学芸会，文化祭などの年中行事も春か秋に催される。また日ごろの課外活動として，スポーツ，音楽，美術などのクラブ活動も授業の後の放課後を利用して行われている。

深刻化するいじめ問題

こうした学校生活の中で，近年非常に深刻な事態になっているのが，いじめ問題である。97年の文部省の調査によれば，全国の小学校の22%，中学校の48%，高校の31%でいじめが発生し，その件数は前年度に比べて減っている。いじめによる自殺も後を絶たない。いじめは日本にかぎらず，欧米諸国にも見られる現象だが，日本では一般にいじめの要因として①一人ひとりの個性を伸ばす教育や教師のいじめへの認識が不十分　②家庭・地域の教育力の低下　③異質なものを排除する同質指向の社会意識が強い——などが挙げられている。いじめ対策は社会全体で取り組む機運が高まってきた。

Student Life

Because Japanese society sets great store by academic credentials and large numbers of students go to college, the competition for entry to the "good" schools is fierce. And because it is easier to get into a good college if you went to a good high school if you went to a good junior high school and so on down the line, many children have no choice but to study hard with one eye on the entrance exams as early as elementary school. Most schools operate on a trimester system with the new year starting in April. Except for the lower grades of elementary school, it is usual to average six hours of school a day one of the longest school days in the world. Even after school lets out, the children have drills and other homework to keep them busy. Vacations are about six weeks in the summer and about two weeks each for winter and spring breaks—and there is often homework to do over these vacations. As such, this is very different from the situation in many Western countries where students have two months or more of summer vacation, Christmas, Easter, and other vacations, and very little homework. With more and more Japanese assigned oveseas, many of the children who have gone to school overseas suffer considerable culture shock upon (re)entering the Japanese system, and some of them have found the adjustment so difficult that they dropped out.

School Activities

Along with this heavy emphasis on academics, schools also offer a variety of extra-curricular activities. There are outings in spring and fall, and the pre-graduation class trips are special favorites with all students. The spring and fall outings are usually one-day trips to a zoo or some historical site in connection with their social science studies, while the pre-graduation trips are longer, about one week, and typically to such places as *Kyouto* (Kyoto) and environs, *Kyuushuu*, *Hokkaidou*, or *Toukyou* (Tokyo)—and lately China, the United States, and other foreign sites— as horizon-expanders.

In addition to these trips, there are also school-wide athletic meets, plays and choral performances, band concerts, and "culture festivals", when all kinds of groups have booths or whatnot, most of them concentrated in the spring and fall. In addition, the school typically has sports teams, musical groups, artistic circles, and other clubs for supervised extra-curricular enrichment.

The Hazing Problem

Yet Japanese school life has lately been marred by reports of vicious bullying and hazing. In a 1997 Ministry of Education survey, 22% of the nation's elementary schools, 48% of the junior high schools, and 31% of the senior high schools reported serious hazing incidents—all of these figures down from 1996. There have even been students who have committed suicide to escape this hazing. While other countries also have similar problems, the main causes of the problem in Japan include teachers who are not sufficiently aware of the problem, families and communities that leave education entirely to the school system, and a general tendency to impose conformity and to smother individuality. Yet society is gradually realizing that this is everybody's problem.

日本の子供たちの受験戦争の厳しさを象徴するものの一つが，学習塾の存在である。いい大学に入って，いい会社に入るためには，小学生のころから受験を意識した勉強をして，進学率の高い有名中学，有名高校に入らなければならない。競争が激しいので，とても学校の勉強だけでは競争に勝ち残れない。そこで多くの子供たちは，学習塾に通って受験のための勉強をするわけである。週3～5日，1日2～3時間も塾で勉強している子供たちも珍しくない。93年度の文部省調査によると，学習塾に通う者の割合は，小学生が24%，中学生が60%にのぼる。

東京など大都市圏の有名な進学塾などでは，塾に入るためのテストがあり，「一般の入学試験より難しい」とさえ言われている。塾どうしの生徒獲得競争も激しく，毎年入学シーズンが過ぎると，有名校への合格者数を載せた塾のチラシ広告がたくさん出回る。

乱塾時代

全国にある学習塾は5万とも10万とも言われ，正確な数はつかめていない。学習塾はだれでも，規模に関係なく自由に営業でき，どの役所も法的な指導権限をもたないことから，詳しい実態把握は難しい。ひと口に学習塾と言っても，大手の進学塾チェーンから個別指導を特徴にする街の補習塾，人間教育をめざすユニークな塾まで千差万別だ。

進学塾業界は，児童数の減少期を迎えて競争が激しくなる中で，寡占化が進み，閉鎖に追い込まれる業者も出始めている。生き残りのカギは有名私立中学などの合格者をどれだけ多く出すかにあるという。「学校5日制で子供たちにゆとりを」と文部省が笛を吹いても，踊れないというのが進学塾経営者の本音である。

学習塾に対する評価はどうだろうか。学校の先生方からよく聞かれるのは，「塾で先取り学習をするので，生徒が学校の授業を聞かなくて困る」「夜遅くまで子供が塾にいるのは，教育上好ましくない」などである。一方，保護者が子供を学習塾に通わせる理由は「子供が希望するから」「家庭で勉強をみてやれないから」「学校の授業だけでは受験勉強が十分できないから」の順だった。いずれにせよ，過度の学習塾通いは子供の発達に必要な遊びや生活体験の機会を制約することになり，望ましい人間形成に悪い影響を及ぼすと懸念されている。

文部科学省は最近まで，塾の存在を無視するような態度を取ってきたが，児童数の減少や，学校5日制の完全実施が間近いという状況の中で，学校と塾の共存を図る政策に転じてきている。

Cram Schools

Called "*juku*," cram schools are symbolic of the fierce competition Japanese children go through to get into good schools. Very often, the competition to get into a good college, and from there into a good company, starts as early as elementary school, when children fight to get into good junior high schools and later senior high schools. Because so many people are competing for so few places, just doing your schoolwork is not enough. Cram schools make the difference, and it is not unusual to see children going to them 2-3 hours a day for three, four, or even five days a week. A fiscal 1993 Ministry of Education study found 24% of elementary school children and 60% of junior high school students going to academic *juku*.

In *Toukyou* (Tokyo) and other urban centers, the better cram schools even have their own entrance exams—tests said to be tougher than most other school entrance exams at the same grade level. At the same time, the *juku* compete to attract the best students, one standard practice being to publicize how many of their students get into which famous high schools and universities each year.

The Era of *Juku*

No one knows how many *juku* there are. Some say 50,000, others 100,000. Anyone can open a *juku*. There are no size requirements and no regulatory authorities. So nobody has detailed records. Likewise, there are all manner of *juku* — from nationwide chains to prepare students for university entrance exams to remedial *juku* offering one-on-one education in specific subjects to counseling *juku* in interpersonal skills.

With a shrinking pool of children to draw upon, the exam-preparation *juku* business has become intensely competitive and a shake-out is under way. The key to their survival lying in how many of their students they can get into the well-known schools, most *juku* are unlikely to go along with the more-free-time-for-students half of the Ministry of Education's call for a shorter school week.

What do their competitors and their customers think of academic *juku*? Non-*juku* teachers complain that students do not pay attention in class because they have already covered the material in *juku*, and that it is not good for students to be out so late at night; parents say they send their kids to *juku* because the kids want to go, because they cannot check their children's schoolwork, and because schools alone are inadequate preparation for passing entrance exams. Yet it seems clear that kids spend so much time at *juku* that they do not get the socialization-through-play and other experiences they need to be mature human beings, and there is concern that *juku* have an adverse impact on personality development.

Until recently the Ministry of Education and Science pretty much ignored the existence of *juku*, but given the present situation with a decline in the number of children and the soon to be instigated five day school week, etc., official thinking is turning towards working out a coexistence between schools and *juku*.

海外旅行ブーム

日本は海外旅行人気が定着した。国内観光がしだいに伸び悩みの傾向を見せているのに対して，海外旅行だけは年々増加の一途をたどっている。総理府の『観光白書』によれば，1999年の宿泊を伴う国内観光の一人当たり年間消費額は6万4700円で，前年に比べ約6％減少している。延べ旅行者数は1億9600万人(国民一人当たり平均1.55回)，延べ宿泊数は3億3300万泊（同2.63泊）で，こちらもそれぞれ前年より減少している。

これに対して，海外旅行者のほうは，1997年には1680万人で史上最高を記録した。日本の海外旅行者数が年間500万人台に乗ったのは86年のことで，毎年うなぎ登りに増え続けたが，バブル崩壊以後は増加率が減少し，1998年には前年の比べて6％減るに至った。

1999年の主な旅行先は，アメリカ(484万人)，韓国(122万人)，中国(210万人）で，アメリカを旅行先とした人の約半数はハワイを選んでいる。

日本人旅行者というと，以前は諸外国の新聞，雑誌で劇画的に描かれたように，カメラを首や肩にぶら下げてかまびすしく練り歩く年配の団体旅行者が多かったが，最近は20歳代の若い女性が増えているのが大きな特徴だ。新婚旅行で海外に出かけるカップルも目立って増えている。

旅行の風習

庶民の間で旅行が一般的となったのは江戸時代のころだが，その始まりは「代参講」という講にある。これは，村落外にある他所の神社や仏閣に参拝するために何人かが寄り集まって懇親する社会集団で，講中で講金を集め，くじ引きで決まった代参者を講の代表として寺社に派遣した。神社を中心とした*伊勢講・*熊野講・*富士講，仏閣を中心とした*身延講(みのぶこう)・*成田講など，枚挙にいとまがないほど多くの講があり，しだいに代参者を派遣するだけでなく，講員それぞれがお金を積み立てておいて団体でお参りするようになったのが，今日の旅行の原型である。こうした講は，今でも年輩者の間では根強い人気がある。

A Boom in Overseas Travel

Overseas travel is a big thing in Japan. While domestic travel has started to taper off, more and more people have been traveling overseas every year. According to the Prime Minister's Office's *White Paper on Tourism*, spending on domestic overnight-or-longer travel averaged ¥64,700 per person for 1999, down approximately 6% from the previous year. The total number of tourists was 196 million (or an average of 1.55 trips per person), and the total number of nights stayed was 333 million (or 2.63 nights per person), both of which represent declines from the previous year.

By contrast, total overseas trips hit a record of 16.80 million in 1997. The number of Japanese overseas travelers topped 5 million in 1986 and increased dramatically each year after that, but the rate gradually flattened after the economic bubble burst. In 1998 it posted a decline of 6% from the previous year.

The most popular destinations in 1999 were the United States (4.84 million people), Korea (1.22 million) and China (2.10 million). About half of the people who went to the United States chose Hawaii.

Foreign media used to depict Japanese tourists as groups of camera-toting old people shuffling along behind their flag-carrying guide, but the main growth in Japanese overseas tourism has been among young women in their 20s and honeymooning couples.

Travel Customs

Travel first spread among ordinary Japanese during the *Edo* period when it was promoted primarily by religious associations called *kou*. Collecting money from all of the members and then drawing lots to see who would go on behalf of the group, these associations served both as social organizations and as a way for everyone to have the chance to make pilgrimages to distant shrines and temples. Innumerable *kou* sprang up, the most prominent being *Shintou* groups such as the *Isekou*,* *Kumanokou*,* and *Fujikou** and Buddhist groups such as *Minobukou** and *Naritakou*.* Later the *kou* not only sent proxy pilgrims, but also organized pilgrimages for members who had saved up enough money to make the trip themselves, and these groups were the forerunners of today's tourist groups. Even now such groups remain very popular among older Japanese.

最もポピュラーな旅

日本で最もポピュラーな旅は，*温泉を巡る旅である。老夫婦が老後の楽しみに名所旧跡を訪ねる旅で，彼らが好んで泊まるのは温泉のある日本旅館だし，職場の社員旅行でも，たいてい近県の温泉が旅の目的地に選ばれる。日中は温泉の近くにあるゴルフ場や釣り場などのレジャー施設で存分に汗を流し，温泉にゆっくりつかって一息入れた後，宴会場にみんなで集まって一献(いっこん)酌み交わしながら社員どうしの親睦(しんぼく)を図るというのが，おおかたのパターンである。若者たちは概して年輩者ほどには温泉好きではないが，それでも，スキーや登山などのついでに温泉につかる，あるいはグループで秘湯や露天風呂を訪ねるというケースが，最近では増えてきている。

湯治の習慣

そもそも温泉巡りは，湯治の習慣に始まった。温泉に含まれるさまざまな成分の薬効によって病気の治療をする湯治は西欧にもあり，主に飲用法によって病人・傷兵の治療に使われていたようだ。しかし，素朴な山奥の秘湯からいくつもの宿が並んだ温泉郷まで2000余もの温泉に恵まれている日本では，湯治はもっぱら入浴法によるもので，しかも持病の治療というだけでなく，日ごろの疲労回復をも兼ねて気軽に出かけられる，最も庶民的なレクリエーションの一つだった。

湯治宿はたいてい自炊だったから，農閑期になると，農民は米・みそ・しょうゆから布団までもって近隣の湯治場へ集まり，毎日ゆっくり湯につかることを日課にしながら，1週間，1か月と長逗留(とうりゅう)をして体を休めたのである。その湯治自体は，近代医療の発達とともにめっきり少なくなったが，日本人の温泉好きだけは相変わらずというわけである。

人気の名湯

どの温泉にもそれぞれ特徴があるが，非常に人気のあるのは伊豆(いず)の熱海(あたみ)温泉。眼前に海を見下ろし，背後に緑濃い坂の町が広がる風情から，東洋のリビエラとも言われ，芸者が多いことでも有名だ。日本最古の湯と言われるのが，神戸の六甲山中腹にある有馬(ありま)温泉。歴史があるだけに付近に名所旧跡が多く，清少納言の『枕草子』にも，「湯は*ななくりの湯，有馬の湯，*玉造(たまつくり)の湯」と，その名湯をうたわれている。別府(べっぷ)・浜脇(はまわき)・亀川(かめがわ)など別府八湯からなる大分の別府温泉郷も，1000余軒もの宿がある世界一の大温泉都市として知られ，その夜景の美しさで多くの観光客を呼んでいる。

Japan's Hot Springs

Widespread Popularity

The most popular outings in Japan are trips to hot springs.* Retired couples visiting famous historical sites usually stay at traditional inns (*ryokan*) with hot-spring baths, and these same inns are also popular with groups of workers on company outings. Most of the company groups spend the day at nearby recreational facilities golfing or fishing and return to the *ryokan* for a relaxing soak before gathering in the banquet room to eat, drink, and reaffirm friendships. Young people are generally not as fond of the hot-spring resorts, but more and more they have been staying at hot-spring inns or indulging in open-air baths while on skiing or mountaineering trips.

Health Spas

The Japanese hot-spring habit began as medical therapy. Many of the minerals in hot-spring waters are said to be good for what ails you. Although hot-spring water has often been drunk in Western Europe, Japan's hot springs are generally only bathed in —and not just by the sick but also by the healthy and hard-working for relaxation. There are now over 2,000 hot-spring inns throughout Japan, ranging from small inns near tiny hot springs deep in the mountains to rows of large hotels near major hot-spring arteries.

It used to be that hot-spring inns offered very inexpensive lodgings to guests who did their own cooking, and farmers would pack up everything from food to *futon* to spend the off season at the local hot-spring inns where they could enjoy the luxury of several weeks of treating tired muscles to daily hot-spring baths. While this custom declined with the advent of modern medicine, today's Japanese are no less fond of visiting hot springs.

Famous Spas

Each hot-spring resort has something different to offer, but one of the most popular resorts is *Atami* on the *Izu* Peninsula near *Toukyou* (Tokyo). Nicknamed the Riviera of the Orient, *Atami* is blessed with a view of the Pacific, a backdrop of lush green hills, and a large contingent of *geisha*. Japan's oldest hot-spring resort is *Arima* spa, located part way up Mt *Rokkou* near *Koube* (Kobe). There are many historic sites in that area, and *Arima* spa is mentioned, along with the hot springs at *Nanakuri** and *Tamatsukuri*,* in *Sei Shounagon*'s *Heian*-period classic *Makura no Soushi* (Pillow Book). The city of *Beppu* in *Kyuushuu*'s *Ooita* prefecture, home of eight famous hot springs including *Beppu*, *Hamawaki*, and *Kamegawa*, is known as the hot-springs capital of the world and has over 1,000 hot-springs inns and a nighttime charm that attracts large numbers of tourists.

*花見

春を表す日本の古いことばに,「桜時」というのがある。昔から,桜の花に特別の愛着をもっている日本人ならではの言い方だが,その桜の花を心ゆくまで眺めて春をめでようというのが,日本の花見である。

格式の高いところでは,「観桜会(かんおう)」といって,皇室や内閣総理大臣が各界の著名人や各国の大使など数千人招いて行う盛大なものもあるが,一般に行われる花見は,家族や町内,職場の気の合った仲間どうしで楽しむ,もっと庶民的なものである。庶民の花見に付き物なのが宴会で,枝ぶりのよい桜の木の下に*ござやビニールシートを敷いて陣取り,料理や酒やカラオケを持ち込んで,飲めや歌えや踊れの大騒ぎとなる。東京の上野公園のような桜の名所となると,その宴席を確保するための陣取り合戦がまたたいへんで,各グループの先発隊が前日から乗り込み,眺めのいい場所を巡って「こっちが先だ」「いや,こっちだ」と小競(こぜ)り合いを演じる狂騒ぶりである。

花見の歴史は古く,平安時代の812年に宮中で行われた桜の花宴がその始まりとされている。豊臣秀吉が1598年に京都の醍醐(だいご)寺で開いた「醍醐の花見」は,その豪華さで史上最も有名だが,花見が庶民の行事となったのは江戸時代に入ってからのことで,葛飾北斎(かつしかほくさい)の『富嶽(ふがく)三十六景』には,花見に興じる江戸町民の様子が鮮やかに描かれている。

桜の名所として有名なのは,日本一の誉れ高い奈良県・吉野山。俗に「吉野千本桜」と呼ばれるたくさんの桜が山すそから頂上まで植えられ,春には山が花で埋まる。京都の嵐山や,世阿弥(ぜあみ)の謡曲「桜川」で知られる茨城(いばらき)県・桜川なども多くの花見客でにぎわう。

紅葉狩り

春の花見に相当する秋の行事が,紅葉狩りである。日本には,楓(かえで)や紅葉など秋に紅葉する樹木が多いため,山紫水明の風土とあいまって,世界で最も紅葉の美しい国の一つとされている。日本人は桜の花を見て春をめでたように,紅葉の名所へ行き,その景観美を眺めて秋を感じるのである。

花見と同様,紅葉狩りも,もともとは宮中で行われる宴だったが,しだいに紅葉を求めて遠出をするようになった。紅葉の美しいのはやはり京都で,桜の名所でもある嵐山,谷が一面の紅葉となる嵯峨野(さがの)近くの栂尾(とがのお),人里離れた秋の風情が楽しめる大原などに人気がある。

Cherry-blossom and Maple-leaf Viewing

Hana-mi*

An old Japanese word for spring is *sakura-doki* or "cherry blossom time"—an indication of the age-old Japanese passion for cherry blossoms and the special delight felt in viewing them at *hana-mi* (flower-viewing) parties each spring.

In addition to the lavish high-society *hana-mi* parties attended by thousands of guests including the imperial family, the Prime Minister and his cabinet, celebrities, and members of the diplomatic corps, there are more plebeian parties at which families, neighbors, or co-workers supplied with food, drink, and groundcloths* stake out claims under the blossoming cherry trees, perhaps singing along to taped accompaniment as the evening progresses in a revelry of drinking, singing, and dancing. At the more popular sites, *Toukyou*'s (Tokyo's) *Ueno* Park for instance, advance parties begin arriving a full day ahead to lay claim to good locations, and territorial disputes sometimes flare up among the more aggressive strategists.

The *hana-mi* tradition is a long one, originating in the *Heian* period when *hana-mi* parties were held at court. In 1598, *Toyotomi Hideyoshi* held a *hana-mi* party at *Kyouto*'s (Kyoto's) *Daigoji* temple which is remembered as the most opulent ever. It was not until the *Edo* period that *hana-mi* parties spread to the commonfolk, but such parties are depicted in the famous "36 Views of Mt. *Fuji*" series of woodblock prints by *Katsushika Hokusai*.

Among Japan's famous *hana-mi* sites, the most highly regarded is Mt *Yoshino* in *Nara* prefecture. Known as the mountain with 1,000 cherry trees, Mt *Yoshino* is graced from top to bottom with cherry trees so that the entire mountain seems to blossom in spring. *Kyouto*'s *Arashiyama* and *Ibaraki* prefecture's *Sakuragawa* (made famous by a popular poem of the same name by *Zeami*) also draw large numbers of *hana-mi* enthusiasts.

Momiji-gari

Autumn's counterpart to spring's flower-viewing is *momiji-gari* (maple-leaf viewing). Japan's autumn season hosts a variety of colorful maple trees such as the *kaede* and *momiji* varieties, painting gorgeous mountain landscapes and making Japan's autumn colors among the world's most beautiful. Just as Japanese love spring for its beautiful cherry blossoms, so do they travel wide and far to drink in the beauty of famous *momiji* landscapes.

As with *hana-mi, momiji-gari* began with the court nobility and gradually became a custom whereby people traveled to renown *momiji-gari* sites. Today's most popular spots for *momiji-gari* include *Kyouto*'s *Arashiyama*, mentioned earlier for its beautiful cherry blossoms; *Toganoo* near *Sagano*; and *Oohara*, a reserve of autumn beauty far removed from human dwellings.

33 野球・サッカー

日本人はスポーツ好きである。四季を通じてあらゆるスポーツが行われるが，中でも人気を博しているのが野球とサッカーである。

高校野球

アマチュア野球の人気のトップは，毎年春と夏に開かれる高校野球の「甲子園大会」だろう。北海道から沖縄まで全国の予選を勝ち抜いた代表校の球児たちが日本一をかけて甲子園球場で熱戦を繰り広げる。このときばかりは日本人も郷土意識に燃えて応援し，テレビも全試合を全国中継する。大会は戦前から行われ，夏は2001年ですでに83回を数え，4000校を超える学校が参加している。

プロ野球

世代を通して広いファンの関心を呼んでいるのはプロ野球である。プロ野球が始まったのは1934年だが，今日のような隆盛は戦後からである。わけても伝統チーム「読売ジャイアンツ」の*長嶋茂雄と*王貞治はプロ野球の生んだ国民的ヒーローであった。日本人にとってはかつては夢であった大リーグで活躍する選手も増え始めた。95年には野茂英雄が大リーグの「ロサンゼルス・ドジャース」に入団し，史上二人目の日本人大リーガーとなった。入団後の野茂は独特の「トルネード投法」で大活躍し，96年と2001年の二度にわたってノーヒット・ノーランを達成するなど偉業を成し遂げた。野茂の後も何人かの選手が大リーグに挑戦し，なかでも2001年に「シアトル・マリナーズ」に入団したイチローは，１年目から首位打者と盗塁王のタイトルを獲得。同僚の佐々木主浩（かずひろ）とともに地区リーグ優勝に大きく貢献した。現在では10人前後が大リーグで活躍している。

日本のプロ野球はセントラル，パシフィックの二つのリーグに各６球団，計12球団があり，両リーグの覇者が日本シリーズを戦い日本一を決める。

サッカー

野球と二分して人気の高いのがサッカーである。そのきっかけとなったのは，93年に開幕した日本初のプロ・サッカーリーグの「Ｊリーグ」である。現在，Ｊ１（16クラブ）とＪ.２（12クラブ）の２部制を採用し，リーグ戦やカップ戦が行われている。またＪリーグで活躍した選手の中からは，ヨーロッパのクラブ・チームに移籍する選手も増え，特に中田英寿（ひでとし）はイタリア・セリエＡで活躍を見せている。世界でもっとも人気のスポーツ・イベントであるワールドカップには，日本も98年のフランス大会に初出場を遂げ，国民的な盛り上がりを見せた。2002年には日本と韓国による共同開催も行われ，ますますサッカー熱が高まりそうである。

Baseball and Soccer

The Japanese are great sports fans. The year is packed with any number of different sports, but by far and away the most popular are baseball and soccer.

High School Baseball

Tops among amateur baseball events are the high school baseball championship games held each spring and summer at *Koushien* Stadium, where regional playoff winners from *Hokkaidou* to *Okinawa* battle it out for the national pennant. This is one of the times when Japanese become nostalgic, rooting for teams from their home prefecture, while every game is televised nationwide. Both these events were begun before WWII, with the summer championship marking its 83rd year in 2001.

Professional Baseball

Professional baseball has a wide following, attracting fans of all ages. Professional baseball got its start in 1934, but really came into its own after the close of WWII. One of the oldest teams, the *Yomiuri* Giants, has produced Japanese baseball's two national heroes, *Nagashima Shigeo** and *Ou* (Oh)*Sadaharu**. The one time dream of many Japanese —to play major league ball—is now being realized by an increasing number of players. *Nomo Hideo* was signed by the Los Angeles Dodgers in 1995 to become the second Japanese ever to make the majors. With his distinctive "tornado" delivery, *Nomo* pitched no-hit, no-run games in 1996 and 2001, and has built quite and impressive record. Following *Nomo* several other Japanese players have taken shots at the majors. Of these, *Suzuki Ichirou*, who joined the Seattle Mariners in 2001, became number one in hits and stolen bases during his first year, and together with teammate *Sasaki Kazuhiro* contributed much to his team's league victory. At present there are about ten Japanese playing in the majors.

Japanese professional baseball has two leagues, Central and Pacific, with six teams each, for a total twelve teams. At the end of the season the two league champions play for the Japan pennant.

Soccer

Soccer shares the same popularity as baseball, and the thing that started it all was the creation of Japan's first soccer league, J League, in 1993. At present J League has two soccer leagues. J1 with 16 teams, and J2 with 12 teams, with league and pennant championships. An increasing number of Japanese players are signing on with various European teams. One of the most popular players to do so is *Nakata Hidetoshi* who plays for Italia Serie A. Japan's debut into the world soccer scene came in 1998 when it reached the World Cup playoffs held in France, arousing nationwide excitement. The most popular sporting event in the world, the World Cup, will be hosted jointly by Korea and Japan in 2002, further infecting the Japanese with soccer fever.

ゴルフ・テニス・釣り

日本人のスポーツ志向は，近年急速に高まりを見せ，中でもゴルフ・テニス・釣りは野球・サッカー・スキーと並んで人気がある。いずれもファッション化が目覚ましく，関連産業は国内需要ばかりでなく，輸出産業の面でも活力を見せるというメリットを生み出している。

ゴルフ

かつて戦前の日本では，ゴルフと言えばごく一部の上流階級のお遊びとされていたが，戦後，とりわけ1960年代ごろから爆発的に普及し，現在のゴルフ人口は1400万人と言われている。15歳以上の人口比で見ると，実に13人に１人がゴルフをする計算になる。ゴルフ場の数は，狭い国土に1800か所もあり，ほとんどが民間経営である。最近は女性も目立って増えてきたが，料金が外国に比べてかなり高い点が泣きどころ。大都市周辺のゴルフ場では，休日料金が平日よりも50％前後高いのが普通で，大衆化はしたものの，日本では依然として金のかかるスポーツである。各種スポーツの年間支出平均の中でも，ゴルフは19万円と群を抜いて高い。プロゴルフも隆盛を極め，世界的プレーヤーとして青木功，岡本綾子などを生み出し，トーナメントの賞金総額は年間15億円を超えている。

テニス

ゴルフに負けず劣らず人気のあるのがテニス。天皇皇后の仲を結び付けるきっかけがテニスだったこともあって，テニス人口は急速に増え，現在では1000万人にも上る。民間のテニスクラブは全国で1000を超えるが，テニス人口が多いため，いつでも，どこでもできるというわけにはいかない。

　もともと1970年代後半から急成長したスポーツだが，現在でも相変わらず人気があり，それにつれてラケットやテニスウエアなどの関連産業も巨大化し，売り上げは年間総額で500億円を上回っている。このテニスブームは都市から地方に広がり，観光地近くでは農家が畑をつぶして，貸しコートを造る例も少なくない。

釣り

釣りブームは30年ほど前から高まり，現在の人口は2000万人と言われている。海に囲まれ，至る所に川や湖，池がある日本だけに，釣りブームはむしろ当然のことと言える。それに業界が次々に質のよい釣り具を開発したことも，ブームに拍車をかけた。女性の間でも釣りの人気は年々高まっている。釣りは完全にスポーツとして定着した。

Golf, Tennis, and Fishing

Japanese have become more sports-minded in recent years, and golf, tennis, and fishing now rank alongside baseball, soccer, and skiing as the most popular sports. All of these sports are strongly fashion-oriented and offer major domestic as well as export markets for sports equipment and sportswear manufacturers.

Golf

In prewar Japan, golf was a game for the very rich. Since the 1960s, however, golf has spread rapidly to become a game for the masses, and there are now about 14 million golfers in Japan. That means one in every 13 Japanese above the age of 14 plays golf, this in spite of the fact that golf is much more expensive in Japan than elsewhere. So far, 1,800 golf courses, most of them private, have been squeezed into Japan's modest land space. There has recently been a sharp increase in the number of female golfers. Golf courses near major cities often charge weekend and holiday premiums that make course fees up to 50% more expensive than on weekdays. Golf has indeed become a mass-consumer sport, but it remains a very expensive one. The average golfer spends ¥190,000 a year on the game, making golf by far the most expensive popular sport in Japan. With world-class players such as *Aoki Isao* and *Okamoto Ayako*, and with about ¥1.5 billion in prize money awarded each year at tournaments, professional golf has also made it big in Japan.

Tennis

Neck and neck with golf in popularity is tennis. A mutual passion for tennis helped tie the wedding knot for the Emperor and Empress, and the increasingly popular game is regularly played by about 10 million Japanese. There are now over 1,000 private racquet clubs in Japan. With so many tennis players, though, getting a court is often still a problem.

Tennis began to boom in Japan in the late 1970s and is still popular. With this growth has come equally rapid growth for manufacturers of tennis equipment and accessories, and these items now enjoy sales of over ¥50 billion a year. The tennis boom began in the cities and spread to countryside resorts, and quite a few enterprising farmers have converted the fields to better-paying tennis courts.

Fishing

Fishing began to jump in popularity about 30 years ago, and there are now about 20 million sport fishermen in Japan. It is only natural that fishing should be popular in Japan, a nation not only surrounded by the sea but full of rivers, lakes, and ponds. The intense competition among fishing-equipment manufacturers and the high-quality equipment that they have developed has further propelled sport fishing's popularity. Fishing is also a very popular women's sport.

相撲

日本の国技である相撲は，日本人ばかりでなく近年は外国人の間にも人気を博している。単なるスポーツ以上に，歌舞伎などに通じる日本的魅力が*土俵にはあると言うのである。

相撲の歴史

起源は遠く神代にまでさかのぼり，『古事記』や『日本書紀』にその記述が見られる。初めは豊作を占う神事相撲の要素が強かったが，しだいに見せるスポーツとして発展し，江戸時代には職業力士が登場した。1909年には初めて国技館が建てられ，25年には東西に分かれていた相撲協会が合併，財団法人大日本相撲協会が誕生した。昭和期前半は不世出の大*横綱*双葉山の人気を中心とした黄金時代だが，敗戦を経て，戦後も勝るとも劣らない隆盛を迎えた。この間，58年からは「年間6場所(1場所は15日)制」，65年からは「部屋別総当たり制」を採用する時代を迎えた。

競技方法

直径4.55mの円形の土俵の中で力士二人が技を競う。力士は*まわしを締めただけの姿で登場し，勝負に入るまでの制限時間(幕内で4分)内に古式にのっとり，四股（しこ）を踏み，また清めのための塩を土俵にまく。土俵上の力士の行為にはすべて意味と由来があり，長く受け継がれた一種の儀式である。外国人が相撲に日本の伝統を見いだすのも，この辺に一因があるのだろう。勝負の決まり手は70手あるが，実際には寄り，押し，突きが全体の半数を占める。15日間の成績で地位は上下する。最高位の横綱は過去60人あまりしか誕生していない。

人気の変遷

相撲のラジオ放送は28年から，テレビ中継は53年から行われ，特にテレビが相撲大衆化に果たした役割は大きい。名力士の輩出も相撲人気の大きな要因である。戦後は栃錦・若乃花の“栃若”，柏戸・大鵬（たいほう）の“柏鵬”，北の富士・玉の海の“北玉”，貴ノ花・輪島の“貴輪”のそれぞれの時代を経て，北の湖に次いで小さな大横綱千代の富士の時代へと推移した。また，ハワイ出身の力士，高見山の活躍は，小錦・曙・武蔵丸・旭鷲山らの外国人力士の輩出をもたらし，相撲人気を国際化した点で特筆される。高見山は引退後は*親方を襲名し，部屋を開設して，ハワイ出身の曙を第64代横綱に育てた。今日，土俵は，武蔵丸と貴乃花の2横綱を中心に絶大な人気を保っている。

Sumou (Sumo)

Japan's national sport, *sumou*, counts not only Japanese but an increasing number of non-Japanese among its fans. Indeed, *sumou* is more than just a sport, and the *sumou* ring* has the same sort of distinctively Japanese appeal as, for example, the *kabuki* theater.

History

Sumou has existed since ancient times, and there are accounts of *sumou* bouts in Japan's earliest extant records. Originally an oracular ritual connected with prayers for the harvest, *sumou* gradually evolved into a spectator sport. Professional *sumou* appeared in the *Edo* period. *Sumou*'s main arena, the *Kokugikan*, was built in 1909 and is the home of the Japan *Sumou* Association formed in 1925. World War II killed *sumou*'s golden age led by the popular *yokozuna** (grand champion) *Futabayama*,* but *sumou* regained its former splendor as Japan recovered from wartime defeat. In 1958, the number of 15-day tournaments was upped to six a year. Other reforms, such as round-robin competition among stables, were initiated in 1965.

Techniques

In *sumou*, two wrestlers face off in the middle of a *dohyou* (ringed platform) measuring 4.55 meters in diameter. Clad only in *mawashi**, they first engage in pre-bout ritual* such as striking fearsome poses and scattering purifying salt on the ring (four minutes at most for upper-division wrestlers), all of which actions are part of *sumou*'s ancient tradition. This ritual is one of the aspects that particularly appeals to foreign fans. Although there are 70 different ways to win a bout, about half are won using the most common *yori-*, *oshi-*, and *tsuki* techniques. Wrestlers are reranked after each tournament on the basis of their won/lost record. The top rank of *yokozuna* has been conferred upon over 60 men.

Renewed Popularity

With radio broadcasts beginning in 1928, and especially with television coverage beginning in 1953, *sumou*'s audience rapidly grew to include the general public, and this renewed popularity led to the appearance of a number of great wrestlers. Following the great rivalries between *Tochinishiki* and *Wakanohana*, *Kashiwado* and *Taihou*, *Kitanofuji* and *Tamanoumi*, and *Takanohana* and *Wajima*, the sport was briefly dominated by *Kitanoumi* and *Chiyonofuji*. Non-Japanese have also done very well, including first *Takamiyama* and then *Konishiki, Akebono*, and *Musashimaru* (all from Hawaii) and *Kyokushuuzan* (from Mongolia). *Akebono*, working out of the stable headed by *Takamiyama* after retirement,* was named *sumou*'s 64th *yokozuna*. Today, the two current *yokozuna* are *Musashimaru* and *Takanohana* (son of the earlier *Takanohana*), and *sumou* continues to enjoy immense popularity.

「柔よく剛を制す」。柔道の原理はこの諺(ことわざ)に象徴されていると言っても過言ではない。「柔(やわら)」とは「柔らか」の意味。その柔の道，それが柔道であり，日本の生んだスポーツである。

柔道の歴史

柔道の源は古代の武術，「柔術」にさかのぼるが，これを「柔道」と命名，明治時代初期にその基礎を確立したのは，当時東京大学の学生だった嘉納治五郎(かのうじごろう)である。嘉納は柔術に関心を抱いて多くの流派を学んだが，これに教育的意義を見いだし，1882年講道館を設立，柔道の研究，指導に励んだ。嘉納によれば，柔道とは「心身の力を最も有効に使用する道であり，攻撃，防御の練習によって身体，精神を練磨修行し，その道の真髄を体得すること」である。柔道に限らず剣道，弓道，空手道など日本古来の武術がいずれも「道」なのはきわめて示唆的だ。つまり，それは単に勝負を競うスポーツではなく，道を求めての精神修行も兼ねた人間形成，それこそが柔道の究極目標なのである。

1951年に国際柔道連盟が発足，日本は52年に加盟した。95年の時点で，国際柔道連盟には約180の国・地域が加盟，柔道人口は世界で500万とも言われる。64年の東京オリンピックからは五輪種目になったほか，女子柔道も普及し，世界柔道選手権など各種国際大会も行われている。

競技の方法

講道館柔道の規定によれば，試合者は柔道着を着用しなければならない。試合場は14.55m四方とし，その中央に9.1m四方(畳50枚)の場内を設け，互いに組み合って技を競う。柔道の技は投げ技，固め技，当て身技の３種類がある。ただし，当て身技は相手の急所を突いたり打ったり蹴る方法で，普通の試合・練習には用いず，形として練習する。練習は「形」と「乱取り」の２形式がある。形は一定の順序，方法に従って行い，乱取りは自由に技を競う。

力量は「段」と「級」で表され，最高は10段で最低は初段，それ以下が級となる。１級を最高に５級までである。段と級は帯の色で区別し，10，９段は紅，８～６段は紅白，５～初段が黒，１～３級は茶，４級～初心者は白色である。

本来は無差別だけであったが，柔道の国際化に伴い，体重別が一般的になっている。常に礼儀作法を重んじ，「礼に始まり礼に終わる」ということばは有名である。

Juudou (Judo)

Softness controls hardness. This ancient wisdom is the fundamental principle of *juudou*. The *juu* in *juudou* means softness and the *dou* way or method, hence the name *juudou* meaning "the way of softness."

History of *Juudou*

Juudou's roots go back to ancient *Juujutsu*, but it was not until early in the *Meiji* period that *Kanou Jigorou*, a *Toukyou* (Tokyo) University student, created and named *juudou* as we know it today. Adept at many *juujutsu* techniques, *Kanou* saw *juudou* as a tool for physical education. Believing that *juudou* makes most effective use of both mental and physical faculties with offensive and defensive techniques practiced to cultivate the whole person and achieve mastery of the discipline, *Kanou* established the *Koudoukan* school of *juudou* in 1882. This holistic orientation is typical not only of *juudou* but also of *kendou* (way of the sword), *kyuudou* (way of the bow), *karatedou* (way of the empty hand), and the many other *dou* (ways) that are collectively called *budou* (way of the warrior, i.e. martial arts).

The International *Juudou* Federation was established in 1951, with Japan becoming a member in 1952. As of 1995, the International *Juudou* Federation has over 180 member nations and regions, and there are an estimated five million wrestlers worldwide. *Juudou* has been an Olympic event since the 1964 Tokyo Olympics, women's *juudou* has become popular, and *juudou* championships and other international competitions are held all over the globe.

Competition

Koudoukan rules require that wrestlers be dressed in regulation uniforms. The floor space must be 14.55 meters square, with a 9.1 meter square center area on which the contestants wrestle. There are three categories of *wazu*: *nage-waza* (throwing), *katame-waza* (grappling), and *atemi-waza* (attacking vital points). However, the *atemi-waza*'s sharp blows are not normally used except in formal shows. Practices are either formal or free-form. While prescribed techniques are used in a prescribed order in formal practice, wrestlers are free to use whatever techniques they like in free-form practice.

Wrestlers are ranked according to ability in a system of *dan* (ranks) and *kyuu* (classes), the highest rank being 10th *dan* and the lowest *shodan* (beginners). Below *shodan* are the *kyuu* with 1 the highest and 5 the lowest. There are different color belts for different ranks: red for 9th and 10th *dan*, red-and-white stripes for 6th through 8th *dan*, black for *shodan* through 5th *dan*, brown for 1st through 3rd *kyuu*, and white for 4th *kyuu* through unranked novices.

As *juudou* has become more international, it has become common to have competitions by weight class. Decorum is heavily stressed in both practice and in matches, as shown in the famous axiom that *juudou* starts and ends with decorum.

剣道

剣道は日本古来の剣術からスタートしたもので，もともと剣術は武士が戦闘技術をマスターするための訓練手段だった。20世紀に入って呼称が剣道と改められ，剣道を通じて心身を鍛える点に主眼が置かれるようになり，やがて戦後は新しい格技形式のスポーツとして変身した。現在では，中学，高校の教育課程にも取り入れられているほか，各地に道場も多い。

1970年には国際剣道連盟が創立されて，国際的スポーツとして認知されるようになった。現在の剣道人口は700万人。有段者は技術の発達によって進級するが，現在は159万人。最高位の10段は過去５人いたものの，今は一人もいない。女性の参加もこのところ増えている。

弓道

弓道も古来から伝わる武道の一つで，弓術とも言う。ほぼ完全にスポーツ化した武道の中にあって，いまだに古い形式を残す数少ない伝統武道で，戦後一時衰えを見せたものの，現在は再び盛んになっている。弓道場は全国に2800か所あり，弓を射る人口は130万人，うち有段者が40万人いて，その50％は女性，それも若い女性が多い。

空手道

空手は武器を一切使わない，徒手空拳の武技である。中国の唐時代に始まった中国拳法が沖縄に伝わり，「手」，「唐手」として発達したと言われている。武器の携帯を許されなかった庶民が，護身の術としてひそかに技を磨くという，独特の歴史によって発展したものである。

日本の空手は４大流派に大別できるが，各々多くの派があり，空手人口は，外国も含めて2300万人に上るという。うち有段者だけで100万人余，その10％が海外と言われるぐらい，柔道と並んで外国人に人気があるスポーツとなっている。

合気道

合気道も日本伝来の武道の一つだが，現代武道の中では唯一ゲーム化していない特異な存在である。守りの武道とも言われるように，心身の鍛錬を基本とし，あくまでも守りに徹する武術で，攻撃技はない。相手を制する技には投げ技，押さえ技がある。歴史は浅く，大正年間に合気道の名で成立，現在は合気会により組織的に統轄されている。全国の道場数は約800か所，合気道人口は国内80万人（うち女性20万人），海外20万人で約60か国に愛好者がいる。

Kendou, Kyuudou, Karate, and Aikidou

Kendou

Swordmanship, or *kenjutsu*, was the means by which *samurai* mastered the techniques of fighting. By the early 20th century, it had evolved into a martial art with equal emphasis on moral and spiritual training, and the name was changed to *kendou*. After the Second World War, *kendou* was established as a major sport in Japan, growing to become part of the regular curriculum at junior and senior high schools. There are also numerous training centers, or *doujou*, throughout the country.

The founding of the International *Kendou* Federation in 1970 firmly established *kendou* as an international sport, and there are some seven million practitioners worldwide today. Within this seven million, people are ranked in *kyuu* and *dan* by level of proficiency. Of the 1.59 million rank-holders, however, none holds the highest rank of 10th dan—a rank held by only five people in history. More and more women are taking part in this traditional sport.

Kyuudou

Also known as *kyuujutsu*, archery is another ancient Japanese sport. Of all the martial arts that have evolved into sports, *kyuudou* has stayed very close to its original form. The sport declined somewhat after the Second World War, but it is now enjoying a revival. There are 2,800 archery *doujou* in Japan with some 1,300,000 archers. Of the 400,000 who hold ranks, 50 % are women, many of them young women.

Karate

This martial art for unarmed combat originated in Tang China and was further developed in *Okinawa*, where it was originally called '*karate*' (lit. "Tang hand"). *Karate* is different from the other martial arts in that it was secretly practiced by the common people who were not allowed to bear arms.

There are four main schools of *karate* and innumerable subschools, with a total of 23 million *karate* enthusiasts worldwide. Over 10% of the million rank holders are foreigners, and *karate* has joined judo as another Japanese sport gone international.

Aikidou

Another uniquely Japanese martial art, *aikidou* is purely defensive and does not lend itself to contests. Largely a spiritual exercise, it relies on throws and holding techniques to protect from attack and has no offensive techniques. Sharing its origins with *juudou* (judo) and other traditional martial arts, *aikidou* is actually relatively new, not having been organized and named until the 1920s. Today there are approximately 800 *aikidou doujou* in the *Aikidou* Federation. There are 800,000 aikido practitioners in Japan (200,000 of them women) and around 200,000 in 60 countries around the world.

日本で初めて映画が輸入公開されたのが1896年，最初の映画撮影は１年後の1897年だから，日本の映画史はちょうど100年余を経過したことになる。

日本映画の黄金時代

戦後の1950年前後は“日本映画の黄金時代”とも言われ，小津安二郎（「東京物語」「晩春」），溝口健二（「山椒太夫」「雨月物語」），成瀬巳喜男（「浮雲」「めし」），黒澤明（「羅生門」「七人の侍」），木下恵介（「二十四の瞳」「日本の悲劇」）など世界的にも認められた監督が輩出し，ベネチア映画祭やカンヌ映画祭など海外の映画祭で激賞された名作が数多く生まれた。これを受けた1960年前後は娯楽性の高い映画を中心として隆盛をきわめ，観客動員は11億人にも達した。

しかし，ブームに乗った粗製濫造の安易さがやがて客を遠ざけ，作品・興行ともしだいに衰退していくことになった。

映画産業の展望

映画界は依然として低調気味にあるとは言え，最近になって新しい傾向も見られ将来への展望が開けようとしている。その一つは，従来の伝統の中からではなく，TVやCFなどから新しい才能が輩出していることがある。北野武，周防正行，岩井俊二，竹中直人などの作品がいずれも好評で，海外でも受賞するなど高く評価されはじめている。アニメーションの分野も活発で，手塚治虫の「鉄腕アトム」「ジャングル大帝」をはじめ大友克洋の「アキラ」，宮崎駿の「風の谷のナウシカ」「もののけ姫」「千と千尋の神隠し」など，内容的に質の高い作品が作られ，内外ともに人気を博している。

興行面では，ショッピングセンターやレストラン街とも一体化された大型映画館シネマ・コンプレックスが増え，また最終回の後に上映されるレイトショーや，車に乗ったまま映画を見るドライブイン・シアターも増加傾向にある。さらにビデオによって過去の映画も手軽に見られるようになるなど，映画の見方も多様化し，ファン層も広がった。1985年に東京国際映画祭が発足して新人育成の新機軸を出したほか，特色をもった映画祭も毎年いくつか開催され，ようやく日本映画の低迷も打開できそうな下地が整いつつあると言えよう。

1996年に，主人公の寅さんを演じた渥美清の死とともに終幕となった「男はつらいよ」シリーズ（1969年第１作）は，日本人が心の底にもっている心情や人間関係のあり方を描いて多くの観客に支持された。その48作に及ぶ最長記録はギネスブックにも記載されている。

The first film shown in Japan was an import shown in 1896, and the first Japanese film was made the next year in 1897. Thus Japanese film history goes back over 100 years.

Golden Age

The postwar period on both sides of 1950 is often referred to as the golden age of Japanese film. Among the outstanding directors who were active then are *Ozu Yasujirou* ("*Tokyo Story*" and "*Late Spring*"), *Mizoguchi Kenji* ("*Sansho the Bailiff*" and "*Ugetsu Monogatari*"), *Naruse Mikio* ("*Floating Clouds*" and "*Repast*"), *Kurosawa Akira* ("*Rashomon*" and "*Seven Samurai*"), and *Kinoshita Keisuke* ("*Twenty-four Eyes*" and "*A Japanese Tragedy*"). This was a prolific period with many films winning awards at the Venice Film Festival, Cannes, and other festivals. Following this era, the 1960s saw many films made for pure entertainment, and film audiences topped 1.1 billion in a good year.

Yet there were also many inferior films made to ride this wave, and these gave Japanese films a bad name and made it very difficult for individual films and film companies to make money.

Outlook for the Industry

Even though the film industry is still lackluster, there have been a few developments recently that appear to bode well for Japanese films. One of these is that new talent has come up, not through traditional channels but in television and even advertising. Among the people whose work has been well received and have won awards overseas are *Kitano Takeshi*, *Suou Masayuki*, *Iwai Shunji*, and *Takenaka Naoto*. Animation is another fertile field, and *Tezuka Osumu's* "*Astroboy*" and "*Kimba the White Lion*" have been followed by *Ootomo Katsuhiro's* "*Akira*," *Miyazaki Huyao's* "*Nausicaa of the Valley of Wind*," "*Princess Mononoke*" and "*Spirited Away*," and a number of other works that are very well done and have won worldwide acclaim.

On the business side, a number of "cinema complexes" have been built—massive theaters integrated with shopping centers and restaurant complexes—and audiences have also been attracted to "late shows" shown after the last scheduled films as well as drive-in theaters. At the same time, the older films are now highly accessible on video, meaning that more people are watching more different films. In 1985, the Tokyo International Film Festival was started to encourage new talent, and there are also a number of special-theme film festivals every year. The ground is being laid for a recovery.

The "*Tora-san*" series starring *Atsumi Kiyoshi* was brought to a sad close in 1996 with *Atsumi*'s death. Starting with the first one released in 1969, this series consistently captured Japanese hearts with its deft portrayal of Japanese psychology. So popular was the series that its 48 installments are enshrined in the *Guinness Book of World Records*.

碁(囲碁)・将棋

碁も将棋も二人で勝ち負けを争う室内ゲームである。

碁は，361目の盤上に交互に白と黒の碁石を置き，最終的にどちらが広く地域を占めたかを競う，きわめて頭脳的な要素をもつゲーム。小学生から年寄りまで，幅広いファンがあり，囲碁人口は1000万人に上る。日本棋院，関西棋院の二つの組織があり，囲碁を職業とするプロ棋士は約500人(うち日本棋院400人) いる。

将棋はチェスの東洋版と考えればいい。盤面で，王将を中心とした各20個の駒(こま)を交互に動かし，相手の王将を捕らえた側が勝ちとなる。古くから大衆ゲームとして広まり，現在でも盛んに行われ，将棋人口は2000万人と言われている。日本将棋連盟に加わるプロ棋士は4段以上で約170人(うち退役は約30人)，新聞社などが主催する主なビッグゲームは10を超える。

碁も将棋も，遣唐使や入唐僧などによって中国から伝えられたものとされ，特に将棋はインドが発祥と言われている。江戸時代には，幕府が専門の棋士を抱えていたほか，町人にも碁や将棋を大いに奨励した。おそらく，庶民の頭脳訓練の手段として考えたのだろう。

碁盤と碁石，将棋盤と駒は，全国どこででも売っていて，数百円という安いものから，数十万円・数百万円という高級品までがある。また，古い家庭には先祖伝来という碁盤や将棋盤がよくあり，家宝になっているケースもある。

マージャン

マージャンも中国からの伝来。4人で楽しむ複雑なゲームで，骨材と竹材を組み合わせたものに彫刻が施された牌(ぱい)が中心。さまざまな種類の牌合わせて136個を使い，親を決めた後，それぞれが順番に牌を取捨し，規定の組み合わせを早く完了したほうが勝ちというルールである。組み合わせはいくつもあって，それにより点数が違う。

日本には1920年ごろに伝わり，比較的後発の伝来遊戯である。1970年ぐらいまではマージャン熱が盛んだったが，近年はゲームセンター，ＴＶゲーム，パソコンなどの登場により若い人の間で人気が薄れ，マージャンはやや下火となっている。

Go (*Igo*), *Shougi*, and *Mahjong*

*Go** and *Shougi**

Both *go* and *shougi* are two-player board games. *Go* is played with black and white stones on a 19 by 19 grid board with 361 intersections. The players alternate in placing stones on intersections and the player who captures the most territory wins. With the nearly infinite variations of moves possible, *go* is a highly intellectual game enjoyed by 10 million Japanese of all ages from grade school children to retirees. Professionally the game is played under the auspices of two organizations, the *Nihon Kiin* and the *Kansai Kiin*. Today there are approximately 500 professional *go* players in Japan, 400 of them in the *Nihon Kiin*.

Shougi is an Oriental version of chess. Each player has 20 pieces, and the object of the game is to capture the opponent's king. Widely played since ancient times, *shougi* remains popular today with an estimated 20 million adherents of the game in Japan alone. As with *go, shougi* players are ranked by skill level. The Japan *Shougi* Association is made up of around 170 professional *shougi* players of the fourth rank and above (approximately 30 of them retired). There are about a dozen major *shougi* tournaments each year, primarily sponsored by the newspaper companies.

Both *go* and *shougi* are believed to have been introduced into Japan in ancient times by Japanese emissaries and monks to China. *Shougi* traces its origins back all the way to India. In the *Edo* period, the *Tokugawa* shogunate established *go* and *shougi* masters and encouraged the playing of these games among the common people as intellectual exercises.

Shougi and *go* sets are sold throughout Japan and range in price from a few hundred yen to hundreds of thousands and even millions of yen. Older households are likely to have *go* and *shougi* boards that have been passed down from generation to generation, many of them treasured as family heirlooms.

Mahjong*

A complex game played by four players using 136 tiles made of ivory and bamboo, mahjong is played with each player alternating in drawing and discarding tiles. Whoever accumulates a complete "hand" of one of the many possible combinations of tiles possible wins the game. A player's score depends on what combination of tiles s/he has.

Mahjong was not introduced into Japan until the early 1920s, but it was very popular for the next half-century. Recently, however, it seems to be in decline as young people drift off to video arcades and computers.

公営ギャンブルの種類

日本では，ギャンブルは法律で禁止されている。ルーレットやダイスなどをギャンブルとして楽しむ場所は日本にはない。ただし，地方公共団体などが行う競馬（けいば）・競輪（けいりん）・競艇（きょうてい）・オートレース・宝くじは特別に許可されていて，人気を集めている。

•競馬　日本では古代から，神社の祭事あるいは宮廷の儀式としての競馬というものはあった。その姿を現在までとどめているのが京都・上賀茂（かみがも）神社の「賀茂の競馬（くらべうま）」と言われている。しかし，近代競馬は，19世紀後半に横浜在住の外国人が始めたのが最初である。日本政府も近代競馬が日本馬の改良に役だつことに着目して認めるようになった。日本にはギャンブルを罪悪視する気風があったため非難もあって，レジャーとして人気を得るようになったのは戦後になってからで，最近では若い女性にも人気がある。欧米の競馬がイギリスの貴族・王室を中心に発達し，上流階級色の強いものであるのに対し，日本の競馬は庶民のギャンブルとなっている点が特徴である。

現在，中央競馬と地方競馬に分かれて開催されており，1995年の売り上げは合わせて４兆5000億円，入場者数は2600万人となっている。

•競輪　プロ選手の自転車競走。戦後の日本経済の復興と，自転車産業の振興を図ることを目的として1948年から行われた競輪は，一時は公営ギャンブルの王座を占めたほどの人気があった。獲得賞金がプロスポーツ選手として初めて１億円を超えたのは，競輪の中野浩一であった。

•競艇　モーターボート競漕で，日本では後発の公営ギャンブル。

•オートレース　自動２輪および自動４輪車の競走。

•宝くじ　番号を記入した抽選券を発売し，抽選に当たった券を当選金と引き換える。宝くじ一枚の当選金最高額は，宝くじ発売価格の20万倍と決められている。江戸時代には「富くじ」と呼ばれる同形式の宝くじが流行していた。

パチンコの隆盛

パチンコは大衆遊戯で，電動式バネで鋼鉄の玉をはじき，特定の穴に入れると多くの出玉を得，それを景品に換えることができる日本独特のゲームである。業界全体の年商は一時は30兆円を超えた。最近はプリペイド・カード（代金前払いカード）を用いたCR(card reader)機が全盛で，ギャンブル性の高い機種が増えたことから批判が高まり，1997年には年商22兆円まで下がった。

Legalized Gambling, *Pachinko*

Legalized Gambling

Most gambling is illegal in Japan, and there are no casinos where you can play roulette or shoot craps for entertainment. However, there is legalized gambling sponsored or sanctioned by various local governments, including racing (horses, bicycles, motorboats, motorcycles, and cars) and lotteries.

• **Horse Races** Japan has a horse-racing tradition going back to the ancient shrine festivals and court ceremonies, and these practices are still to be seen in the *Kamo no Kurabeuma* at *Kyouto*'s (Kyoto's) *Kamigamo* Shrine. Modern horse racing was introduced into Japan in the late 19th century by the foreign community in *Yokohama*, and it was quickly approved by the Japanese government in the hope that it would contribute to improving the breed for Japanese horse ranches. Yet it was not until after the war that racing became widely popular – recently among young women as well – even though there was still considerable criticism from people who saw gambling as a vice. In contrast to the aristocratic air which pervades horse racing in the United States and England from its association with the British nobility, Japanese racing is decidedly a gambling pursuit for the average man.

With separate associations for metropolitan circuits and rural circuits, horse racing grossed ¥4.5 trillion in 1995 from a total gate of 26 million.

• **Bicycle Racing** Powered by professional bicyclists, bicycle racing was started in 1948 to stimulate Japan's economic recovery and promote the bicycle industry, and it caught on to become the top gambling sport at one point. Indicative of the sport's popularity, the first Japanese professional athlete to win over ¥100 million was *Nakano Kouichi*—a professional bicycle racer.

• **Other Racing** Motorboat racing is a latecomer to the world of Japanese gambling, but it has made considerable advances with racers competing for rich purses. In addition, Japan has both motorcycle and automobile racing.

• **Lotteries** Lotteries in Japan sell tickets, each with a different number, and the holders of the lucky numbers win prizes. At present, lotteries are not allowed to give a top prize more than 200,000 times the price of a ticket. Vestiges of the *tomi-kuji* under the *Tokugawa* shogunate, these lotteries are just as popular now as they ever were.

Pachinko

Pachinko is a very common entertainment. Basically, it uses a spring device to shoot a small metal ball across a vertical panel with holes in it. Depending on what holes the balls go into, the players get bonus balls that can later be exchanged for prizes. In the past total annual sales in this industry regularly topped 30 trillion yen. Faced with criticism that recently introduced machines that take prepaid cards have increased the element of gambling, the industry has suffered a decline in revenue. In 1997 sales were down to 22 trillion yen.

現代の遊び

日本の子供たちがしだいに外遊びをしなくなっていることが，各種の調査で明らかになっている。ベネッセ・コーポレーションの調査（1994年）によると，「外遊びが多い」は小学校4年生の男子で48.6%，女子で33.1%であったのに対し，小学校6年生の男子では39.4%，女子では17.7%であった。逆に「室内遊びが多い」は小学校4年生の男子で19.0%，女子で23.1%に対し，小学校6年生の男子では26.0%，女子では50.8%であった。この結果から，室内遊びは小学校中学年から高学年にかけて，特に女子で急激に増加していることがわかる。

「遊びの体験」を見ても，「テレビゲームで遊ぶ」「一人でテレビやマンガを見る」が上位にあり，「どろんこ遊びをする」は「何回もある」5.9%，「わりとある」14.3%と最下位を示している。テレビゲームで遊ぶ子供は70%以上おり，街のゲームセンターやパソコン店，デパートのテレビゲーム売り場でゲームに打ち興じる子供たちも多い。家庭でも，小遣いをためたり親にねだったりして，数種類のゲームマシーンや子供専用の高価なパソコンをもっている子供もいる。日本の現代っ子たちが，いかにブラウン管などによる間接的な遊びに熱中しているかがわかるだろう。

こうした子供たちの「遊びの室内化」の背景には，「受験戦争の低年齢化」による塾通いのために時間的なゆとりがないことや，かつてはどこにでもあった空き地などの「遊びの空間」の減少，また「子供の数」の減少などがあると考えられる。

昔の遊び

昔は，子供どうし誘い合って家の外で体を動かすことが遊びだった。男の子なら，歴史上の英雄や漫画の人気者が書かれた丸や四角のボール紙をお互いに地面に置いて，自分のもので相手のものを裏返したりはじき飛ばしたりする「*メンコ遊び」や，小さな模様付きのガラス玉を，これも相手のものにぶつけて取ったり取られたりする「ビー玉遊び」。女の子なら，目隠しをした子の周りを歌を歌いながら輪を作って回り，歌が終わったときに後ろに来た子の名を当てて遊ぶ「かごめかごめ」，鬼を一人決めて，みんなは鬼に捕まらないよう逃げ回る「鬼ごっこ」などをして過ごすのがつねだった。家の中での遊びには「*あやとり」や「*お手玉」などもある。こうした友達との遊びを通じて，子供は子供なりにルールを守ることや，人との付き合い方を学んだのである。

お正月に見られた「凧(たこ)上げ」や「*羽根付き」なども年々見られなくなり，遊びながら学ぶという遊びの原点が忘れられつつある。

Modern Amusements

Japanese children do not play outside as much as they used to. A 1994 Benesse study asking elementary school children if they played mostly outside or inside got "outside" responses from only 48.6% of the boys and 33.1% of the girls at the fourth-grade level. By sixth grade, these figures were 39.4% for boys and 17.7% for girls. By contrast, "inside" got 19.0% of the boys and 23.1% of the girls at the fourth grade level and 26.0% of the boys and 50.8% of the girls in sixth grade. The older the child, the more likely s/he—especially she—is to play indoors.

The top responses to "how do you spend your free time?" were "playing video games" and "watching TV or reading *manga* (comics) by myself." At the bottom of the list was "getting dirty playing" with only 5.9% saying "frequently" and 14.3% "not infrequently." Over 70% of the children said they play video games, and children crowd the game arcades and eagerly try out the latest games at the computer stores and department stores. A lot of children have their own game machines that they either saved up for or wheedled their parents into buying for them. Japanese children are playing, but it is virtual games on monitors, rather than real games out with their friends on the playground.

Among the many reasons advanced to explain this indoor shift are that children are too busy studying, that they only have little bits and pieces of time here and there, that there are fewer vacant lots and other places to play outdoors, and that there are fewer other children to play with.

Old-fashioned Games

Play used to be something physical that kids got together to do outdoors. One of the games boys played is *menko*, in which two or more opponents would lay out small circular or square pieces of cardboard decorated with pictures of popular historical heroes or cartoon characters and then each boy would throw other similar pieces (*menko*) down on the ground to create a gust which would flip his opponent's over. Another game boys played is marbles. Girls' games included *kagome-kagome*, in which several girls dance and sing in a circle around a blindfolded girl who tries to guess who is behind her when they stop. Another was *tag (oni-gokko)* with the *oni* being "it" and trying to catch the others. *Ayatori* (cat's cradle) and *otedama* (a form of juggling) were also popular indoor games. In all of these activities, the games helped the children learn how to follow rules and get along with other people. Yet these games are largely forgotten today, and even the traditional kite-flying and Japanese battledore at New Year's have largely disappeared. Play is no longer the socializing process it once was.

Notes

■2. The Japanese Day

NHK Japan's national broadcasting system. It is the only public broadcasting company in Japan, and it is supported solely by subscriber fees paid by television owners. NHK has two AM stations, one FM station, two television stations (one for general broadcasting and another for educational programming), and two satellite channels. It also handles Radio Japan's international broadcasts.

■5. Housing

condominiums (マンション) *Manshon* is a generic term referring to reinforced concrete multi-unit dwellings. *Manshon* can be either rented or purchased. While more impressive-sounding than apartment, *manshon* does not have the same meaning of a large, impressive residence that mansion has in English.

tile roofs (瓦屋根) The traditional Japanese home is built of wood and has a tiled roof.

sliding-door partitions (ふすまや障子) *Fusuma* are sliding doors separating rooms in a traditional Japanese home. Made of wooden frames covered on both sides with paper or cloth, *fusuma* slide along grooves cut into wooden beams in the ceiling and floor. *Fusuma* are usually decorated with pictures and patterns. *Shouji* are gridded sliding doors covered with a single layer of paper on one side. Some *shouji* are partially fitted with glass instead of paper. In contemporary Japanese homes, which usually have both Japanese- and Western-style rooms, *shouji* are only used in the Japanese-style rooms, where they fulfill the same function as curtains or blinds.

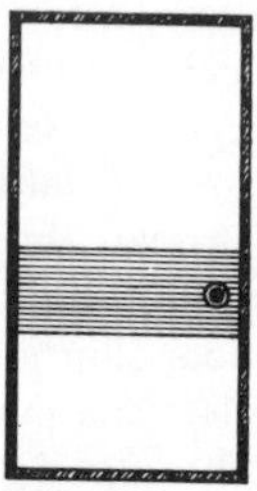

△*Fusuma*

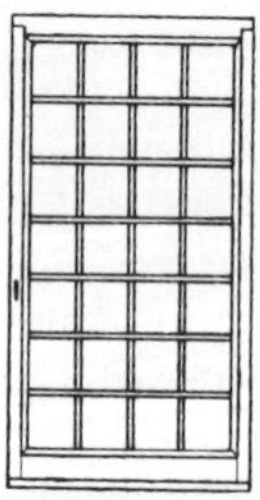

△*Shouji*

■6. Consumer Durables

closet (押し入れ) A closet in a typical Japanese-style room. A recess with its *fusuma* door flush with the wall, the *oshiire* is used to store bedding during the day and other things year-round.

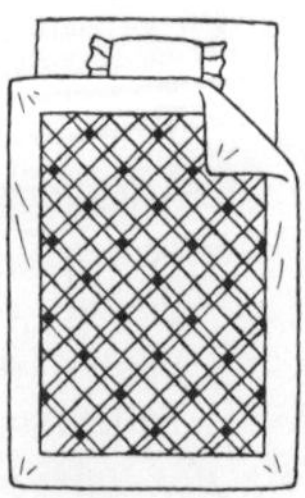

△*Futon*

△*Kotatsu*

■7. Western Clothing and the *Kimono*

***sumou* wrestlers** (力士) The *rikishi* is also called a *sumoutori*.

obi (帯) A broad sash worn around the waist with a

●*Kimono*

kimono. There are several variations, and men and women wear distinctly different styles of *obi*.

hakama (袴) A pleated, skirt-like garment worn over a *kimono*. Worn by men on formal and highly ceremonial occasions. Worn by some women only upon graduation from a school.

furi-sode (振袖) *Kimono* with sleeves between 95 and 115 cm deep. Worn by unmarried women for the coming-of-age ceremony, upon graduation, and on other special occasions such as a friend's wedding. Usually decorated with vibrant, colorful motifs.

■8. The Japanese Diet

***miso* soup** (みそ汁) A soup made of *miso* stock with vegetables, fish, and other ingredients. *Miso* is a bean paste made of steamed soybeans and a fermenting agent, and is a basic flavoring in Japanese cooking.

soba (そば) Fine noodles made of buckwheat flour kneaded with wheat flour. Eaten either steeped in a hot broth or cold with a soy sauce-based dip.

udon (うどん) Thick white noodles made from wheat flour.

△*Soba (mori-soba)*

△*Udon*

△*Sushi*

△*Tenpura*

△*Inari-zushi*

■9. Japanese Food

non-glutinous rice (うるち米) This is different from the glutinous rice pounded into *mochi* rice cakes.

abura-age (油揚げ) A common food, *abura-age* is often an ingredient in *miso* soup. *Inari-zushi* is *abura-age* cut in half to form small pouches which are stuffed with vinegared rice.

seasoned with soy sauce (おひたし) This is a simple side dish of boiled greens, usually a leafy green vegetable such as spinach, seasoned with soy sauce and topped with *katsuo-bushi* dried bonito flakes.

■10. Traditional Japanese Dishes

△*Honzen-ryouri*

△*Cha-kaiseki*

△*Kaiseki-ryouri*

△*Shoujin-ryouri*

△*O-sechi-ryouri*

△A set of lacquer boxes

■11. Marriage and Divorce

△*Shintou*-style wedding

wedding (結婚式) Three types of marriage ceremony are common in Japan: *Shintou*, Buddhist, and Christian. The choice of ceremony depends less on a couple's religious inclinations than on which ceremony they find most attractive. The marriage ceremony is usually followed by an elaborate reception.

■12. Funerals

△Burning incense

posthumous Buddhist name (戒名) *Kaimyou*, a posthumous Buddhist name, is usually based on the deceased's social status and quality of life. *Kaimyou* are commonly purchased, the larger the payment the more illustrious the name. The *kaimyou* is engraved on the gravestone and the deceased's tablet kept in the home altar.

■13. *Shougatsu* and *Bon*

first week of January (松の内) *Matsu-no-uchi* is the period of time around New Year's during which pine decorations are displayed. Formerly 15 days, *matsu-no-uchi* is today usually observed for only seven days.

zouni (雑煮) A soup with *mochi* as its main ingredient, *zouni* is prepared in many different ways according to regional and family custom.

nengajou (年賀状) The post office stocks New Year's cards mailed in late December and delivers them during the first days of the year. Many people use special *nengajou* issued

△*Kado-matsu*

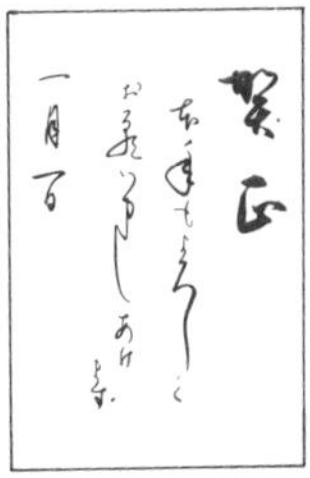

△*Nengajou*

△**Traditional Japanese hair styles**

by the Post and Telecommunications Ministry and printed with lottery numbers. In 1996, 4.1 billion *nengajou* of this type were issued.

bon-odori (盆踊り) Originally these were dances to console departing spirits, but today *bon-odori* are simply enjoyed as entertainment.

△**Flute and drum**

■14. Children's Festivals

sekku (節句) Originally days marking seasonal changes, there were five officially recognized *sekku* in the *Edo* period. Only the March 3 *Momo no Sekku* (Doll Festival) and May 5 *Tango no Sekku* (Children's Day) are still observed today.

armor (よろい) A suit of armor usually made of metal or leather strips sewn together with silken cords.

koi-nobori (こいのぼり) Made of paper or cloth, these are streamers made to look like carp and strung on poles outside of the house. Because the carp will swim upstream and jump waterfalls to get to its spawning grounds, it is considered a symbol of perseverance and valiant effort.

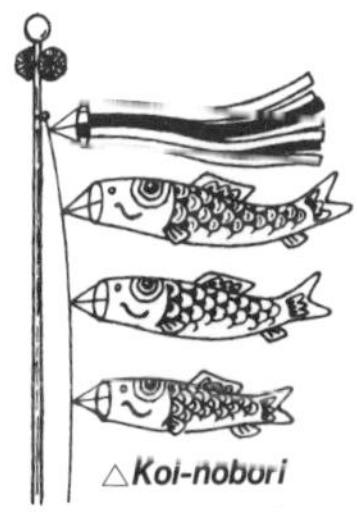

△*Koi-nobori*

kashiwa-mochi (かしわもち) A *mochi* rice cake wrapped in an oak leaf.

birthday (数え年) *Kazoe-doshi* is an arcane method of counting age by which a child is considered one year old at birth and a year is added every New Year's instead of on the child's actual birthday.

△*Hina-ningyou*

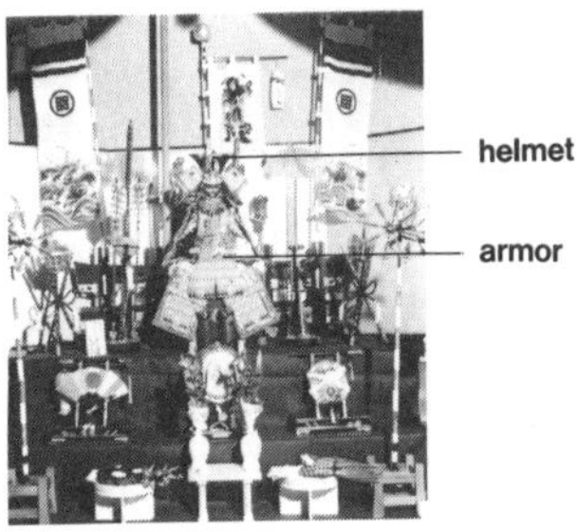

△*Gogatsu-ningyou*

△Rice paddle

△*Binzasara no Mai*

■15. *Tanabata* and Christmas

shuuji (習字) The practice of penmanship, primarily calligraphy executed with a brush.

multicolored streamers of paper (短冊) Thin strips of paper used to write *haiku*, *waka*, and other forms of poetry.

■16. Japanese Festivals

yukata (浴衣) *Yukata* is an informal cotton *kimono* worn in the summer. White *yukata* with stenciled patterns are common.

famous warrior-heroes from ancient China (三国志) Heroes from the Chinese historical novel, *Sanguo zhi yanyi* (Romance of the Three Kingdoms).

Katou Kiyomasa (加藤清正) (1562-1611) A *daimyou* of the *Azuchi-Momoyama* and early *Edo* periods, *Katou Kiyomasa* led both of *Hideyoshi*'s invasions of Korea and later served under *Tokugawa Ieyasu*.

mikoshi (みこし) A portable shrine carried in festivals.

binzasara (びんざさら) A long, rattle-like percussion instrument made by stringing numerous wooden clappers together.

Kamo no Kurabeuma (賀茂の競馬) A horse race held annually at the *Kamigamo* Shrine in northern *Kyouto* (*Kyoto*) on May 5.

Aoi Matsuri (葵祭り) An annual joint festival of the *Kamigamo* and *Shimogamo* Shrines in *Kyouto* (*Kyoto*) held on May 15.

△*Nebuta* Festival

△*Sanja* Matsuri

△*Gion* Festival

△*Hakata Dontaku*

△*Hachimaki*

△*Koban*

■18. Gift-giving

small towels (手ぬぐい) A rectangular piece of cotton cloth (about 30×80cm). In addition to functioning as a towel, the *tenugui* is also sometimes worn on the head (*hachimaki*) in different styles especially during festivals and by craftsmen and workers in various fields.

■19. Newspapers

nation's conscience (木鐸) *Bokutaku* is a bell with a wooden clapper used in ancient China to summon people whenever a new decree or law was to be announced. It is often used in Japanese as a simile for a leader who guides the people.

■24. Public Order in Japan

koban (交番) See picture.

■27. The Japanese Education System

University of *Toukyou* (東京大学) Japan's oldest national university, the University of *Toukyou* is considered an elite school and its entrance examinations are extremely difficult.

rounin (浪人) Originally meaning masterless *samurai*, *rounin* today is used to refer to someone who failed to get into the school (or company) of his/her choice and is devoting himself/herself to another try next year.

△University of *Toukyou*

■30. Tourism

Isekou*, *Kumanokou*, *Fujikou (伊勢講, 熊野講, 富士講) The *Isekou* traveled to *Ise* Shrine; the *Kumanokou* to the shrines of *Kumano Honguu Taisha*; and the *Fujikou* to Mt *Fuji*.

Minobukou*, *Naritakou (身延講, 成田講) The *Minobukou* visited the temple of *Kuonji* on Mt. *Minobu* and the *Naritakou* went to *Naritasan Shinshouji*.

△Hot springs

■31. Japan's Hot Springs

Nanakuri* and *Tamatsukuri (ななくりの湯, 玉造の湯) *Nanakuri*, now known as the *Sakakibara* hot springs, is in *Mie* prefecture, and the *Tamatsukuri* hot springs is in *Shimane* prefecture.

■32. Cherry-blossom and Maple-leaf Viewing

groundcloths (ござ, ビニールシート) The *goza*, a mat of woven rush reeds, is commonly used as a groundcloth, as are plastic *furoshiki*. The *furoshiki* is a square cloth used to wrap and carry things. Called a *furoshiki* because it was originally a cloth used to stand on after getting out of the bath.

△*Hana-mi*

■33. Baseball and Soccer

Nagashima Shigeo (長嶋茂雄) (1936-) *Nagashima* joined the *Yomiuri* Giants in 1958. Known as Mr Giants up to his retirement in 1974, *Nagashima* was a flamboyant and highly popular player. He was manager of the *Yomiuri* Giants until his retirement in 2002.

Ou Sadaharu (王貞治) (1940-) A Tokyo-born and -bred Taiwanese, *Ou* is famous for his home run record. He managed the *Yomiuri* Giants for several years and is now manager of the *Daiei* Hawks.

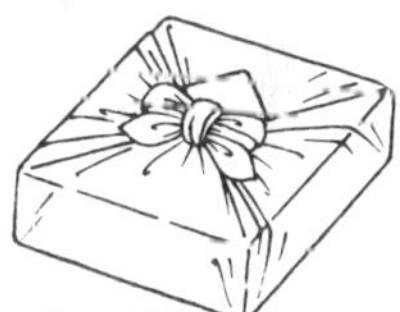

△*Furoshiki*

●Pre-bout ritual

■35. *Sumou*

***sumou* ring** (土俵) A raised dais of packed earth with a ring of sand in the middle.

yokozuna (横綱) The highest rank in *sumou*, a *yokozuna* is so-called because of the twisted rope (*yokozuna*) he is privileged to wear.

Futabayama (双葉山) (1912-68) *Yokozuna Futabayama* is credited with winning a record 69 bouts straight.

retirement (親方) Retired *sumou* wrestlers who remain active in the sport even after they retire are called *toshiyori*. The term of address for a *toshiyori* is *oyakata*.

■39. *Go, Shougi*, and Mahjong

△*Go*

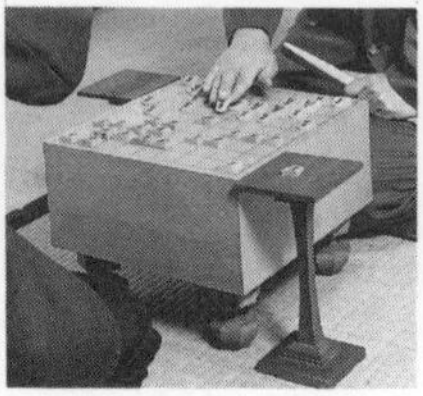

△*Shougi*

△Mahjong

■41. Children's Games

△*Menko*

△*Ayatori*

△*O-tedama*

△Japanese battledore

PART・3

日本の社会
JAPANESE SOCIETY

天皇制

日本の統治のしくみは「天皇」抜きでは語れない。日本が国家として誕生して以来，国家の「象徴」としての地位を維持し続けてきたのは天皇である。ただ，天皇が直接，具体的に国家を統治したのは，古代を除いてほとんどなく，現実の政治を行っていたのは，貴族であり，武家を中心とした幕府であった。近代になって，いわゆる「明治憲法」が施行され，天皇が憲法上の統治者となったが，政治制度は「議院内閣制」が採られ，政治の責任は政府が担っていた。

第二次世界大戦で日本が敗戦となり，マッカーサー司令部の主導で憲法が改正され，1947年*5月3日に新憲法が施行された。この新憲法で，主権者は「天皇」から「国民」になった。しかし憲法第1条には，天皇は「日本国の象徴であり日本国民統合の象徴」とうたわれ，憲法第6条で総理大臣，最高裁判所長官の任命，また第7条で次の10項目の国事行為を行うことになっている。①憲法改正，法律・条約の公布　②国会の召集　③衆議院の解散　④選挙の公示　⑤国務大臣などの任免と認証　⑥大赦などの実施　⑦栄典の授与　⑧批准書・外交文書の認証　⑨外国大・公使の接受　⑩儀式の執行。いずれも内閣の助言・承認によって行うもので，実体的には，天皇には何らの権限はなく，本来の伝統的な「天皇制」の姿に戻ったと言われている。この「権威(天皇)」と「権力(政府)」の並立して機能していたのが，日本の統治のしくみの大きな特色である。

日本国憲法の特色

新憲法と旧憲法との相違は，主権が天皇から国民に移ったことのほか，基本的人権の尊重が強く打ち出されたこと，「戦争の放棄」(第2章9条)が明記されたことである。また行政，立法，司法の三権分立が明確にされ，立法府としての国会は，国民の選挙によって定数480人の衆議院，定数242人の参議院との二院制で，国会議員の中から首相を指名する議院内閣制をとっている。首相は，各省庁の長である国務大臣を任命し，国会議員を過半数とする内閣を組織する。司法府である裁判所は，地方(または簡易)，高等，最高の三審制を採っている。

国民の政治参加は，投票によって国会議員を選ぶこと，最高裁判所の裁判官の国民審査，地方自治体の首長・議会議員の選挙・罷免，さらに憲法改正の際の国民投票への参加(衆参両院の各3分の2以上，国民の過半数)などが行えることになっている。

Government

Imperial Foundations

The Imperial structure is an integral part of government in Japan, and the Emperor has served as the symbol of the state ever since the Japanese nation was founded. Yet the Emperor has seldom exercised direct rule, except for the very ancient past, and it has been the nobility and the warrior class that has actually run the government. Even after the promulgation of the *Meiji* Constitution in 1889 making the Emperor the titular ruler, the system was actually run by the Cabinet with the ministers responsible for national government.

Following defeat in World War II, a new constitution was drawn up at the direction of the occupation forces headed by the Supreme Commander for the Allied Powers, Douglas MacArthur, and went into effect on May 3,* 1947. Under this postwar constitution, sovereignty shifted from the Emperor to the people. Yet Article 1 states that the Emperor is "the symbol of the State and of the unity of the people", and Article 6 declares that the Prime Minister and the Chief Judge of the Supreme Court are to be appointed by the Emperor. Article 7 follows this by enumerating ten acts in matters of state that the Emperor performs: (i) promulgating amendments to the constitution, laws, and treaties, (ii) convoking the Diet, (iii) dissolving the House of Representatives, (iv) proclaiming general elections, (v) attesting the appointment and dismissal of Ministers of State and other officials, (vi) attesting general amnesty and other reprieves, (vii) awarding honors, (viii) attesting instruments of ratification and other diplomatic documents, (ix) receiving foreign ambassadors and ministers, and (x) performing ceremonial functions. All of these duties are performed with the advice and approval of the Cabinet, and the Emperor himself does not have any independent powers. Japan has, so to speak, reverted to the tradition in which the Emperor reigns but the government rules.

Constitution of Japan

In addition to the shift of sovereignty, the *Meiji* and postwar constitutions also differ in that the postwar constitution embodies strong respect for basic human rights and (in Article 9) clearly renounces war. There is also a clear distinction among the three branches of government: legislative, executive, and judicial. The legislative branch has a 480-member House of Representatives and a 242-member House of Councilors, all 722 members being elected by direct vote of the people. Because it is a cabinet form of government, the Prime Minister is designated by the Diet from among its members. In turn, the Prime Minister appoints the Ministers of State (a majority of whom must be Diet members) to head the executive ministries and agencies, and the Cabinet serves at the Diet's sufferance. The judiciary is a three-tier structure with district courts, high courts, and the Supreme Court.

The people participate in politics through voting to elect Diet members, to approve or disapprove Supreme Court judges, to elect and dismiss local officials, and to decide national referendums on amendments to the Constitution (passage requiring the approval of two-thirds of each house of the Diet and a majority of the popular votes cast).

万世一系，125代目の当主

日本最古の歴史書『古事記』，『日本書紀』などによれば現在の天皇は，「万世一系」の125代目の当主である。古代国家の成立以来日本を支配していた天皇家，つまり「皇室」は，政治的権力者というよりも宗教的・文化的支柱として，国民の尊敬を集めていた。時には，実質上の権力に利用されながら，歴史上存続してきた。日本の歴史は天皇の歴史，天皇と新しい時代の権力者との政治史であると言える。その一つの証拠に，日本には*元号という天皇の時代ごとの年号の数え方がずっと続いている。武士の時代（鎌倉時代～江戸時代）には天皇は不遇な存在だったが，下級武士が革命を起こした明治維新では，天皇はおみこしのように担ぎだされて強力に復活した。天皇は時代の中で浮き沈みしながら，権力や権威の度合いを強めたり弱めたりして存続してきたが，その本質は，宗教的な起源と関係がある。

天皇と文化遺産

日本人の宗教観は，一神教でなく，多神教だと一般的に言われている。日本には，八百万（やおよろず）の神がおり，その神の中心にあるのが，天皇家の先祖である「天照大神（あまてらすおおみかみ）」である。天皇の神格化は，ここから生まれたものである。戦前は「現人神（あらひとがみ）」と言われ神道の象徴であったが，戦後天皇自ら「人間宣言」をして，その神格化を否定した。神格化は，明治維新を起こした下層武士，また軍部が，自分たちの権威づけのため天皇を利用したもので，庶民は「天皇さん」と親しみをこめて天皇を呼んでいた。ただ天皇家には古代からの日本の神々を祭る祭司としての役割，また奈良の正倉院が象徴するような文化遺産の継承者，歌会・雅楽・神事など日本古来の芸術・文化が今も天皇家に継承されている。現在の天皇も皇居にある水田で，水稲の田植えや稲刈りを宮中神事として行っている。

日本が第二次世界大戦で連合国に降伏したとき，受諾にあたって日本政府が最も気にしたのは，「国体の護持」，つまり「天皇制」の維持であった。占領政策においても，天皇を中心とする立憲君主制にするか共和制を採るかが大きな焦点になったが，「天皇制を廃止すれば，日本は混乱しアメリカの占領は失敗する」という米国政府の判断から天皇制が維持された。ただ，旧憲法では主権は天皇にあったが，新憲法では，主権は国民に，天皇の地位は第１条で「天皇は日本国の象徴であって，この地位は，主権の存する日本国民の総意に基づく」と日本の「象徴」となった。日本人は，天皇家を民主主義との整合性において矛盾を感じながらも，それに相反する天皇家に「権威」を置くことのメリットを選択している。

The Imperial Institution

Unbroken Lineage

If the *Kojiki* and *Nihon Shoki*, Japan's oldest chronicles, are to be believed, the current Emperor is the 125th in an unbroken line. Ruling Japan ever since its founding as a state, the Emperor (which is to say the Imperial Court) has won the respect of the people more as a spiritual and cultural leader than as a political leader. As such, the institution has survived, at times in the service of the country's actual rulers, and it may be said that the history of Japan is also the history of its Emperors and how the Emperor has interacted with the political rulers in every age. Symbolizing the Emperor's centrality is *gengou**—the practice of counting history in terms of Imperial reigns. Although the Emperor was largely ignored when the warrior class ruled (from the *Kamakura* period through the *Edo* period), the lower-ranking *samurai* who led the revolution known as the *Meiji* Restoration in the mid-1800s forcefully thrust the Emperor to the political forefront. The Emperor has had more or less temporal authority depending upon the era, but his essential spiritual nature has remained unchanged.

The Cultural Legacy

It is generally accepted that the Japanese sense of religion is not monotheistic but is polytheistic. Japan is a land of innumerable gods, and at their center is *Amaterasu Oomikami*, said to be the direct ancestor of the Imperial line. It is this belief that has given rise to the idea of the Emperor's divinity. Before the war, the Emperor was assumed to be a living god and was at the center of State *Shintou*, but the Emperor renounced his divinity in 1946. Even before that, the idea of the Emperor's divinity was merely a convenient fiction created in the *Meiji* Restoration, and the people viewed the Emperor as a familiar figure to be referred to as "*Tennou-san.*" Yet the Imperial Household has long had an important role in religious ceremonies dedicated to the Japanese gods, has been an important repository of Japan's cultural legacy as seen in *Nara*'s *Shousouin*, and is today the patron of such traditional arts as the *utakai*, *gagaku*, and *shinji*. Even now, the Emperor has a rice paddy on the Palace grounds where he performs ceremonial rice planting and harvests.

When Japan accepted the Potsdam Declaration to end World War II, the biggest sticking point was Japan's desire to retain the Japanese "state"—which meant the Imperial institution. Although the Occupation was divided over whether to push for a constitution with the Emperor at its center, or to push for an Emperor-less republic, the Imperial system was retained because the United States government felt that abolishing it would make it impossible to achieve the Occupation's other aims. That said, the new constitution took sovereignty away from the Emperor and located it with the people, stipulating in Article 1 that the Emperor was simply a symbol of the State. Even though it was recognized that the Imperial institution might not be fully compatible with democracy, Japanese accept the idea that political authority should be based in part on the authority of the Imperial institution.

GHQの介入と吉田内閣誕生

日本を占領した米軍の占領政策は，戦前の日本を否定することから始まった。アメリカの狙いは，日本が再び世界に脅威を与えないことにあり，そのため非軍事化と欧米的民主主義制度の導入を最重要政策に掲げた。まず行ったのは極東国際軍事裁判で，*東条英機元首相ら戦時中の指導者の戦争責任の追及を通して，日本の戦前までの歴史的価値観を悪として断罪した。と同時に，憲法改正に着手，非武装中立の思想を盛り込もうとした。具体的な政策では旧日本軍の解体，天皇の神格化の否定，思想犯の釈放，大地主からの農地解放などを日本政府を通して実施させた。

米軍政は当初日本社会党の育成を目指し，社会党政権が実現したものの，政権担当能力に欠けていたうえ，汚職事件を引き起こしつぶれた。これに代わって登場したのが，*吉田茂の率いる保守系の自由民主党の前身である自由党だった。吉田は外交官出身で，戦時中，戦争を批判したとして憲兵隊に逮捕された。こうした経歴から総司令官のマッカーサー元帥の信頼を得た吉田は，巧みな政治手腕で戦後日本政治の指導的地位を確立していった。

「安保」闘争と自民党長期政権

アメリカは朝鮮戦争とソ連との冷戦を契機に，日本に自衛力保持を認めるなど占領政策をしだいに変更し，その政策の比重も「革新」から「保守」に移していった。1951年，講話条約が締結されたが旧ソ連圏諸国が調印しなかったため，左翼勢力が講和条約に反対し保守勢力との対立が激化した。この講和条約の扱いで社会党が左右に分裂したが，やがて統一に向かった。この統一と東西冷戦の激化で，保守系政党が合同，自由民主党(自民党)が誕生した。1960年日米安保条約改定を巡って，与野党が激しく対立，国論も分裂，国会は連日のように「安保反対」のデモに囲まれた。自民党はこの条約を国会で成立させた後，所得倍増計画を打ち出し，その後の石油危機も巧みに乗り切って，38年にわたる長期政権の基礎を築いた。しかしリクルート事件などの汚職，消費税の導入，農産物の自由化などで国民の批判を受け，1989年の参議院選挙に敗北した。また，政治改革を巡って党内対立から分裂し，1993年の衆議院選挙でも破れ，自民党による一党支配体制に終止符が打たれ，ついに連立政権時代に入った。自民党は選挙後下野したが，１年半後に，非自民政権の与党内の分裂をついて政権に復帰し，96年自民党単独内閣を復活させた。

SCAP and the *Yoshida* Cabinet

Postwar occupation policy toward Japan was predicated on rejecting prewar systems. Determined that Japan should not again threaten world peace, the Supreme Commander for the Allied Powers (SCAP) made demilitarization and democratization its top priorities. The first concrete step was to convene the Tokyo Military Tribunal to fix responsibility for the war on former Prime Minister *Toujou Hideki** and other wartime leaders and hence to make a clean break with wartime values. At the same time, work was begun on constitutional reform and a policy of unarmed neutrality propagated. The Occupation disbanded the Japanese military, had the Emperor renounce his divinity, freed political prisoners, redistributed agrarian land from large landholders to tenant farmers, and guided the Japanese government through other reforms.

At first, the Occupation authorities tilted toward the Japan Socialist Party (JSP), but that collapsed when the JSP proved corrupt and unable to govern. In its stead emerged the conservative Liberal Party (forerunner of today's Liberal Democratic Party [LDP]) led by *Yoshida Shigeru*.* A former diplomat, *Yoshida* had been arrested during the war for opposing government policies, credentials which won him General MacArthur and SCAP's trust. Once in office, *Yoshida* proved himself an adroit politician as he consolidated his place in postwar Japanese political history.

Fighting over the Security Treaty and the LDP's Long Reign

With the Korean War and the start of the Cold War, SCAP reversed field and urged Japan to militarize. At the same time, the U.S. shifted from emphasizing reform to promoting conservative policies. The Soviet bloc nations' refusal to join in the signing of the 1951 San Francisco Peace Treaty threw many Japanese leftists against the treaty and squarely in conflict with the pro-U.S. conservatives. Although the left split over policy toward the treaty, it soon reunified. This coalition on the left, and the worsening of the Cold War, in turn prompted a grand conservative union to form the Liberal Democratic Party (LDP). In 1960, the government and opposition parties clashed bitterly over the revision of the Japan-U.S. Security Treaty. Public opinion was also split, and the Diet was ringed by anti-treaty demonstrators daily. Almost as soon as the LDP rammed treaty ratification through the Diet, they announced economic plans to double people's incomes. This prosperity, plus the fact that the LDP got Japan through the subsequent oil crises without major damage, sustained 38 years of LDP rule. However, the LDP came in for heavy criticism in connection with the Recruit scandal and other wide-spread corruption, the imposition of the consumption tax, the liberalization of agricultural imports, and other policies, and ended up losing the 1989 House of Councilors election. Soon after that, the LDP split over the issue of political reform and the party lost its majority in the 1993 election for House of Representatives, bringing the LDP's one-party rule to an end. After a year and a half in opposition, the LDP capitalized on a split in the anti-LDP forces to form a coalition government in 1994 and then to become the sole ruling party in 1996.

総理大臣選出と組閣

日本は議院内閣制を採っている。日本国憲法によると,「総理大臣その他の国務大臣は文民でなくてはならない」と文民優位が定められている。これは軍国主義の復活をおそれた占領軍の意思の反映である。また総理大臣は「国会議員の中から,国会の議決で指名」され,そして総理大臣は国務大臣を任命するが,その「過半数は,国会議員から選ばなくてはならない」と憲法で決められている。総理大臣以外の閣僚のポストは,総務大臣・法務大臣・外務大臣・財務大臣・文部科学大臣・厚生労働大臣・農林水産大臣・経済産業大臣・国土交通大臣・環境大臣・内閣官房長官・防衛庁長官などである。2001年1月から1府21省庁を1府12省庁に再編された。同時に,政務次官を廃止し,副大臣や大臣政務官を新設して,従来の官僚主導による政策決定から政治家主導に戻そうと試みている。

1955年保守政党の統合で,自由民主党(自民党)が誕生,93年まで自民党による政権が続いたが,この自民党単独政権時代には,閣僚のポストは自民党内の各派閥の大きさによって配分されていた。したがって,適材適所の「人材」を閣僚に据えると言うより派閥内の年功序列によって,しかも任期が1年強というローテーションで閣僚が決まるというケースが多かった。

1993年,自民党の単独政権が終わり,細川護熙(もりひろ)を首相とする反自民の連立内閣が生まれ,さらに自民党・社会党・新党さきがけの3党連立内閣が誕生したが,ここでも与党各党の議席数によって閣僚ポストの配分が決められた。

内閣の運営

日本は伝統的に官僚組織が極めて強固なうえ,政党が政策立案能力を官僚に依存しているため,政党政治と言われながらもこれまで政治家主導の政治が行われていなかったのが実状である。この傾向は,多党化・連立内閣時代に入ってむしろ各政党が政策を牽制(けんせい)しあって妥協を重ねるようになったため,かえって強まった。

毎週火曜・金曜の2回,政府は閣議を開くが,その前日に開かれる事務次官会議で閣議の内容が決まってしまう。ということで「政治主導」の政策を打ち出すため,内閣の機能,特に首相官邸の機能強化を図ることが検討されている。しかも大蔵省,厚生省などで汚職などの不祥事が起きたことから,国民の間からも官僚批判の声が高まり,行政改革と規制緩和を推進して,官僚政治を打破し,政治家のリーダーシップによる政治の実現が,各政党の政策課題になっている。

The Cabinet*

Election of the Prime Minister and Cabinet Formation

Japan has a cabinet system, and reflecting SCAP's determination to prevent a revival of militarism, the constitution states that the Prime Minister and other Ministers of State must be civilians. Designated by the Diet from among its members, the Prime Minister then appoints the other ministers, a majority of whom must be Diet members, and these include the Minister of Public Management, Home Affairs, Posts and Telecommunications, Minister of Justice, Minister of Foreign Affairs, Minister of Finance, Minister of Education and Science, Minister of Health, Welfare and Labor, Minister of Agriculture, Forestry and Fisheries, Minister of Economics and Industry, Minister of Lands, Infrastructure and Transport, Minister of the Environment, Chief Cabinet Secretary and Director General of Defense, etc. As of January 2001 the government bureaucracy was streamlined from Prime Minster's Office plus 12 ministries and 9 agencies to Cabinet Office plus 10 ministries and 2 agencies. At the same time the post of parliamentary vice minister was done away with, and the new posts of senior vice minister and parliamentary secretary were created. These changes represent an attempt to move leadership in government policy decision making away from the bureaucrats back to the politicians.

From the party's formation in the 1955 conservative union until 1993, the Liberal Democratic Party had a Diet majority and formed the governments —which meant that cabinet posts were doled out to the party factions proportionate to their strength. Rather than tapping "the right person for the right post," seats were allocated on the basis of seniority within the factions —and the cabinets were shuffled every year or so on average.

In 1993, the LDP lost its majority and *Hosokawa Morihiro* became Prime Minister heading a non-LDP government. Following that, the LDP returned to power in a coalition with the Socialist Democratic and Harbinger parties, with cabinet seats apportioned to the parties based upon Diet strength.

How the Cabinet Works

Japan has traditionally had a very strong bureaucracy and the politicians have relied upon the bureaucrats to draft new legislation, with the result that the parties do not actually govern even though we speak of "the ruling parties." If anything, this tendency has been even more pronounced with coalition governments, as the parties seek to thwart each other's ambitions and to reach acceptable compromises.

The cabinet meets every Tuesday and Friday, with the agenda for these meetings set by the Administrative Vice Ministers' meetings on Mondays and Thursdays. Looking for ways to enhance political leadership, there has been considerable talk of giving the cabinet greater powers and particularly of beefing up the Prime Minister's Residence's functions. Compounding this has been the public outcry over scandals at the Finance, Health and Welfare, and other ministries, and all of the parties are looking at ways to promote administrative reform and deregulation, to break the bureaucracy's hold on power, and to achieve a government driven by political leadership.

55年体制の解消

1955年から1993年までの38年間，自由民主党による政権が続いた。この時期は，自由民主党(自民党)，日本社会党(社会党)，公明党，社会党右派を母体とした民社党，日本共産党の5党が主要政党で，自民党が政権与党として過半数を維持し，社会・公明・民社・共産の各党は少数野党であった。このうち社会党はつねに野党第1党の地位を保持し，その結果国会運営は自民・社会両党を軸に行われていた。この間の政治体制を特に「55年体制」と呼んだ。

1990年代に入ると，自民党による長期政権から生まれた政治の停滞や汚職事件で，「自民党の長期政権の打破，55年体制の解消」をかかげる政治改革運動が起きた。92〜93年には，自民党から分裂した2党を含む保守系の3新党が生まれた。その結果，93年7月の総選挙で自民党が衆議院の議席数の過半数を割ると共に，社会党の議席も半減した。同年8月に自民党・共産党を除く8党の連立政権が生まれ，「55年体制」は崩壊した。この時期から，政党の分裂・合同が頻繁に行われるようになった。

現在のおもな政党

自由民主党　1955年に自由党と民主党が合同して成立。単独で長期政権を維持してきたが，93〜94年に野党を経験して以後は，他党と連立政権を組んでいる。

民主党　1998年に旧民主党（96年結成）を中心とした結成。野党第一党として，自民党に代わる政権交代の軸となることを目指している。

公明党　1964年に創価学会（仏教の一宗派である日蓮正宗(にちれんしょうしゅう)の信徒団体）を母体として結成。70年に政教分離を宣言した。99年より自民党中心の連立政権に参加している。

自由党　1998年に新進党が解党した際，元新進党党首の小沢一郎を中心に結成。一時期は自民党・公明党と連立政権を組んだ。

日本共産党　1922年結成。たびたび激しい弾圧を受け，35年に消滅。45年12月再建。64年にソ連共産党と，66年に中国共産党と決裂して以来，自主独立路線を歩んでいる。

社会民主党　1945年11月に日本社会党として結成。46〜50年および94〜96年には，党委員長が首相を務めた。96年1月現党名に改称。

保守党　2000年4月，自由党が自民党・公明党との連立政権を離脱したときに，離脱反対グループが分かれて結成し，与党に留まった。

Political Parties

Dissolution of the 1955 Framework

For 38 years, from 1955 to 1993, the Liberal Democratic Party formed the Cabinets and ran the government. The main parties during this period were the LDP, Japan Socialist Party, *Koumei* Party, Democratic Socialists (formed by a JSP right-wing split-off), and Japan Communist Party, and the four smaller parties were arrayed in opposition to the majority LDP. Of the opposition parties, the JSP was consistently the largest, meaning that Diet machinations revolved around the LDP-JSP axis in what came to be called the 1955 framework.

Moving into the '90s, the political stagnation and numerous graft scandals arising from the LDP's having retained power for so long resulted in the birth of a reform movement under the banner of, "Down with the LDP! Dissolution of the 1955 Framework!" In 1992～93 three new conservative parties were formed, two of which splintered off the LDP. As a result, the LDP failed to win a majority of seats in the House of Representatives in the July 1993 election, while the Japan Socialist Party lost half its seats. In August of that year an eight party coalition, excluding the LDP and Communist Party, came into power, thus ending the 1955 Framework. Since then the fragmentation and merging of political parties has become a common occurrence.

Present Major Political Parties

Liberal Democratic Party (LDP)···Formed in 1955 by joining the then Liberal and Democratic Parties. Remained in sole power for nearly 40 years. After a short stint as the opposition party in 1993～94, has governed in coalition with other parties.

Democratic Party of Japan···Formed in 1998 out of the old Democratic Party (formed in 1996). As the leading opposition party it seeks to become an axis of alternate political power in place of the LDP.

***Koumei* Party**···Formed in 1964 from its parent, *Soukagakkai*, an organization of followers of the *Nichiren Shoushuu* Buddhist sect. Proclaimed a separation of religion and politics in 1970. Since 1999 has participated in government as part of an alliance centering on the LDP.

Liberal Party···Formed in 1998 upon the dissolution of the New Frontier Party around party chief *Ozawa Ichirou*. For a time was part of a ruling coalition together with the LDP and *Koumei* Party.

Japanese Communist Party···Formed in 1922. Under constant attack, was dissolved in 1935. Reformed again in December 1945. Has tread a solitary path since its split with the Soviet Communist Party in 1964 and the Chinese Communist Party in 1966.

Social Democratic Party···Formed in November 1945 as the Japanese Socialist Party. Its party head served as Prime Minister from 1946～50, and from 1994～96. The present party name was adopted in 1996.

New Conservative Party···Formed in April 2000 by a faction of the Liberal Party opposed to the party's backing out of the coalition with the LDP and *Koumei* Party, and remained as part of the coalition.

選挙制度

選挙は，国政選挙と地方選挙に大きく分けることができる。国政選挙は衆議院選挙と参議院選挙，地方選挙は，都・道・府・県・市・町・村・区の地方首長選挙とその地方自治体の議会選挙である。

衆議院は，1994年に選挙法が改正され，長く続いた中選挙区から小選挙区比例代表並立制となった。定数は480で，選挙区選出が300，残り180は全国11ブロックからの比例代表選出である。参議院は定数242，日本全国を1選挙区とする比例代表選出が96，各都道府県を1選挙区とし定員1～4の選挙区から146人が選出される。被選挙権は衆議院議員と地方議員が25歳から，参議院議員は30歳から，選挙権は20歳以上の男女に与えられている。

政党に助成金

選挙法の改正の狙いの一つは，かかりすぎる選挙資金をいかに少なくするかにあった。このため政党に国から「政党助成金」がでることになった。2001年は，総額313億円。交付資格は，国会議員が5人以上か直近の国政選挙で，2％以上の得票数，いずれかの要件を満たした政党が対象である。これによって各議員の政治資金は軽減されると見られていたが，96年の選挙では，依然として個人の選挙資金は減らず，むしろ多くかかった。しかし今後は，政治資金が党に集約されるため，選挙は「党営選挙」の色彩が濃くなることが予想され，それと同時に政治資金を握る党執行部の権限が強まると思われる。

議員の任期

議員の任期は参議院が6年で，ほかは4年。地方議会はリコールなどによるほかは任期いっぱいで改選される。ただ衆議院議員は，任期いっぱいの4年で自然解散するのはむしろ例外で，平均2年半で解散選挙が行われている。選挙の時期は，解散のある衆議院を除くと，参議院が3年ごとの半数改選で7月，地方選挙は4年ごとに，4～5月に集中的に行われる。これは「統一地方選挙」と呼ばれている。投票率は各選挙とも最近の若者たちの選挙離れを反映し，年々減少の傾向にある。平均は60％ぐらいで，このうち都市部は50％前後と低く，農村部は高くなっている。

衆・参両院議員は一部の例外を除いて，政党に所属しているが，地方議員は所属政党を明確にするのを避ける傾向にある。特に首長選挙の場合はその傾向が強い。それは「県民党」「市民党」と名乗るほうが幅広く支持者を集められ，選挙に有利だからである。しかしその大多数は自由民主党系の保守派であって，野党は少ない。

Elections

The Election System

Elections may be broadly divided into national elections for the Houses of Representatives and Councilors and local elections for town, city, prefectural, and other local government councils.

Under the 1994 Election Law the old multirepresentative constituencies were abolished. The House of Representatives has 480 members—300 elected from single-representative districts and the remaining 180 from party lists in eleven electoral blocs nationwide, each voter having two votes (one candidate vote and one party-list vote). The House of Councilors' 242 members are elected—96 nationwide with voters voting for parties' pre-announced candidate slates, and the other 146 in prefectural polls electing 1 to 4 Councilors per prefecture. While all Japanese 20 or older can vote, candidates must be at least 25 years old for the House of Representatives and local councils and 30 or older for the House of Councilors.

Public Funding

One of the objectives in reforming the election law was to make political donations less important to the process. Provision was thus made for public funding to the parties. In 2001, this amounted to ¥31,300 million. This funding is available to parties that either have five or more seats, or have won 2% or more of the votes in the most recent election. While it was hoped that politicians would not be as dependent on private donations as a result, there was, in fact, an increase in such private contributions in the 1996 election. Because the public funding goes to the parties, it is expected that parties will become more important in elections and that party leaders will wield more control since they have their hands on the money.

Terms of Office

Terms of office are six years for the House of Councilors and four years for all other offices. Unlike local council members, who usually serve out their full terms, members of the House of Representatives typically find their terms interrupted by House dissolution and general elections—on average every two and a half years or so. While the House of Representatives can be dissolved and new elections called any time, the House of Councilors elects half its members every three years, usually in July, and local council elections are every four years, usually concentrated in April and May. With the growing political apathy among young people, voter turnout has been slipping at all levels. Today, the average turnout nationwide is about 60%—about 50% in urban areas and somewhat higher in the countryside.

Almost all Diet members belong to one of the major parties, but there is a tendency to downplay political affiliation in the local elections, especially at the prefectural level. Instead, local politicians prefer to cast themselves at the head of "citizen parties" for broader appeal. Even so, most of these "independent" candidates are actually conservatives aligned with the Liberal Democratic Party.

日本では，３人集まると派閥ができると言われている。派閥とは，仲間を作って特定の利益を追求するというのがその定義である。仲間を作る場合，出身地・出身校・縁戚（えんせき）によるケースが多く，それは「藩閥」「学閥」「門閥」とそれぞれ呼ばれている。このうち「藩閥」「門閥」はほとんどなくなっているが，「学閥」は残っている。例えば，各省庁の高級官僚の多くが東京大学の出身者であるため，彼らグループは“東大閥”と言われている。しかし現代の日本では，派閥と言うと自由民主党内のグループを指す場合が多い。

党内派閥の成り立ち

自民党の長期政権が続いたことで，政権維持を目的に結集した議員の中には，相反する考えを持つ者もいて，党内でグループ化していった。

しかし，派閥の長の死亡・引退，政治資金法の改正などで，従来どおりの派閥維持が困難となり，その結果，結束力を弱めている。現在自民党内には，橋本派，宮沢派，森派，江藤・亀井派，山崎派などがあるが，派閥解消の動きもあり，政策を中心とした「政策集団」にやがて再編される流れとなっている。

自民党内に派閥ができたのは，日本の選挙区制が原因だと言われている。選挙区の定員が１名の欧米諸国と相違して，これまで日本は２～６人の中選挙区制を採っていた。したがってつねに過半数をめざす自民党は同一選挙区に同党の候補者を複数，選挙区によっては定員いっぱい立候補させていた。このため必然的に選挙では党員どうしがライバルとなり，同じ党員どうしが激しい選挙を戦うことになる。そこで党首をめざす党内の実力者は，自分の勢力を拡大するために系列化し，系列に入った候補者に資金援助するなどして支援する。候補者は当選するとその派閥の所属議員として，派閥の親分の政権実現のために努力していた。

派閥の功罪

議員が派閥に入るのは，選挙の資金援助のほか，政務次官や大臣のポストを得るために大いに役立つからである。というのは自民党内の内閣は派閥の連合内閣であり，閣僚のポストはその派閥の大きさによって配分されているからで，無派閥議員が閣僚になることはきわめて難しかった。

2001年４月に誕生した小泉純一郎内閣は，派閥にとらわれない閣僚ポストの選任を行い，これまでの旧弊に大きな風穴を開けた。しかし，今後も定着するかどうかは流動的である。

Political Factions

A faction is generally defined as a gathering of people to press for special interests, and the old Japanese saying has it that three people make a faction. Many factions are formed of people from the same city or the same school, or people who are related by marriage or blood. Although geographical and blood alliances have become less important recently, old school ties retain their strength. For example, because many of the top bureaucrats in the various ministries and agencies are University of *Toukyou*(Tokyo) graduates, they as a group are referred to as the "Tokyo clique". However, the term "faction" in modern Japan most commonly calls to mind the political factions within the powerful Liberal Democratic Party (LDP).

Formation of Factions

With the LDP remaining in power for so long, the only thing unifying many of its members was the common goal of winning elections and remaining in power. Their otherwise conflicting views resulted in a solidification into intra-party factions. Yet it is difficult for such factions to maintain cohesion as old leaders die or retire, or public funding laws are revised, etc. Currently the main factions in the LDP are the *Hashimoto* faction, *Miyazawa* faction, *Mori* faction, *Etou-Kamei* faction and the *Yamazaki* faction. But future development seems to be toward dissolution of such factions, and eventual reshaping into policy oriented groups.

Japan's electoral system is said to be at least partly responsible for the factions' existence. Whereas most Western countries elect one person from each district, Japanese voters returned 2-6 people per electoral district until just recently. As a result, a party (e.g., the LDP) hoping for a majority in the Diet had to run more than one candidate in every district, sometimes fielding as many candidates as there were seats available. As a result, candidates from the same party ended up competing with each other for votes, and established politicians vying for the party presidency contributed endorsements and money in the expectation that successful candidates would return the favor later. Once a candidate was elected, he teamed up with his patrons and worked to help the group leader get elected Prime Minister.

Pros and Cons

The main advantage of belonging to a faction is that it promises electoral support as well as a better shot at vice-ministerial and ministerial posts. LDP cabinets are basically coalitions among the various LDP factions. Cabinet posts are distributed proportional to each faction's strength, and it has always been very difficult for a non-aligned politician to become a cabinet member.

Junichirou Koizumi became the new Prime Minister in April 2001 and proceeded to choose cabinet members without regard for what faction they belonged to, thus putting a dent in the old faction set up. Whether this new idea will catch on, however, remains to be seen.

8 官僚

日本では官僚という場合は，中央省庁の高級公務員，国家公務員採用試験Ⅰ種・外交官試験を通った行政のテクノクラートを指すのが普通である。

官僚制度の歴史

日本の官僚制度は非常に古い。千数百年前，大和（やまと）朝廷(政権)が中国から導入した律令（りつりょう）制が，時代とともに整備され，それに伴って官僚も育っていった。特に江戸時代は，戦乱のない平和な時代が二百数十年の長期にわたって続いたため，武士たちは，しだいに行政テクノクラートとなり，官僚制度はいっそう成熟していった。明治になって日本は，欧米の思想・技術を積極的に取り入れ，急速に近代化したが，その原動力となったのが武士出身の行政官たちだった。彼らはこれまでの官僚組織を基礎に，欧米の行政制度を巧みに導入する一方，国立大学を設立，官僚の養成を図った。特に中央省庁の高級官僚養成を目的とした東京大学には，全国から優秀な学生が集まった。こうした伝統が今も生きており，現在の中央省庁の官僚には東京大学出身者が少なくない。

官僚制度の功績

官僚と言うとどこの国でも融通のきかない，杓子（しゃくし）定規，冷たいというイメージがもたれている。日本もその例外でなく，「官僚的」と言えば形式的で独善的の同義語として使われている。しかし日本の官僚の場合，その能力は高く評価されている。例えば近年欧米の学者やジャーナリストたちの間で，日本研究が盛んになっているが，彼らが「日本の繁栄と奇跡的な高度成長」の秘密を語るとき，例外なく挙げるのが官僚の功績であり，官僚機構である。

しかし1990年代に入って，日本の経済が停滞すると共に国による規制の緩和が叫ばれるようになった。そして，新規産業が生まれない原因として官僚による規制が指摘された。さらに，大蔵省の行政指導の失敗による住宅金融専門会社（住専）の破綻（はたん），エイズ薬害問題における厚生省と製薬会社との関係など，官僚がもつ規制と権限が引き起こした業界と官僚との癒（ゆ）着（ちゃく）と汚職で，官僚批判が急速に高まった。2001年には外務省職員が機密費を横領した容疑で逮捕されるなど，外務省関連の不祥事が相次いで明らかになり，国民の官僚批判はかつてない高まりを見せている。

2001年１月からは，それまでの１府21省庁から１府12省庁に再編された。硬直化した行政組織の効率化が狙いだが,「数を減らしただけで中身は変わらない」との批判も多い。

The Bureaucracy

In Japan, "the bureaucracy" usually refers to government technocrats who have passed the qualifying examinations for high-level posts in the central government offices, and diplomats.

History

Japan has a long history of bureaucracy. Well over 1,000 years ago, the *Yamato* Court adopted rules of government patterned after the Chinese model. With time, a bureaucracy grew up to service these regulations. This was especially conspicuous during the *Edo* period when peace prevailed for over 250 years and the warrior class gradually metamorphosed into a bureaucracy. Although Japan modernized rapidly with the introduction of Western thinking and technology in the late 19th century, the driving force remained these warrior-scion bureaucrats. Building upon the indigenous Japanese government structure, they grafted on Western administration and founded national universities in an effort to build a strong bureaucratic corps. The University of *Toukyou* (Tokyo), for example, was founded to train elite bureaucrats, and drew outstanding students from throughout the country. Even today, many of the top government bureaucrats are University of *Toukyou* graduates.

A Successful System

Worldwide, bureaucrats are perceived as uptight and unfeeling people who rigidly go by the book. Japan is no exception, and the adjective "bureaucratic" is synonymous with paperwork and arbitrariness. Yet the Japanese bureaucracy is also perceived as highly capable. Western scholars and journalists have recently done considerable research on Japan, and without exception they give much of the credit for Japan's prosperity and miraculous economic growth to the skilled bureaucracy.

In the 1990s, however, as the Japanese economy seemed to falter, there were increased calls for government deregulation. Bureaucratic regulation was widely blamed for stifling entrepreneurship and the emergence of new industries. Compounding this, the bureaucracy came under heavy criticism in connection with the bankruptcy of the housing loan corporations under Ministry of Finance tutelage, and the incestuous relationship between the Ministry of Health and Welfare and pharmaceutical companies that led to patients being treated with HIV-infected blood products.

In 2001 a series of unpleasant affairs surrounding the Ministry of Foreign Affairs was uncovered, including some of its employees being arrested on charges of stealing secret funds. These and other incidents have escalated public criticism of the bureaucracy to new heights. As of January 2001 the cabinet was reduced from Prime Minister's Office and 12 ministries and 9 agencies to Cabinet Office and 10 ministries and 2 agencies. The aim of this move was to increase efficiency in a governmental organization that had grown rigid. But critics contend that,"Even though you decrease the number, content-wise things remain the same."

地方自治体の種類

日本自治体は，主に次の種類からなる。

①都（東京都）・道（北海道）・府（大阪府・京都府）・県（神奈川県・千葉県など43県）

②市・町（まち・ちょう）・村（むら・そん）

③特別区（東京の23区）

日本の地方自治は「3割自治」

国と地方の関係は明治以来，行政システムが築かれてきた。両者の立場は「主従・上下」の関係にあったが地方自治の理念が日本に導入されたのは，日本国憲法に条項が盛り込まれた戦後になってからだ。しかし，実体的には国の機関委任事務が80％を占めていたほか，国の歳入全体に占める地方税の比率が約30％だったことから，「3割自治」と揶揄（やゆ）され続けてきた。

「主従・上下」から「対等・協力」へ

1990年代の長引く不況により，地方自治体も歳入の減少が続き，地方経済テコ入れを狙った公共事業の投入に伴う地方債の増発は，自治体を深刻な財政危機状態に陥れており，健全な財政状況の回復が急がれている。

2000年4月に施行された地方分権一括法は，国と地方自治体との関係を「対等・協力」に切り替えるのが狙いだ。地方分権一括法により機関委任事務の約55％は自治体が責任を持って行う「自治事務」に組み入れられた。残りの約45％に当たる部分は国が自治体に委託させる「法定受託事務」となった。新たな権限委譲によって，学校の自由選択制や少人数学級の編成などに動く自治体が出始めている。

自治体の自立を保つための方法の1つは課税自由権だ。石原慎太郎東京都知事による銀行への外形標準課税の導入は，各自治体の独自財源創設のきっかけとなるものだった。この動きも従来は法定外普通税の新設や変更には自治大臣の許可が必要だったが，「同意を要する協議」に変わり，法定外目的税も可能となったことが背景にある。自治体は様々な課税を検討し始めており，国に依存した財政体質からの脱皮を狙った動きが少しずつだが始まっている。

また，自治体の効率性を追求しようと，市町村の合併の動きも強まっている。

Local Autonomy

Types of Local Government

The main types of local government found in Japan include:

①*To*=metropolitan(Tokyo Metropolis); *Dou*=provincial(*Hokkaidou* Province);*Fu*=prefectural(*Oosaka-fu*, *Kyouto-fu*); *Ken*=prefectural (*Kanagawa* Prefecture, *Chiba* Prefecture, etc., 43 *Ken* in all)

②*Shi*=city; *Machi* or *Chou*=town; *Mura* or *Son*=village

③*Ku*=ward(Tokyo Metropolis has 23 wards)

30% Autonomous

Since the time of *Meiji* there evolved a system of government founded in dependence on central authority, with national and local in the positions of master and follower.

The idea of local autonomy was first introduced to Japan at the close of WWII by way of the new constitution. But in actual fact, however, 80% of the activities of local governments consisted of business commissioned by the national government. 30% of all tax revenues collected by the national government consists of money collected in the form of local taxes, and this money went directly to local governments to use as they saw fit. Any other money required to carry out business had to be applied for from the national government and could be used only as the national government directed. For this reason local governments were ridiculed as being "30% autonomous".

From Master-Follower to Equality and Cooperation

At present many local governments are in serious financial difficulty because of the continuing decline in revenues due to the drawn out recession of the '90s, together with an increasing debt incurred through public works projects intended to act as a lever on the local economy. Recovery to a healthy financial state remains a top priority.

In April 2000 a new decentralization act was passed, aimed at replacing the master-follower system with one based on equality and cooperation. Under this act approximately 55% of the business formerly commissioned by the national government is now the sole responsibility of local governments. The remaining 45% is commissioned from the national government. Many local governments have been using their new power to introduce elective courses into the school curriculum, create smaller classes, etc.

One means for ensuring the independence of local governments is their power to levy taxes. When the mayor of Tokyo, *Ishihara Shintarou*, introduced the idea of taxing banks according to their size rather than their earnings, it was like a spark setting off various other local governments to create their own personal sources of revenue. Before the decentralization law, local governments had to get official authorization from the Minister of Home Affairs before imposing or changing taxes. Now it possible to create a specific purpose tax after "consultation".

Also there is a strong tendency toward merger between cities, towns and villages in order to further increase the effectiveness of local governments.

日本の裁判制度は，戦後大幅に変わったものの一つである。戦前は天皇の裁判所であったが，戦後は国民の裁判所として，行政，立法とともに三権の一つとしての地位を確立した。日本の司法は戦前まで「ドイツ法」の影響が強かったが，戦後は「英米法」の制度が導入された。しかし，陪審制度の採用は見送られた。

司法の組織

裁判所には最高裁判所，高等裁判所，地方裁判所，家庭裁判所，簡易裁判所がある。裁判は三審制で，地方裁判所が一審，高等裁判所が二審，最高裁判所は最終審である。家庭裁判所は離婚などの裁判，簡易裁判所は地方裁判所の下部機関で，交通違反などの軽い犯罪を扱う。最高裁判所は判事と長官を含め15人，全判事で裁判を行う大法廷と，3人の判事で構成する小法廷がある。通常は小法廷で扱われるが，大きな問題のときは大法廷が開かれる。最高裁判所はこうした裁判のほか裁判官の人事など全裁判所の司法行政事務の最高機関でもある。高等裁判所は全国で8か所，地方裁判所は50か所にあり，それぞれ刑事，民事の裁判を行っている。

裁判の方法

まず，裁判は一審を担当する地方裁判所で争われる。刑事犯罪に例を取ると，検察官が起訴，不起訴を決め，起訴が決まると裁判が始まる。

通常の場合，地方・高等裁判所の裁判は，裁判長と陪席（ばいせき）判事二人の計3人の裁判官と検事，弁護人で構成する。証拠調べの後，検事の求刑，弁護人の最終弁論，そして裁判官の合議で判決が下される。見解が分かれたときは多数決で決まるが，少数意見は明らかにされない。高等裁判所の裁判は，一審裁判に不満をもった被告人，あるいは検察官の控訴によって行われる。裁判の方法は一審と同じだが，書面審理の比が大きくなる。最高裁判所は，憲法にかかわる問題と重大な事実誤認が明らかになったとき法廷が開かれる。

「国民に開かれた司法を」との国民の声を受け，司法制度改革の動きも強まっている。陪審制度の導入が検討されているほか，司法試験の合格者数の拡大などが提言された。犯罪被害者側の人権保護が放置されている問題でも，対策が急務となっている。

The Japanese Judicial System

The judicial system is one of the Japanese institutions that changed most after the war. In place of the prewar imperial courts, popular courts were established (along with the executive branch and the legislature) as one of the three main pillars of authority in Japanese society. The prewar court system had been strongly influenced by German law, but now it is closer to the Anglo-American system, albeit without juries.

Structure

The judicial system consists of the Supreme Court, high courts, district courts, family courts, and summary courts. The appeals process has three levels, the 50 district courts having first jurisdiction, the eight high courts acting as appellate courts, and the Supreme Court the court of last appeal. Family courts handle such things as divorce cases, while summary courts handle only such minor cases as traffic violations. The Supreme Court is made up of 15 judges, including a chief judge, and is divided into the grand bench consisting of all supreme court judges and petty benches of three judges each. Most cases are decided by the petty benches, but the grand bench may be convened for especially important cases. In addition, the Supreme Court is responsible for administering the judicial system, including personnel appointments, and is the highest judicial administrative body.

Procedures

Cases go first to the district courts. In criminal offenses punishable by imprisonment, the case begins in the district court when the public prosecutor decides to indict the defendant.

Ordinarily, cases in the high courts and district courts are tried by three judges, one of whom presides, with prosecution and defense attorneys present. After the judges have heard the evidence, they hear the prosecution's sentencing recommendations and the defense's final argument and hand down their verdict. When the judges are divided, the majority opinion is adopted and no dissenting opinion announced. The high courts try cases which have been appealed, by either the defendant or the prosecution, after a previous trial. Procedures are similar to those in the district court, except that record of the previous trial also plays an important part. The Supreme Court considers constitutional questions and other matters deemed important enough to require the highest court's attention.

Yielding to public outcry for an administration of justice open to the public, a movement to reform the judicial system is gaining momentum. Besides considering the adoption of a jury system, it has been suggested that a greater number of persons be passed on the bench examinations. Another problem in need of urgent attention is the infringement on personal rights of persons injured by criminal acts.

消費税の導入

日本の税制は，所得税，法人税など直接税が主体である。酒税，ガソリン税，関税などの間接税はあったが，「消費税」が導入されたのは，1989年と最近で，税率も3％と低く押さえられていた。97年4月から5％にアップされたが，それでもヨーロッパ諸国に比べると低い。

日本の税制が，直接税を中心に組み立てられてきたのは，伝統的な税制の他，戦後の占領期，直接税主体の米国の主導で，税制改革が行われたためである。税制の基本的原則は「公正にして公平」，そして申告納税(のうぜい)を土台にしている。しかし，日本の場合は税の徴収が容易な「源泉徴収」方式が主流である。この方式は，サラリーマンなど勤労者の毎月の月給から所得税を天引きするもので，100％近い税が捕捉される。

一方自営業者などは自己申告制で，申告しない人もいるし，申告内容にも必要経費などの面で裁量が効く。このため自営業者の場合半分程度，農民の場合は30％程度しか捕捉出来ないというのが実状だった。いわゆる「10・5・3（トウゴーサン）」といい，不公平税制の代名詞になっていた。こうした理由のほか日本は累進課税のため，高額所得になるに従いきわめて高い税率になること，さらに73年の第1次石油危機以来，景気の後退などの税収の落ち込み，景気対策のための財政支出の膨張で財政赤字が慢性化した。

膨大な財政赤字

国の歳入に占める税収は70％台が続いた。このためそれを補う国債の発行が増大した。70年代後半の景気対策として，公共事業の追加や所得税の減税が続いたことも，国債の大量発行につながった。国債残高は90年度末には166兆円であったが，2001年度末には389兆円に達する見通しである。この額は国税収入の約7年分にあたる。都道府県の公債を加えた長期債務残高も，国内総生産（GDP）を大きく上回る666兆円にのぼると見られている。国債残高は減る見通しがなく，2005年度末には491兆円に達する試算が出ている。国の予算に占める国債利子などの「国債費」が占める比率が高まり，財政が硬直化し，新規事業への支出がしだいに少なくなってきた。また，高齢化に伴う医療・年金など社会保障費の増大で，日本の財政は悪化の一途をたどっている。

そこでこれまでの政府は，3％の消費税を導入し，さらに5％にアップした。これからも財源は消費税のアップしかなく，財政当局は10～15％に引き上げることを狙っている。国民の抵抗にあうことは必至で，税制の改革が大きな政治課題の一つとなっている。

Taxes

The Consumption Tax

Japanese taxes are mainly such direct taxes as income taxes and corporate taxes. There are also such indirect taxes as the liquor tax, gasoline tax, and customs duties, but there was no consumption tax until 1989. At first, this consumption tax was a low 3%, but it was raised in April 1997 to 5% (which is still low by international standards).

This primary reliance on direct taxation both follows the Japanese tradition and accords with the postwar reforms instituted by the U.S.-led Occupation (the U.S. also relying primarily on direct taxation). The guiding principle is that of "fair and equitable taxes," and the system relies upon self-reporting. Yet because office workers and other salaried personnel have their taxes withheld (i.e., deducted at the source) every month, the collection rate on these people is nearly 100%.

By contrast, self-employed people file their own returns, and some of them either fail to file or claim excessive deductions. The upshot, it is claimed, is that self-employed entrepreneurs pay only half of their real taxes and farmers only 30 % of what they should, and this has in turn led to mistrust in the tax system's fairness. At the same time, the fact that tax rates are progressively graduated by ability to pay means that people in the higher income brackets end up paying heavier taxes. Further complicating this situation, the sluggish economy and the economic stimulus programs since the 1973 oil crisis have meant that the government has been spending more than it has been taking in, and government debt is another serious problem.

Bloating Government Debt

Economic strategy adopted in the late '70s offered increased public works projects and reduced income taxes as incentives to the economy. Entering the '90s, however, tax revenues have amounted to only three-fourths of government spending, so the government is increasingly going into debt. At the end of 1990 the value of outstanding national bonds was ¥166 trillion, and is expected to reach ¥389 trillion by the end of 2001, which equals roughly 7 years worth of tax revenues. Add to this the debts of the various local governments, and the figure for outstanding public debt soars to ¥666 trillion, which is greater than gross domestic production. With more and more of the budget going toward interest payments on national bonds, less money is available for new projects and the economy freezes. Add to this the ever-growing medical, old age pension and other welfare costs of an aging society, and the projected national debt for 2005 climbs to ¥491 trillion, with no end in sight except financial ruin.

Conditions like these caused the government to introduce a 3% consumption tax, which it then raised to 5%. Further hikes in the consumption tax seem to be the only likely source of revenue, and the Ministry of Finance is aiming at 10～15%. Such a move will of course meet with strong resistance from the public. Tax reform then is another major problem on the political agenda.

日本の外交が戦後本格的にスタートしたのは1951年，サンフランシスコで講和条約が調印されたときからである。講和条約を締結するに当たって，ソ連圏を含めた関係諸国のすべてと締結する全面講和論と，とりあえず欧米諸国だけとの講和をするという多数講和論が激しく対立，国論も二分された。当時の吉田内閣は多数講和を選択したが，現在もこれが日本外交の原点となっている。すなわち日本外交の基軸はまず「日米友好」であり，欧米民主主義諸国と協調を図りながら，外交を展開するという現在の外交方針がこのとき確立したのである。

日米関係

日米関係はこれまで大きなトラブルもなく推移してきたが，近年アメリカの対日貿易赤字が膨大になるにつれ，自動車・鉄鋼・農産物を中心とした貿易摩擦，また防衛問題で，日本の防衛力整備がアメリカの希望どおりに進んでいないことなど，日米間に摩擦が起きている。しかし日本の外交の中で，日米間の友好は最優先で，毎年明らかにされる政府の外交青書では，「日米安全保障条約に基礎を置く，アメリカとの友好協力関係は，日本外交の基軸であり，政治・経済・防衛をはじめ，広範な分野にわたり，アメリカは日本の重要なパートナーである」と強調している。

アジア諸国との関係

日米関係とともに日本が重視しているのは，韓国，中国，ASEAN諸国である。韓国との関係は隣国でありながら，必ずしもスムーズな外交関係が確立されているとは言えなかった。このため日本の首相は在職中必ず韓国，中国，ASEAN諸国を歴訪しており，その友好関係に心を砕いている。

日ロ関係

日ロ関係については，まだ平和条約が締結されていない。これは北方領土の択捉(えとろふ)・国後(くなしり)・歯舞(はぼまい)・色丹(しこたん)返還問題が解決していないためである。日本の方針は「経済，文化の交流を維持しながら，粘り強く北方領土の返還を求める」というものである。

国連

日本外交の大きな柱の一つは，国連外交である。国連分担金は安保理事会の多くの常任理事国より多い。常任理事国でないために十分な発言力を行使できないなどの理由から，常任理事国入りを狙っている。しかし，日本国内には「常任理事国になると，海外派兵の義務を負う」と消極的な意見もあるが，国民の多数意見は常任理事国を望んでいる。

Foreign Policy

Japanese postwar foreign policy was shaped in 1951 with the signing of the San Francisco Peace Treaty. At the time Japanese public opinion was split between advocates of waiting for a comprehensive peace treaty including the Soviet Union and all other principals, and advocates of going ahead with a partial peace treaty signed by the Western powers. By establishing the basic orientation of a foreign policy premised upon friendship with the United States and cooperation with the other Western democracies, the government's decision to go with the partial peace determined Japanese foreign policy to this day.

U.S.-Japan Relations

U.S.-Japan relations have been largely trouble-free so far, but there has been increasing trade friction recently in automobiles, steel, agricultural products, and other items as the U.S. trade deficit with Japan has soared. Also defense is a problem, as Japanese defense build-up has not been as fast as the United States would like. However, friendship with the United States remains Japan's highest foreign policy priority. The *Diplomatic Bluebook* has annually emphasized that the relations of friendship and cooperation with the United States based upon the security arrangements are the cornerstone of Japanese foreign policy, and the two countries are important partners in a wide range of political, economic, defense, and other areas.

Relations with the Countries of Asia

Japan also emphasizes its relations with the Republic of Korea, China, and the Association of Southeast Asian Nations (ASEAN) countries. Although Korea is right next door, Japan-Korea relations have not always been the smoothest. Major efforts have been made to strengthen Japan's friendly relations with China, Korea, and the ASEAN countries, and these areas are musts for Prime Ministers traveling overseas.

Relations with Russia

Given the unresolved status of the Northern Territories of Kunashir, Etorofu, Habomais, and Shikotan, Japan and Russia have yet to sign a peace treaty. Japan is pushing tenaciously for the Territories' return even as it maintains economic and cultural relations with Russia.

Participation in the United Nations

The United Nations figures prominently in Japanese foreign policy. Yet looking at the amount Japan contributes to the UN (more than many of the Security Council's permanent members), and its relative lack of voice and influence, Japan has begun campaigning for a permanent seat in the Security Council as a way of rectifying this disparity. Although there are many people in Japan who want to go slow on this, fearing that permanent membership might entail an obligation to commit Japanese forces overseas, most Japanese favor the idea of permanent membership.

専守防衛と安全保障条約

日本の防衛政策は，各国に比べてきわめて大きな制約を受けている。憲法第９条に，戦争放棄，戦力の不保持と交戦権の否定に関する規定があること，核については「もたず，作らず，もち込ませず」という非核三原則があるからである。したがって，日本の防衛は専守防衛を基本的な方針として，自衛隊を創設，その整備を推進し，運用を図ってきた。

専守防衛ということばについての確定された定義はないが，①相手から武力攻撃を受けたとき，初めて防衛力を行使する　②その行使は必要最小限度にとどめる　③装備も攻撃的なものでなく，自衛的な武器に限る　など「受動的な戦略である」と日本政府は説明している。具体的には，性能上，もっぱら他国の国土の壊滅的破壊のためにのみに用いられる兵器，例えばICBM，長距離戦略爆撃機などはもてない。

こうしたことから戦闘行為を伴う海外派兵はできない。政府は，後方支援の国連平和監視部隊の一員なら，自衛隊の派遣は許されると解釈，カンボジア，ゴラン高原の国連平和維持活動要員として，自衛隊を派遣した。

また政府は「集団的自衛権は憲法違反」という憲法解釈を採っている。しかし日本は，さまざまな制約をもつ日本の防衛力を補完するため，アメリカと安全保障条約を結んでいる。いわゆる日米安保条約である。こうした憲法解釈では，アメリカだけが日本の防衛に義務を負うという片務的状況が起きることが避けられず，「このままでは日本防衛の基盤である，日米同盟にひびが入りかねない」と日米両国内から，この解釈の変更を求める声がでている。

自衛隊と防衛力の拡大

自衛隊の規模は，陸上が８個師団，６個旅団，１個機甲師団，１個空挺団（くうていだん）などで，隊員は14万6000人。海は４個護衛隊群などを基軸に護衛艦50隻，潜水艦16隻，作戦用航空機170機，隊員４万3000人。空は17飛行隊を中核に約400機（うち戦闘機が約300機），隊員４万4000人。アメリカは，「日本の防衛力はまだ不十分」として，さらにその整備を求めている。

防衛力の整備をするに当たって，日本政府は防衛計画大綱を作り，それに基づいて充実を図っているが，その上限をGNP１％としていた。しかし装備費，人件費の上昇で，１％の枠を守るのはしだいに困難になってきて，1987年度の予算で１％の枠を超えた。しかし1995年につくられた新防衛大綱によると，日本の防衛費は，今後ともGNP１％前後に推移することになっている。

Japanese Defense Policy

Defense-orientation and the Security Treaty

Japanese defense policy operates under many more restrictions than exist in most other nations. Article 9 of the Japanese Constitution is a declaration that "land, sea, and air forces, as well as other war potential will never be maintained," and a renunciation of the right of belligerency of the state. Added to this is the government's Three Non-nuclear Principles which state that Japan will not produce, possess, or allow the entry of nuclear weapons. Japan's stance is thus purely defensive, and the establishment and maintenance of the Self-Defense Forces (SDF) has been in line with this fundamental policy.

Although Japan's defense strategy has no official definition, it is to be reactive in that (i) Japan will employ its self-defense capability only when attacked, (ii) such a response will be limited to the absolute minimum force required, and (iii) all weapons will be defensive weapons only. More specifically, weapons capable of being used in an attack on a foreign nation, such as ICBMs and long-range strategic bombers, will not be maintained.

As a result, Japan cannot send forces overseas to engage in combat. However, the government has interpreted this as allowing the dispatch of SDF personnel to provide logistics support for UN peace-keeping operations, and has sent forces to take part in UN operations in Cambodia and the Golan Heights.

The government has also taken the position that the constitution prohibits collective defense efforts. Despite this, Japan has concluded security arrangements with the United States to offset the various constraints the SDF operates under. As a consequence, the treaty provides that the U.S. is bound to defend Japan but Japan does not incur a reciprocal obligation, and there are many people in both countries calling for a rethinking of these constitutional positions lest the non-reciprocity create fissures in the Japan-U.S. alliance that underpins Japan's defense.

Expansion of the SDF and Defense Capability

The Japanese Self Defense Forces (SDF) are comprised of a ground force including 8 divisions, 6 brigades, 1 armored division and 1 airborne unit, and totaling 150,000 men; a navel force of 4 escort fleets including 50 escort vessels, 16 submarines and 170 strategic aircraft, and totaling 43,000 men; and an air force of 400 aircraft (300 of which are fighters) divided into 17 squadrons, and totaling 44,000 men. The U.S. continues to insist, that Japan's defense capabilities are inadequate and must be further enhanced.

As to the matter of defense capability, the Japanese government formulated a defense budgeting schedule by means of which it proposed to fulfill all its defense needs. But the upper limit it placed was 1% of the GNP. Given the rising costs of equipment and personnel, however, it became increasingly hard to remain within this limit, and the 1987 budget actually went beyond the 1% ceiling. A new budgeting schedule was drawn up in 1995, so that now Japan's annual defense spending can be anywhere in the neighborhood of 1% of the GNP.

世界第1位のODA供与国

先進国から発展途上国に与える経済援助のうち，政府・政府機関によって行われるものをODA（政府開発援助）という。これには二国間の贈与（無償資金協力と技術協力）・貸し付け，国際機関への資金拠出などが含まれる。日本は1999年に米貨で154億ドルのODAを供与した。これはOECD（経済協力開発機構）のDAC（開発援助委員会）加盟22か国のODA総額の約4分の1（27.2%）を占め，日本は1991年から9年連続して世界第1位のODA供与国となっている。

二国間ODAの地域別・分野別内訳

99年の二国間ODAの総額約105億ドルのうち，アジア向けは約63%を占めた。最大の供与国はインドネシアで，中国・タイ・ベトナムがそれに次ぐ。その他の地域では，アフリカが約9%，中南米が約8%，中東が約5%，オセアニアとヨーロッパがともに1%台となっている。

日本の二国間ODAを分野別で見ると，道路・鉄道・港湾・空港・電力などの経済インフラ整備が多く，全体の31.5%を占める。また，住宅・上水道・教育などの社会インフラ整備は18.9%である。

日本のODAの課題

日本のODAは，金額では世界一でも，対GNP比率が低い。例えば，99年の日本のODAの対GNP比率は0.35%であり，国連総会で決定された0.7%という目標には遠く及ばない。DAC加盟22か国の平均の0.24%よりは高いが，第7位である。また，国民一人当たりのODAは98年に84.1ドルで，DAC諸国中第9位である。また，贈与の比率が低いなどの批判がある。贈与の比率は98～99年平均で45.4%であり，DAC加盟国中最下位である。ODA供与の条件の緩やかさを示すグラン・エレメント比率も83.6%と最下位である。国内でも巨額の財政赤字が続き，また景気の悪化から失業者が増加する状況のなかで，多額のODAを供与することに対する不満や，ODAが有効に使われていないのではないかという疑問が出てきている。政府が今後，財政赤字を減らす努力をするなかで，ODAをどう見直していくかが注目されている。

Economic Cooperation

The World's No. 1 ODA Nation

Among the various types of assistance offered by developed countries to developing countries is that which is given by a government or governmental agency, and is termed Official Development Assistance, or ODA. ODA may take the form of a gift (financial or technical assistance with no strings attached) or a loan from one government to another, or consist of funds deposited with an international agency. In 1999 Japan offered ODA totaling US$15.4 billion. This is approximately one fourth (27.2%) of the total ODA figure for all 22 member nations of the Development Assistance Committee (DAC) of the Organization for Economic Cooperation and Development (OECD), making Japan the world's number one giver of ODA for the ninth straight year since 1991.

Breakdown of ODA to Other Governments by Region and Use

Of the approximately US$10.5 billion in ODA given by the Japanese government to other nations in 1999, roughly 63% went to Asia. Indonesia received the largest share of this, followed by China, Thailand and Viet Nam. Other parts of the world receiving Japanese assistance included Africa (approximately 9%), Central and South America (approximately 8%), the Middle East (approximately 5%) and Oceania and Europe (each approximately 1%).

A sizeable portion, 31.5%, of Japan's ODA to other countries goes into improving the economic infrastructure, with such projects as roads, railroads, harbors, airports, electric power plants, etc. 18.9% of Japan's ODA goes to improving the social infrastructure, in the form of housing, water, education and other projects.

Criticism of Japanese ODA

Although Japanese ODA might be number one in the world dollar-wise, it often comes under criticism for being low compared to Japan's GNP. In 1999 Japan's ODA was 0.35% of its GNP, which is far below the 0.7% goal set by the UN General Assembly. Percentage-wise it is above the 0.24% average for all 22 member nations of DAC, but ranks Japan only seventh. Or take a look at per capita ODA. In 1998 this worked out to US$84.10, ranking Japan ninth among DAC member nations. Another criticism is that the percentage of Japanese ODA in the form of gifts is low. For 1998~99 gifts averaged 45.4% of total ODA, placing Japan last among DAC member nations. The grand element ratio, used to express the leniency of the conditions of ODA giving, also puts Japan in last place, with 83.6%. At home Japan continues to be plagued with huge deficit spending, while the economy deteriorates and unemployment grows. There is growing criticism of huge ODA spending, and concern that ODA is not being used effectively. It will be interesting to note just how attitudes toward ODA are redefined as the Japanese government makes an effort to decrease deficit spending in the years to come.

第二次世界大戦により混乱に陥った日本経済は，1947年ごろから急速に復興をとげ，55年ごろからは約20年にわたり高度成長と呼ばれる持続的な経済成長を記録した。70年代の２度の石油危機を経て，日本経済は安定成長の時代に入ったが，80年代後半の地価・株価の高騰(バブル)とそれに続くバブルの崩壊，急速な円高の進行などによって，90年代初めには長期不況に陥り，21世紀に入った現在も低成長に直面している。

敗戦後の経済的混乱

敗戦直後の日本経済は悲惨な状況にあった。工業生産の水準は戦前の10分の１に落ち込み，その後も３分の１前後の水準で推移した。国民の生活は食べるのが精一杯であり，消費の中にしめる食費の割合を示すエンゲル係数は，戦前でも30％にすぎなかったのが，46年には68％にもなった。インフレも激しく，45年の物価水準は37年の4.4倍となり，48年には100倍を超えた。外国貿易もほとんど停止の状態にあった。

このような経済的混乱に対し，なによりも生産力を回復し，インフレを抑えることが優先された。生産力の回復のためにとられた措置が傾斜生産方式である。これは石炭と鉄鋼の増産に集中的に資源を投下し，これらの生産の増加分を順次，他の生産に振り向けていくという方式であった。また，消費を抑制し，重要な物資の生産を優先させるために，経済安定本部という強力な機関を設け，物資ごとの配給をするなど，統制的な手段も用いられた。消費の抑制には一定額以上の預金の引き出しを禁止することなども行われたが，インフレを抑えることはできなかった。

混乱からの回復

傾斜生産方式による生産の増加などにより，日本経済は47年ごろから急激な復興が始まり，48年には17.5％の経済成長率の最高記録が達成された。しかし，この回復が「国内の補助金とアメリカからの援助の２本足で立つ竹馬経済のそれ」であると断じた占領軍経済顧問のドッジ公使は，均衡予算の編成，円レートの360円への一本化など，厳しい緊縮政策を指示した。この結果，49年から不況色が強まったが，インフレの原因は一掃された。

その後，50年に始まった朝鮮戦争による特需などによって国内需要が盛り上がり，日本経済は50～52年には戦前の水準に回復した。技術水準の遅れを取り戻そうとする日本企業の高い投資意欲と，それまで抑えられていた消費需要が所得の増加により解放されたことが背景にある。

復興期には，財閥の解体，農地改革による自作農の創出，労働組合の結成などによる労働者の地位向上などの経済体制の改革が行われ，戦後の経済発展のための枠組みが整備された。

Japan's Postwar Economic Recovery

Chaotic ruins in the wake of World War II, the Japanese economy began its remarkable come-back around 1947. By 1955, the foundations had been laid and the economy started nearly two decades of rapid growth. Although this growth was slowed by the two oil crises of the 1970s, the economy experienced a period of excess liquidity and asset inflation in the late 1980s and then the bubble's inevitable bursting. Even as Japan enters the 21st century the economy has yet to shake its post-bubble recession.

Postwar Turmoil

The economy was a disaster at the end of the war. Industrial production was only 1/10 of prewar levels and was seemingly unable to get back beyond 1/3. The people lived hand to mouth and the Engel coefficient (the share of total consumption going to food) was 68% in 1946 — even though it had never before been any higher than 30%. Inflation was rampant, with 1945 consumer prices up 4.4-fold—and 1948 prices up 100-fold—over 1937 levels. Foreign trade had come to a virtual standstill, and the nation was thrown back on its own inadequate resources.

The first imperatives were thus to restore industrial productivity and to rein in inflation. In seeking to restore industry, it was decided to focus on the most important industries first by concentrating resources on coal and steel and then to allocate output to other industries as it became available. On the inflation front, an Economic Stabilization Board was established and given wide-ranging powers to discourage consumption and to direct resources to favored industries. Among the measures taken to discourage consumption was one setting a ceiling on savings withdrawals, yet not even these heavy-handed controls could stop inflation.

Recovery

These measures resulted in increased production and the Japanese economy jumped back on its feet around 1947 and achieved an unprecedented 17.5% economic growth in 1948. However, Joseph Dodge, sent to Japan to advise SCAP on economic policy, criticized the economy as looking strong simply because it was propped up by domestic subsidies and U.S. assistance. Far from satisfied with the economy's performance, Dodge demanded harsh austerity, including balanced budgets for the government and an official exchange rate of ¥360/$. As a result, inflation was tamed, but the economy was limping toward stagnation in 1949.

However, the outbreak of the Korean War in 1950 sparked massive procurement demand from the U.S. military, and by 1950-52 the Japanese economy had regained its prewar levels. This was further boosted by technological advances as Japanese companies invested heavily in research and development, and by consumer demand as people rushed to enjoy their wealth.

During the years when SCAP ruled, it effected a number of reforms—including *zaibatsu* dissolution, agrarian land reform to give tenant farmers the land they farmed, and legal guarantees for the rights of workers—that changed the economic climate and helped the postwar recovery.

高度成長の理由

高度成長期と呼ばれる1955年から73年までの期間の日本の実質経済成長率は9.1%にもなった。同期間にアメリカで３%前後，ヨーロッパ主要国で５～６%の実質成長率であったから，日本の成長はきわめて高かった。需要面で成長をリードしたのは設備投資，消費，輸出であった。設備投資はこの間に年率で16.5%伸び，15.7倍もの規模になった。このような高い投資の伸びをもたらしたのは，第１に新製品，新技術がめざましい勢いで開発され，これらを生産に結びつける設備投資が拡大したこと，第２に戦後復興期には既存の設備の稼働率を引き上げることで済んだのが，この時期には能力の限界に突き当たり，能力拡大の投資が他の投資を呼ぶメカニズムができたことによる。消費の拡大は耐久消費財の急速な普及によるところが大きい。50年代には白黒テレビ，洗濯機，冷蔵庫が「３種の神器」と呼ばれ，60年代にはカラーテレビ，ルームクーラー，乗用車が「３Ｃ」と呼ばれて，需要が急拡大した。輸出は年率13.5%と，世界貿易の1.6倍のスピードで増加した。輸出の高い伸びは，国内市場のみでは不可能であった規模の経済を実現させ，設備の近代化と技術革新の積極的導入により，日本製品の国際競争力は飛躍的に高まった。

供給面からみると，人口の増加率が1.4%と比較的に高かった上に，農業からの人口の移動があり，さらに教育水準の高まりによる質の改善があった。高い投資の伸びは貯蓄によって支えなければならないが，この時期には家計の貯蓄率が20%を超えるまでに高まるなど，国内貯蓄の増加があった。技術においては，日本は欧米諸国へのキャッチアップの過程にあり，旺盛な技術導入の意欲が技術進歩を支えた。また，平和な世界で自由貿易の体制が整備されていったことが，日本の輸出環境を改善し，エネルギー・原料の安定的確保を可能にしたことも大きい。

安定成長期への移行

70年代の２度にわたる石油危機，外国との通商摩擦，80年代の円高の進行などにより，日本経済が高度成長期の成長を続けることは不可能となった。これは，輸出を大幅に伸ばして貿易黒字を拡大することが困難となり，技術水準も欧米水準に追いついて，技術革新のスピードが低下したことによる。労働力の伸びも低下し，農業からの移動もほぼ枯渇し，日本経済は安定成長へ移行する。80年代後半には地価と株価などの資産価格が急騰（きゅうとう）し，90年代には逆に急低下した。バブルの発生と崩壊である。バブルの発生期に過剰に行われた実物，金融両面の投資はその後に不良資産として残り，日本経済はなおその影響から抜けきっていない。

From Rapid to Stable Growth

Rapid Growth

In the rapid-growth period of 1955-73; Japan had a real economic growth rate averaging 9.1% per annum. This was very rapid growth, the equivalent figures during the same period being about 3% for the U.S. and 5-6% for Europe. On the demand side, this growth was fueled by capital investment, consumption, and exports. Facilities investment grew 16.5% p.a. during this period, while production capacity expanded 15.7 times. The two main factors sustaining this growth in capital investment were (i) the drive to commercialize and produce the new products made possible by rapid technological advances, and (ii) the fact that production lines could no longer simply be expanded but had to be replaced with new equipment if industry was to satisfy the booming demand. Much of the growth in consumption was due to the popularization of consumer durables. In the 1950s this focused on black-and-white television sets, washing machines, and refrigerators; and in the 1960s the focus changed to color television sets, air conditioning, and automobiles. On the export front, exports were up 13.5% p.a., growing 60% faster than world trade. This export growth then made it possible for Japan to achieve an economy of a scale that the domestic market alone would not sustain, while factory modernization and agressive introduction of new technology made Japanese products much more competitive on the international market.

On the supply side, the population was growing at a strong 1.4% p.a., and there was a considerable flow of labor from the farms to industry. In addition, educational advances meant that the labor force was of higher quality. Heavy investment has to be financed by strong savings, and during this period domestic savings increased, with a household savings rate of over 20%. Technologically, Japan was still catching up with the West, and ambitious efforts were made to learn from other countries. Finally, the fact that free markets were established in a world at peace dramatically improved the climate for Japanese exports and made it possible for Japan to import the oil and other resources it needed.

Economic Slowdown

Yet the two oil crises of the 1970s brought this rapid growth to a halt, and the slowdown was consolidated with trade friction and subsequent yen appreciation. For one, it was no longer possible to keep expanding exports and building ever greater trade surpluses, and for another Japanese technology caught up with world levels and could no longer achieve its quantum leaps forward. At the same time, the labor force grew more slowly as there were fewer people left to leave the farms. For all of these reasons, the Japanese economy entered a period of slower growth. In the late 1980s, a liquidity glut fueled asset inflation and rampant speculation. When the speculative bubble burst, the economy plunged into recession in the 1990s. Many of the "bubble investments" in land, financial products, and other assets had to be written off as losses, and the economy has yet to recover from this trauma.

産業・就業構造の変遷

戦後の日本の産業構造は，きわめて大きく姿を変えていった。それは，まず，農業から工業へ，さらにはサービス業へという流れであった。その結果，1999年の日本の国内総生産（GDP）の合計512兆円のうち，第1次産業（農林水産業）は8兆円，第2次産業（鉱業，製造業，建設業）は150兆円，第3次産業（サービス業ほか）は354兆円を生み出すようになっている。GDPにおける構成比の変化を1955年と1999年で比べると第1次は20%から2%へ，第2次は33%から29%へ，第3次は47%から69%となった。

就業者の構成をみるとその変化はよりはっきりしている。全就業者に対する第1次，2次，3次産業のシェアは，55年のそれぞれ41%，25%，34%から，99年には5%，31%，64%へ変わった。

進むサービス産業化，知識集約化と空洞化

産業構造のサービス化が進むのは，所得水準の上昇に応じて消費の内容が衣食住の必需的なものから，文化，教育，レジャーなどに多様化するためで，先進国に共通の現象である。

第2次産業の構成比の変化がそれほど大きくなかったのは，このうちでウエートが大きい製造業の製品の価格が技術革新の成果の恩恵を受けてあまり上昇せず，生産金額が増えにくかったからである。価格を固定して数量的な増加で比べると，1955年から1970年の間にGDP全体の年平均伸び率が8.9%であったのに対し，製造業は13.8%であった。高度成長期において，数量面では製造業が経済成長をリードしたと言える。

しかし，1998年にはGDP全体の対前年比−1.2%に対して製造業は−5.0%，1999年にはGDP全体−0.6%に対して製造業−2.6%と，製造業の生産の落ち込みがGDPをマイナス成長にする一因となってしまった。これは，バブル崩壊後の不況下で，デフレに陥ったことが原因である。メーカーは安値競争の中で生き残るため，人件費の安い中国に生産拠点を移して，コストの削減を図るようになり，産業の空洞化が急速に進み始めた。

製造業の中では，1950年代から60年代には金属，化学，機械などへ重点が移る「重化学工業化」が見られたが，石油ショックを経た70年代後半以降は，金属などの基礎素材型から，工作機械，電気機械，自動車などの加工組立型へウエートが移った。さらに半導体，情報機器，高度通信機器などへとつながる流れは，「技術集約化」，また「知識集約化」と言われる。

Changing Industrial Structure

Changes in Industrial and Employment Structure

Japanese industrial structure changed dramatically after the war, first from agriculture to manufacturing, and then from manufacturing to services. As a result, of the total GDP of ¥512 trillion in 1999, ¥8 trillion was in the primary sector (agriculture, fishing, etc.), ¥150 trillion in the secondary sector (mining, manufacturing, construction), and the remaining ¥354 trillion in the tertiary sector (trading, finance, etc.). As percentages of the total, the primary sector fell from 20% in 1955 to 2% in 1999, the secondary fell slightly from 33% to 29%, while services grew from 47% to 69%.

The changes in the different sectors' shares of total employment between 1955 and 1999 are even more dramatic : primary down from 41% to 5%, secondary up from 25% to 31%, and tertiary up from 34% to 64%.

Increasing Reliance on Services and Knowledge-Intensive Industries

This shift to the tertiary sector is common to all industrial countries and is caused by the fact that rising incomes have enabled people to meet their basic food, shelter, and clothing requirements and to diversify demand into cultural, educational, recreational, and other non-essential areas.

One of the reasons that the secondary sector's share of GDP did not change as much as might be expected from the fact that Japan is now a manufacturing powerhouse is that technological advances allowed companies to hold prices down even as they expanded production volume. If we not worry about price but just compare increase in volume of production, we see that volume-wise GDP as a whole increased at an average of 8.9% per year during the period 1955 to 1970, while the average increase in industrial output was 13.8%. In other words, it was industrial output that powered economic growth as far as volume of production is concerned during Japan's high-growth years.

In 1998 however, GDP as a whole was −1.2% compared to the previous year, while industrial output was −5.0%. Again in 1999 total GDP was −0.6% compared to the previous year, while industrial output was −2.6%. Thus decline in industrial output has become a factor in the minus growth of the GDP. This is a result of deflation brought about by the bursting of Japan's economic bubble. In order to keep prices competitive businesses have had to move their manufacturing facilities to China where labor is cheap, thus cutting production costs, but at the same time escalating industrial hollowing.

In the 1950s and 1960s, industry tended to focus on metals, chemicals, machinery, and other heavy industry. Yet with the oil crises, this changed in the late 1970s, moving away from metals and other basic industries to machine tools, electrical equipment, automobiles, and other assembly industries. Since then, the center has further shifted to semiconductors, data processing, high-speed telecommunications, and other technology-intensive, knowledge-intensive fields.

日本の輸出構造

輸出品は，かつて繊維製品が中心であったが，現在は機械機器が中心で，1999年には73.4%を占めている。その他の輸出品は，化学品が7.4%，金属品が6.3%である。輸出される機械機器の第1位は，輸出総額の20.3%を占める自動車（主に乗用車）で，自動車部品を含めると25.0%にもなる。第2位は電子部品（主に集積回路）で，10.7%を占める。輸出先はアジア諸国向けの伸びがめざましく，1999年で37.3%を占め，アメリカ向けの30.7%を大きく上回った。

日本の輸入構造

輸入品は，かつては原油・石油製品・天然ガス・石炭などの鉱物性燃料が中心であったが，最近は機械機器の伸びがきわめて高く，99年には輸入総額の31.3%を占めた。その他の製品を含めた製品輸入のシェアは，99年には62.4%にまで上昇した。鉱物性燃料は16.1%，繊維原料・金属原料・木材などの原料品は7.2%に過ぎない。輸入先でもアジア諸国が躍進しており，99年のシェアは39.6%で，アメリカの21.6%を大きく上回った。アジア諸国の中では中国が最大の輸入先で，輸入総額の13.8%を占める。

頻発する貿易摩擦

1960年代以降，日本の輸出が急増する中で，外国との貿易摩擦が繰り返された。古くは62年以降の繊維から，66年の鉄鋼，77年のカラーテレビ，81年の自動車，85年の半導体，98年の鉄鋼と，主としてアメリカとの間の問題解決のための交渉が続けられた。

1990年代から不景気の続く日本では，一方では日本企業が中国で農産物や工業製品を作って，日本へ輸入するケースが増えており，農家や衣料・タオル・機械部品などのメーカーに大きな打撃を与えている。中国の労働者一人に要する人件費は，日本の10分の1と言われており，価格競争では日本はとても太刀打ち出来ない。2001年には，中国からのネギなど農産物3品目の輸入が，国内の農家に大きい損害を与えているとして，日本では初めてセーフガードの適用に踏み切り，中国との貿易摩擦が発生した。日本のセーフガード適用に対して，中国も日本製自動車などの輸入に効率の関税をかける対抗措置を開始した。日本では更に他の品目のセーフガード適用も検討されており，日中間の貿易摩擦がますます拡大することが懸念されている。

Trade Structure and Trade Friction

Japan's Export Structure

At one time textiles were the major export, but today Japan's major export is machinery and equipment, comprising 73.49% of total exports for 1999. Other export items include chemicals (7.4%) and metal products (6.3%). The leading exported piece of machinery is the automobile—mainly family cars—comprising 20.3% of total export value. When automotive parts are added to this, the figure becomes 25.0%. The second largest export item is electronic parts—mainly integrated circuits—comprising 10.7%. As to export destinations, there has been a spectacular growth in exports to Asia, which received 37.3% of Japan's exports in 1999. This is well above the 30.7% which went to the U.S.

Japan's Import Structure

At one time crude oil, petroleum products, natural gas, coal and other fossil fuels were the major import item, but recently there has been a rapid growth in machinery and equipment, which comprised 31.3% of total imports in 1999. Combined with other manufactured products, manufactured imports comprised 62.4% of all imports in 1999. Fossil fuels comprised 16.1%, while raw materials for textiles, metal ores, timber and other raw materials comprised only 7.2%. Imports from Asia are climbing rapidly, and made up 39.6% of total imports in 1999, far outstripping imports from the U.S. at 21.6%. China is the largest source of imports from Asia, supplying 13.8% of Japan's total imports in 1999.

Recurrent Trade Friction

Since the '60s when Japanese exports began to soar, Japan has repeatedly experienced trade friction with other nations. First it was textiles in '62, then it was steel in '66, color TVs in '77, automobiles in '81, semiconductors in '85, steel again in '98. And usually it was problems with the U.S. that Japan had to negotiate and iron out.

With Japan's continuing recession starting in the '90s, more and more Japanese businesses have begun producing agricultural and manufactured products in China and importing them back to Japan, causing hard times for domestic farmers and manufacturers of clothing, towels, machine parts, etc. Wages for a Chinese worker are said to be one tenth that of the wage in Japan, and thus Japanese prices are nowhere near competitive in a price war.

In 2001 leeks and two other produce items imported from China caused considerable harm to domestic farmers, and for the first time Japan took to applying safeguards, resulting in trade friction with China. In reply to Japan's safeguards China took countermeasures, placing a high customs duty on Japanese made automobiles, etc. Japan is now considering applying safeguards to other items as well, and there is concern that Japanese-Chinese trade friction will escalate even further.

海外直接投資が一時拡大

海外での工場の建設などの日本企業の直接投資は，1985年の先進５か国蔵相会議での行き過ぎたドル安を是正しようとするプラザ合意の後，円高の進展とともに急増が始まった。円高により日本からの輸出の価格が切り上がり，輸出先で現地生産したり，海外工場から輸出したほうが有利となる場合が増えたからである。89年には675億ドルのピークを記録し，多くの投資受け入れ国で日本が最大の直接投資国となったが，バブルのピークとも一致しており，やや行き過ぎの感があった。日本の直接投資はその後低下するが，円高の一層の進行もあって，93年から再び拡大する傾向を示している。80年代後半の直接投資ブームにおいては，金融・保険業，不動産業の，地域別にはアメリカ向けの投資が積極的に行われたが，現在は製造業のアジア向けの投資が活発になっている。特に中国への投資の拡大が目立ち，93年度の製造業直接投資の増加の半分は中国向けだった。製造業の中では，家電や半導体などの電気機械，自動車などの輸送機械の投資のウエートが大きい。

国内経済の空洞化と国際的生産ネットワークの強化

海外への直接投資は，投資が国内から海外へ「流出する」ことであり，日本企業の海外工場で生産された製品が日本へ「逆輸入される」ことでもある。企業の海外進出は，国内工場の海外移転という形で国内経済の空洞化を招く，と心配されてきた。事実，94年度には海外工場からの「逆輸入」額は総輸入額の13％を超えた。日本企業が海外で生産する比率は，製造業で95年度には10％になったと見られるが，アメリカ企業の25％，ドイツ企業の21％に比べれば，まだ低いものの着実に上昇している。

90年代後半からは，日本企業の海外への工場進出は少なくなり，現地企業との提携による海外展開の比重が強まっている。

しかし，工場の海外進出は日本からの部品，材料の輸出を増加させるなどの効果もある。国内経済の空洞化といわれる現象は，最適な立地点を世界に求め，より競争力のある国際的ネットワークを構築するという企業の戦略の反映でもあり，マイナスとばかりみることは適切ではない。経済のグローバル化の一つの過程とみることもできるだろう。

Overseas Production and Industrial Hollowing

Temporary Increase in Foreign Direct Investment

There was a sharp increase in foreign direct investment by Japanese companies intent on building plants and other facilities overseas with the yen's appreciation in the wake of the G-5 Plaza Agreement of 1985 designed to align exchange rates with reality. With the yen appreciation, dollar-denominated prices of exports from Japan went up and it became more advantageous in many cases to manufacture in the market countries or to export from other overseas production facilities. FDI peaked at $67.5 billion in 1989, at which point Japan was the major foreign investor in many countries. However, this was also at the height of the speculative bubble's excesses, and there was a feeling of excess here too. Following that, Japanese FDI slowed considerably, but the continuing yen appreciation put it on an upward curve again starting in 1993. In the late 1980s, most of this FDI was in the financial, insurance, and real estate sectors, and was mainly in the United States. At present, however, the bulk of FDI is for production purposes and is directed at Asia. There has been especially strong investment in China, as fully half of the manufacturing sector's growth in FDI for fiscal 1993 was to China. Much of this manufacturing investment is in consumer electronics, semiconductors, and other electrical machinery and in automobiles and other transport machinery.

Domestic Hollowing and Economic Globalization

Many people have expressed the fear that FDI is money leaking out of Japan and that goods produced at overseas facilities will then be imported into Japan and the economy will be hollowed out. In fact, imports from Japanese facilities overseas accounted for 13% of total Japanese imports in fiscal 1994, and it is estimated that approximately 10% of Japanese production took place overseas in fiscal 1995. While this is still much less than the United States' 25% or Germany's 21%, it is nonetheless a considerable figure and rising.

Since the latter half of the '90s, however, Japanese businesses have been building fewer plants and factories abroad. The present trend in overseas development is toward partnerships with businesses in those countries.

On the other hand, however, the exodus of Japanese factories to other countries in effect also increases the need for parts and materials from Japan. The so-called hollowing phenomenon is also a reflection of business strategy, whereby a company seeks out the most ideal location in the world in an attempt to create a more competitive production network, and in this sense should not be viewed as entirely bad. It is best considered as one necessary feature of economic globalization.

バブルの発生と崩壊

1990年代は日本経済にとって「失われた10年」と言われている。バブル崩壊後の不良債権（融資先から金利の支払いが遅れたり，経営破綻（はたん）で回収できなくなった債権）の処理が遅れ，経済は低成長を余儀なくされた。不良債権の処理の遅れは21世紀に入っても続き，景気回復の見通しが立たない状態に陥っている。

バブルの発生

もともとバブルの発生は，日本経済の構造に起因していた。株式や不動産への過度の投資から，本来の利回りや収益性以上に価格が膨らみ，バブル経済となったのだ。

80年代の輸出の拡大は，アメリカなどの貿易相手国との激しい摩擦を引き起こした。85年のプラザ合意で円高が急進すると，輸出主導の経済成長は困難となり，金利を引き下げて内需を増やそうとする動きに転じた。87年のブラックマンデー（アメリカの株価急落）の影響を避けようとした金利引き下げも行われて，国内での資金供給が拡大し，膨大なマネーが土地や株式などに投入された。

地価上昇を背景に，金融機関は不動産担保貸し出しを急増させた。調達された資金は，設備投資や新たな不動産投資に向けられ，のちの不良債権につながっていった。株価の上昇は個人消費を活発化され，新たな需要を生んでいった。

バブル崩壊後の景気低迷

ところが90年代初めのバブル崩壊で，地価と株価は一転して下落した。高値で買った不動産や設備が利益を生まない不良資産となり，企業などを圧迫した。このあおりは個人にも及び，個人消費が低迷を続ける結果となった。98年のGDPの対前年増加率は，ついに－0.6％とマイナス成長になった。

99年には1.4％とやや持ち直したものの，個人消費は相変わらず低迷を続けて，従来の商品価値を大幅に下回る価格で販売する価格破壊が進行し，ついにはデフレに陥った。商品のコストを下げるために，国内工場を閉鎖し，人件費の安い中国などで生産して輸入し，国内で販売する企業が増え，産業の空洞化が急速に進んだ。そのため2001年半ばには，失業率がついに５％を超えた。

The Bubble Expands and Bursts

The '90s are known as the "lost years" as regards the Japanese economy. There was difficulty in disposing of bad debts (debts for which interest payments are late, or which are not recoverable because of bankruptcy), and the economy was inevitably forced into low growth. This difficulty in disposing of bad debts has continued even on into the 21st century, and the economy has fallen into such a state that there is no saying when it will recover.

The Bubble Expands

Essentially the bubble has its origin in the structure of the Japanese economy. Excessive investment in stocks and real estate inflated values all out of proportion, thus creating the bubble economy.

A sharp rise in Japanese exports in the '80s generated a great amount of friction between Japan and the U.S. and other trade partners. With the G-5 Plaza Agreement of 1985 and the rapid appreciation of the yen, Japan's export bolstered economic growth ran into difficulty. Interest rates were lowered in an attempt to increase domestic demand. There was another lowering of interest rates in 1987 in an attempt to avoid the effects of Black Monday when the U.S stock market crashed. The expanded supply of domestic capital resulted in huge amounts of money being invested in land and stocks.

Against this background of increasing land values finance companies sharply increased the number of loans with real estate as security. Capital secured through such loans was invested in facilities and equipment, or used for purchasing more real estate (later to become a factor in bad debts). A rise in stock value acted as an incentive for people to increase consumption, thus creating an increased domestic demand

The Bubble Bursts, The Economy Crashes

Japan's economic bubble burst, however, at the start of the '90s and land and stock values nose-dived. Real estate, facilities and equipment purchased at high bubble prices were unable to pay for themselves, putting pressure on the businesses that owned them. Individuals felt the pressure as well, and personal consumption has continued to flounder. The 1998 GDP (gross domestic product) ratio compared to the previous year was — 0.6%, indicating minus economic growth.

The figure for 1999 was + 1.4%, a slight improvement, but personal consumption was still down and more and more goods were being sold at prices below their original price, bringing about deflation. In order to lower production costs, more and more businesses were closing down domestic plants, manufacturing their goods in China and elsewhere where labor is cheap, importing them back to Japan and selling them domestically, further exacerbating economic hollowing. As a result the middle of 2001 saw the unemployment rate in Japan exceed 5%.

ゼロ金利政策

日本銀行のゼロ金利政策は，金融機関同士が資金をやり取りする短期金融市場（無担保コール翌日物）の金利をほとんどゼロに近い水準に下げることにより，市場に潤沢な資金を流して景気を下支えする政策で，99年２月に開始した。これにより個人の預貯金の金利はほとんどつかなくなり，年金生活者らに多大な影響が出た。日銀は2000年８月にゼロ金利を一旦解除したが，景気の回復が遅く，2001年に再びゼロ金利に戻らざるを得なくなった。

不良債権処理

21世紀に入って，日本経済再生の最大のポイントになっているのが，不良債権の処理だ。全国の銀行が抱える不良債権の残高は，2000年度末で32兆円。銀行はそれまでの８年半の間に，累計で68兆円の不良債権を処理してきたが，一向に減らないどころか，融資先企業の倒産・業績悪化や担保価値下落などで，増える傾向が続いている。

　不良債権処理の原資は，銀行業の本業のもうけにあたる業務純益や，保有する株式の含み益だが，全国の銀行の業務純益は年間５兆円前後で，有価証券含み益も減少しており，処理はままならない状況である。

　不良債権は発生してから２～３年で帳簿から切り離すのが課題だが，銀行は問題先送り体質が根強く，解決が遅れてきた。

　このほかには，海外の機関投資家に不良債権を安く買ってもらう方法や，民事再生法や会社更生法による法的な処理がある。

小泉内閣の構造改革

2001年に誕生した小泉純一郎内閣は，経済・財政運営の基本方針として，不良債権の２，３年以内での処理を打ち出した。整理回収機構の機能を強化するほか，企業の倒産や失業者の増加には，規制緩和による新規雇用創出でカバーする方針である。特殊法人・郵政事業・国立大学の民営化を含む見直しも含めている。またIT（情報技術）や環境に予算を重点的に配分して，従来の公共事業偏重を是正する姿勢を強調している。

0% Interest Rate Policy and Disposing of Bad Debts

0% Interest Rate

The Bank of Japan announced its interest rate policy in February 1999. The aim of this policy is to pour an abundant flow of capital into the market and bolster the economy by means of lowering to nearly 0% the interest rate in the short-term financial market (unsecured transactions payable the following day) in which financial businesses transfer capital amongst themselves. But this meant that nearly 0% interest was earned on personal savings accounts as well, and had a great adverse affect on people living on old age pensions. The Bank of Japan tentatively lifted its 0% interest rate in August 2000, but economic recovery remained slow, and it was forced to return to 0% interest in 2001.

Disposing of Bad Debts

The greatest barrier to rebirth of the Japanese economy at the start of the 21st century is the disposal of bad debts. The total value of uncollected bad debts held by Japanese banks at the end of fiscal year 2000 was ¥32 trillion. Over the eight and a half previous years banks managed to dispose of a sum total of ¥68 trillion in bad debts, but instead of decreasing, bankruptcies, poor business results and a fall in mortgage values have combined to actually increase the value of outstanding bad debts.

Normally a bad should be written off the books in two to three years from the time it is incurred. The cost of the bad debt must be subtracted from the bank's net operating profits and latent profits from negotiable securities in its possession. However at present the annual net operating profits of all the banks in Japan totals somewhere around ¥5 trillion, while the latent value of securities remains low. Thus banks would have to admit to heavy losses, something they are reluctant to do, and so the problem drags on and on.

Other means for disposing of bad debts include selling them off at low prices to foreign institutional investors, or disposing of them through application of the Civil Rehabilitation Law or Corporation Reorganization Law.

The Koizumi Cabinet and Structural Reform

The *Koizumi* Cabinet was formed in 2001, and its basic economic and financial policy calls for the disposal of bad debts within two to three years. Besides strengthening the operation of the structure for handling and recovering debts, its policy also aims at offsetting the rise in business bankruptcy and unemployment by creating new employment through the relaxing of regulations and restrictions. Also under consideration is the privatization of various semi-governmental agencies, the postal service and national universities. The cabinet also emphasizes its intention to weight budget allocations towards information technology and the environment, and to correct the hitherto evils of public works and services.

変貌を遂げる日本の流通

日本の流通は，伝統的に次のような多段階構造になっていた。まず，1次卸，2次卸というようないくつかの卸売業者があって，その先にエンドユーザーに接する小売業がある。さらに，小売業には，日常的な買い物に対応する個人商店と，衣料・装飾品・家具などを中心に豊富な品揃えをするデパートからなっていた。戦後，スーパーと呼ばれる量販店が急速に拡大していくことになり，その結果価格競争のため小さな個人商店への影響が大きくなった。それを緩和するための大規模小売店舗法(大店法)によって，スーパーの出店が抑えられ，価格競争は停滞した。しかし，1990年になって大店法が改正になり，規制が大幅に緩和され，大型店や郊外型ショッピングセンターが相次いで開店した。2000年6月には，大店法から大規模小売店舗立地法（大店立地法）に改正された。大型店が出店する際に，騒音対策，ゴミ対策，駐車場整備など，周辺の生活環境への影響を審査することとなった。そのため，改正前に出店する大型店が続出した。このため，1990年に個人商店は激減している。

一方，90年代後半には新しい小売業の形態も次々に登場した。大手メーカーや専門店の売れ残り品や規格外品を30～70％引きで売るアウトレット(在庫処分)モールが郊外にできた。商店街には，文房具や生活雑貨などを100円で売る100円ショップが現れた。これらの新しい小売形態や価格の下落は，長びく不況と消費の低迷を反映しているといえる。また，こういった消費形態の変化で，一時は売り上げで百貨店のトップだった「そごう」が，民事再生法の適用を申請し，事実上倒産したほか，地方百貨店などが閉店に追い込まれた。

高い物価，残る内外価格差

日本の物価の水準は，外国に比べてかなり高い。例えば，ガソリン・スタンドで2，3人がかりで接客するサービスに見られるような過剰なサービスがコストを押し上げていることもあるが，あまりに速く円高になったからでもある。95年の経済企画庁の調査による東京の物価水準は，ニューヨークの1.59倍，ロンドンの1.52倍，パリの1.34倍，ベルリンの1.35倍，ジュネーブの1.02倍とされている。

バブル崩壊以降，低成長が続いた日本は，物価が比較的安定した動きとなった。内閣府は2001年3月，「緩やかなデフレーション(持続的な物価下落）にある」と，戦後初めてデフレにあることを認定した。

Distribution and Consumer Prices

Changing Patterns of Distribution

Japanese distribution has traditionally been multi-layered. At the top are the primary wholesalers who take delivery from the manufacturers and pass the products along to the secondary wholesalers and so on down the chain until they reach the retail outlet and finally the consumer. Before the war, the main retail outlets were the mom-and-pop stores catering to everyday needs and the department stores with their full line of up-scale clothing, furnishings, furniture, and more. After the war, however, this started to change as supermarkets appeared with their wide assortment and competitive prices, and these general merchandise stores had a major impact on the mom-and-pop stores. Responding to the small retailers' cries, the government enacted the Large-scale Retail Store Law in 1973 restricting new store openings and reducing the incentives for price competition. The Large-scale Retail Store Law was amended in 1990, however, leading to a rash of new large scale stores and suburban shopping centers being opened. In June 2000 this law was further revised to become the Large-scale Retail Store Location Law. Under this law a newly opening large store must undergo inspection for its effect on the surrounding environment and residents, including how it deals with noise pollution and waste disposal, its parking facilities, etc. Therefore anyone planning to open a shopping center did it before the new legislation came into effect.

The latter half of the '90s saw many new styles of retailing appearing on the scene as well. Outlet malls sprang up in the suburbs offering leftover and non-standard merchandise from major manufactures or specialized dealers at 30～70% off regular prices. Urban shopping avenues saw the appearance of ¥100 shops selling stationary supplies and sundries. These new styles of retailing and lower prices proved to be more in tune with the dragging economy and consumption. Sogo Department Store, for example, at one time ranked number one among department stores in sales, but was forced to apply under the Civil Rehabilitation Law, essentially going bankrupt. Several other department stores in cities throughout Japan have been forced out of business.

Prices Higher in Japan than Elsewhere

Commodity prices are quite high in Japan compared to prices in other countries. Some of this price differential is also a service differential—as seen in the fact that several people rush out to service your car at the typical Japanese gas station—but part of it is also because prices have not kept pace with the yen's rapid appreciation. According to a 1995 survey by the Economic Planning Agency, *Toukyou* (Tokyo) prices were 1.59 times New York's, 1.52 times London's, 1.35 times Berlin's, 1.34 times Paris's, and 1.02 times Geneva's. Since the bursting of the economic bubble Japanese economic growth has continued to be low and prices have tended to remain stable. In March 2001 the Prime Minister's Office announced a moderate deflation (lasting drop in prices) for the first time ever since the close of WW II.

進む規制緩和

1980年代後半から，各分野で規制緩和が進められた。

•運輸　日本国有鉄道が7つの民間企業（JR7社）に分割された。96年には43年ぶりに国内航空路線に新会社が就航した。

•電気通信　国内の電信電話はNTT（日本電信電話公社）が，外国との電信・電話はKDD（国際電信電話株式会社）が独占するという体制を廃止した。NTTはNTT東日本・NTT西日本の2民間企業に分割されたうえ，KDDI，日本テレコムなどと競争することになった。

•電力・ガス　製造業など電力以外の分野の企業が独自に発電を行い，電力会社に電気を売る「卸売り」が自由化され，入札が始まった。ガスでも，従来の事業者以外の新規参入が，大口需要家向けで認められた。

•金融　銀行，証券会社，信託銀行は，子会社を通して互いの業務に進出できるようになった。

企業系列や国境を越えた企業再編

近年，諸業種で企業再編の動きが加速し，三井・三菱・住友などの旧財閥の枠組みをも越えるようになった。

•金融　銀行は，みずほフィナンシャルグループ，三井住友銀行，三菱東京フィナンシャル・グループ，UFJ（ユナイテッド・フィナンシャル・オブ・ジャパン）グループなどに再編された。

•自動車　1999年にルノー社（フランス）が日産自動車に出資した。2000年には三菱自動車がダイムラー・クライスラー社（ドイツ）の傘下に入った。すでにマツダがフォード・モーター社（アメリカ）の系列下にあり，いすゞ自動車・スズキ・富士重工業はゼネラル・モーターズ社（GM。アメリカ）のグループに属している。国内の自動車メーカーのうち，資本面で独立しているのは，トヨタ自動車とホンダの2社だけとなった。

•鉄鋼　新日本製鐵がユジノール社（フランス）と包括提携した。NKKと川崎製鉄が共同持ち株会社を設立した。

•化学　住友化学工業と三井化学が，2004年に経営統合をする予定。

•造船　石川島播磨重工業と川崎重工が，2002年に造船事業を統合する。

•家庭電器　松下電器産業と日立製作所，三洋電気とシャープが，2001年に洗濯機・冷蔵庫・掃除機などの白物家電の相互供給を開始することを決めた。

•住宅関連　大手住宅設備機器メーカーのINAXと大手建材メーカーのトステムが事業統合を決めた。

Deregulation and Business Reorganization

Continuing Deregulation

Deregulation has continued in various areas since the latter half of the '80s.

• **Transportation**—Japanese National Railways was broken up into seven privately owned railways. 1996 saw the opening of a new domestic airlines, the first in 43 years.

• **Telecommunications**—The formerly state run domestic telecommunications corporation, NTT, and the overseas telecommunication corporation, KDD, have both been stripped of their monopoly status. NTT was divided into two privately owned companies, NTT Eastern Japan and NTT Western Japan, which now have to compete with KDDI and Nihon Telecom.

• **Electric Power and Gas**—It is now possible for manufacturers and concerns in fields other than electric power to produce their own electricity and sell it to electric power utilities, and the bidding has begun. For gas as well, newcomers other than established suppliers are being welcomed by large-scale consumers.

• **Finance**—It is now possible for banks, security companies and trust banks to own subsidiaries in each other's fields.

Business Groups and Corporations Crossing International Boundaries

The trend toward business reorganization within the various industries has gained momentum in recent years, and has even crossed over the old *zaibatsu* framework of *Mitsui*, *Mitsubishi*, *Sumitomo*, etc. This movement is part of the process of economic globalization, and represents and attempt to remain competitive in a wider international arena.

• **Finance**—Companies all using the same main bank have formed into business groups, which include the *Mizuho* Financial Group, *Mitsui-Sumitomo* Bank, *Mitsubishi-Tokyo* Financial Group, and United Financial of Japan (UFJ) Group.

• **Automotive**—In 1999 the French auto manufacturer, Renault, invested capital in Nissan Motors. In 2000 Mitsubishi Motors came under the wing of Germany's Daimler-Chrysler. Already Mazda is part of Ford Motors Group (US), while *Isuzu*, *Suzuki* and *Fuji* Heavy Industries belong to the General Motors Group (US). Of the Japanese auto manufacturers, only Toyota and Honda have remained independent of foreign capital investment.

• **Steel**—*Nippon* Steel Corporation has gone into partnership with Usinor of France, while NKK and *Kawasaki* Steel Corporation have formed a joint holding company.

• **Chemicals**—*Sumitomo* Chemical Industries and *Mitsui* Chemicals are scheduled to merge operations in 2004.

• **Shipbuilding**—*Ishikawajima Harima* Heavy Industries and *Kawasaki* Heavy Industries will join their shipbuilding operations in 2002.

• **Home Appliances**—*Matsushita*, *Hitachi*, *Sanyo* and *Sharp* have decided on a mutual supply agreement for washing machines, refrigerators, vacuum cleaners and other home appliances.

• **Housing Related**—The major home furnishings manufacturer, INAX, and the major building materials supplier, TOSTEM have agreed to combine operations.

地下資源に乏しい日本のエネルギー供給は，1950，60年代に石油への依存度を高めた。しかし，70年代の石油ショックの教訓から，その後は天然ガスや原子力などに多様化が進んだ。98年の発電電力量は，原子力36.3%，天然ガス24.4%，石炭14.9%，石油13.0%，水力10.8%となっている。

原子力発電に関する長期計画の停滞

最近は，真夏に冷房のための電力需要が増大することから，そのピークに合わせた，より大きな設備能力が求められている。しかし，原子力発電所の新規立地は地元住民の反対でなかなか進まないのが現状である。

近年，原子力発電への信頼が大きく揺らぐ事件が続いた。1995年には福井県敦賀（つるが）市の高速増殖原型炉「もんじゅ」が，冷却剤のナトリウムが漏れる事故を起こした。97年には茨城県東海村の核燃料再処理施設が火災・爆発事故を起こした。99年には同じ東海村のウラン濃縮工場で臨界事故が発生し，2人の職員が亡くなった。スリーマイルズ島（アメリカ合衆国）やチェルノブイリ（旧ソ連）の原子力発電所の事故に次ぐ深刻な原子力事故だったことから，住民の不安が大きくかきたてられることとなった。

プルトニウムを使う高速増殖炉の実用化が後退したことで，原子炉（軽水炉）から発生するプルトニウムの活用法が課題となった。プルトニウムとウラン燃料を混合し，MOX燃料として軽水炉で利用するプルサーマル方式が計画された。しかし，MOX燃料を製造したイギリス核燃料公社が，品質データを捏造（ねつぞう）したことが発覚し，この計画も停滞している。

また，日本の原子力発電は，使用済み核燃料の処理や再利用の問題を解決しないまま始まったので，現在も多くの問題が存続しており，「トイレなきマンション」と揶揄（やゆ）されている。

新エネルギーの利用

1997年に太陽光発電や風力発電など，クリーンエネルギーの利用の促進を目指す法律が施行された。しかし効率がよくないことから，まだ補助的な利用にとどまっている。これらの新エネルギーの開発は，始まったばかりである。

日本の電源別の発電電力量（98年，旧通産省調べ）

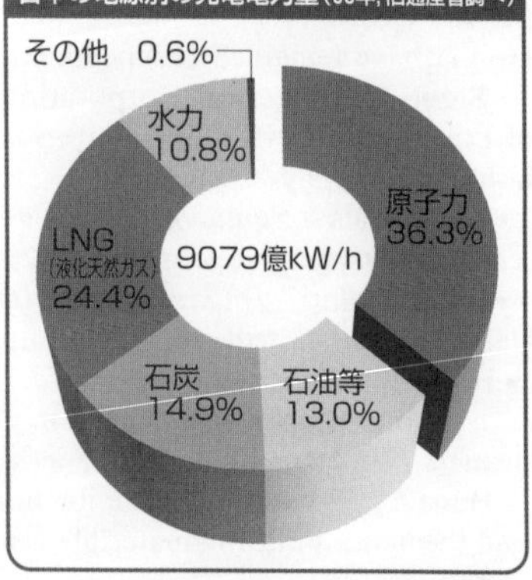

Japan's Energy Situation

Lacking in underground natural resources, Japan became increasingly dependent on petroleum during the '50s and '60s. But after the lesson learned during the oil shock of the '70s, Japan has diversified into other energy sources such as natural gas and nuclear energy. Of the total electric power produced in 1998, 36.3% was by nuclear power, 24.4% by natural gas, 14.9% by coal, 13.0% by petroleum and 10.8% by water.

Short Half-life for Plans for Nuclear Power Stations

Along with the ever-growing demand for more electricity for those midsummer air conditioners comes a need for larger facility capabilities to cope with this. However finding sites for new nuclear power plants is very difficult due to protesting by local residents.

The past few years have brought a string of accidents that have shaken the public's faith in nuclear power plants. In 1995 there was a leakage of the sodium coolant from the "*Monju*" high-speed breeder reactor in *Tsuruga* City. In 1997 there was a fire and explosion at the nuclear fuel reprocessing plant in *Toukaimura*, *Ibaraki* Prefecture. And again at *Toukaimura* in 1999 there was a critical accident at the uranium refining plant which claimed the lives of two workers. This accident ranks next after Three Mile Island in the U.S. and Chernobyl in the former Soviet Union in seriousness, and has stirred up a great feeling of uneasiness among the Japanese people.

With the setback in plans for operation of the plutonium fueled "*Monju*" high-speed breeder reactor, there remains the problem of how to use the plutonium produced in the light-water reactor. At first plutonium thermal use, that is, mixing the plutonium with uranium to form MOX (mixed oxide) fuel that could be used in the light-water reactor, appeared to be a promising solution. It was discovered, however, that the British government operated nuclear fuel manufacturer that produced MOX fuel had falsified its data, and so this plan too has been put on hold.

The entire Japanese nuclear power program was put into operation without ever having solved the problem how to dispose of or reuse spent nuclear fuel, and this continues to vex the program today. Indeed critics of the program liken it unto a huge "housing complex with no toilets".

New Energy Sources

A new law was passed in 1998 aimed at promoting a greater use of solar, wind and other clean energy sources, but poor efficiency has limited them to largely auxiliary use. The development of clean energy is still in its infancy.

Japan's Electric Power Production by Source
(former Ministry of Trade statistics for 1998)

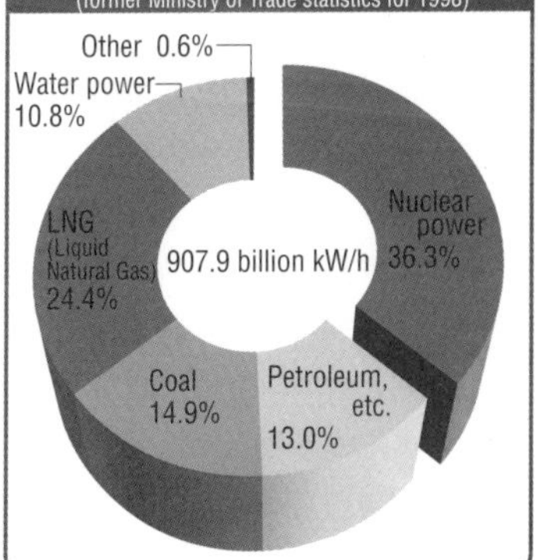

4人に1人が65歳以上

総人口のうち65歳以上の高齢者が占める割合は西ヨーロッパ10か国の平均で1960年の11.4%から1995年には14.9%に上昇した。アメリカでは同じ期間に9.2%から12.3%への上昇が見られた。日本では60年に5.7%で，西ヨーロッパのちょうど半分の水準にあったが，95年には14.5%となり追いついた。日本の高齢化はEUの2倍のスピード，アメリカに比べると3倍のスピードで進行した。2000年には17.2%に至った。

旧厚生省の予測によると，日本のこの比率は2020年には26.9%に高まり，国連の予測によるアメリカの16.1%，西ヨーロッパの20.2%を大きく上回ることになる。日本は今世紀にはずば抜けた高齢者大国になるということだ。

伸びる寿命，低下する出生率

日本の急速な高齢化は，平均寿命が伸びたこと，出生率が低下したことによる。日本人の平均寿命は，47年には男50.06歳，女53.96歳であったのが，99年には男77.10歳，女83.99歳まで伸びた。人口が一定の水準を保つためには，一人の女性が生涯に平均して2.09人の子供を生む必要があるが，89年にはこの指標が1.57人にまで低下し，「1.57ショック」と言われた。その背景には，都市部の女性の高学歴化・晩婚化の傾向や，仕事と子育てが両立しにくい社会環境などが挙げられる。93年には1.46まで低下し，99年は，1.34に落ち込んだ。旧厚生省の人口予測は，出生率が1.53人まで回復することを前提としているが，現実は同省のもっと悲観的な予測に沿って展開している。

高齢化への対応

95年には一人の高齢者の生活を15～64歳の生産年齢にある4.8人が支えていた計算になるが，2015年にはその半分の2.4人で一人の高齢者を支えなければならない。15～64歳の生産年齢人口はすでに95年から減り始めている。今後は高齢者就業を高める制度が必要になる。また，現役世代の負担が重くなりすぎないように，年金を受け取り始める年齢を引き上げるなどの措置も必要となる。さらに，医療や介護サービスなどを最も必要とする75歳以上の高齢者も増えるため，これらサービス供給のコスト削減や人員の確保などが重要な課題となっている。2000年4月からは，介護が必要な人が介護サービスを受けられるようにするため介護保険法がスタートした。

Rapidly Graying Population

One in Four 65 or Older

In the ten countries of Western Europe, the average percentage of the population 65 or older rose from 11.4% in 1960 to 14.9% in 1995. In the United States, the percentage rose from 9.2% to 12.3% during the same period. In Japan, these figures were 5.7% in 1960 (about half of the European average) and 14.5% (about the same as the European figure) in 1995. Thus in Japan aging has advanced twice as fast as in the E.U. and three times as fast as in the U.S. In 2000 the percentage of Japanese aged 65 or older reached 17.2%.

Former Ministry of Health and Welfare forecasts indicate that by the year 2020 26.9% of the Japanese population will be 65 or older, as compared with 16.1% in the U.S. and 20.2% in Western Europe (UN estimates). During this century Japan will be by far and away the country having the highest percentage of people at 65 or over.

Longer Lives, Lower Birthrate

Japan's rapidly aging population is the result of people living longer, plus fewer people being born. In 1947 the average lifespan for Japanese males was 50.06 years, and for females 53.96 years. By 1999 this had risen to 77.10 for males and 83.99 for females. In order for a population to maintain itself at a steady level, one woman must give birth to an average of 2.09 children during the course of her life. Yet in 1989 the figure for Japan had fallen to 1.57, and was spoken of as the "1.57 crisis". Factors often cited as probable causes include the trend toward a higher education and a later age for marrying among urban women, as well as a social environment that makes it difficult for women to work and raise children at the same time. By 1993 the figure had fallen to 1.46, and in 1999 it was 1.34. Population projections by the Ministry of Health and Welfare assume the birthrate will recover to 1.53, but in fact things are proceeding according to the Ministry's worst-case scenario.

Dealing With an Aging Population

It works out that in 1995 one elderly person was supported by 4.8 working age persons (15 ~ 64 years of age). By 2015 only one half that number, or 2.8 working age persons, will have to support one elderly person. The 15—64 year old working age population has already started to shrink as of 1995. In the future it will become necessary to increase employment for elderly persons. Also measures such as further raising the age when old age benefits begin will be necessary, so that the burden on the working age population does not become too great. Moreover the number of elderly persons 75 and over, the age group in most need of medical and nursing care services, will also increase, so another important task will be to cut the cost of providing these services, and at the same time securing personnel to perform them.

終身雇用制と忠誠心

ひとたび企業に採用されたら，上司の命令に従い，同僚たちとの協調を保ち，無難に仕事をしていれば，特に際だった業績を上げなくとも，その会社が倒産でもしないかぎり解雇されない。また，さまざまな付加給付を受けることができるとともに，身分，生活とも保障される。いわば会社は，定年まで個人の生活を丸抱えするのである。それは給与とそれに付随する諸手当にはじまり，社宅や独身寮といった住居の提供，また，さまざまの福利厚生施設を備えるなど，企業規模が大きくなればなるほどその恩恵も大きい。

就職してから定年まで丸抱えで生活を保障してくれるということは，安心して働けるわけで，その意味では会社と従業員は運命共同体である。すなわち，企業が存続し，かつ発展成長することが，自らの生活基盤を安定させ，より豊かにさせることにほかならない。したがって，一つの企業に対する勤労者の定着率は高く，忠誠心が強いのも当然のことと言える。

採用と人事

採用については，原則的に新卒者を対象にした年１回の定期採用である。採用人員については，業績により毎年変わるものの，組織としての年代構成のバランスなどを配慮し，計画的にある一定数は定期採用している。

入社後は，会社の必要とする能力を身に付けさせるための教育訓練を定期的に行うとともに，数年ごとに配置転換をして，多面的な経験を積ませ，そうした蓄積された能力を定年までの長期にわたって活用するやり方が多い。

このような雇用慣行は1990年代初めから変容し始め，リストラによる従業員削減や，成果型賃金の導入などで転職や中途採用に動く企業が増えた。また，契約制や人材派遣などの形で雇用形態の多様化も進み始めた。

女性の労働力と差別

一般的に女性の労働力は，男性と区別され，仕事も男性の補助的作業が主である。最近ではこれを差別として改善の動きも強まり，1986年４月に「男女雇用機会均等法」が施行された。現実には数年で離職するケースも多いが，キャリア・ウーマンとしての道を選択する女性も増えている。

Lifetime Employment Security

Under Japan's employment system, an employee who does what he is told, gets along with his fellow workers, and makes no major blunders can reasonably expect to be employed with the same company guaranteeing his social standing and income for the rest of his working life even if he is not an especially outstanding performer—a condition that holds under almost all conditions short of corporate bankruptcy. Among the benefits he is eligible for in addition to his basic salary are special allowances, company-owned housing or dormitories for single employees, and various health and welfare benefits, their generosity directly proportional to the size of the company.

Because the Japanese company guarantees its workers' livelihoods until retirement, people can concentrate on their work in the realization that they and their company share a common fate. Working for the same company for all of their working lives, and knowing the company's success will mean enhanced livelihood, security and an improved standard of living, many Japanese identify strongly with their companies.

Recruitment and Promotion

Most Japanese companies hire new people in once-a-year recruitment drives during which prospective graduates are tested, interviewed, and finally hired. Each company decides beforehand how many people it intends to hire given its business outlook, the demographic balance within the company, and other considerations. Once hired, employees are trained on-the-job and reassigned every few years to give them broad, generalized experience and ensure their long-run competence.

Such established employment practices began to change in the '90s, however, as economic conditions forced more and more companies to start laying off employees in order to reduce their workforce. Companies also began adopting a wage schedule adjusted to worker productivity. The pattern of employment began to diversify as companies did more and more contract hiring and made greater use of temporary staff.

Female Employment

Most Japanese companies hire women under a separate system and assign them jobs as assistants to male employees. However, pressure is building to end this discrimination, and an Equal Employment Opportunity Law was passed in April 1986. While many women still quit in several years to get married or for other reasons, the woman career executive is increasingly common in Japan.

年功序列制度は終身雇用制度とともに日本的経営の大きな特質と考えられているが，この年功序列と終身雇用は一体不可分の関係にあり，企業の個人丸抱えによる身分，生活保障上のセットとして考えられている。

年齢給と職能給

日本の企業の賃金体系は年齢給が基本となっており，これに役職手当や専門職などによる職能給，家族手当が加算される。こうした年功序列賃金は，終身雇用による従業員の生活を保障するという観点に立つ賃金体系として定着してきたものである。

しかし，高齢化社会の到来が急速に迫り，しかも高度経済成長期に大量に採用したため，今日の低成長時代にあって人件費の支出が経営を圧迫するに至っている。そのため，ほとんどの企業で賃金体系の見直しがなされている。

その主たる対策は，年齢給を抑え，職能給の割合を増やしていこうというものである。具体的には，年齢序列賃金制度に年齢の上限を定めて一定にし，その分は職能給で補おうというもので，職能についても細かく規定するとともに資格制度を導入し，それぞれの給付水準を定めるなどの改訂が進められている。

昇給制度の問題

戦後の日本経済の発展に大きく貢献したのは民間企業であり，とりわけ企業の推進力となったのは，当時の中堅社員以下の活力だった。そして，彼らの動機付けとなったのが出世志向，昇進志向の実現であった。高度経済成長期には，そういった志向に対して企業も十分に対応でき，年功による昇進も可能だったが，第１次石油危機以来の低成長期に入ると，とたんに対応しきれなくなり，ポスト不足が深刻な問題となった。

一方，今までの年功序列制度はいい意味での出世競争による活性化が図られていたが，今日のポスト不足による出世意欲の減退や企業に対する忠誠心の欠如などが懸念されるに及び，企業によっては課制の廃止や職制の代わりに試験により上級資格を得るといった資格制度の導入を図るなど活性化につとめている。とはいえ，年功序列という制度そのものが徐々に消滅しつつあることは否めない。その意味で，日本のサラリーマンにとって実力主義の厳しい時代を迎えつつあると言えよう。

Seniority-based Rewards

Seniority-based rewards (both occupational title and wages) go hand in hand with lifetime employment as a distinguishing characteristic of Japanese management, and these two elements are often seen as the two sides of the single coin of the company's total embrace of the individual.

Wages

In most Japanese companies, employees receive basic salaries geared to their entry-level salaries and how long they have been with the company. These basic salaries are then supplemented by special allowances for managerial or technical expertise, family size and structure, and other special factors. This system of seniority-based wages was devised as a means of guaranteeing the livelihoods of all employees throughout their lifetime careers with the company.

However, with a working population skewed toward the older age groups and with the large number of workers hired during the rapid-growth 1960s, many Japanese companies, large and small, are finding their earnings squeezed by high personnel costs in today's slow-growth era. As a result, most companies have been forced to review their seniority-based wage systems.

Many companies have thus chosen to curtail the seniority-based share of wages (such as by putting a cap on age-based wage increases) while increasing the share that is ability-based. Companies are increasingly linking salary schedules to the individual's qualifications and abilities.

Problems with Seniority-based Promotions

Japanese industry was the driving force behind the nation's amazing postwar recovery, and capable middle- and lower-level workers were the main force behind industry. These people were motivated by the promises of promotion and improved social status as their companies grew. During the rapid-growth 1960s, corporate growth made it possible to accommodate these promotion needs with a steadily-expanding number of posts. However, with the slower growth in the aftermath of the 1973 oil crisis, there are fewer top posts being created and companies can no longer adequately reward all of their deserving employees.

Although this seniority-based system worked well by stimulating healthy competition for promotions, the shortage of higher-level openings has eroded employee motivation and even company loyalty. Some companies are attempting to maintain employee morale by restructuring their organizations to allow wider involvement and by basing promotions more on ability to reward the better-qualified people. Ultimately, the entire system of seniority-based rewards is on its way out, and Japanese company employees will increasingly have to face the pressures of performance-based competition.

企業別組合の体質

日本の労働組合の大多数は，その組織単位が企業または事業所別に編成され，組合員の資格も原則としてその企業の正式な従業員に限定されている。したがって，組合員の賃上げなどによる生活権の要求も，終身雇用制度，年功序列制度によって一応の水準は確保されている。また，組合員と言っても企業別組合では，企業の存続が前提であるため，経営者側とある程度の協調を図っていかざるを得ないしくみになっている。そのため，経営状態が悪い場合などには組合は強い要求を出さず，逆に経営者側に積極的に協力することすらある。こうした体質は会社側との癒着を生じやすく，御用組合化の危険性がつねに付きまとう。

また，日本の企業内組合では，一般に下級管理職以下が組合員の資格を有し，それ以上の管理職は非組合員であり経営者側となる。昨日まで組合員として組合の利益を代表していたのが，昇進によって今度は経営者側のテーブルに就くなどということもよくある光景である。

団体交渉の方式

使用者と労働者個人との交渉に代わり，組合組織が組合員の利益を代表して使用者側と労働条件などに関して交渉を行い，協定を結ぶという方式は，戦後の日本では一般化している。

ただ日本の場合，労使は運命共同体的関係にあり，組合側も経営状態を把握していることもあって，企業そのものの存立を危うくするような対立は避ける。労使ともにどこまで譲歩し，どこで妥協するかが交渉のポイントとなる。

組合の経営参加

組合の経営参加は戦後の経営民主化に伴って進んできたが，形式としては労働協約で定める経営協議会方式が一般的である。これは，経営者側が経営に関する諸事項について労働組合に参加させる機関であって，討議事項としては，生産，福利厚生，人事に関する協議などが主要である。

かつては，「春闘」と称して大幅な(2けた台の)賃上げ率を勝ち取ってきた組合も，雇用情報が悪化した90年代半ば以降は賃上げよりも雇用確保，あるいは労働時間の短縮などを重視する傾向が強まってきた。労働組合の政治的発言力は低下している。

Enterprise Unions

The vast majority of Japan's labor unions are organized not along craft or skill lines but as enterprise (or enterprise-branch) unions with membership restricted principally to regular, full-time employees at the specific company. These enterprise unions seek to maintain and improve their members' standard of living by bargaining for pay raises and defending employees' rights within the framework of lifetime employment and seniority-based rewards. Because it is an enterprise union, the union knows that its survival depends on the company's survival. When times are rough, the union refrains from making aggressive demands and cooperates to help the company through the crisis. Inherent in this posture is the danger that the union will identify too strongly with the company and become a rubber stamp "company union."

Membership in Japan's enterprise unions is limited to lower-level management people and below, meaning that a union member who is promoted to middle management is no longer eligible for membership. Thus it is not unusual for someone who was on the union side of the negotiating table yesterday to find himself on the management side today.

Collective Bargaining

The postwar Japanese pattern in industrial relations has been for management and union representatives to negotiate agreements regarding working conditions and other matters on behalf of all union members.

Realizing that their members' long-term prosperity is linked to the prosperity of the companies where they work, Japanese union leaders make an effort to be well versed in business conditions affecting the industry and to avoid doing anything that might jeopardize the company's survival. As a result, contract negotiations are always a delicate compromise between confrontation and cooperation.

Worker Participation in Management

Unions gained a greater voice in management during the postwar democratization, and most companies now make formal provisions for labor-management consultative committees or other arrangements enabling the union to participate in a variety of management decisions, mainly in such areas as production schedules, employee welfare, and personnel policy.

While past spring labor offensives won significant (double digit) percentage pay raises for union members, deterioration in the job market since the mid-1990s has caused a shift in emphasis from wage increases to job security and shorter working hours, with laber unions losing much of their political pull.

労働時間

1990年の製造業の一人当たり年間総労働時間は2124時間と，先進国の中で2000時間を超えるのは日本だけであったが，99年には1842時間に減少した。週法定労働時間が段階的に引き下げられ，週休２日制が普及したことなどによる。また，90年代は景気低迷により残業時間も大幅に減少したことから時短が急進展した。

週休２日制と有給休暇

週休２日制をなんらかの形で導入している企業の割合は，98年には90.5%に及んでいる。適用労働者の割合は95.6%だが，このうち完全週休２日制は59.2%と，90年に比べて20ポイント上昇した。しかし，企業規模別，産業別に普及の状況には差が出ており，98年の完全週休２日制の適用労働者割合で見ると，1000人以上の企業で81.9%，100〜999人50.1%，30〜99人32.4%と，中小企業での普及が遅れている。

有給休暇は98年に15.6日与えられていたが，実際の取得日数は7.2日であり，取得率は45.9%にすぎなかった。これは，企業規模によらず共通の傾向がある。長い休みをまとめてとる習慣がないことや，実際には仕事が忙しく，休みを取りづらいことが反映している。

賃金

給与所得者の賃金は，ふつう月給と年２回（夏冬）のボーナスによって支払われる。ボーナスは本来，会社の業績に応じて支給される報奨的性格のものであり，日本でも月給に比べてやや弾力的ではあるが，年間の給与の重要な一部として組み込まれている。労働省の調査によると，99年の年間給与総額の平均（30人以上の事業所）は476万円，そのうちボーナスは108万円であった。定期昇給は，企業ごとの賃金体系の中で毎年１回行われるが，最近は管理職を中心に年俸制を採用するところも現れている。

世帯の収入面からみると，労働者世帯の99年の月平均の収入は57万円であった。税金・社会保険料などを差し引いた可処分所得は48万円で，これから35万円の消費支出を行い，貯蓄率は19.4%であった。

Working Hours and Wages

Working Hours

In 1990, the average number of hours worked per person was 2,124, making Japan the only industrial country where people averaged more than 2,000 hours of work a year. By 1999, however, this had come down to 1,842 hours, mainly because the legal limit on hours worked per week was lowered and because five-day weeks have become more common. In addition, the recession, of the '90s sharply reduced the amount of overtime.

Five-day Workweek and Paid Vacation

As of 1998, 90.5% of all companies had adopted a five-day workweek in some form or another, affecting 95.6% of the business labor force. Of these, 59.2% had out and out adopted a five-day workweek, up 20% from 1990. Differences exist, however, depending on company size and industrial sector. The percentage of workers on a five-day workweek with every weekend off was 81.9% for companies with 1000 or more employees, 50.1% for 100～999 employees, and 32.4% for 30～99 employees. Thus small and medium sized companies are slower in adopting a five-day workweek.

Japanese workers were entitled to an average of 15.6 days of paid vacation in 1999, but in actual fact took only an average of 7.2 days, or 45.9% of what they were permitted. This tendency holds true regardless of the size of the business. This is a reflection of the fact that it never was customary in Japan to take long vacations, and that people are in truth so busy that they find it difficult to take so much time off.

Wages

Japanese salaried workers normally receive a monthly salary plus two bonuses annually, one in the summer and one at year's end. Begun as a kind of supplementary profit-sharing incentive, bonuses retain some of that flexibility but are today an integral part of the Japanese salaried worker's earnings. Ministry of Labor surveys show that the average wage for 1999 (at companies with 30 or more employees) was ¥4,760,000, of which bonuses accounted for ¥1,080,000. The base wage goes up once a year across the board at each company. Recently, however, there has been a shift away from this monthly-wage-plus-bonus structure as more executive level people have opted for annual compensation packages.

The average monthly income for wage-earner households in 1999 was ¥570,000. After deducting for taxes, social security, and other non-discretionary items, the household's disposable income was ¥480,000 / month. Of this, ¥350,000 was spent and 19.4% was put into savings.

定年年齢

日本の企業の定年は，長い間55歳であった。55歳の定年で，人生50年と言われていた間はほぼ一生働くことができ，生活も保障されていた。しかし，戦後日本人の平均寿命が急速に伸び，1999年現在，男性77.10歳，女性83.99歳となり，定年以後約20年余も働く機会のないまま生活しなくてはならないという事態になってきた。高齢化社会の到来と合わせ，老後の生活という観点からも定年の年齢延長問題が，ここ数年議論されている。

政府は，企業に定年を60歳に引き上げるよう指導しており，99年には定年制を定める企業の91.2%が60歳定年制を実施している。60歳定年は，公的年金の支給年齢が60歳であることから設定されたものだが，年金財政の問題から，公的年金の支給開始を65歳に引き上げることが決定されており，これに伴い，定年もさらに65歳にすることが議論されている。

退職金制度

退職金制度は終身雇用・年功序列制度とともに，雇用慣行として定着している。これは，永年勤続に対する報奨と老後の生活を保障しようという性格のもので，一時金として支払われる。最近では，定年延長，あるいは従業員の高齢化とともに，退職金の見直しが図られている。その一つが退職金を年金として支払う基金の設立で，公的年金を補完する制度として，また企業の資金の効率的運用という面から急速に普及した。しかし近年は，低金利による運用利回りの低下から，解散する基金が増えている。

老後の生活設計とカウンセリング

老後の生活保障問題は，日本では単に企業の問題としてではなく，社会全体の問題として政治，行政，労使ともに真剣に取り組んでいる。企業では，定年延長，企業年金制度の導入とともに，従業員の老後についての相談制度やカウンセリングを行っている。終身雇用という慣行から，退職後の生活設計の相談に乗り，適切なアドバイスをしようというもので，退職後の就職斡旋(あっせん)から老後に備えての財産形成の方法などを企業内制度として設置している。

老後の問題でいちばん切実なのは，雇用機会がないことであり，あるいはあっても，これまでの能力や技術を生かした再就職の道が閉ざされていることなどである。老後の生きがいの問題には，課題は多い。

Retirement Age

For a long time, the Japanese retirement age was 55. This standard, set at a time when people thought of the average life span in terms of two score and ten years, was premised upon providing workers guaranteed livelihoods for virtually their whole lives. Yet life expectancy has improved remarkably since the war—to 77.10 for men and 83.99 for women in 1999. Thus the average worker retiring at 55 can expect over 20 years as an unemployed retiree. Accordingly, there has been much debate in recent years over whether or not to raise the retirement age, especially since the population center is also growing older.

In response, the government is urging corporations to raise their official retirement age to 60, and as of 1999, 91.2% of the nation's private companies have complied. Although this age-60 retirement was set in consideration of the fact that public retirement pensions begin at age 60, severe fiscal problems have forced the government to postpone the start of such payments until age 65, which suggests the retirement age may be raised again—this time to 65.

Retirement Allowances

Along with lifelong employment and seniority-based wages, lump-sum retirement allowances are a traditional part of Japan's employment system. When most workers were working their entire lives, these rewards for long and loyal service were sufficient to see them through their post-retirement years. Today, however, there is increasing concern that, along with postponing retirement, pensions may also have to be revamped. One such revision called for the establishment of a pension fund to replace lump-sum retirement payments. This idea was rapidly adopted on the premise that pension payments would supplement public pension funds, and that companies could make more effective use of their capital. Yet recently many such funds have been liquidated due to low capital returns caused by the low interest rate policy.

Retirement Planning and Counseling

The problems plaguing Japan's senior citizens are of serious concern to all of Japanese society, and politicians, bureaucrats, and labor-management groups are all working hard to find solutions. Besides raising the retirement age and switching from lump-sum payments to annuities, companies are setting up in-house counseling services to help retired employees with everything from finding re-employment to financial planning.

Post-retirement work opportunities are few and far between, and those that do exist often fail to draw upon the skills learned in a lifetime of working. Nevertheless, many people believe that something is needed to make their lives fully meaningful, and this is another problem which must be solved as the Japanese population grows older.

日本の企業は集団主義と言われるように，人間関係の和を重要視する。そのために，企業内ではフォーマルおよびインフォーマルなさまざまな催し物が行われる。

一般に人生の大半を一つの会社で過ごすために，おのずと付き合いは会社中心となり，こうした人間関係を円滑にすることは，ビジネスマンにとって重要な条件でもある。しかし，以下のような慣行も雇用形態の多様化などから，過去のように盛んではなくなる傾向にある。

運動会，忘年会など

多くの会社では，定期的に組織全体，あるいは各セクションごとの行事が行われる。それは，従業員の家族も参加する運動会であったり，社員旅行，転勤者に対する送別会，歓迎会，年末の忘年会などさまざまである。

このような行事は，日本の会社の家族主義的習慣で，人間関係を緊密にするとともに，組織は運命共同体であるという意識をもたせ，組織の活性化を図るという効果もある。

会社内にはさまざまな同好会がある。スポーツから文学，囲碁，将棋といった趣味の分野に至るまであり，社内の厚生施設を利用し，活動している。こうした活動では労使の区別はなく，経営幹部も一般社員といっしょになって楽しむのが普通である。

赤ちょうちん

日常的な付き合いで最もよく利用されるのが，居酒屋(いざかや)や赤ちょうちんと言われる大衆酒場である。就業時間が終わると同僚，もしくは上司たちと連れ立ち，酒を飲みながら雑談するわけだが，インフォーマルな席として日ごろの不満などを言い合うなど，一種のストレス解消の場ともなっている。赤ちょうちんとともにマージャンも終業後の付き合いや楽しみの一つであるが，最近は減っている。特に若い世代は，こうした付き合いを敬遠する傾向にある。

ゴルフ

ビジネスマンの付き合いで，欠かせないのがゴルフである。商取引において，日本ではふだんの付き合いが重要とされ，しばしば接待と称して酒席に招待するが，この酒席とともに多いのがゴルフ接待である。そのためビジネスマンは，こぞってゴルフを始める。したがってゴルフは，必ずしも純粋に個人的趣味ではなく，仕事上の利益をも伴っている場合が多いのである。

Socializing

Japanese companies are very harmony-conscious, and this emphasis on people shows up most clearly in their emphasis on good interpersonal relations and the numerous formal and informal social events that most companies sponsor.

Since the Japanese worker spends the greater part of his life with the same company, his friends tend to be people he knows from work, and being able to get along well with the rest of the people at the office or the factory is an important prerequisite for business success. This remains basically true even though business-practice diversification and other changes are making this (and the practices explained below) much less important than they used to be.

Athletic Competitions, Parties, and More

Most Japanese companies sponsor a number of regular company- or section-wide social events, including athletic competitions for employees and their families, employee excursions, farewell parties for people being transferred out and welcoming parties for newcomers, and year-end bashes.

All part of the family-like atmosphere that pervades many Japanese companies, these events are encouraged as a way of strengthening interpersonal relations, underscoring the group's shared destiny, and improving organizational morale.

Many Japanese companies also provide facilities for active in-house hobby groups, ranging from sports to literature and board games such as *go* and *shougi*. Rather than having separate groups for managers and ordinary workers, employees from all levels gather together in these groups to share in the enjoyment of their common interests.

Stopping off at the Pub

The most common kind of socializing in many Japanese companies is outside the company and after hours—when a group of workers, with or without their boss, stops off at a local watering hole after work to relax over a cold one and talk off the stress of everyday work. Another favorite after-hours diversion is mahjong, a board game played in small parlors catering to the evening throngs of businessmen. Recently however, especially among the younger generation, there is a tendency not to participate so much in such forms of socializing.

Golf

Golf is another indispensable part of the Japanese businessman's social life. With entertaining clients and potential clients alike such a very important part of the ordinary run of business, many clients are not only wined and dined but also taken out for a round of golf. As a result, businessmen often consider golf a business skill, and they see a trip to the local course as not so much a personal pleasure as a means to success in business.

通勤・会議

ビジネスマンの朝は早い。始業時間は8時半～9時というのが一般的であるが，通勤時間の平均が1時間以上もかかるため，7時ごろには家を出なくてはならない。おまけにこのラッシュアワーの通勤電車はかなり混雑を極め，ほとんど立ちっぱなしで，会社に着くまでにかなりの疲労を強いられる。そして，タイムカードを押し，仕事が始まる。

週に1度，あるいは月に1度といった定例会議から，販売会議，宣伝会議など各セクションごとの会議，また，部課長会議，支店長会議などの職制別の会議など，実にさまざまな社内会議が行われる。会議に参加する回数は職制が上がるほど多くなる傾向にあり，一日中会議などということも珍しいことではない。会議の時間は，一応決められてはいるものの結論がなかなか出ずに延びてしまう，あるいは後日改めて会議を開くということもよくある。

社員食堂・喫茶店

昼食時ともなると，オフィス街周辺のレストランなどは，ビジネスマンで満員となるが，会社には社内に社員用の食堂を常設しているところが少なくない。社員食堂は，会社が業者と契約して設置しており，財政的にも何割かを負担しているため，値段は市価よりも安い。いわば，社員食堂は福利厚生の一環であると同時に，社内にあることで業務効率を図る―例えば，社内コミュニケーションの促進，すぐ仕事に戻れるなど―意図をも含んでいる。

商談は社内で行われるのが普通である。商談の重要性や相手との関係にもよるが，一般的には，簡単な打ち合わせ程度の場合は喫茶店でお茶を飲みながら，あるいは雑談しながら行われることも少なくない。ビジネスマンにとっては，仕事であると同時に一種の息抜きにもなっている。もちろん経費は会社もちである。

退社後

所属するセクションにもよるが，退社時間がくると仕事をやめて，すぐ帰宅するという社員はほとんどいない。やりかけの仕事を終えるまで残業をするのが普通である。また，夜は取引先の接待も多く，帰宅が深夜に及ぶことも珍しいことではない。もっとも90年代初めの不況後は，接待費あるいは交際費を削減した会社が増え，いわゆる社用族は大幅に減ってきた。

A Day in the Life of a Japanese Businessman

The Morning Commute and Meetings

The average Japanese businessman's day begins bright and early. Although not expected at work until 8:30 or 9:00, most businessmen live at least an hour away and must leave the house soon after 7:00. Invariably finding his rush-hour train packed with other commuters streaming into the city, he often has to stand most of the way and is worn out even before his workday begins. Once he gets to the office or factory, however, he punches in and gets right to work.

Aside from the regular weekly or monthly meetings, there are sales meetings, advertising meetings, and other meetings within each department, as well as interdepartmental management meetings at all levels. Generally, the higher you go on the corporate ladder, the more meetings there are to attend, and it is not uncommon for top executives to spend all day in meetings. Although meetings are scheduled well ahead of time, they often run over or have to be reconvened later when things take longer than expected.

Company Cafeterias and Coffee Shops

Come lunch time and the numerous restaurants in and around the business district are filled, even though many employees eat at in-house cafeterias run by outside contractors offering food at subsidized prices. An extra benefit for employees, the company cafeteria also pays off for the company by promoting smoother intra-company communication, shorter lunch breaks, and better work efficiency

While most business takes place in the office, a considerable portion is also transacted at nearby coffee shops where people can enjoy a cup of coffee and talk in a more relaxed setting. The decision on where to meet depends upon how important the meeting is and how relaxed an interpersonal business relationship there is. Generally, however, only relatively minor matters are worked out over coffee. Businessmen find coffee shops good places to combine business with pleasure by getting away from the office for a while. As you might expect, the company picks up the tab for this.

Clock-out Time

It is the rare employee who manages to quit work and head home at the official quitting time every day. More often than not, people stay to see the job through to completion. Even when he does manage to get away from his desk, the businessman frequently has entertaining to do and often does not get home until the wee hours of the morning. With the recession since the early 1990s, however, there has been a considerable decline in the number of people living high on expense accounts as more and more companies have moved to rein in expense account entertaining.

学歴偏重社会

一流会社への就職には，学歴が大いに重要となる。つまり，一流大学を卒業することがきわめて重要な条件となるとともに，入社以後の出世にも影響を与えるというのが実情である。そして，こうした一流大学に入るためには一流高校に入ること，というように学歴問題はエスカレートし，今では，小中学校の受験競争にまで及んでいる。

こうした受験競争は，つまりは一流企業に入り，一生安定した生活を獲得せんがためであるが，このような学歴社会に対して，教育のゆがみによる青少年の落ちこぼれ，非行化などが顕在化し，社会問題となっている。そのため，まだごく一部にすぎないが，採用時に学歴を考慮しない企業も現れている。

配転・転勤

入社後は，終身雇用，年功序列のもとで一応の生活は保障されるものの，その一方では，会社の命令に対しての拒否権，あるいは選択権はほとんどないと言ってよい。まず，どのセクションに配属されるかは会社が決める。転勤も辞令一つで，従わなければならない。特に，日本の企業では，ある一定の期間ごとに配置転換を行うので，勤めている間に何度かの配転，転勤を経験するのが一般的である。会社の命令に従わないと，社内においてきわめて不利な状況に追いやられる。

家族との関係

ビジネスマンの生活が会社中心であるため，家庭は妻を中心に運営される。家計，子供のしつけ，教育などは妻に任せ，月給も全額妻に渡し，必要な小遣いを妻からもらうというのが一般的なビジネスマン家庭である。

単身赴任

転勤はビジネスマンにとって避けられないことであるが，中年になっての転勤で多いのが単身赴任である。これは，マイホームを建てたためにその地を離れたくないという家族の希望とともに，子供の教育上の問題がその背景にある。それと，転勤の期間が数年であり，いずれ戻って来るという見込みもあるからで，我慢をするというのが実態である。しかし，任地が海外であったり，また，家族が離れて生活するというのは何かと問題があり，企業によっては制度的に見直しを図っているところもあるが，なかなか実効は上がっていない。

The Life of a Businessman

Academic Credentials

Academic credentials are very important to succeeding in business in Japan. Not only is graduation from one of the nation's top universities an important consideration for anyone hoping to get hired by a big blue-chip company, it is also important in climbing the corporate ladder. As the competition for admission to the leading colleges and universities has escalated, intense competition has developed for admission to the better high schools and even the more academic-oriented junior high and elementary schools.

The goal of all this fierce competition on entrance examinations is to attain the lifetime security that goes with working for a big company, but the extreme pressure this has generated has distorted the educational process and sparked such major problems as school drop-outs and increased delinquency. As a result, a few companies have decided to ignore academic credentials in the selection process.

Transfers

Once employed by a "good" company, the Japanese businessman enjoys lifetime employment and seniority-based wages, yet this lifelong security is balanced by the company's demand for unquestioning loyalty and acquiescence. Ultimately, the company decides what kind of work he will do and where he will do it, and most employees are put through a long period of regular job rotation, often involving transfers to other cities. Trying though this is, to balk would be a blot on the employee's record, and few are so brave.

Family Life

With the businessman devoting most of his attention to his work, it is usually up to his wife to manage the household. She is the one who takes care of the family budget and the children's socialization and education. Typically, the husband gives her his entire pay check and she then doles out his weekly or monthly allowance.

Living away from Home

Relocations are a fact of life for many Japanese businessmen, and some middle-aged transferees reluctantly decide to leave their families behind. This decision is often based not only on the family's personal desire to remain in the community where they may own their own home but also on a desire to avoid the problems which relocations can pose for the children's education. Even though the assignment may last for several years, the businessman sticks it out alone in the knowledge that he will be able to return home eventually. Although companies are studying ways to alleviate the hardships connected with overseas postings and the various problems which arise from such split-family living, they have yet to find any effective institutional solutions.

信用第一主義

欧米では，仕事を通じて付き合いが始まったとしても，ビジネスと個人的付き合いは区別するが，日本の商談ではそういった区別はあいまいで，たとえ，仕事の話が全くされない酒席や遊びの場でも，それは商談の一つのプロセスと考えられている場合が多い。つまり，商売上の信用は契約内容や契約条件を検討し，それに基づいて確実に実行することであるといった欧米の契約第一主義は，日本の商売では第二段階的な問題と考えられている。

日本の商売で第一に重要な点は，交渉相手が人間的に信用できるかどうかに懸かっている。したがって，外国人が日本の企業と商売をする場合は，直接会って交渉することが肝要となる。日本人担当者は，何度か面接の機会を作るだろうが，それは，契約条件を詰めるという目的以外に，個人として信用がおける人間かどうかを観察しているのである。

時間のかかる合意決定

日本では，商談の開始から契約成立までに非常に時間がかかる。意思決定までに，現場の人間の合意をも得るといった形が取られることが多いからである。

日本との交渉は気長に，誠意をもって当たることである。契約内容に対して性急にイエスかノーを迫ったところで交渉はスムーズにいかない。逆に関係を悪くすることすらある。日本の契約事項の検討というのは，単に契約書に書かれていることだけではなく，人間関係と同様に契約相手と長期的に取引していけるかということが重要なので，この点でも合意に時間がかかるのである。

ビジネスの家族的志向

商売である以上，契約の履行は当然であるが，日本的商売においては最初から詳細な取引規定をせずに，大枠で合意することを好む。日本的合意というのは相手を信用したということである。いわば今後親戚(しんせき)としていっしょにやっていきましょうという意味であり，問題が起きたらそのつど話し合いで解決し，困ったときは助け合いましょうというわけである。したがって，いったん取引が始まると，その関係は長期的に継続される場合が多い。こうしたことが，外国の会社にとって新規参入を難しくする要因にもなっているようである。

Japanese Business Practices

Mutual Trust

Western businessmen tend to make a clear distinction between business and pleasure, but this dividing line is a very fuzzy one in the Japanese business world. Socializing, for example, can be considered an integral part of the business relationship even if not a word of business is spoken, for such informal socializing contributes to establishing personal trust—and such personal trust is far more important in Japan than specific contractual relationships are. While the Western businessman builds trust in the negotiation and fulfillment of contractual obligations, the contract is a secondary issue for the Japanese businessman.

The most important thing in a Japanese business relationship is whether or not the people involved are comfortable and feel they can trust each other. Thus non-Japanese who establish ties with Japanese companies soon learn that face-to-face contacts are by far the most effective. Japanese businessmen meeting together repeatedly are not only working out the terms of the deal but are sizing each other up as human beings.

Reaching an Agreement

This need to establish trust among the people concerned is one reason it often takes a long time to go from the start of negotiations to the signing of the contract in Japanese business. While there are many other reasons as well, a prime one is that the Japanese decision requires the informed consent of all of the people who will be involved in its actual implementation.

Japanese business decisions are made with an emphasis on sincerity and trust, and pressures for a quick decision are counterproductive in the Japanese context. In Japan, working out a business deal means more than simply hammering out the terms of a contract; it includes an effort to build mutual trust and a long-term relationship. Naturally, this cannot be done overnight.

People-oriented Business

Fulfilling the contract is obviously an important part of any business deal, but in Japan the contract is not so much a detailed tome of specifics to cover every contingency as it is a general statement of the framework of the business relationship. Because business relationships are founded on mutual trust, they are somewhat like family ties. In the ideal situation, there is a deep and basic agreement to work together. If problems arise, they can be talked about and worked out, and if one side runs into trouble the other will often lend a helping hand. Once initiated, such business ties often last for many years. Conversely, the need for and existence of such ties makes it more difficult for newcomers — Japanese and foreign companies alike—to break into the Japanese market.

Notes

■1. Government

May 3 (5月3日) May 3 is a national holiday commemorating the Constitution. November 3, when the Constitution was first promulgated, is a national holiday designated Culture Day.

●National holidays

Jan. 1	*Ganjitsu* (元日) New Year's Day
Jan. 2nd Mon.	*Seijin no Hi* (成人の日) Adults' Day
Feb. 11	*Kenkoku Kinen no Hi* (建国記念の日) National Foundation Day
(Mar. 21)	*Shunbun no Hi* (春分の日) Vernal Equinox Day
Apr. 29	*Midori no Hi* (みどりの日) Greenery Day
May 3	*Kenpou Kinenbi* (憲法記念日) Constitution Memorial Day
May 5	*Kodomo no Hi* (子供の日) Children's Day
July 2nd Mon.	*Umi no Hi* (海の日) Marine Day
Sep. 2nd Mon.	*Keirou no Hi* (敬老の日) Respect-for-the-Aged Day
(Sep. 23)	*Shuubun no Hi* (秋分の日) Autumnal Equinox Day
Oct. 2nd Mon.	*Taiiku no Hi* (体育の日) Sports Day
Nov. 3	*Bunka no Hi* (文化の日) Culture Day
Nov. 23	*Kinrou Kansha no Hi* (勤労感謝の日) Labor Thanksgiving Day
Dec. 23	*Tennou Tanjoubi* (天皇誕生日) Emperor's Birthday

■2. The Imperial Institution

Gengou (元号) *Gengou* (a.k.a. *nengou*) are imperial reign names. Until the *Meiji* period, some emperors changed their reign names several times, but now only one *gengou* is used for each emperor's reign. *Heisei* has been in use since the present Emperor ascended the throne in 1989.

■3. Postwar Politics

Toujou Hideki (東条英機) (1884-1948) Army general and Prime Minister between 1941 and1944, *Toujou* was convicted at the *Toukyou* (Tokyo) Military Tribunal for the Far East and executed in December 1948.

Yoshida Shigeru (吉田茂) (1878-1967) Head of the Liberal Party, *Yoshida* was Prime Minister between 1946 and 1954 and played a pivotal role in Japan's postwar reconstruction.

●Some important *gengou*

Taika (大化)	645-650	*Genroku* (元禄)	1688-1704
Tenpyou (天平)	729-749	*Kyouhou* (享保)	1716-1736
Engi (延喜)	901-923	*Kansei* (寛政)	1789-1801
Hougen (保元)	1156-1159	*Tenpou* (天保)	1830-1844
Heiji (平治)	1159-1160	*Ansei* (安政)	1854-1860
Bun'ei (文永)	1264-1275	*Keiou* (慶応)	1865-1868
Tenshou (天正)	1573-1592	*Meiji* (明治)	1868-1912
Keichou (慶長)	1596-1615	*Taishou* (大正)	1912-1926
Genna (元和)	1615-1624	*Shouwa* (昭和)	1926-1989
Kan'ei (寛永)	1624-1644	*Heisei* (平成)	1989-

■4. The Cabinet

●Postwar Prime Ministers

Higashikuni Naruhiko (東久邇稔彦)	Aug. 1945 ～ Oct. 1945
Shidehara Kijuurou (幣原喜重郎)	Oct. 1945 ～ Apr. 1946
Yoshida Shigeru (吉田茂)	May 1946 ～ May 1947
Katayama Tetsu (片山哲)	May 1947 ～ Mar. 1948
Ashida Hitoshi (芦田均)	Mar. 1948 ～ Oct. 1948
Yoshida Shigeru (吉田茂)	Oct. 1948 ～ Dec. 1954
Hatoyama Ichirou (鳩山一郎)	Dec. 1954 ～ Dec. 1956
Ishibashi Tanzan (石橋湛山)	Dec. 1956 ～ Feb. 1957
Kishi Nobusuke (岸信介)	Feb. 1957 ～ July 1960
Ikeda Hayato (池田勇人)	July 1960 ～ Nov. 1964
Satou Eisaku (佐藤栄作)	Nov. 1964 ～ July 1972
Tanaka Kakuei (田中角栄)	July 1972 ～ Dec. 1974
Miki Takeo (三木武夫)	Dec. 1974 ～ Dec. 1976
Fukuda Takeo (福田赳夫)	Dec. 1976 ～ Dec. 1978
Oohira Masayoshi (大平正芳)	Dec. 1978 ～ June 1980
Suzuki Zenkou (鈴木善幸)	July 1980 ～ Nov. 1982
Nakasone Yasuhiro (中曽根康弘)	Nov. 1982 ～ Nov. 1987
Takeshita Noboru (竹下登)	Nov. 1987 ～ June 1989
Uno Sousuke (宇野宗佑)	June 1989 ～ Aug. 1989
Kaifu Toshiki (海部俊樹)	Aug. 1989 ～ Nov. 1991
Miyazawa Kiichi (宮沢喜一)	Nov. 1991 ～ Aug. 1993
Hosokawa Morihiro (細川護熙)	Aug. 1993 ～ Apr. 1994
Hata Tsutomu (羽田孜)	Apr. 1994 ～ June 1994
Murayama Tomiichi (村山富市)	June 1994 ～ Jan. 1996
Hashimoto Ryuutarou (橋本龍太郎)	Jan. 1996 ～ July 1998
Obuchi Keizou (小渕恵三)	July. 1998 ～ Apr. 2000
Mori Yoshirou (森喜朗)	Apr. 2000 ～ Apr. 2001
Koizumi Junichirou (小泉純一郎)	Apr. 2001 ～

PART・4

日本の文化
CULTURAL HERITAGE

建築は，その土地の気候，風土，習慣に大きく制約される。日本は，湿潤で四季のある気候であることと，素材として木材が豊富であることなどから，建物は木造で，床下および室内の風通しをよくし，屋根には勾配（こうばい）をつけ，軒を出して気候に合わせている。座る生活に合わせて床上には畳を敷いている。

仏教建築

寺院建築は中国の影響を強く受けているが，屋根の反りが少なく，軒が深い点，優美な曲線と直線のコントラストなど，日本化したものとなっている。*法隆寺，唐招提寺など，7～8世紀の遺構が現在，奈良県下に数多く残されており，法隆寺は世界最古の木造建築である。

神社建築

日本建築の最も古い様式を残しているのは神社で，高床式，彩色を施さない白木（しらき）造り，かやぶき，地面に直接柱を立てる掘っ立て柱で，典型的なのは*伊勢神宮，出雲（いずも）大社，住吉神社などである。上述の神社以外の神社は，神社建築の特徴のいくつかを残しながら，仏教建築の影響を受けた建築となっている。

住宅建築

住宅建築は奈良時代までのものは遺構もないので明確ではないが，平安時代になると，寝殿造りが貴族の間では一般的になる。主人の起居する寝殿を中心に，対屋（たいのや），池に臨む釣殿を造り，それぞれを廊下でつないだもので，家内は板敷きだった。室内に畳を敷きつめるようになったのは室町時代末期からで，さらに桃山時代になると書院造りが完成する。これは現代の日本建築に見られる*床の間，*違い棚，ふすまなどを備えた建築で，*桂（かつら）離宮，修学院（しゅがくいん）離宮などがその代表的なものである。

城郭建築

戦国時代から造られた城は，石組みと木骨に白壁で，3～5層の高層建築を造り上げた。*姫路城がその典型である。

西洋建築

明治維新後，*鹿鳴館（ろくめいかん）などレンガ造りの西洋建築が新国家の威信を示すものとして建てられた。現存する明治の代表的建築の多くは，愛知県の犬山にある「明治村」に移築されている。昭和になると，造形学校のバウハウスや建築家ル・コルビュジエに学んだ建築家も現れたが，それが花開くのは戦後のことで，谷口吉郎，丹下健三らがコンクリートの素材を生かした仕事をし，さらにその後は白井晟一（せいいち），黒川紀章らが，多様に発展させて世界的に活躍している。

Architecture

Architecture is shaped by circumstances of climate, geography, and customs. In Japan with its high humidity, seasonal change, and plentiful forests, wood has been the traditional building material. Traditional Japanese architecture has good foundation ventilation, airy rooms, slanted roofs, long overhangs, and *tatami*-covered floors.

Buddhist Architecture

Buddhist temple architecture is heavily influenced by Chinese aesthetics, but some features are purely Japanese—the gentle curve of the roof, the deep eaves, and the general contrast between curved and straight lines. Typical is *Houryuuji** in *Nara*, the world's oldest wooden structure, and such 7-8th century temples as *Toushoudaiji*.

***Shintou* Architecture**

Shintou shrines represent the oldest Japanese architectural style. They are generally placed high above the ground, made of plain, unpainted wood, topped with thickly thatched roofs, and supported by pillars driven directly into the ground. *Ise*,* *Izumo*, and *Sumiyoshi* Shrines are typical, but other shrines show signs of Buddhist influence.

Residences

There are very few private residences left from before the *Nara* period. By the *Heian* period a style called *shinden-zukuri* was popular with the nobility. Centered around the *shinden* (master's quarters), this style is characterized by an annex, open pavilion by a pond, and long connecting corridors. Floors were wooden, *tatami* not coming into common use until the end of the *Muromachi* period. In the *Momoyama* period a style called *shoin-zukuri* emerged incorporating many features now accepted as traditionally Japanese, including the *tokonoma** alcove, staggered shelves,* and *fusuma* paper sliding doors. *Katsura** and *Shugakuin* Detached Palaces are superior examples.

Castle Architecture

Castles were built throughout Japan during the tumultuous civil wars. Stone and wood with white plaster walls, castles were usually three to five stories high. *Himeji* Castle* is typical.

Western-style Architecture

The earliest example of Western-style architecture was the *Rokumeikan*,* a brick structure built soon after the *Meiji* Restoration and epitomizing the new zeal for Westernization. Today, much of the architecture of that period is preserved in *Meiji* Village at *Inuyama*, *Aichi* prefecture. Japanese architects influenced by the Bauhaus school and Le Corbusier appeared by the 1930s, but they were unable to show their full talents until after World War II. *Taniguchi Yoshirou* and *Tange Kenzou*, for example, are known for their work in concrete, and they have been joined by *Shirai Seiichi*, *Kurokawa Kishou*, and other internationally recognized architects in a multitude of styles.

欧米の庭園が，樹木や石材を幾何学的に整然と配置するのに対し，日本の伝統的庭園は，自然の一部を再現する風景式庭園である。水流，池，石組み，樹木，*築山（つきやま）などの取り合わせで変化をつけ，自然のままの風情（ふぜい）を出している。その考えが行きついたところが借景（しゃっけい）で，遠方の山や，そこから見える風景そのものを，庭の景色の一部として取り入れたものである。日本の伝統的庭園はこのように自然の景色の一部を織り込んだものであり，この日本庭園の様式が現代にも生きている。作庭の思想の上からは，日本の庭園は自然中心主義のものと，宗教性を帯びたものとの二つの流れに大別できる。

自然中心主義の庭園

自然中心主義の庭園は飛鳥（あすか）時代にさかのぼり，その日本庭園の様式を結晶させたのが寝殿造り庭園である。寝殿造り庭園は，築山，池，遣（や）り水に樹木を配したものだが，現在，その完全な遺構は残っていない。自然中心主義の庭でもう一つ代表的なのは，江戸時代に造られた大名庭である。諸国の大名が，その国元や江戸の屋敷に造らせた大規模な庭園で，回遊式の庭に天下の名所を模した景観を造り，また名石，名木を豊富に使っている。日本三庭園と呼ばれる水戸の偕楽（かいらく）園，金沢の兼六園，岡山の後楽園などがそれであり，都市の中に大面積をもつ近代公園の性格をもち，現代ではすべてが公園として一般公開されている。

宗教性を帯びた庭園

宗教性を帯びたものとしては，平安時代後期から鎌倉時代にかけて造られた浄土庭園がある。当時流行した極楽（ごくらく）浄土への信仰から生まれたもので，浄土曼荼羅（まんだら）などに描かれているように，池を掘り，その中に中島を造って橋で結び，その向こうに阿弥陀（あみだ）堂，*金堂（こんどう）を設けたもので，京都宇治の平等院鳳凰堂（ほうおうどう）庭園はその初期のもの，京都の金閣寺庭園は，浄土庭園と住宅庭園とが融合した末期のものである。

室町時代から禅宗寺院になって，「任運無作（にんぬんむさ）」という，ありのままにこだわらないことを本旨とし，山川草木すべてが仏の相（すがた）を備えているという禅の精神にのっとり，抽象化，象徴化された庭が造られた。石組みを仏像になぞらえ，流れる水は白砂で表し，超自然的な深山幽谷の趣（おもむき）を表現した。それが石庭であり，枯山水である。京都の*竜安（りょうあん）寺の石庭，大徳寺・大仙院の庭園などがこれで，その抽象性は現代芸術における抽象性と相通ずるものが多い。

In contrast to the geometric arrangements of trees and rocks in Western-style gardens, the traditional Japanese garden is a scenic composition mimicking nature. Elements of the Japanese garden include flowing water, ponds, groupings of stones, trees and shrubs, and artificial hills,* each in as natural-looking a state as possible to evoke the feeling of artlessness. The ultimate in Japanese garden philosophy is probably the concept of *shakkei* or "borrowed view"—a still-used ruse in which background elements such as mountains are incorporated into the garden's composition. Japanese gardens can be broadly divided into those which focus on naturalism and those with religious symbolism.

Natural Gardens

Among the natural-style gardens is the *shinden-zukuri* garden, a crystalization of extremely ancient Japanese garden motifs. The oldest recorded garden of this type—which includes artificial hills, ponds, and man-made streams among the foliage—dates back to the *Asuka* period. While no perfect examples of this type of garden exist today, the *kaiyuu* gardens created for the feudal lords during the *Edo* period are also representative of this naturalist school. These *kaiyuu* gardens, built both in their home fiefs and at their residences in *Edo*, often used exquisite stones and trees to create miniature reproductions of famous scenes. *Kairakuen* in *Mito*, *Kenrokuen* in *Kanazawa*, and *Kourakuen* in *Okayama*—often called Japan's three best gardens—are of this type. Broad expanses of green in crowded cities, these three gardens are today popular public parks.

Religious Gardens

Among gardens having religious significance are those in what is known as the *Joudo* style. Taking its name from the *Joudo* Buddhist sect, this garden style was developed in the late *Heian* and *Kamakura* periods and draws its symbolism from the belief in the *Joudo* paradise popular at the time. The focal point of this type of garden is the pond with a bridge arching to a central island, a major motif of the *Joudo* mandala. Behind the pond is the *Amidadou* housing the figure of the *Amida* Buddha or the *kondou*.* The *Hououdou* garden at *Byoudouin*, a temple in *Uji* south of *Kyouto* (Kyoto), is an early example of the *Joudo* style garden; and the *Kinkakuji* (Golden Pavilion) garden in *Kyouto* a later example combining the *Joudo* and the residential styles.

Beginning in the*Muromachi* period, garden design was strongly influenced by *Zen* Buddhism and abstract symbolism became increasingly important. Groupings of rocks represented figures of Buddhas, and white sand replaced flowing water in the sand and rock gardens of this period. Examples of this style include the rock garden at *Kyouto*'s *Ryouanji** and *Daitokuji*'s *Daisen'in* garden, also in *Kyouto*. The extreme abstraction of these gardens echoes abstract modern art.

外国のものを次々と貪欲なまでに吸収してきた日本人の特性は，音楽の分野にも発揮されている。クラシック，ジャズ，ロック，シャンソン，歌謡曲，*民謡，そして邦楽……。いまや日本ではコンサートをはじめ，CD，ビデオなどを通して，世界のあらゆる種類の音楽を居ながらにして楽しむことができる。

ポップス全盛の現況

若年層を中心とした人々に楽しまれている音楽は一般にポップスと言われる。これは，ロックからジャズ，映画音楽などクラシック以外のポピュラー音楽全般を指すあいまいなことばであるが，新しい曲が盛んに作られていく一方，古い曲もオールディーズとして再び登場している。アイドル歌手が人気の若者向けポップスでは，売り上げ枚数が200万枚とか300万枚といった“メガヒット”CDが続出し，国民的行事とさえ言われる年末恒例のNHKテレビ番組「紅白歌合戦」にも進出した。中高年層では演歌やナツメロが不変の人気を保っている。

こうした状況を反映して，伴奏だけのテープやLDに合わせて歌うカラオケは，初期には中年層が盛り場で歌うのが中心であったのに，若者や中高生，さらに家族ぐるみと広範囲に楽しまれるものとなり，歌うことだけが目的のカラオケ・ボックスが普及するようになった。

また，香港，台湾，韓国，中国などのアイドル歌手によるアジアン・ポップスも若者の人気を得つつあり，どちらかというと西欧寄りの日本の文化傾向を崩すものとして注目される。

クラシック音楽

クラシックは，ポップスほどは一般的ではないが，多くの固定ファンがいて人気がある。また，ピアノやバイオリンは児童の稽古ごととして普及していて，世界の音楽コンクールでの入賞者も相次いでいる。日本人のプレーヤーや団体も国際的に活躍を続けており，「Ｊクラシック」とよばれる邦人演奏家のＣＤも増えた。

“バブル景気”が去ったあとも盛んにコンサートが開かれ，“バブルの落とし子”ともいうべきオペラ・ファンも少ないながら定着し，外国のアーティストやオペラ・カンパニーの来日も成功している。また古楽器演奏の世界的なブームも日本を襲っており，各種の企画コンサートやＣＤが目白押しとなっている。しかし演奏会の入場料は高騰する傾向にあり，ファンを悩ませている。

Music is one of the areas where Japanese have shown a particular aptitude for assimilating Western culture. Without ever leaving home, Japanese can hear everything from classical, jazz, rock, chanson, *kayoukyoku* (Japanese popular music), *min'you** (Japanese folk songs), and *hougaku* (traditional Japanese music). Besides the constant stream of foreign musicians visiting Japan, there are CDs, video tapes, and all manner of other musical media.

Pops

The kind of music most-played and enjoyed by everyone, especially young people, is called pops. This is a very broad category embracing rock, film scores, and almost everything else except classical music. Just as new songs are being written daily, the old favorites are being revived. The more popular singers' mega-hit CDs can easily sell several million, and this music has even gotten onto NHK's New Year's eve song-fest—one of the "must do" ceremonies in modern Japan. Among older listeners, *enka* and "*natsumero* (Japanese oldies)" are the favorites.

Karaoke—with just the accompaniment on tape, laser disc, or whatever—started out as something middle-aged people sang when they were out drinking but has now expanded to attract young people, older people, and whole families. As a result, this is now big business, and there are "*karaoke* box" places where you and your friends can go just to sing.

"Asian pops" sung by popular singers from Hong Kong, Taiwan, Korea, China, and elsewhere in Asia have also become very popular with young people of late, and this is being watched as a possible indicator of a cultural shift away from the West.

Classical Music

While classical music does not have the same broad appeal that pops does, it has a large and loyal audience. Japanese children often take piano and violin lessons, and there are many Japanese musicians entering overseas competitions, playing with world-class orchestras, and otherwise active in the classical field. In fact, there are so many Japanese active in this field that record stores have racks of "J-classics" with Japanese artists performing the classics.

There were numerous opera and other concerts in Japan when the economy was booming, and the people who "discovered" this music then have stuck with it even though the economy has cooled. As a result, Japan remains a profitable stop for foreign artists and opera companies. Japan has also been swept up in the global fascination with older musical forms, and these CDs and concerts are also strong-sellers. Yet the high prices are a deterrent to many enthusiasts.

邦楽の種類

邦楽は，一般的には，日本の音楽の総称であるが，普通には洋楽の対語として用いられ，洋楽以外の日本の伝統音楽すべてを指す。用いる楽器の種類によって次のように分類することができる。

- **雅楽**　宮廷の行事の際に演奏される儀式音楽。古代に中国・朝鮮半島から入った音楽で，日本音楽の最も古い姿を残しているものと言える。
- **声明**（しょうみょう）　仏教の典礼音楽で，声楽。仏教伝来とともに輸入され，その後の日本音楽に大きな影響を与えた。
- **琵琶楽**（びわ）　戦国時代以降，戦記物などを*琵琶の伴奏で語る音楽として発達した。弾き語りで演奏される声楽曲である。
- **能楽**　現在の「能」の形式が大成したのは，室町時代初期である。能は，音楽と舞踊と劇の総合芸術であり，能の音楽は，「謡（うたい）」という声楽と，「囃子（はやし）」という器楽から成り立っている。
- **箏曲**（そうきょく）　箏曲とは，*琴の曲のほか，琴・*三味線（しゃみせん）・*尺八の合奏曲も指す。琴は13弦の撥弦（はつげん）楽器。江戸時代に三味線音楽と結び付いたことによって発達した。大正から昭和初期にかけて数多くの名曲を残した宮城道雄は，箏曲界に大きな影響を与えた。
- **尺八楽**　尺八は鎌倉時代から*虚無僧（こむそう）が読経（どきょう）の代わりに吹いた立笛。長さが１尺８寸(約55cm)であることから，尺八と呼ばれた。
- **三味線音楽**　三味線は，３弦で，猫か犬の皮を張った胴をもつ日本の代表的な楽器。江戸時代に広く使われるようになった三味線は，歌舞伎・*人形浄瑠璃（じょうるり）などの劇場音楽として，また数多くの歌い物音楽の伴奏として現在も使われている。
- **民謡**　各地で歌い継がれてきたもの。労働歌が多い。

邦楽の特色

洋楽の音階が７音音階であるのに対し，近世邦楽は５音音階である。リズムは，２拍子，４拍子の偶数拍子が大部分で，３拍子はほとんどない。歌が多く，純器楽曲は少ない。楽器は，ふつう声楽の伴奏楽器として用いられるが，声楽の進行と微妙に一致しない複雑なズレがある。また，三味線・琴・尺八など，楽器の構造に由来する雑音的要素も邦楽の複雑な音色として好まれる。

明治に洋楽が入って以降，洋楽が日本の音楽の主流で，邦楽は洋楽に圧倒されてきた。しかし，近年，邦楽が見直され，愛好者も増えている。外国人の愛好者も多くなった。

Traditional Japanese Music

Types

Hougaku, traditional Japanese music, is classified by the type of instruments used.

- ***Gagaku*** Ceremonial court music introduced from China and Korea, *gagaku* is the oldest type of traditional Japanese music.
- ***Shoumyou*** Buddhist liturgical chants are called *shoumyou*. Introduced into Japan at the same time as Buddhism, *shoumyou* had a profound impact on the development of native Japanese music.
- ***Biwa-gaku*** A type of short lute, the *biwa** was a favored instrument of accompaniment for long chanted ballads about great battles and heroic deeds, and this music is called *biwa-gaku*.
- ***Nou-gaku*** *Nou* (noh) as it is performed today gelled in the *Muromachi* period. An art combining song, dance, and drama, *nou* is characterized by its *utai* chorus and *hayashi* flute and percussion instrument accompaniment, all of which combine to form *nou-gaku*.
- ***Soukyoku*** *Soukyoku* is music performed on the *koto** (a 13-string zither) or by an ensemble of *koto*, *shamisen** (three-stringed long lute), and *shakuhachi** (vertical flute) players. *Koto* music flowered in the *Edo* period along with *shamisen* music. *Miyagi Michio*, a composer of *soukyoku* active in the early years of the 20th century, had a major influence on this type of traditional music.
- ***Shakuhachi*** *Shakuhachi-gaku* is all of that music played on the *shakuhachi*, a bamboo flute formerly played by wandering Buddhist monks.* The name for this instrument derives from the fact that it is one *shaku* and eight (*hachi*) *sun* (total: approximately 55cm) long.
- ***Shamisen-ongaku*** Made of cat or dog hide and having only three strings, the *shamisen* is a uniquely Japanese instrument and its music the uniquely Japanese *shamisen-ongaku*. An extremely popular instrument in the *Edo* period, the *shamisen* is an important accompaniment to *kabuki* and puppet theater drama,* and it continues to be used today as accompaniment for many Japanese songs.
- ***Min'you*** Folk songs are called *min'you*. Found throughout Japan, many *min'you* are work songs.

Characteristics

In contrast to the seven-note scale of Western music, traditional Japanese music is based on a five-note scale and has primarily two- and four-beat rhythms as opposed to a three-beat time. Most traditional music consists of songs with instrumental accompaniment, and there are very few purely instrumental compositions. The instrumental accompaniment seldom progresses exactly in step with the song. The "noise" that is an inevitable part of the sound of the *shamisen, koto, shakuhachi*, and other traditional instruments is appreciated for the unique tone it gives to the music.

Since it was first introduced into Japan full-force in the late 19th century, Western music has become very popular, overshadowing traditional music. Still, interest in traditional music has been reviving in recent years, and many audiences include appreciative non-Japanese.

5 能*

能は歌にあたる「謡」と，それに伴う演技(型と言う)と舞から成る仮面劇である。能の美しさは様式的な美しさで，劇的な演技はなるべく抑えて緊縮された動きの中に幽玄な趣を出そうとするところにある。能は台本に相当する謡本によって上演され，演者のほかに謡の合唱の部分を受けもつ「地謡」があり，演奏は笛・大鼓・*小鼓によって行われ，演ずる曲によっては太鼓が加わることがある。役は，シテ方・ワキ方・狂言方・囃子方がそれぞれ分担し，ほかの役を演ずることはしない決まりになっている。シテ方は主役の登場人物とそのツレを受けもつほかに地謡を担当する。ワキ方はワキとそのツレ，狂言方は間狂言と言って１曲の能の前場と後場をつなぐ役を演ずるほか，能の間に番組を挟んでユーモラスに演じて見せる。囃子方はそれぞれ上記の楽器を受けもつ。これらの役で仮面をつけるのはシテ方(能面)と狂言方(狂言面)だけで，ワキ方はつけないことになっている。

能の歴史

能は先行芸能の散楽や田楽能から発展し，室町時代に観阿弥・世阿弥父子によって大成を見た伝統芸能で，社寺や時の将軍足利義満などの庇護のもとにしだいに完成した。特に豊臣秀吉がこれを好み，自ら演じたのは有名な話である。能は江戸時代にも大名たちの保護を受け，武家の武楽として栄えた。そのため，明治になって武家社会が廃れると能も衰微の運命を甘受することになる。しかし，関係者の努力でなんとか生命を保ちながら今日に及び，最近は古典芸能見直しの気運もあって，若い人々の間に愛好者が増えている。

舞台と能組み

能の舞台は普通の劇場のように額縁舞台ではなく，正面と脇正面が観客席(見所と言う)にはり出していて，演者が登場してくる橋懸という通路(歌舞伎の花道に当たる)をもって楽屋と通じている。特に舞台装置はなく，必要があれば簡素な形をした家屋や岩屋の作り物が運び出される程度で，舞台背景には１本の老松が描かれている。

能の現行曲はほぼ250番あるが，大きく「神・男・女・狂・鬼」の５つに分けられ，プログラム(能組みと言う)を作成するときはこの順序に従う。「神」は祝言性の勝ったもの，「男」は武人の修羅の悲劇を描き，「女」は能の美の中心的なもの，「狂」は異常な情況に置かれた心理葛藤を，切能の「鬼」は文字通り鬼畜が登場する。

Nou (Noh)*

Nou is a type of masked dance-drama in which extreme stylization of the actors' movements and the narrative music evoke a beautiful, mysterious atmosphere. The only script for a *nou* play is a song book called an *utai-bon* with narrative chants and songs sung by a chorus to the accompaniment of flutes, large and small hand drums,* and, at times, a large drum.

The performers are defined by their roles. These are the *shite* principal actor, the *waki* subordinate actor, the *kyougen* comic actor, and the chorus and musicians, none of which are interchangeable. The principal actor directs not only his own performance in the leading role, but also that of his companion, the *tsure*, and the singing of the chorus. In the same way the *waki* or subordinate actor oversees his own role and that of his *tsure*. The *kyougen* actor will sometimes provide a brief explanation of events between acts, and he performs in humorous sketches, also called *kyougen*, which provide comic relief between plays. Music plays an important role throughout, for the musicians and chorus are as vital to a *nou* performance as the actors. Masks may sometimes be worn by the *shite* and the *kyougen* actors, but never by the *waki*.

History

Originating in dramatic performances at religious festivals in the middle of the 14th century, *nou* as it is known today was developed in the *Muromachi* period by *Kan'ami* and his son, *Zeami*, and flourished under the patronage of *Shintou* shrines and Buddhist temples and such authoritative figures as the *Ashikaga shougun Yoshimitsu*. *Toyotomi Hideyoshi* was an enthusiastic supporter of *nou* who delighted in playing leading roles himself. *Nou* continued to flourish in the *Edo* period under the patronage of the *daimyou* and became a favored entertainment of the military class. Because of this close association with the *samurai*, however, *nou* declined rapidly in the *Meiji* period when the *samurai* lost their position of supremacy. Still, devotees have managed to keep the *nou* theater alive, and it is enjoying renewed popularity as Japanese people today evidence a growing interest in their traditional arts.

Stage

Unlike the conventional stage, the *nou* stage has an extension on one side that acts as a side stage and a bridge connecting it to hidden dressing rooms and providing an entrance for actors similar to *kabuki*'s *hana-michi*. Very few stage props or settings are used, although there is always a single pine tree painted on the back wall of the stage.

The 250 or so *nou* plays which continue to be performed today are divided into five groups: plays about gods, warriors, women, the deranged, and demons.

6 歌舞伎*

東京・銀座にある*歌舞伎座，京都・四条通にある南座などは，いつも観客でにぎわっている。数百年からの歴史をもつ日本の代表的伝統芸能は，今なお脈々とその生命力を保っている。

歌舞伎の歴史

起源は出雲大社の*巫女，*阿国が江戸時代初期，京都で歌舞伎踊りをしたのに始まる。「かぶき」とは「傾く」のことで，異様な容姿・所作を意味した。今日の総合演劇としての歌舞伎の原型は，それまでの，容色をもって観客の人気を得ていた女歌舞伎，若衆歌舞伎から脱皮し，技芸をもって俳優の本分とした野郎歌舞伎からである。特に元禄・享保年間には専門の脚本作家が登場，俳優も京阪には坂田藤十郎，芳沢あやめ，江戸には市川団十郎という名優が輩出し，一つの頂点に達した。その後一時人形浄瑠璃劇に人気を譲るが，18世紀後半には再び盛り返した。また，回り舞台やせり上げなど，舞台装置も工夫開拓された。一方，活動の中心は上方から江戸に移った。

代表的作者には近松門左衛門，鶴屋南北，河竹黙阿弥らがいる。中でも江戸時代から明治にかけて活躍した河竹黙阿弥は，それまでの歌舞伎劇を集大成した第一人者である。明治以降は大きな変化を見ることなく今日に至っている。近世の名優としては明治に尾上菊五郎（5代），市川団十郎（9代），市川左団次（初代）が，大正に尾上菊五郎（6代），中村吉右衛門（初代）がいる。昭和に文化勲章の受章者として，松本白鸚（初代），中村歌右衛門（6代），中村勘三郎（17代），尾上松緑（2代）がいる。

歌舞伎の特色

歌舞伎は役者中心の演劇であり，役者のもっている魅力に支えられている。特に女形のもつ独特の雰囲気は多くの外国人をも引き付ける。女歌舞伎が禁止され，やむをえず男が演じたわけだが，長い歴史の中で独自の世界を作り上げるに至った。今日，若手女形として人気のある坂東玉三郎は海外公演でも大成功を収めた。歌舞伎役者はほとんど世襲で，幼時から厳しい稽古を積み，伝統を守っている。

舞台の役者は*屋号で声援される。主な屋号には，市川団十郎＝成田屋，松本幸四郎＝高麗屋，中村歌右衛門＝成駒屋，尾上菊五郎＝音羽屋などがある。舞台下手（客席から向かって左）に観客席を貫いて作られた花道（役者の通り道）を入退場しながら役者と観客はいっそうの一体感を味わう。

脚本の種類は大きく分けて貴族や武士の世界を描いた時代物と，庶民の生活を描いた世話物とがある。

*Kabuki**

Toukyou's (Tokyo's) *Kabuki-za** and *Kyouto*'s (Kyoto's) *Minami-za* consistently play to full houses as *kabuki* continues to draw upon its centuries-old tradition to remain a vital force in Japanese theater today.

History

Kabuki's roots go back to an *Izumo* shrine maiden* named *Okuni** who performed "*kabuki*" (the name taken from the word *kabuku* meaning to act in an unusual manner) dances in *Kyouto* during the early *Edo* period. On the way to today's mature genre, *kabuki* passed through a number of stages, including *onna kabuki* with women dancing provocatively, *wakashuu kabuki* in which young men replaced the women, and *yarou kabuki* performed by older men for its artistic merits. By the late 17th century, authors were writing specifically for the *kabuki* stage and great actors were emerging, among them *Sakata Toujuurou* and *Yoshizawa Ayame* in the *Oosaka-*(Osaka-)*Kyouto* district and *Ichikawa Danjuurou* in *Edo*. After later losing audience to puppet plays, *kabuki* came back stronger than ever in the late 18th century. As staging became more elaborate with revolving stages and hoists, the center of action shifted from the *Oosaka-Kyouto* area to *Edo*.

Among the best-known *kabuki* playwrights are *Chikamatsu Monzaemon*, *Tsuruya Nanboku*, and *Kawatake Mokuami*. *Kawatake* especially is remembered for carrying on the spirit of *Edo kabuki* and writing some of the best *kabuki* plays. Some of the best-known greats of the modern *kabuki* stage are *Onoe Kikugorou* V, *Ichikawa Danjuurou* IX, *Ichikawa Sadanji* I, *Onoe Kikugorou* VI, *Nakamura Kichiemon* I. *Matsumoto Hakuou* I, *Nakamura Utaemon* VI, *Nakamura Kanzaburou* XVII, and *Onoe Shouroku* II. All have been awarded the Order of Culture.

Characteristics

Kabuki is an actor's theater, and the actor's skill is all. Many foreign observers have been drawn to *kabuki* for its women's roles gracefully performed by male *onna-gata* in conformity with *kabuki*'s longstanding tradition of banning women from the stage. *Bandou Tamasaburou*, for example, the most popular *onna-gata* in *kabuki* today, has also been lionized overseas. *Kabuki* names are generally hereditary, and actors' children undergo rigorous training from a very early age.

Every *kabuki* actor has a *yagou*,* called out by appreciative members of the audience when he cuts an especially striking figure. Some of the most famous *yagou* are *Naritaya (Ichikawa Danjuurou)*, *Kouraiya (Matsumoto Koushirou)*, *Narikomaya* (*Nakamura Utaemon*), and *Otowaya* (*Onoe Kikugorou*). Another unique feature of *kabuki* is the *hana-michi*, a long passageway running directly through the audience at the left of center stage, and having principal actors make their entrances and exits along the *hana-michi* helps to draw the audience into the performance itself.

Kabuki's main themes include both tales of war and court life and everyday psychological conflicts that townspeople could identify with.

*文楽

歌舞伎とともに近世演劇を代表する文楽は，文楽座から発祥した操り人形芝居の名称で，別に人形浄瑠璃とも呼ばれる。歌舞伎ほどポピュラーではないが，生身の演者によるよりも人形の演じる芝居にいっそうの魅力を見いだす通的外国人も多い。

文楽は起源は室町時代で，江戸時代になり，京阪を中心に発展し，完成した。*太夫・三味線弾きが義太夫浄瑠璃を演奏するのに合わせて人形を遣う。しかも一つの人形を３人がかりで遣う。人形は首・肩板・胴・手から成り，足は原則として男にしかない。1ｍから1.5mの大きさで，重いものは10kgにもなる。主遣いが首・胴・右手，左遣いが左手，足遣いが足を受けもつ。女の人形には足がないのが普通だが，着物のすそをつまんでさばくことによってそれらしく見せる。本来表情のない人形は，黒い頭巾，黒い衣服をまとった人形遣いによって魂を吹き込まれたかのように，嘆き，笑い，怒る。

代表的作家近松門左衛門は江戸時代に，『国性爺合戦』『曽根崎心中』『心中天網島』など不朽の名作を残し，それは今も観客の胸を打つ。武家社会を題材にした時代物にしろ，庶民を主人公にした世話物にしろ，人間や人間関係の本質を詩情豊かに追究したところに，時代を越えて人々の心を動かさずにはおかないものがあるのだろう。また文楽は人形劇とは言え，大人を対象にしているところにも特色がある。文楽は現在，*重要無形文化財となり，*人間国宝に数人が指定されている。

日本舞踊

発生は古代までさかのぼり，『古事記』にアメノウズメが舞ったという「天岩屋伝説」が記されている。現在の日本舞踊の代表と言えば，歌舞伎とともに歩み，古くからの各種の舞踊の要素が集大成されている歌舞伎踊りを挙げることができる。一方，19世紀に京阪の宴席を中心に，能の影響を受けて発達した，上方舞も忘れることができない。共に三味線を主体の伴奏音楽によって演じられる。前者は当然劇的要素が濃く，動きも活発。後者の動きは極端に少なく，一畳の畳の中で舞うとさえ言う。

日本舞踊が，西洋の舞踊，すなわちバレエと最も異なる点は，バレエがトーシューズでつま先立ち，跳躍するのに対し，日本舞踊はすり足で，むしろ腰を入れて足拍子を踏むところにある。家元制度の下に西川，藤間，花柳，井上など多数の流派があるが，現在，最大の流派は花柳流。生け花，茶道同様に習い手の大半は女性である。

Bunraku and Buyou

*Bunraku**

The traditional Japanese puppet theater is known as *bunraku*, a name derived from *Oosaka*'s (Osaka's) *Bunraku-za* theater. While not as popular as *kabuki*, *bunraku* with its all-puppet cast appeals to a discriminating audience that includes many non-Japanese.

Although the earliest forms of *bunraku* appeared in the *Muromachi* period, it was in the *Edo* period that it became popular in *Kyouto* (Kyoto) and *Oosaka*. *Bunraku* demands close cooperation among the ballad-reciting chanter,* the *shamisen* accompanist, and the three operators required for each puppet. *Bunraku* puppets measure 1-1.5 meters high and can weigh up to 10 kg. Each of the three operators is responsible for different parts—the principal operator for the head, torso, and right hand, the first assistant for the left hand, and the second assistant for the feet—and all have devoted many years to their art of bringing the puppets to life. While dolls for female characters do not usually have feet, the hems of the *kimono* are moved to give the illusion of feet. Even though the puppets have little facial expression, the operators manage to make them weep, laugh, and get angry very realistically. Onstage, the operators are inconspicuously clothed in black.

The greatest *bunraku* playwright was *Chikamatsu Monzaemon*, who wrote such classics as *Kokusen'ya Kassen* (Battles of Coxinga), *Sonezaki Shinjuu* (Love Suicides at *Sonezaki*), and *Shinjuu Ten no Amijima* (Love Suicides at *Amijima*). Modern audiences find that many of these plays still possess dramatic power and themes — romantic love, the star-crossed lovers' suicide, and war—that transcend time. Even though these are "puppet plays", there is nothing childish about them. *Bunraku* has been designated an Important Intangible Cultural Asset,* and several *bunraku* artists have been named Living Cultural Treasures.*

Nihon Buyou

Nihon buyou is a generic term used to refer to traditional Japanese dance forms. The earliest mention of Japanese dance is in the *Kojiki*. Best-known are the *kabuki* dances which use elements from the *kabuki* stage, although the *kamigata* dance which developed in the 19th century *Kyouto-Oosaka* area and is patterned after *nou*(noh) dance is also an important tradition. Both are performed to *shamisen*-centered accompaniment, the *kabuki* dancing retaining the stage's vigorous movements and the *kamigata* dance showing powerful restraint and taking place in a small area.

Nihon buyou differs conspicuously from ballet and other Western dance forms in that, while ballet dancers wear toeshoes to dance and perform leaps, *Nihon buyou* performers tend to move in shuffling motions. Among the many *Nihon buyou* schools existing today under the traditional *iemoto* system of master-led schools are the *Nishikawa, Fujima, Inoue*, and (most popular) *Hanayagi* schools. As with flower arrangement and the tea ceremony, most *Nihon buyou* students are women.

8 大衆芸能

大衆芸能は寄席を舞台に，庶民の娯楽として栄えてきた。テレビ・ラジオの台頭とともに娯楽の王座は奪われたが，今日では寄席ばかりでなく，テレビ・ラジオにも進出し，再び現代の娯楽として大きな位置を占めている。以下，主な大衆芸能を挙げると——

落語*

江戸時代初期に起こり，江戸，大坂を中心に栄え，多くの流派を生む。世相人情を風刺しながら，こっけいな話の展開と話術で聴衆を笑わせ，話の最後には巧みに「落（おち）」をつけるのが定型である。まだ駆け出しの落語家は「前座」と呼ばれ，高座では初めのほうに出演する。また，一座の主たる格の芸人は「真打ち」と呼ばれ，最後に出演する。真打ちとは，それだけの値打ちがある落語家を言う意味で付いたが，今日では一人前になり，披露を済ませた芸人は「真打ち」と呼ばれている。

講談

落語と並ぶ日本特有の話術芸能で，江戸・元禄（げんろく）時代に『太平記』を講じた名和清左衛門が祖とされる。政談や武勇伝，御家騒動，あだ討ち，侠客（きょうかく）伝，人情物語などを語り聞かせる。当初は「講釈」と言い，明治に入って「講談」と呼ばれるようになった。全盛期は大正までで，宝井馬琴（ばきん），一龍斎貞山などを輩出した。昭和の後半には女性にも講談師として活躍する者が現れ，再び注目を浴びている。

漫才

古くは13，14世紀ごろ，初春などに太夫（たゆう）と才蔵の２人が連れ立ち，おもしろおかしく掛け合いを演じ悪魔を払い，新年の繁栄を祝った「万歳」に端を発している。漫才はその現代化であり，明治末期に関西で始まり，発展してきた。出し物は作者が別にいる場合もあるが，自作自演も多い。また最近は２人にこだわらず，多数で演ずるものや，楽器などバンド入りのものもある。時代の進展とともに漫才も影響を受け，若手コンビによるテンポの速い漫才が人気を得ている。

浪花節（なにわぶし）

講釈，物語，演劇，文芸作品などを材料とし，三味線（しゃみせん）を伴奏に，独特の節回しで歌い，語るもので，独演である。江戸中期大坂に出た浪花伊助からこの名で呼ばれ，明治に入り桃中軒雲右衛門（とうちゅうけんくもえもん）が盛り上げた。義理人情，勧善懲悪を内容としたものが多く，「浪花節的」と言えば，義理人情に傾きがちなことの代名詞である。「浪曲」とも言う。

Popular Entertainment

Popular entertainment was once the specialty of the *yose* theater. Though the *yose* has been supplanted by television and radio, *yose* entertainment continues to survive as staple fare in the new media.

*Rakugo**

This comic monologue originated in the early *Edo* period in the stories of human foibles told with vivid expression and ending with skillfully delivered punch lines called *ochi* (the character *ochi* is also read *raku* to give *rakugo* its name). *Rakugo* flourished in *Edo* and *Oosaka* (Osaka), and many schools of storytelling evolved. Novice performers are called *zenza*, and open the bill in the typical *yose* program, and experienced storytellers of exceptional skill are called *shin-uchi* and perform last. *Shin-uchi* was formerly a title reserved for only the best *rakugo* artists, but today it is accorded any *rakugo* storyteller who has finished his apprenticeship.

Koudan

This form of storytelling is said to have begun with the recitation of tales from the 14th-century *Taiheiki* military ballad in the *Edo* period as perfected by *Nawa Seizaemon. Koudan* stories are of historical events, military exploits, succession disputes in *daimyou* households, vendettas, heroic figures and sentimental tales of human nature. Originally called *koushaku*, this type of storytelling or recitation has been known as *koudan* since the *Meiji* period. At its height in the *Taishou* era, when such artists as *Takarai Bakin* and *Ichiryuusai Teizan* were in their prime, *koudan* declined during the war years, but has since recovered somewhat with help from female storytellers and other innovations.

Manzai

Comic banter usually performed by two artists, *manzai* goes back to the 13th and 14th centuries when such performances were a common entertainment for ushering in the new year and exorcising devils, and the name is said to come from the "*banzai*" at the end. Modern *manzai* developed in the late 19th century in the *Kansai* region. Though some *manzai* acts are scripted by professional writers, most are thought up by the performers. Recent *manzai* acts have sometimes included more than two people and have even had musical accompaniment. *Manzai* has changed considerably with the times. Today rapid-paced dialogues by young performers are especially popular.

Naniwa-bushi

Japanese narrative ballads, *naniwa-bushi* (also called *roukyoku*) are recited by a solo chanter to the accompaniment of a single *shamisen*. Stories are derived from *koushaku*, drama, and literature. Originated by *Naniwa Isuke* in the *Oosaka* area in the mid-*Edo* period, *naniwa-bushi* was popularized by *Touchuuken Kumoemon* at the turn of the century. Most *naniwa-bushi* tales are of sacrifice, sentiment, and morality, and the term is often used to mean tear-jerking self-sacrifice.

9 生け花（華道）

茶の湯と同様，生け花も室町時代，将軍足利義政の下，東山文化の中で華道として成立した。四季に恵まれた日本には四季の花々があり，野にあるそれらの素材を単に切り取って飾るだけでなく，そこに一つの芸術的理念を展開させたもの，それが生け花である。つまり自然の容姿風体を生かし，あるいは生ける際の花材の構成に天地人の形式を取り入れて華道の理念としている流派が多い。

生け花は，時代に応じてさまざまな様式を生んできた。そして今日なお生き続けているものに，立華（りっか），生花（せいか），投入（なげいれ），盛花（もりばな）がある。流派は2000〜3000あるが，最大のものは池坊で，弟子の数100万人と言われる。これに次ぐのは小原流，草月流などである。

• *立華　書院の床の間の飾り花として，池坊専慶が室町時代に創造した。松・桃・竹・柳・紅葉（もみじ）・ヒノキなどが使われ，後述の生花のように，必ずしも瓶口に直接挿して水を揚げる形を取らない。立華と称するのは，草木の立ち伸びる姿から，立てる形を取ったためで，花や木を素材に針金などを用いて容姿を整え，一つの風景の再現を意図している。

• *生花　花を生けるという表現は，もともとは生花に対して使われていた。江戸時代中期，客をもてなす生け花として生まれ，主として床の間に置かれた。投入や盛花と異なり，花を挿す器は大地を象徴し，草花の部分的な美しさよりも，草木が伸びゆく生命力を表そうとする。品格の高さ，流麗，端正さが生花の特徴である。

• *投入　深い花器に花枝を自然の姿のまま，無造作に投げ入れたように挿したところからこの名が生まれた。床の間につるす場合と，柱にかける場合，床の間に置く場合の３通りの形式がある。生花同様江戸時代から。

• *盛花　*水盤やかごを用い，器に花を盛るような形で生けるところからこの名がついた。明治末期，洋花の栽培や洋風建築の増加により，床の間の装飾に限らないものとして考案された。小原流，草月流，安達式など，盛花は現代の生け花の主流と言える。　戦後の住宅環境の変化――洋風建築や小さな間取り――は，生け花にも影響を及ぼした。伝統にとらわれない新しい様式の創造は，前衛生け花として市民権を得，華道から造形芸術へと変貌しつつある。また，流派にこだわらずフラワーデザインを楽しむ人も増えている。

Flower Arrangement

Together with the tea ceremony, *ikebana* (also known as *kadou* or way of the flower) was established in the *Muromachi* period as a central part of the *Higashiyama* culture under the *shougun Ashikaga Yoshimasa*. Because Japan is blessed with changing seasons and plentiful flora, it was not enough simply to go out and pick flowers from the field. They had to be displayed artistically, and this is the heart of *ikebana*. At times this artistic arrangement entails making them look as close to their ideal natural state as possible, and at times the elements of the arrangements are used to represent the heavens, earth, and man; both of these being important principles in many schools.

Ikebana has developed numerous styles over the years. Some of the most common today are explained below. All told, there are 2-3,000 different schools of *ikebana*. The largest of these is *Ikenobou*, with over a million students. Other important schools include *Ohara* and *Sougetsu*.

• ***Rikka**** This style was developed by *Ikenobou Senkei* in the *Muromachi* period for decorating the *tokonoma* with flowers. Using pine, peach, bamboo, willow, maple, cypress, and other plants, this style is not as concerned as, say, *seika*, with putting the stems in contact with the vase or even the water. Because *rikka* is a "standing" or vertical style, and indeed the name derives from the use of protruding branches, it uses supporting materials in an attempt to recreate an entire landscape.

• ***Seika**** This style of using flowers as they appear in "real life" developed in the mid-*Edo* period as a *tokonoma* arrangement for the delight of guests Unlike *nageire* or *moribana*, *seika* uses the vase to represent the earth and attempts to portray not beauty but rather the power of flowers in the field. *Seika* is characterized by its elegance, flow, and breadth.

• ***Nageire**** This style derives its name from the fact that flowers are simply "thrown into" a tall vase and allowed to fall naturally. These tall vases can be hung from the ceiling, hung on a pillar, or placed in the *tokonoma*. Like *seika*, it developed in the *Edo* period.

• ***Moribana**** This style uses water trays* or even basket-clad containers and derives its name from the fact that flowers are "piled up" for show. It was conceived in the late *Meiji* period as a modern reaction to the traditional *seika* and to make use of Western flora and forms outside of the *tokonoma*. Favored by the *Ohara*, *Sougetsu*, *Adachi*, and other schools, *moribana* is perhaps the pre-eminent modern form.

The postwar shift to Western-type housing with smaller rooms has also affected *ikebana*. New forms have been created ignoring traditional rules, and avant-garde *ikebana* has come to be a recognized form as some styles even use artificial flowers. At the same time, increasing numbers of people are enjoying flower design unfettered by tradition.

日本人の書いた英文書として，今なお名著と言われる『茶の本』の中で，著者*岡倉天心は，「茶道とは，日常生活のむさくるしい諸事実の中にある美を崇拝することを根底とする儀式である」（桶谷秀昭訳）と簡にして要を得て書いている。奈良時代に中国から伝えられた茶が，異国・日本で茶道として独自の文化を開花させたのはなぜか。茶の湯にこそ，日本文化の特質が内包されているのかもしれない。

茶の湯の歴史

日本に初めて茶が渡来したのは，奈良時代，遣唐使たちによってである。一時廃（すた）れたが，鎌倉時代には再び広まり，室町時代，将軍足利義政の下で，村田珠光（じゅこう）が四畳半の侘（わび）茶方式を始めるに及び，茶は芸術性を高め，茶道となった。そしてこれを大成したのが，安土・桃山時代の千利休である。利休は豊臣秀吉の庇護（ひご）を受けたがやがて対立，1591年，秀吉の命により切腹した。茶道は子孫に受け継がれ，表千家，裏千家，武者小路千家の，いわゆる三千家を生んだ。流派としてはこの三千家を中心に，藪内（やぶのうち）家，遠州（えんしゅう）流，宗徧（そうへん）流など多くの流派を生み，今日に至っている。中でも淡交会を組織する裏千家は，戦後いち早く海外へ進出し，茶道の国際化に大きな役割を果たした。

作法と心得

庭園や寺社の境内（けいだい）などに臨時の席を設けて行う野点（のだて）の形式もあるが，茶道に茶室は欠かせない。そしてこの茶室という狭い空間こそが茶文化をはぐくんだ。茶を点（た）てることは*点前（てまえ）と言い，その手順は，*茶碗（ちゃわん）に*抹茶を入れて*釜（かま）の湯を注ぎ，*茶筅（ちゃせん）でかき回し泡立てる。飲み方は右手で茶碗を取り，左の手のひらにのせ，茶碗を向こうから手前に回す。飲んだ後は指先でぬぐい，指は懐紙（懐中の紙）でふく。しかし，茶道とは単に茶を飲むのではなく，茶碗をはじめとする茶道具，茶室の調度，露地（茶庭）などの鑑賞，そして主人と客との心の交流にこそ本質がある。

千利休は茶の湯の心得を，「四規七則」と説いた。「四規」とは和敬清寂で，和敬は茶会での亭主と客相互の心得。清寂は茶室，茶庭の清らかで閑寂な雰囲気を言う。「七則」は他人に接するときの心構えで，「茶は服（飲みかげん）のよきように点て，炭は湯の沸くように置き，冬は暖かく夏は涼しく，花は野にあるように入れ，刻限は早めに，降らずとも雨具の用意，相客に心せよ，の7つが秘事」と言う。

The Tea Ceremony

One of the best English-language books by a Japanese author is *Okakura Tenshin*'s* *The Book of Tea* (1906), in which *Okakura* characterizes teaism as "a cult founded on the adoration of the beautiful among the sordid facts of everyday existence."

History of the Tea Ceremony

The tea ceremony was introduced into Japan from China during the *Nara* period. After initially fading into obscurity, it was revived in the *Kamakura* period and spread during the *Muromachi* period thanks to the enthusiasm of the *shougun Ashikaga Yoshimasa* and his tea master *Murata Jukou*, who originated the *wabicha* style of using a 4½-mat room and enhanced the artistic and spiritual aspects to develop a discipline known as *sadou* (the way of tea). In the *Azuchi-Momoyama* period, *sadou* was further refined by *Sen no Rikyuu*. *Rikyuu* gained the patronage of *Toyotomi Hideyoshi*, but the two later had a falling-out and in 1591 *Hideyoshi* ordered *Rikyuu* to commit ritual suicide. His teachings were carried on by his descendants, three of whom established the three *Senke* schools of tea: *Omote Senke*, *Ura Senke*, and *Mushakouji Senke*. In addition to these three main schools, other influential schools include the *Yabunouchi*, *Enshuu*, and *Souhen* schools, all of which are active today. *Uru Senke* began being taught overseas immediately after the war and has played a major role in *sadou*'s internationalization.

Etiquette

Traditionally, the tea ceremony is held outside or in a small room set apart from other buildings, and it is this simplicity of setting more than anything else which epitomizes the spirit of tea. In the serving of the tea, the *temae*,* the host spoons some powdered green *matcha** tea into a ceramic teabowl,* adds hot water from the kettle,* and stirs briskly with a small whisk.* In receiving the tea, the guest takes it with his right hand and, steadying it on his left palm, turns it once or twice before drinking. After drinking, the guest wipes the rim with his finger and then his finger with a small napkin. In addition to the tea, appreciation of the utensils, the room decor, and the garden, as well as the chemistry between host and guests, are all essential elements of *sadou*.

Sen no Rikyuu established four rules for the rapport between host and guests and the simple beauty and tranquility of the tea room and garden and seven guidelines for the host's attitude: "Serve the tea with insight into the guest's soul, prepare the charcoal to heat the water best, make your guest feel warm in winter and cool in summer, arrange the flowers so they look like wild flowers, be quick and efficient, be prepared for rain even on a clear day, and be attentive toward all guests. These are the seven keys."

書道は*毛筆と*墨を使い，漢字や仮名（かな）文字を書く一種の造形芸術である。西洋でも，文字を象形化したり装飾化するカリグラフィーの伝統はあるが，書道のもつ芸術的奥深さには及ばない。アルファベットと比べ，文字それ自体がもつ意味や毛筆の多様性などが，書道を芸術へと高めた。昨今は外国人にも関心が高まっている。正月の２日，新年に初めて文字を書く書き初めの儀式は今日も残っており，吉方に向かってめでたいことばや詩歌（しいか）を書く。小中学生の大がかりな書き初め大会も，例年催されている。

書道の歴史

日本の書道はもともと中国の王羲之（おうぎし）が祖と言われ，中国の書が日本に入ったのは奈良時代である。平安時代前期には空海，嵯峨（さが）天皇，橘逸勢（たちばなのはやなり）の３人が特に三筆と言われ，中国風の雄勁（ゆうけい）な書風を代表した。さらに中期には小野道風（おののとうふう），藤原佐理（すけまさ），藤原行成（ゆきなり）が現れ，三蹟（さんせき）と言われた。彼らはそれまでの中国風に対し，優美典雅な日本風の和様書道（上代様とも言う）の創造に功績があった。藤原行成は世尊寺流を興し，また，小野道風は青蓮院流（後の御家流）など後代の書道に大きな影響を与えた。南北朝時代に興った御家流は，江戸時代には一切の公文書に採用され，また寺子屋でも習字にもっぱら使われた。

このように，書は時代を象徴する雰囲気を有し，今日，書道ブームと言われるほどの隆盛の中で，バラエティーに富んだ自由な書が愛好され，また，女性書家の進出が目だっている。

書体の種類

文字の書体には，*楷書（かいしょ），*行書，*草書，それに仮名がある。楷書は字形が方正で，動きが少なく，安定した書体のため，真書とも言われる。行書は楷書と草書の中間的存在で，楷書では固すぎ，草書では難解であるために考え出された書体。草書は行書をさらに崩し，点画を略したものを言い，最も早く書くことができる。と同時に，造形上の自由が大きいために，芸術性も高いところから，書家に好まれている。

この草書体の究極に生まれたのが仮名で，平安時代，主に女性によって使われたので，女手とも呼ばれ，和歌の流行とともに発展した。漢字の雄渾（ゆうこん）に対して，優美，流麗である。書は表現美（線，形，流れ，余白，墨色など）と内容美（風格，意味），さらに書家の人となりがあいまって成立，鑑賞される。

Calligraphy

Japanese calligraphy, *shodou*, is a highly developed art form using brush* and black ink* to write Japanese and Chinese characters. While similar to the decorative calligraphy of the West, *shodou* is more deeply rooted as a fine art form, in part because every character has meaning in and of itself and in part because of the great diversity of character shapes. *Shodou* is increasingly admired by Japanese and foreigners alike.

The *kakizome* held on January 2 marks the first writing of the new year and is still regularly performed today. Facing an auspicious direction, participants write out felicitous words and phrases. *Kakizome* competitions are annual elementary and junior high school events.

History

Shodou traces its origins to China, where the master calligrapher Wang Xizhi is traditionally credited as the father of the art. It was introduced into Japan in the 8th century. The early *Heian* contemporaries, *Kuukai*, Emperor *Saga*, and courtier *Tachibana no Hayanari* are respectfully referred to as the *Sanpitsu* or Three Great Brushes, and their calligraphy is considered representative of Chinese calligraphy's classic beauty. In the 10th and 11th centuries these three were succeeded by the *Sanseki* (the Three Traces): *Ono no Toufuu*, *Fujiwara no Sukemasa*, and *Fujiwara no Yukinari*. These three masters developed the first uniquely Japanese calligraphy style, known as *wayou* (also *joudaiyou*). *Fujiwara no Yukinari*'s style led to the formation of the *Sesonji* school and *Ono no Toufuu* served as a model for the *Shouren'in* school which later evolved into the *Oie* style of calligraphy. The *Oie* style was used for official documents in the *Edo* period and was the predominant style taught in the *terakoya* schools of that period.

Just as calligraphy has changed over the ages, the revived interest in calligraphy today is characterized by its broad latitude for creativity and the increasing number of women masters.

Calligraphy Styles

There are three basic styles, *kaisho*,* *gyousho*,* and *sousho*,* with *kana* added as a fourth style. *Kaisho* is an unabbreviated block style with little movement, is also called *shinsho. Gyousho* is an intermediate style neither as stiff as *kaisho* nor as flowing as *sousho. Sousho* is a highly cursive or abbreviated style written with swift strokes. Its freedom and aesthetic appeal has made *sousho* very popular with calligraphy masters.

Kana originated from the more extreme forms of *sousho*. Because it was the primary script for *Heian* women, *kana* was at one time referred to as *onnade* (women's writing). *Kana* developed with the growing popularity of *waka* poetry. Compared to the boldness of Chinese characters, *kana* is elegant and refined. Japanese calligraphy is judged not only by its surface beauty and meaning but also by the calligrapher's character.

日本画は緑青，辰砂などの岩絵具や墨を，*にかわ水で溶いて，毛筆で紙，絹布，などに描くものである。西洋絵画の油絵は，顔料を油で溶くことによって色を自由に混ぜ合わせ，好みの色彩が得られるが，日本画ではそれはできず，また，重ね塗りもできない。

日本画には単色画と彩色画がある。単色画には，墨の線だけによる「白描」と，墨の濃淡によって物体の量感や空間を表す「水墨画」がある。いずれも中国から伝わった技法であり，白描は平安時代末の「鳥獣戯画」絵巻が代表的なもので，水墨画は室町時代の雪舟によって日本的な水墨画が生み出されたとされている。

彩色画は当初は仏画として移入された。この技法が根付くのは平安時代になってからで，四季の草花や自然，風俗などが柔らかい線と穏やかな色彩で描かれた。これを「大和絵」と言う。

絵巻物

中でも，平安時代末，鎌倉時代初めから盛んになった日本独自の型式が絵巻物である。絵画と，その説明を何枚も並べて，長い巻物にしたもので，寺の縁起や人物の歴史が，時間を追って展開され，全体で一つの物語を作っている。『源氏物語絵巻』などが代表作。

障屏画

室町時代末期から安土・桃山時代にかけて，中国・宋の絵画と大和絵とを融合させた*狩野派の絵画が寺や城の装飾に用いられた。これらは「障屏画」と呼ばれ，障子や*屏風などの大画面に，花鳥や人々の風俗などを豪華けんらんに描いた。狩野永徳，長谷川等伯らが代表的画家。さらに江戸時代初期には，俵屋宗達，尾形光琳などが現れ，それまでのさまざまな伝統的な画風を自由な立場で独自に発展させた。

洋画

日本に洋画がもたらされたのは江戸時代末期で，オランダから写実的画法が入ってきた。明治維新後，黒田清輝，浅井忠らがフランスへ留学し，当時最新の印象派の影響を受けて帰り，藤島武二，青木繁，坂本繁二郎らに伝えた。

他方日本画も，岡倉天心に率いられた菱田春草，横山大観らが，写実を加えて近代化を図った。だが，今日も日本の絵画は版画，抽象画を除き，日本的な感性と市場性ゆえに，国際舞台に出る画家は少ない。

Painting

Traditional-style Japanese paintings, or *nihon-ga*, are executed by brush on paper or silk with such pigments as verdigris (green copper rust), cinnabar, and black ink diluted with liquid glue.* Unlike Western oil painting in which colors can be mixed and applied in thick layers, *nihon-ga* is limited in its colors and their application.

Nihon-ga can be broadly divided into mono- and poly-chrome works. Monochrome ink paintings include simple line sketches as well as elaborate washes with subtle differentiations of tone. Both are techniques introduced from China, and are represented, respectively, by the late *Heian*-period *Choujuu Giga* (Scrolls of Frolicking Animals and Humans) and the purely Japanese-style of *Sesshuu*, a *Muromachi*-period painter.

The earliest polychrome paintings in Japan were of Buddhist subjects, and it was not until the *Heian* period that a truly Japanese style of polychrome painting known as *yamato-e* evolved. In addition to its subtle lines and soft colors, *yamato-e* is distinguished by its depicting the changing seasons and people involved in various activities.

E-makimono

Many of the best-known *yamato-e* are *e-makimono*, horizontal scrolls which first appeared in the late *Heian* period and early *Kamakura* period. They consist of long scrolls with alternating text and pictures telling a story in chronological order. The *Genji Monogatari E-maki* (Tale of *Genji* Scrolls) are among the most famous *e-makimono*.

Shouhei-ga

From the end of the *Muromachi* period well into the *Azuchi-Momoyama* period, the *Kanou* School,* which combined Chinese and *yamato-e* styles, supplied the primary decorative painting for temples and castles. Known as *shouhei-ga*, this decorative painting was executed on sliding doors and folding screens.* Subjects included birds and flowers and people painted in a sumptuous style. Major artists of the period include *Kanou Eitoku* and *Hasegawa Touhaku*. Later, in the early *Edo* period, such artists as *Tawaraya Soutatsu* and *Ogata Kourin* imbued this kind of decorative art work with freedom and vitality.

Western-style Painting

At the end of the *Edo* period, realistic Western-style painting was introduced by the Dutch. Following the *Meiji* Restoration, Japanese artists such as *Kuroda Seiki* and *Asai Chuu* traveled to France and were influenced by the impressionist painters. The new art concepts these men brought back to Japan were avidly pursued by such people as *Fujishima Takeji*, *Aoki Shigeru*, and *Sakamoto Hanjirou*.

Influenced by Western techniques, artists such as *Hishida Shunsou* and *Yokoyama Taikan* created modern *nihon-ga* under the patronage of *Okakura Tenshin*. Except for those working in woodblock printing and abstract painting, few Japanese artists are active internationally today, in part because of the uniquely Japanese sense of their work.

13 浮世絵*

江戸時代に，江戸を中心に風景や庶民の風俗などを描いた，主として多色刷りの版画を浮世絵と呼ぶ。当時「浮世」と呼ばれていた歌舞伎や遊里(ゆうり)の風俗を描いたためにこの名がある。こうした風俗画が現れるのは江戸時代初期の1670年代で，菱川師宣(ひしかわもろのぶ)が墨一色摺(ず)りによる木版画を売り出し，師宣は浮世絵の創始者と呼ばれている。

春信，歌麿(うたまろ)，写楽

18世紀半ば，歌舞伎の繁栄，出版の隆盛などから浮世絵の人気が高まり，また木版技術の進歩もあって，多色刷りの浮世絵である錦絵(にしきえ)が鈴木春信によって作られた。春信は美人画を描き，また，多色刷りゆえ，背景も描けるようになった。この美人画の様式を独自に発展させたのが喜多川歌麿で，雲母摺(きらずり)という，背景に雲母(うんも)を入れて輝きを出した美人の上半身像で(これを大首絵(おおくびえ)と言う)，女性の肉体美を優美に描き出した。大首絵で女性美を表した歌麿に対し，歌舞伎の役者の表情の変化から内面の性格までを，芸術性高く描き出したのが東洲斎写楽である。1794年５月から翌年２月までの10か月間に，江戸で上演された歌舞伎の役者の絵ばかり約150種を描いて，すい星のように消えていった写楽が，どんな人であったのかわかっていない。

北斎(ほくさい)，広重

19世紀に入ると，美人画・役者絵は多数描かれるが，芸術性の高いものは失われていく。この時代に浮世絵に新風を送り込んだのが葛飾(かつしか)北斎と安藤広重で，新しいテーマとして風景画を創出した。北斎は西洋銅版画の影響を受けて風景画を志したと言われており，『富嶽(ふがく)三十六景』で，大胆な構図と色彩を見せて人気を得，以後各地の名所などのシリーズを描いた。90歳まで生きて，木版画ばかりでなく，肉筆画も多く残している。広重は『東海道五十三次』のシリーズで，日本の自然と旅行く人々を叙情豊かに描いて北斎をしのぐ人気があった。後に『木曽街道六十九次』など，日本各地に題材を取ったシリーズものを作った。

浮世絵は，19世紀末のヨーロッパにもたらされ，その大胆な構図や色彩のコントラストだけで陰をつけない画法などが，ドガ，マネ，ゴッホらの印象派の画家に衝撃を与えた。近代美術への影響の大きさは，日本国内よりも欧米で高く評価されている。

Ukiyo-e*

This term is used to describe the pictures, many of them color prints, depicting *Edo*-period scenes and customs. The name comes from the fact that many showed the *ukiyo* (floating world) of the theater and pleasure quarters. The first such pictures appeared in the 1670s when *Hishikawa Moronobu* discovered a way to make monochromic woodblock prints.

Harunobu, Utamaro, and Sharaku

Ukiyo-e became very popular in the mid-18th century with the flowering of *kabuki* and the spread of publishing. As printing technology evolved, it became possible to print full-color art, and *Suzuki Harunobu* created the full-color *nishiki-e* prints. *Harunobu* drew pictures of beautiful women in full color and with great background detail. Yet it was for *Kitagawa Utamaro* to bring these pictures of beautiful women to their full glory. *Utamaro* was particularly skilled at depicting beautiful women from the waist up, and these superb portraits often used backgrounds sparkling with mica. In contrast to *Utamaro's* sensual pictures of beauties, *Toushuusai Sharaku* turned his skills to powerfully depicting the expressive character of the *kabuki* theater. In a meteoric career, he produced about 150 different pictures from the leading *kabuki* plays in *Edo* between May 1794 and February 1795, but little is known about his person.

Hokusai and Hiroshige

Going into the 19th century, there were vast numbers of inferior prints of beautiful women and *kabuki* actors, and the genre seemed beset with imitation and exaggeration until *Katsushika Hokusai* and *Andou Hiroshige* breathed new life into it by turning their talents to the virgin field of landscapes. *Hokusai* is thought to have started doing landscapes under the influence of Western copper plates. He later became famous for his 36 Views of Mt *Fuji* with their dynamic compositions and gorgeous colors, and he followed this success up with other series of pictures of famous tourist sites. *Hokusai* lived to be 90 and has left behind many woodblock prints and even paintings. *Hiroshige*'s *53 Stations on the Toukaidou* won him a place as *Hokusai*'s main rival for their rich depiction of Japanese scenery and the sights of travelers, and he also went on to do other series of other famous spots, including *69 Stations on the Kiso Kaidou*.

Many *ukiyo-e* pictures were taken to Europe in the late 19th century, where their sweeping composition and striking colors, plus the fact that they did not use shadows, attracted the interest of Degas, Manet, van Gogh, and other impressionists. A major influence on modern art, *ukiyo-e* are more appreciated in the West than in Japan.

日本では約１万年前から土器が作られ，その時代・様式によって縄文土器，弥生土器の名が付けられているが，陶磁器が作られるのはずっと後になる。日本では木工が盛んであるうえ，漆の技術が早くから発達していて，日常雑器にはこれらを用いていたからである。

陶器

日本最初の陶器は，奈良時代に中国の唐三彩を模して作られたと思われる，奈良三彩と呼ぶ白・緑・茶の釉薬を用いたものである。その多くが*正倉院に伝わっているものであるため，正倉院三彩とも呼ばれている。奈良三彩の後，日本では約500年近く陶器は作られず，この間は須恵器と呼ぶ灰黒色の硬く焼き締めた土器が日本全国で作られたが，それも平安時代末期にはほとんど姿を消してしまった。

本格的な陶器が焼かれるのは鎌倉時代で，瀬戸の藤四郎という人が，中国から技術を移入したもので，壺や水差し，香炉，仏具などが作られた。この後室町時代に至るまでの間に瀬戸のほか，信楽，常滑，丹波，備前，越前で陶器が作られるようになり，これらを日本の六古窯と呼んでいる。

戦国時代を経て豊臣秀吉により天下統一が成され，茶の湯が盛んになるに従い，瀬戸の陶工が移った美濃で志野，黄瀬戸，織部など，日本独特の味わいをもつ茶陶が作られ，ほかに信楽，伊賀，備前，京都などでも茶器が盛んに焼かれた。加えて，秀吉による朝鮮侵略の際，大名たちが朝鮮の陶工たちを連れ帰って各地に窯を作り，陶磁器作りはたいへん盛んになった。

磁器

日本の磁器作りは，1616年朝鮮の陶工李参平が肥前有田で磁器焼成に成功した時をもって始まったと伝えられる。さらに酒井田柿右衛門が色絵を始めたことにより，有田の磁器はたいへん有名になり，その後オランダとの貿易を通じて，ヨーロッパにも伝えられるようになった。その積み出し港が*伊万里であったため，「伊万里焼」とも呼ばれ，ヨーロッパでももてはやされた。特にドイツのザクセン王アウグスト２世は，ドレスデン城内に陶磁器研究所を作り，多くの伊万里焼のコレクションを研究し，後にマイセン窯を作って，ヨーロッパでも磁器を作るようになった。

日本の陶磁器作りは時代を下るに従い盛んになり，全国各地に窯が築かれ，江戸末期には日常雑器もすべて陶磁器を用いるようになった。ことに瀬戸では有田から磁器製法を学び，日常雑器を盛んに作ったため，陶磁器一般を「せともの」と呼ぶようになり，現代に至っている。

Ceramics

Earthenware was made in Japan some 10,000 years ago. Despite the centuries of earthenware production, glazed pottery and porcelain were not made until much later, partly because it was possible to meet daily needs with advanced woodworking techniques and lacquer ware.

Pottery

The first Japanese glazed pottery was a white, green, and brown ware imitation of Tang three-colored ware. Called *Nara* three-colored ware, this is also known as *Shousouin* three-color ware because many representative pieces are in the *Shousouin** depository. Until the next glazed ware appeared nearly 500 years later, a hard, gray ware known as *Sue* was made nationwide. *Sue* disappeared in the late 12th century.

True mass production of glazed ware began in the *Kamakura* period when a potter named *Toushirou* used Chinese techniques to make urns, pitchers, incense burners, and Buddhist liturgical instruments in the *Seto* district. By the *Muromachi* period, potting had spread beyond *Seto* to kilns in the *Shigaraki*, *Tokoname*, *Tanba*, *Bizen*, and *Echizen* regions. Today these are known as the Six Ancient Kilns.

Potting took on new sophistication with the unification of the country under *Toyotomi Hideyoshi* and the spread of the tea ceremony. *Seto* potters moved to new clay deposits at *Mino* where they produced distinctly Japanese tea implements in *Shino, Kiseto, Oribe*, and other styles. Tea utensils were also made in *Shigaraki, Iga, Bizen*, and *Kyouto* (Kyoto). Although their efforts to invade Korea ended in failure, *Hideyoshi*'s generals brought back many skilled prisoners, among them potters who breathed new life into Japanese ceramic manufacture, building new and better kilns and producing high-quality wares.

Porcelain

It is said one of these Korean potters, Ri Sampei, discovered porcelain clay in *Arita* and succeeded in firing porcelain ware in 1616. This was the first Japanese porcelain production. Another *Arita* potter, *Sakaida Kakiemon*, painted his porcelains with brilliant colors, and soon *Arita* and *Kakiemon* porcelains were famous nationwide. *Arita* ware was exported by Dutch traders in the *Edo* period, becoming known in Europe as *Imari** ware because it was shipped out of *Imari* port. Augustus II of Saxony collected *Imari* ware and commissioned the experts at his Meissen kiln near Dresden to study it and find out how it was made. The result was the first true porcelain produced in Europe.

Pottery and porcelain production spread throughout Japan in the 18th and 19th centuries, and ceramics were in common daily use by the late *Edo* period. Using porcelain production technology from the *Arita* kilns, the *Seto* kilns turned out such a volume of dishes and utensils of all kinds that the term *seto-mono* is today synonymous with ceramics.

漆器は木・竹・布などの製品の上に，漆(うるし)の木から取った天然のラッカー(塗料)を塗り付けたもので，日本，中国をはじめ東南アジア一帯で2千数百年も昔から用いられてきた生活工芸品である。英語で陶磁器がchinaと呼ばれるのに対し，漆器はjapanと呼ばれる。それは，陶磁器が中国で高度に発達し，元時代から世界に輸出されていたのに対し，漆器は日本で家具・武器・食器・生活雑器などに幅広く使われ，さらに美術工芸品としても発達し，15，16世紀にポルトガル・オランダとの貿易によってヨーロッパに広く紹介されたからである。

漆器の歴史

漆の木の原産地は中国またはチベットと言われ，これがアジア各地に広まったものである。漆器は，日本では約2000年前の縄文(じょうもん)時代のものが出土しているが，漆器作りの技法が中国から伝わったものか，日本で独自に発展したものかは意見が分かれている。ただ，技術が飛躍的に進歩したのは，6世紀に入って大陸との交流が活発になり，中国の優秀な技術が輸入されたためである。このころになると，実用品ばかりでなく，美術工芸品としての価値をもつものも作られるようになった。

しかし，それまで漆器の用途として最も多かった食器は，江戸時代末ごろから陶磁器が広く使われるようになり，また明治以後は金属器も使用され，塗料も化学塗料が作られたため，漆器は伝統工芸品や，美術工芸品としてのみ生き残るようになった。現在も輪島塗，会津(あいず)塗，春慶塗などが作られている。

漆器の利点

古来，漆が使われてきたのは，接着剤としての機能，塗料として木・竹・布などを保護する機能，そして色素を混ぜることによって装飾の機能をもつからである。出土品の例から見ると，古代には主に武器の接着・保護剤として弓，刀のつかなどに用いられ，次いで，木製の食器類などの保護塗料として，後に装飾性も加わり，家具などにも広く用いられるようになったようである。乾燥した後の漆は非常な強度をもっており，奈良時代には，木芯(しん)の上に麻の布で成型し，漆を何度も塗り，さらに麻布を重ねるという技法で，仏像を作ったほどである。これらは乾漆仏と呼ばれているが，奈良・興福寺の国宝八部衆立像，十大弟子立像など，等身大の像が1200年後の現在も細部に至るまで完全な形を保っている。

Lacquer Ware*

Lacquer ware is made of wood, bamboo, cloth, or other material coated with layers of lacquer extracted from the lacquer tree. Lacquer ware was being produced in China, Japan, and throughout Southeast Asia more than two millennia ago. In Japan, lacquer-making was developed to such a degree of sophistication that the term japan has become the generic term for lacquer ware just as china is used for porcelain ware. By the time Yuan-period China (1271-1368) was exporting sophisticated porcelains and celadons, Japan was using lacquer for furniture, weapons, dishes, and other daily utensils and producing exquisite works of lacquer art. In the 15th and 16th centuries japan was exported to Europe by Portuguese and Dutch traders.

History

Indigenous to China and Tibet, the lacquer tree has been widely cultivated throughout Asia. Japanese lacquer ware dating back more than 2,000 years to the *Joumon* period has been discovered in archaeological digs, but opinion is divided on whether lacquer-making techniques were introduced from China or developed spontaneously in Japan. In either case, rapid advances in lacquer-making technology were made when active trading with the continent was initiated in the 6th century and superior technology was introduced from China. It is from about this time that lacquer ware acquired an aesthetic as well as a practical value.

Near the end of the *Edo* period utilitarian lacquer ware was widely replaced by ceramic ware. From the *Meiji* period lacquer ware was further supplanted by metal ware and artificial varnishes. Today the best Japanese lacquer ware (dishes and eating utensils) is preserved primarily as an art form. Well-known types of contemporary lacquer ware include *Wajima*, *Aizu*, and *Shunkei* ware.

Characteristics

Lacquer has been used since ancient times as an adhesive and as a varnish to protect wooden, bamboo, and cloth objects. It has also been mixed with color pigments for decorative effect. Early examples are to be found in the use as an adhesive and protective varnish for bows and sword hilts. It was later applied as a protective coating to wooden utensils, this use gradually developing into an elaborate decorative technique for many other objects such as furniture.

Dried lacquer is extremely strong and durable, and it was used in the *Nara* period to make dry-lacquer sculptures. The basic form, shaped with hemp fabric covering a wooden core, was coated with repeated layers of lacquer and cloth. Well-preserved specimens of this type of Buddhist sculpture over 1,200 years old include the *Hachibushuu* (Eight Supernatural Guardians of the Buddha) and the *Juudai Deshi* (Ten Great Disciples of Buddha), both National Treasures at *Koufukuji* in *Nara*.

日本刀の特徴

西洋の刀が「突き，刺す」を目的とする両刃の剣であるのに対し，日本刀は「切る」を目的とする片刃の刀である。日本刀は，刀剣の必要条件である「折れず，曲がらず，よく切れる」という機能を備えていることと，美術工芸品としても十分に鑑賞にたえるできばえを見せているところに特徴がある。

日本刀は，２種または３種の地金を何度も何度も打ち延ばして鍛練し，焼き入れによって硬度を増し，最後に研磨するという日本独自の製法で出来上がっている。これは諸外国に例を見ない優れた技術で，ぴんとはった曲線，均整のとれた形，地肌・刃文の変化などに美しい魅力をもっている。

日本刀の歴史

片刃で反(そ)りをもつ日本刀の基本形式は平安時代に完成し，鎌倉時代には優れた刀工が輩出した。16世紀半ばに鉄砲が伝来するまでは，日本刀は主要な武器であった。鉄砲に武器としての主役の座を譲って後，江戸時代300年の太平の世の中で，実際の戦闘に使われることはなかった。そして明治維新後の近代社会では，刀を帯びることは禁止され，現在では，美術工芸品として鑑賞されることが主となっている。

武士の魂

江戸時代，儒教思想に裏付けされた武士の道徳律である武士道が大成されると，日本刀は，その象徴とされた。刀を帯びることは武士だけに許された特権であり，一般の商人，農民には許されなかった。それはすなわち，国民の１割弱の武士が９割を占める農民や商人を支配する体制を維持するためにも必要なシンボルであり，またそのための小道具でもあったのである。

武士たちは刀を神聖なものとし,家の名誉と誇りを示すものとして,代々の宝とした。曇りやすくさびやすい刀をいつも光らせ，武士の魂としてたいせつに扱った。

日本の時代劇映画や，1970年の三島由紀夫の割腹(かっぷく)自殺から，日本刀に切腹の道具としてのイメージをもつ人がいるかもしれない。この切腹も江戸時代には刀を持つ武士にだけ許された刑で，名誉な死に方であった。

The Japanese Sword*

Characteristics

Whereas the Western sword is a two-edged weapon for penetrating and stabbing, the Japanese sword is a single-edged weapon for slashing and cutting. In addition, the Japanese sword must fulfill the three functional requirements of not breaking, not bending, and cutting well—as well as being an aesthetically pleasing work of craftsmanship.

Japanese swords are made by repeatedly heating, flattening, folding, and tempering two or three different metals to produce a strong blade which is then honed to a razor-sharp edge. The technology used in making these ancient blades surpassed anything available in the West at the time, and the Japanese sword's graceful curve, well-balanced shape, and the changes in the *jihada* (blade) and *hamon* (temper patterns) make it a work of art.

History

The Japanese sword achieved its basic single-edged curved shape in the *Heian* period and reached new heights of excellence with many outstanding swordsmiths in the *Kamakura* period. For centuries, the sword remained the primary weapon for fighting. Yet once firearms proliferated in the mid-16th century, swords came to be used more and more for ceremonial purposes and less and less for combat. Finally, swords were relegated to museums and private collections in the modern period when the *Meiji* government banned their wearing after the Restoration of 1868.

Soul of the Swordsman

Although peace prevailed in the *Edo* period, the sword remained a symbol of *bushidou* (the way of the warrior) and its Confucian-based ethic. The wearing of swords was a class privilege restricted to the *samurai* class and forbidden to merchants and farmers. In effect, the sword served as both symbol and instrument of the *samurai* 10% of the population's domination over the 90% of the people engaged in commerce and agriculture.

The true *samurai* revered a good sword, and superior blades were passed down from generation to generation as treasured heirlooms. Yet this elegantly powerful work of art has a propensity to tarnish and rust, and it was a mark of pride for the *samurai* to spend the time and care needed to keep his sword ever-gleaming.

Despite this many-faceted history, there are still some people who think of the sword solely as an instrument for disembowelment, both because of the cut-em-up *samurai* movies and because of author *Mishima Yukio*'s dramatic *seppuku* (hara-kiri) in 1970. However, it should be noted that such ritual *seppuku* was limited to the *samurai* in the *Edo* period, since they were the only ones permitted to carry swords, and was perceived as an honorable and atoning death.

日本人形*

日本人にとって人形は，大昔から縁の深いものであった。古墳(こふん)時代の埴輪(*はにわ)はその好例だし，文楽は，人形が芸術にまで高められたケースである。子供たちが人形相手に遊ぶのも，平安時代にすでに始まっているし，魔よけや呪術(じゅじゅつ)的意味合いからも，人形は用いられてきた。

ひな人形と武者人形

年中行事のなかにも，人形は組み込まれている。なかでも女の子の祭りである3月3日のひな祭りにはひな人形を家庭に飾り，子供たちの幸福を願って白酒などを飲む。

また5月5日は男の子の節句で，雄々(おお)しく育つようにと武者人形を飾る。ひな人形も武者人形も，いずれもその期間に限って飾られ，後はまた翌年までしまわれる。中には代々何百年も伝えられた，家宝のような人形もある。今日では多分に儀式化し，またデパートなどの商業主義に利用されがちだが，人形に託しての夢や幸せへの願いは，依然生きていると言えよう。

博多(はかた)人形とこけし

郷土玩具(がんぐ)にも，人形は多数見られる。中でも今日，最もポピュラーなものは，博多人形とこけしである。博多人形は九州・博多の特産で，粘土で型を作り，素焼きにしてから彩色を施したもの。写実的で彩色も繊細，題材は子供から老人，歌舞伎役者，力士などきわめて幅広く，観賞用に愛好されている。こけしは東北地方の木製人形で，ろくろでひいた円筒状の胴に丸い頭を付け，女の子の顔を描き，胴体には赤や紺，黄などの2，3色で花や線の模様を描く。同じ東北でも場所によって形と模様が異なり，8～10の系統に分かれ，こけしを見れば産地がわかる。こけしは子消しに由来するという説もあるが，今日ではもっぱら観賞用に製造販売されている。

木目込(きめこみ)人形・嵯峨(さが)人形・御所(ごしょ)人形

今日もなお日本人形として広く愛されているものに，木目込人形，嵯峨人形，御所人形などがある。木目込人形は，木彫の人形原型に各種のきれ地をはって，端を溝に埋め込む手法で作り，これをきめ込むと言うところからこの名がある。嵯峨人形は，木彫に金箔(きんぱく)や絵具で色彩を施した小人形。御所人形は，江戸時代に京都の公卿(くぎょう)たちが大名に対する贈答の返礼として与えていたもので，肌の白い，頭の大きな幼い男児の裸人形である。さらに現代はこうした伝統的な日本人形ばかりでなく，新しい人形の創作活動も盛んに行われている。

Japanese Dolls*

Japanese history contains many references to dolls. One ancient example is the *haniwa** of the *Kofun* period. Dolls have even been used as an artistic medium, as in the *bunraku* puppet theater. In the *Heian* period, some dolls were used as children's toys and others as talismans to dispel demons or work voodoo.

Festival Dolls

Dolls are also featured in traditional Japanese festive events. One of these is the *Hina Matsuri* (Doll Festival) on March 3 when girls place *hina* dolls on step-like tiers in the family living room, offer prayers for good fortune, and drink a sweet *sake*-based drink called *shiro-zake*.

Boys have their turn on May 5, when they ornament their homes with warrior dolls inspiring them to be strong and brave. On both of these days, the dolls are put away the following day until next year. Some of these traditional dolls are heirlooms handed down for several centuries. Even though these festivals have become highly ritualized and commercialized, the dolls continue to represent parents' hopes for their children.

Regional Dolls

Dolls are an important part of the toy-craft traditions associated with various regions of Japan. The most popular regional dolls today are the *hakata* and *kokeshi* dolls. *Hakata* dolls, named after the historic area in *Fukuoka*, *Kyuushuu*, where they were produced, are painted figures made of bisque-fired clay. Painted realistically and in fine detail, *hakata* doll motifs range from children to old people, *kabuki* actors, and *sumou* (sumo) wrestlers, and they are collected as ornaments. *Kokeshi* dolls, products of the *Touhoku* region, are made of wood and include a cylindrical torso decorated with multicolor floral and linear patterns and a spherical head on which a young child's features are painted. *Kokeshi* shapes and patterns vary depending on exactly where they come from, and each of the eight to ten different types of *kokeshi* is distinctive to its place of origin. Although some people have theorized that the name *kokeshi* may have originally symbolized infanticide, *kokeshi* dolls are today manufactured and sold merely as decorative ornaments.

Collector's Items

Other dolls popular with collectors include *kimekomi*, *saga*, and *gosho* dolls. *Kimekomi* dolls are carved from wood and clothed with real fabric wedged into narrow grooves. *Saga* dolls are wooden figures gilt in gold or painted. *Gosho* dolls, usually chubby baby boys with white skin and oversized heads, were favored by *Edo*-period court nobles in *Kyouto* (Kyoto). Today, the traditional-doll industry is still alive and flourishing alongside manufacturers of new doll designs.

最古の歴史書

日本語の表記は，5世紀ごろ朝鮮半島を経て日本に伝えられた（中国の）漢字と，シラブルの音をしめす仮名の組み合わせで行われる。漢字が伝来する以前は日本には文字はなく，したがって文献的なものも見られず，民族の伝承は人から人へ語り伝えられていた。また，漢字が伝えられて以後仮名文字が草案されるまで，しばらくは漢字による日本語の表記が行われた。日本の古い歴史書と言われる『天皇記』や『帝紀』などは残念ながら残っていないが，古代皇室の皇位継承を中心とした記録であったらしい。

『古事記』と『日本書紀』

現存する最古の歴史書『古事記』は全3巻より成り，上巻は神の系譜と神話，中巻は*神武(じんむ)天皇から応神(おうじん)天皇，下巻は仁徳(にんとく)天皇から推古(すいこ)天皇までの叙述である。天武(てんむ)天皇の命により*稗田阿礼(ひえだのあれ)・*太安万侶(おおのやすまろ)が712年に完成した。続いて*舎人親王(とねりしんのう)・太安万侶らにより720年，『日本書紀』全30巻が成立した。神代から持統(じとう)天皇の代までを漢文の編年体でつづったもので，前書同様，皇室の系譜や民族の古い伝承を明らかにする政治的目的のもとに完成した。以後『続日本紀(しょくにほんぎ)』(797年)，『古語拾遺(しゅうい)』(807年ごろ)，『日本後紀(こうき)』(840年)，『続日本後紀』(869年)というように編纂(へんさん)されている。

初の地誌『風土記(ふどき)』

元明天皇の713年，各地に地方のありさまを編述させた『風土記』は，日本では初めての地誌で，今日完全な姿で残っているものは『出雲国(いずものくに)風土記』(今の島根県)だけ。常陸(ひたち)(茨城(いばらき)県)，播磨(はりま)(兵庫県)，肥前(ひぜん)(長崎県)，豊後(ぶんご)(大分県)は一部欠落して伝わっている。内容は地名起源の説話，伝説，生活習慣，信仰と行事，産業と産物など多岐にわたり，民俗学的にも貴重な史料となっている。

『万葉集』と『懐風藻(かいふうそう)』

現存する最古の歌集『万葉集』は全20巻あり，*大伴家持(おおとものやかもち)が中心となって編纂した。8世紀中ごろまでの，上は天皇から下は無名の民衆まで，長歌・短歌含めて約*4500首が集められ，万葉仮名と呼ばれる表記法が用いられている。この万葉仮名は意味よりも音(おん)を表す漢字で，仮名文字の発達の前ぶれとなるものである。また，『懐風藻』は当時の公式表記に漢文が用いられていたことを反映して，盛んに詠まれた漢詩を集めた日本最古のもので，751年の採録である。撰者(せんじゃ)も諸説あり，詩文も大陸詩の模倣の域を出ないものが多い。

Japanese Literature (1) (Beginnings)

Oldest Historical Records

Written Japanese is a combination of Chinese ideograms, or *kanji*, brought to Japan via the Korean peninsula sometime around the 5th century AD, and *kana* symbols to represent syllable sounds. Because Japan had no written language prior to *kanji*'s introduction, there are no records remaining from before the 5th century. Even after *kanji* were introduced, it still took a while to devise *kana*, and early Japanese literature was all written in *kanji*. Among the oldest works are the *Tennouki* and the *Teiki*, thought to have been genealogical records of the imperial clan. Unfortunately there are no known copies of these works in existence, although they are mentioned in later writings.

Kojiki and *Nihon Shoki*

The oldest historical work which still exists is *Kojiki*, a three-volume text with volume one recounting Japanese mythology, volume two depicting the reigns of Emperors *Jinmu** through *Oujin*, and volume three describing the reigns of Emperors *Nintoku* through *Suiko*. It was compiled by *Hieda no Are** and *Oo no Yasumaro** in 712 for the Emperor *Tenmu*. Soon afterward, in 720, *Toneri Shinnou** and *Oo no Yasumaro* completed the thirty-volume *Nihon Shoki*. This was a chronology of the emperors from earliest times and was clearly intended to legitimize the emperor as a political authority. It was later reedited and reissued as *Shoku Nihongi* (797), *Kogo Shuui* (c. 807), *Nihon Kouki* (840), and *Shoku Nihon Kouki* (869).

Fudoki

In 713, the Emperor *Genmei* ordered local regions to record conditions there, and these records became Japan's first comprehensive local records, *fudoki*. Today, the only volume which remains intact is the one on *Izumo no Kuni* (now *Shimane* pref), and parts are missing from the records from *Hitachi* (*Ibaraki* pref), *Harima* (*Hyougo* pref), *Hizen* (*Nagasaki* pref)* and *Bungo* (*Ooita* pref). Explaining the area's name, recounting local legends, depicting lifestyles, outlining religious beliefs and rites, and detailing local industry and products, the *fudoki* are invaluable reference sources for cultural anthropologists.

Man'youshuu and *Kaifuusou*

Man'youshuu, the oldest extant anthology of poems, is a 20-volume work. The approximately 4500 poems were written by people from all walks of life, from exalted emperor to humble peasant, up until the mid-eighth century. *Man'youshuu* was written with Chinese characters to represent sounds rather than meaning, foreshadowing the development of *kana* symbols. *Kaifuusou* was compiled in 751 and is the oldest collection of poems written in *kanbun*, that is to say Chinese as written by Japanese, and testifies to the fact that official documents of that time were written in Chinese. It is not clear who compiled *Kaifuusou*, and the poems themselves are generally nothing more than imitations of Chinese poetry.

王朝文学の先駆け

8世紀の終わり近く，都が平城(奈良)から平安(京都)に移され，以後12世紀後半の武家政治の台頭まで，政治はこの地を中心に行われ，皇室をめぐる貴族社会は全盛を極めた。この時代は公式文書に用いられた漢文に対し，生活に即した仮名文字の発達もあって，和歌や物語文学がけんらんたる花を開く。その先駆けとなったのが，美しい天女かぐや姫を主人公とする『竹取物語』(9世紀ごろ)である。

王朝文学の傑作『源氏物語』

『竹取物語』と同じころ書かれ，『源氏物語』に影響を与えたと言われる『伊勢物語』は，*在原業平ではないかと思われる人物を主人公とする歌物語である。和歌を物語の軸に据えたものとしては『大和物語』『平中物語』などがその後に続く。王朝文学の傑作と言われる『源氏物語』は，日本文学の代表作としても定評がある。作者は*紫式部がほぼ定説になっており，1010年ごろ成立した，全54帖という大長編小説である。天皇の子でありながら母が身分の低い女性であったため臣籍に降った光源氏という貴公子を主人公とする正編44帖と，その子の薫君を主人公とする10帖から成る，宮廷生活を中心とする女性遍歴の恋物語である。

女流の日記文学

『源氏物語』の作者が著したものに『紫式部日記』がある。当時の宮廷サロンに仕えて暮らしていた女性には和歌をよくし，そのころ盛んに編まれた勅撰の和歌集に入集するものもたいへん多かったが，日記や随筆が書かれたのも王朝文学の特色である。このほか，代表的なものに『蜻蛉日記』(藤原道綱母作)，『和泉式部日記』，『更級日記』(菅原孝標女作) などが知られ，随筆文学では*清少納言の『枕草子』(11世紀初) がある。こうして見ると王朝文学は女流の花盛りの観を呈するが，これも男性文学と言われた漢字に対する仮名文字の発達があったからである。男性による最初の仮名書きの作品に『土佐日記』(紀貫之作・10世紀) という旅日記がある。

説話文学『今昔物語』ほか

けれども王朝文学の花盛りの陰には，庶民生活の不安を反映する物語も生まれている。『日本霊異記』(9世紀)，『今昔物語』(12世紀)，『宇治拾遺物語』『古今著聞集』(ともに13世紀)などで，これらの説話文学は仏教の教えを説く因果応報をはじめ，動物と人間の婚姻譚，妖怪譚などで埋められている。

Japanese Literature (2) (Court Literature)

Prelude

In the late 8th century, the capital moved from *Heijoukyou* in *Nara* to *Heiankyou* in Kyoto, and Kyoto became both the home of the imperial court and the center of political power until the rise of the military governments in the late 12th century. During this period, *kanbun* (Chinese) was used for official documents, while *kana* came to be used for private communications. *Waka* and narrative literature flourished. Harbinger of this new age was *Taketori Monogatari* (Tale of the Bamboo Cutter) written in the 9-10th centuries about the beautiful princess, *Kaguya*-hime, from the moon.

Tale of *Genji*

Ise Monogatari (Tales of *Ise*), written about the same time and thought to have influenced *Genji Monogatari* (Tale of *Genji*), is a collection of poems featuring a hero probably patterned after *Ariwara no Narihira*.* Subsequent works such as *Yamato Monogatari* and *Heichuu Monogatari* continued this pattern of building novels around a core of *waka*. Yet the real flowering of *Heian* court literature is *Genji Monogatari*, acclaimed as a Japanese literary classic. Most scholars accept that this was written by *Murasaki Shikibu** around 1010 in an epic 54 volumes. With 44 volumes on *Hikaru Genji*, an imperial son relegated to low rank because of his mother's lowly status, and 10 volumes on his son *Kaorunokimi*, it is a rich depiction of the life of men and women at court.

Women's Diaries(*Nikki*)

Another work by the same author is *Murasaki Shikibu Nikki*. While many court women wrote *waka*, as collected in the *Chokusen* anthology, this era in Japanese literature is typified more by the many essays and diaries which they wrote. Among the best-known of the diaries are *Kagerou Nikki* (The Gossamer Years) by *Fujiwara no Michitsuna*'s mother and *Izumi Shikibu Nikki* and *Sarashina Nikki* by *Sugawara no Takasue*'s daughter. *Sei Shounagon*'s* early-11th-century *Makura no Soushi* (Pillow Book) is representative of the essays. Much of this rich literature written by women was written in the *kana* script while *kanji* was left to men for use in official writings. The first book written by a man in *kana* was the 10th-century *Tosa Nikki* travel diary by *Kino Tsurayuki*.

Konjaku Monogatari and Other Epics

Along with this flowering of court literature, there was also a literature being born telling of the common man's plight. These include the 9th-century *Nihon Ryouiki*, the 12th-century *Konjaku Monogatari* (Tales of a Time That is Now Past), and the 13th-century *Ujishuui Monogatari* and *Kokon Chomonjuu*. These bizarre tales of fantasy included stories with morals illustrating Buddhist teachings, fables of marriages between animals and people, and accounts of strange, fantastic beasts.

軍記物語の誕生

12世紀半ばに起こった*保元の乱を契機として，武士階級による中央政権への進出が始まり，やがて*源氏や*平家による武家政治の実現を見る。もちろんそこには源平両軍の流血の政権交替劇が行われたわけで，その中から起こってきたのがいわゆる軍記物語である。保元の乱を扱った『保元物語』，*平治の乱の『平治物語』，源平合戦と平家の滅亡を描いた『平家物語』などがあるが，これらの3書は初めから筆で書かれたものではなく，いずれも*琵琶法師(びわほうし)によって街頭で語られたものを原型として成立を見たユニークなものである。もともと「語り物」として発生したものなので，音読しても快い語感の響きをもっている。特に『平家物語』は軍記物語の最高傑作と言われ，盛衰と興亡を一身に担った平家一門の滅びゆく姿は，美しくもまた哀れ深い。

その他の軍記物語

平家を滅ぼした源氏は現在の鎌倉市に幕府を開き，以後北条(ほうじょう)氏が執権として政治を掌握し，次の足利(あしかが)氏が京都・室町に幕府を樹立するという，武家政治にもそれなりの変遷がある。そうした世相を反映して軍記物語が世に歓迎され，13世紀半ばに成立を見た『源平盛衰記』，14世紀の『曽我(そが)物語』『太平記』，15世紀初めの『義経(ぎけい)記』などが代表的作品である。特に『太平記』は江戸時代には「太平記講釈」と言って太平記読みが流行し，庶民の間にまで親しまれた。

そのほか，歴史物語としては『大鏡』『今鏡』『水鏡』(いずれも12世紀)があり，異色の書としては僧慈円が仏教の理念に立ってまとめた『愚管抄(ぐかんしょう)』(13世紀)がある。また，鎌倉幕府の公的記録と言われる『吾妻鏡(あずまかがみ)』も武家社会を知る上で，重要な史料となっている。

隠者の文学『方丈記』『徒然草(つれづれぐさ)』

武士の身分を捨て，遁世(とんせい)の道に生きた西行(さいぎょう)の歌集『山家(さんか)集』(12世紀)や，大火，辻風，遷都，飢饉(ききん)，大地震などを体験したことから，これを末世の世相として市井(しせい)の暮らしに無常を感じ，山家に隠棲(いんせい)した鴨長明(かものちょうめい)の随筆集『方丈記』(13世紀)，神官の家に生まれながら出家し，自由な生活に身を置いた吉田兼好の，為政者の徳や宗教家のあり方，人の進むべき道などを説いた随筆集『徒然草』(14世紀)は，今日もなお人生の思索の書として，広く読まれている。

Japanese Literature (3) (Medieval)

Tales of Battle

With the *Hougen* Disturbance* of the mid-12th century, the warrior class seized power and military governments were installed under first the *Heike** and then the *Genji** clans, each transfer accomplished by bloody fighting between the opposing camps. The literature that emerged from this were the tales of battle, including *Hougen Monogatari*, *Heiji Monogatari* about the *Heiji* Disturbance,* and *Heike Monogatari* (Tale of the *Heike*) about the rise and fall of the *Taira* clan. These three tales are distinctive in that they originated not as written literature but as ballads sung by traveling *biwa-houshi** minstrels—and they are still stirring when read aloud. Of the three, *Heike Monogatari* is acclaimed as an epic tale of battle par excellence, and it impresses readers even today with its elegantly compassionate tales of how the *Taira*s fell into decline and ruin.

Other Tales of Battle

Having vanquished the *Taira*s, the *Minamoto* established their military government in what is now *Kamakura*. This was soon followed by a string of military rulers including the *Houjou* regents and then the *Ashikaga*, who set up their government in *Kyouto* (Kyoto). Military epics were favored in these turbulent times, among them the 13th-century *Genpei Seisuiki* (Rise and Fall of the *Genji* and *Heike*), 14th-century *Soga Monogatari* (Tale of the *Soga* Brothers) and *Taiheiki*, and 15th-century *Gikeiki* (*Yoshitsune*). *Taiheiki* was especially well received, and *Taiheiki* readings were popular among the townsfolk as late as the *Tokugawa* shogunate.

Other historical works include the 12th-century mirror books *Oo Kagami* (Great Mirror), *Ima Kagami* (Mirror of the Present), and *Mizu Kagami* (Water Mirror), and the 13th-century *Gukanshou* (Notes on Foolish Views), which is somewhat different in expounding Buddhist teachings. *Azuma Kagami*, said to be the official record of the *Kamakura* government, is invaluable for historians seeking to learn more about that period's warrior society.

Tales of Seclusion

At the same time, this period also saw *Sanka-shuu* (The Mountain Hermitage), a 12th-century anthology of poems by *Saigyou*, a warrior who became dissatisfied with the way things were and withdrew from the secular world; 13th-century *Houjouki* in which *Kamo no Choumei* recounts the fires, storms, famines, earthquakes, and other disasters which convinced him of the futility of man's constant struggle for aggrandizement; and the 14th-century *Tsurezuregusa* (Essays in Idleness) by *Yoshida Kenkou*, a hermit who was raised in a shrine but left to seek his freedom and ended discussing the principles that should govern the way we live. All of these are read and studied by people even today for their insights into human nature.

町人文学の起こり

徳川氏が政治の実権を握っていた江戸時代は，江戸（今の東京）や大坂を中心に栄えた町人文化の時代でもあった。それというのも，太平に慣れた武家に代わって経済の基盤に根を据え，主導権を握っていたのは商人たちのほうであったからである。特に印刷技術が開発され，木版刷りの技術が普及すると出版業者・職業作家が現れ，いきおい町人ものの文学，読み物が出版されるようになった。十返舎一九の滑稽本『東海道中膝栗毛』や式亭三馬の『浮世風呂』，滝沢馬琴の伝奇小説『南総里見八犬伝』（ともに19世紀）などは空前のベストセラーになっている。

井原西鶴の文学

江戸時代町人文学の代表的作者と言ったら，井原西鶴を真っ先に挙げなくてはなるまい。愛欲小説『好色一代男』『好色一代女』，町人の経済生活を描いた『日本永代蔵』『世間胸算用』などは彼の代表作で，特に『色好一代男』は現実主義的な近代小説に先駆けた作品とも言われ，主人公・世之介の，7歳から60歳までの女性遍歴を描いた物語で，『源氏物語』を下敷きにしてストーリーが展開する。

日本のシェークスピア・近松門左衛門

西鶴と同じころ活躍した浄瑠璃・歌舞伎狂言作者の近松門左衛門も忘れてはならない人である。当時市井に頻発した心中事件にヒントを得て書いた『曽根崎心中』『心中天網島』，*飛脚問屋の忠兵衛と遊女梅川の悲恋を描いた『冥途の飛脚』，中国・明朝の遺臣と日本女性の間に生まれた男子がやがて明朝を復興しようとする『国性爺合戦』などは今日もよく上演され，大向こうをうならせている。そのほか江戸時代の劇作家では近松半二，鶴屋南北，河竹黙阿弥などが知られている。

怪談集『御伽婢子』と『雨月物語』

浅井了意の『御伽婢子』（1666年）は怪異談集で，この中には*三遊亭円朝が高座にのせて評判をとった『怪談牡丹灯籠』の原話も入っている。これは18世紀の中ごろ成立した上田秋成の『雨月物語』にも多大の影響を与えている。秋成には，このほか『春雨物語』という怪異談集がある。ところで，歌舞伎の『東海道四谷怪談』（鶴屋南北作）もそうであるが，このように怪異談が好まれた世相の背景には，庶民の不安感があったことも見逃せない。

Japanese Literature (4) (Town Pleasures)

Prelude

The *Edo* period of *Tokugawa* rule was a time of renaissance centered on the townsfolk of *Edo* (now *Toukyou* (Tokyo)) and *Oosaka* (Osaka). When peace returned to the land, actual control passed from the warriors to the merchants who held the economic reins. At the same time, the development of printing technologies and the appearance of publishers made it possible for people to make a living by writing, and this in turn spurred the emergence of literature for the masses. Among these 19th-century best sellers were *Jippensha Ikku*'s *Toukaidouchuu Hizakurige* (Shank's Mare), *Shikitei Sanba*'s *Ukiyoburo* (Bathhouse of the Floating World), and *Takizawa Bakin*'s *Nansou Satomi Hakken-den* (*Satomi* and the Eight Dogs).

Ihara Saikaku

Ihara Saikaku is perhaps the single most important popular writer of the *Edo* period. Among his works are *Koushoku Ichidai Otoko* (Life of an Amorous Man) and *Koushoku Ichidai Onna* (Life of an Amorous Woman), depicting the floating world of people who live for sexual gratification, and *Nihon Eitaigura* (The Japanese Family Storehouse) and *Seken Munesanyou* (Worldly Mental Calculations) on the lifestyle of the merchant class. *Koushoku Ichidai Otoko*, for example, is almost modern in its realism as it details the hero *Yonosuke*'s 54-year quest for pleasure much in the manner of the *Genji Monogatari*.

Japan's Shakespeare

Another figure who deserves recognition is *Chikamatsu Monzaemon*, who wrote for both the puppet and *kabuki* theaters. Even today, his *Sonezaki Shinjuu* (Love Suicides at *Sonezaki*) and *Shinjuu Ten no Amijima* (Love Suicides at *Amijima*) drawing upon the many love suicides of the time, *Meido no Hikyaku* telling of the tragic love between the shopowner* *Chuubei* and the courtesan *Umegawa*, and *Kokusenya Kassen* (Battles of Coxinga) of the attempt by the Chinese-Japanese son of a Ming descendant to reestablish the Ming dynasty are popular. Among the other well-known playwrights of the *Edo* period are *Chikamatsu Hanji*, *Tsuruya Nanboku*, and *Kawatake Mokuami*.

Tales of the Supernatural

Published in 1666, *Asai Ryoui*'s *Otogibouko* is a collection of horror tales including the original *Botan-dourou* as popularized by the raconteur *San'-yuutei Enchou*.* This work also had a major influence on the 18th-century *Ugetsu Monogatari* by *Ueda Akinari*, who also wrote the *Harusame Monogatari* (Tales of the Spring Rain) collection of hair-raisers. Also in this same genre is *Tsuruya Nanboku*'s *Toukaidou Yotsuya Kaidan* (Ghost Story of *Toukaidou Yotsuya*), and the popularity of horror stories seems to reflect the anxiety of the city people concerning their livelihoods and status.

近代文学への歩み

江戸時代の鎖国政策から脱し明治に入ると，日本の近代化への歩みは着実に進められ，文学もまた二葉亭四迷のツルゲーネフに関する翻訳紹介や上田敏の訳詩集『海潮音』などに見られるように，海外の文芸思潮を取り入れ，新しいあり方を探ってきた。そうした運動推進の代表的な人に坪内逍遥がいる。逍遥は小説・戯曲・評論・翻訳に幅広く活動した人であるが，1885年に『当世書生気質』という小説を発表するとともに，従来の勧善懲悪主義を排し，写実主義を提唱した文学論『小説神髄』を世に問い，一躍注目を浴びた。そのほか逍遥には戯曲『桐一葉』『役の行者』などがあり，また『シェークスピア全集』の翻訳は高く評価されている。

森鷗外と夏目漱石

明治も中ごろになると，二葉亭四迷の『浮雲』，幸田露伴の『五重塔』，樋口一葉の『たけくらべ』『にごりえ』，徳富蘆花の『不如帰』などの小説が評判になった。そうした中でも森鷗外，夏目漱石の創作活動は際立っている。鷗外は陸軍軍医としてドイツに留学した体験を生かし，処女作『舞姫』を1890年に発表，２年後にはアンデルセンの『即興詩人』を翻訳している。また，その後に書かれた『雁』は現代小説のサンプルとして不動の評価を得ている。一方漱石はロンドンに留学し，帰国後代表作『吾輩は猫である』『坊っちゃん』『草枕』などを次々に発表，近代文学のひとつの頂点を極め，その門下から多くの有力作家が輩出した。

自然主義の作家

日露戦争前後，島崎藤村や田山花袋などの自然主義を唱える作家が台頭し，藤村の『破戒』，花袋の『蒲団』などが代表的役割を果たした。自然主義は，その後も近代文学の最も大きな運動として，広く影響を及ぼしていく。

明治の詩歌

1882年に訳詩・創作詩で編んだ『新体詩抄』が出版され，以後新体詩と呼ばれる新しい詩の領域が開かれる。代表的詩人としては島崎藤村・土井晩翠などがいる。19世紀も終わりに近いころ，与謝野鉄幹が短歌革新運動を起こし『明星』を創刊するや，鉄幹夫人となった晶子や石川啄木・北原白秋・高村光太郎などの俊秀が結集した。同じころ正岡子規も空想や偶像を排して写実を尊ぶ短歌・俳句運動を展開している。

Japanese Literature (5) (Post-restoration)

Toward a Modern Literature

With the opening of the country shortly after the *Meiji* Restoration, Japan began a process of modernization that involved a receptiveness to imported ideas and a search for new modes, as epitomized by *Futabatei Shimei*'s translated introduction to the life and work of Turgenev and *Ueda Bin*'s *Kaichouon* (Sound of the Tide) anthology of translated poems. Foremost among the experimenters is *Tsubouchi Shouyou*. While he was active as a novelist, playwright, critic, and translator, he is best known for the 1885 novel *Tousei Shosei Katagi* (The Character of Modern Students) and for *Shousetsu Shinzui* (Essence of the Novel) in which he rejected the hoary traditions and called for a more realistic fiction. In addition, he is also known for his plays such as *Kiri Hitoha* and *En no Gyouja* and his translation of the complete works of Shakespeare.

Ougai and *Souseki*

The popular novels near the turn of the century were *Futabatei Shimei*'s *Ukigumo* (Drifting Clouds), *Kouda Rohan*'s *Gojuu no Tou* (Five-storied Pagoda), *Higuchi Ichiyou*'s *Takekurabe* (Growing Up) and *Nigorie* (Muddy Bay), and *Tokutomi Roka*'s *Hototogisu* (*Namiko*). Yet the two luminaries of the period were *Mori Ougai* and *Natsume Souseki*. Drawing upon his years as an army physician in Germany for study, *Ougai* published his first novel *Maihime* (Dancing Girl) in 1890 and followed that two years later with a translation of Andersen's *Improvisators*. His later *Gan* (Wild Geese) still stands as an exemplary modern novel. *Souseki*, returning home from his studies in London, marked new heights in modern literature with his outpouring of *Wagahai wa Neko de Aru* (I am a Cat), *Botchan*, *Kusamakura*, and more. He was a prolific writer who had a profound influence upon many later writers.

Naturalism

Around the time of the Russo-Japanese War, there was a spate of naturalist writers including *Shimazaki Touson*, prominent for his *Hakai* (Broken Commandment), and *Tayama Katai* (known for *Futon*). This naturalist school has since been a major component and influence in modern Japanese literature.

Poetry

The 1882 *Shintaishi Shou* (Collection of New Style Poetry) of translated and original poetry opened up new vistas for poetry. *Shimazaki Touson* and *Tsuchii Bansui* were among the best-known poets. In the late 19th century, *Yosano Tekkan* urged radical reforms in the *tanka* and founded *Myoujou* magazine in *Toukyou*(Tokyo) as a vehicle for such brilliant poets as his wife *Akiko*, *Ishikawa Takuboku*, *Kitahara Hakushuu*, *Takamura Koutarou*, and others. About the same time, *Masaoka Shiki* was campaigning for *tanka* and *haiku* able to deal with the fantastic and grotesque in realistic terms.

大正期の『白樺(しらかば)』

1910年創刊された同人雑誌『白樺』で活躍した作家に武者小路実篤(むしゃのこうじさねあつ)・志賀直哉・里見弴(とん)・有島武郎(たけお)・有島生馬らがいる。『白樺』は*関東大震災後に廃刊するまで，文芸・美術雑誌として大正期の文壇や画壇に大きな影響を与えた。中でも志賀直哉の長編小説『暗夜行路』は現代文学の金字塔とも言われ，高い評価を得ている。

芥川龍之介(あくたがわりゅうのすけ)と永井荷風(かふう)

虚構の世界での自己表出に生きた作家としては芥川龍之介がいるが，彼は長編には全く手を染めず，終始短編作家で通した異色の存在である。代表作に『今昔(こんじゃく)物語』や『宇治拾遺(うじしゅうい)物語』に材を得た『羅生門(らしょうもん)』『地獄変』『鼻』などがある。永井荷風の長編小説『腕くらべ』や『濹東綺譚(ぼくとうきだん)』は遊廓や私娼窟(くつ)に材をとった作。

谷崎潤一郎と佐藤春夫

永井荷風の推称を受けて世に出た作家に谷崎潤一郎がおり，谷崎と親交があった作家に佐藤春夫がいる。春夫と谷崎夫人の恋愛は二人の友情を裂く不幸な出来事となったが，ともに大正から昭和の戦後まで活躍した代表的作家である。

川端康成と横光利一

1924年創刊された『文芸時代』により，新感覚派運動を起こした作家に川端康成・横光利一らがいる。彼らは既存の現実主義にあきたらず，官能や神経に病的な敏感さを見せ，意匠や装飾に新しいものをねらった。川端の代表作『伊豆の踊子』『雪国』，横光の『日輪』『旅愁』などは今日も広く読まれている。川端は日本人では初めてのノーベル文学賞を受賞(1968年)している。

現代の詩人

明治に起こった新体詩は大正に入るとしだいに影をひそめ，代わって日常使用されていることばで音律を踏まずに書く自由律口語詩が普及する。萩原朔太郎(はぎわらさくたろう)の『月に吠(ほ)える』『青猫』『氷島』，高村光太郎の『道程』『智恵子抄』，宮沢賢治の『春と修羅』などの詩集は，その代表的なものである。また，この時期にフランスの詩人アンドレ・ブルトンの提唱する超現実主義(シュールレアリスム)，ベルレーヌ，バレリーやマラルメを指導者とする象徴主義が日本詩壇を真っ向から揺さぶった。

そのほか大正から戦後にかけては，外国文学の翻訳紹介が次々に行われ，カフカ，フォークナー，マルロー，ドストエフスキー，トルストイなどがよく読まれている。

Shirakaba

Founded in 1910, the literary magazine *Shirakaba* was home to *Mushanokouji Saneatsu* , *Shiga Naoya*, *Satomi Ton*, *Arishima Takeo*, *Arishima Ikuma*, and many others; and it was both lectern and showplace for the artists of the era until it ceased publication after the Great *Kantou* Earthquake* of 1923. Especially notable was *Shiga Naoya*, whose long novel *An'ya Kouro* (Dark Night's Passing) is acclaimed as the masterpiece of early-20th-century literature.

Akutagawa and Nagai

Perhaps the writer who best expressed himself in fiction was *Akutagawa Ryuunosuke*, who is also unusual for having written only short stories. He is famous for *Rashoumon, Jigokuhen* (Hell Screen), *Hana* (Nose), all patterned after *Konjaku Monogatari* and *Ujishuui Monogatari*, and others. *Nagai Kafuu* is known for his long novels such as *Udekurabe* (*Geisha* in Rivalry) and *Bokutou Kidan* (Strange Tale from the East of the River) set in Japan's red-light districts.

Tanizaki and Satou

Among the writers drawn to literature by *Nagai Kafuu* is *Tanizaki Jun'ichirou*, and among those encouraged by *Tanizaki* is *Satou Haruo*. While the two men's friendship was poisoned by *Satou*'s affair with *Tanizaki*'s wife, they were major literary figures even as late as the postwar period.

Kawabata and Yokomitsu

Two of the novelists who took part in the neo-sensationalist literary movement launched by the magazine *Bungei Jidai* in 1924 were *Kawabata Yasunari* and *Yokomitsu Riichi*. Rebelling at the prevailing realism, they invented new styles and forms in an effort to stimulate both mind and spirit. Even today, *Kawabata* is widely read for *Izu no Odoriko* (*Izu* Dancer) and *Yukiguni* (Snow Country), as is *Yokomitsu* for *Nichirin* (The Sun) and *Ryoshuu* (Traveler's Sadness). In 1968, *Kawabata* became the first Japanese to win the Nobel Prize in Literature.

Modern Poets

After an early popularity, the new-style poetry movement began to fade, and a free poetry using everyday language in unmetered lines took its place. Typical are *Hagiwara Sakutarou*'s *Tsuki ni Hoeru* (Howling at the Moon), *Aoneko* (Blue Cat), and *Hyoutou* (Frozen Island); *Takamura Koutarou*'s *Doutei* and *Chieko Shou* (*Chieko*'s Sky); and *Miyazawa Kenji*'s *Haru to Shura* (Spring and Asura). At the same time, Japanese poetry was shaken by the surrealism of the French poet Andre Breton and the symbolism of Stephane Mallarme, Paul Verlaine, and Paul Valery.

Translations of foreign works were also very much in vogue, and Kafka, Faulkner, Malraux, Dostoevski, Tolstoi, and many others were widely read in Japan.

敗戦国日本の文学の担い手

第二次世界大戦が終わったとき，敗戦の虚脱から最も早く立ち上がったのが文学ではなかろうか。言論の自由，出版の自由がそれに拍車をかけた。作品の内容も戦争の悲惨さ，残虐さに材を求めたものが多い。第1次戦後派と呼ばれるそれらの人々を挙げると梅崎春生（はるお）・大岡（おおおか）昇平・武田泰淳（たいじゅん）・椎名麟三（りんぞう）・中村真一郎・三島由紀夫などがおり，それに続く第2次戦後派として安部公房（あべこうぼう）・堀田善衛（ほったよしえ）などがいる。特にフィリピンにおける戦争体験をつづった大岡昇平の『俘虜（ふりょ）記』や『野火』などは，戦後文学の一時期を画するものである。典雅な文体の中に，不倫・背徳といった時代に先行する観念によって出発を見せた三島由紀夫は『仮面の告白』『金閣寺』など，次々に問題作を発表するかたわら，劇作家としても『鹿鳴館（ろくめいかん）』『十日の菊』といった評判作を書いた。現代における人間行動の意味を追求する作品で戦後文学の花形となった井上靖は，日本文学の伝統をひく私小説のほかに歴史小説・社会派小説・詩・エッセーなど幅広く題材を手がけた。

太陽族の流行

特需景気をあおった朝鮮戦争を境として，敗戦の様相がしだいに薄れてくると，文学にもそれなりの動きが現れ，既成の道徳や価値観を否定し，あるいは打破しようとする若者を描く小説が登場してくる。石原慎太郎の『太陽の季節』がそれで，「太陽族」や「慎太郎刈り」などの流行語やヘアスタイルまで生んだ。『死者の奢（おご）り』『飼育』などの作品で登場した大江健三郎は，戦後青春の疎外感などを定着させた作家で，1994年わが国二人目のノーベル文学賞を受賞している。

民主主義文学の動き

しかし，また一方では社会主義的民主化運動を反映した作家も登場した。『播州（ばんしゅう）平野』『風知草』などの作品を戦後いち早く発表した宮本百合子（ゆりこ）は，すでに戦前に『貧しき人々の群』『伸子』などの長編で知られたプロレタリア文学の旗手でもあった。佐多稲子や徳永直（すなお）もプロレタリア文学の戦前戦後を支えた代表的作家である。

戦後文学の広がり

戦後の混乱期を経てしだいに世相が落ち着いてくると，読者の要求もさまざまな広がりを見せ，純文学と大衆文学の距離が縮まり，中間小説と呼ばれる作品の流行を見るに至った。推理小説なども昨今は全盛期を迎えた感がある。

Bearers of the Torch

Literature was one of the first fields to recover from Japan's defeat in World War II. Encouraged by freedom of the press and freedom of expression, literature flourished, much of it depicting the suffering and misery of war. The first wave of postwar authors included such people as *Umezaki Haruo*, *Oooka Shouhei*, *Takeda Taijun*, *Shiina Rinzou*, *Nakamura Shin'ichirou*, and *Mishima Yukio*; and this was soon followed by a second wave including *Abe Koubou*, *Hotta Yoshie*, and others. Among the landmark works of the first wave were *Oooka Shouhei*'s *Furyoki* (Prisoner of War) and *Nobi* (Fires on the Plain) based upon his wartime experiences in the Philippines. Employing an elegant style to depict vice and depravity, *Mishima Yukio* caught the temper of the time with *Kamen no Kokuhaku* (Confessions of a Mask), *Kinkakuji* (Temple of the Golden Pavilion), and other sensationalist works. At the same time, he was also active as a playwright of such highly acclaimed works as *Rokumeikan* (Deer Cry Pavilion) and *Tooka no Kiku*. The star of post-war literature was *Inoue Yasushi*, whose works examine the meaning of man's actions in the modern age. He carries on the Japanese literary tradition with his stories based on personal experience, historical and socially conscious novels, poems and essays, dealing with a broad spectrum of themes.

Taiyou-zoku

As the prosperity induced by the Korean War took hold and people forgot the despair of defeat. Literature also took a new turn with novels depicting a new breed of Japanese who rejected the old values and moral standards. With *Ishihara Shintarou*'s *Taiyou no Kisetsu* (Season of Violence), the term *taiyou-zoku* (sun tribe) was born and *Shintarou* haircuts became all the rage. Soon afterward, *Ooe Kenzaburou* appeared as one of the most perceptive observers of this postwar alienation, as depicted in *Shisha no Ogori* (Lavish are the Dead) and *Shiiku* (The Catch). In 1994, *Ooe* became the second Japanese to win the Nobel Prize for Literature.

Democratic Literature

Yet there were also other authors who wrote to propagate their ideals of socialist democratization. *Miyamoto Yuriko*, who came out with *Banshuu Heiya* (Banshu Plain), *Fuuchisou*, and other works soon after the war, had established her reputation as a proletariat writer before the war with such novels as *Mazushiki Hitobito no Mure* (A Flock of Poor People) and *Nobuko*. Other proletariat writers active in both the wartime and postwar eras were *Sata Ineko* and *Tokunaga Sunao*.

Spread of Postwar Literature

As things settled down after the war and more people started reading again for more diverse purposes, the wide rift between pure literature and popular literature narrowed, and a very popular form developed called in-between novels. Mysteries and other mass-appeal literature entered a golden age.

和歌の形式

日本で最も古く，しかも中世・近世・現代を問わず多くの歌人たちに強い影響を与えているのは，何と言っても8世紀に編纂(へんさん)された『万葉集』である。その中には長歌・短歌が含まれていて，今日なおその形式が重視されている短歌は「あかねさす(5音)，紫野行(むらさきのゆ)き(7音)，標野(しめの)行き(5音)，野守(のもり)は見ずや(7音)，君が袖(そで)振る(7音)」(額田王(ぬかだのおおきみ)の歌)のように31音で構成されている。今日では長歌はまったく影をひそめ，短歌が主流となっている。短歌の形式がいつどのような経過をたどって古代歌謡の世界に愛用され，定着したのかは，いまだにはっきりとは解明されていない。

勅撰(ちょくせん)和歌集の意味

天皇の命により公的に編纂された歌集を「勅撰和歌集」と呼んでいるが，その中に撰(えら)ばれ，入集するということはたいへん名誉とされた。勅撰の最初のものは10世紀初めに編まれた『古今和歌集』で，以後『後撰和歌集』『拾遺(しゅうい)和歌集』というように続き，16世紀の室町時代まで21集に及ぶ。内容はどの集もほぼ春・夏・秋・冬・賀歌・別れの歌・旅の歌・恋の歌などで構成され，きわめて広範囲にわたっている。

宮廷のサロン化

これらのことからもうかがわれるように，特に平安(今の京都)に都があった8世紀から12世紀までは，皇室を中心に貴族の間で和歌がもてはやされた。判者(審判者)を設けて歌合わせの座で作の優劣を競ったり，意中の女*房へ手紙に代えて恋歌を贈ったり，歌を詠むことはさながら日常茶飯事のように扱われ，宮廷そのものが歌の一大サロン化するほど盛んだった。

しかし，それも空想や想像の産物としてしだいにあきたりなく思う者も現れ，12世紀に活躍した歌僧西行(さいぎょう)の『山家(さんか)集』のように，実際に自然の中に身を置いて詠んだ歌が尊ばれるようになってくる。

現代の短歌

今日も短歌は手軽にだれでもできる文芸として愛されているが，その中には俵万智(まち)のように日常生活の基盤に立ち，ふだん着の用語を駆使する手法も出てきており，また必ずしも音律の形式にこだわらない自由律短歌の運動もないではないが，やはり主流を成しているものは依然古語の幽玄性を尊ぶ31文字の形式であり，その伝統の根強さと，色あせぬ短歌の魅力には，不思議な感銘さえ覚えさせられる。

Waka (Tanka)

Form

The *Man'youshuu* compiled in the 8th century is the oldest and most influential collection of Japanese poetry. In it are two types of poetry: *chouka* and *tanka*. While the *chouka* has nearly disappeared as an art form, the shorter 31-syllable *tanka* has been popular throughout Japanese history and is today in the cultural mainstream, although it remains unclear exactly how the ancient poets developed the *tanka*. The following *tanka* by Princess *Nukada* (7th century) is a classical example of the *tanka* verse form.

A-ka-ne-sa-su	In the purple field
Mu-ra-sa-ki-no yu-ki	Of blooming madder,
Shi-me-no yu-ki	In the forbidden meadow you run.
No-mo-ri wa mi-zu ya	Won't the guard see
Ki-mi ga so-de fu-ru	You waving to me ?

Imperial Anthologies

Imperial anthologies were frequently compiled over the centuries and it was considered a great honor to have one's poems included. The earliest imperial anthology is the *Kokin Wakashuu* (Collection of Ancient and Modern Times) compiled in the early 10th century. It was followed by the *Gosen Wakashuu* (Later Collection) and by the *Shuui Wakashuu* (Collection of Gleanings). By the *Muromachi* period, 21 such anthologies had been compiled of poems treating a wide range of subjects and themes; verses on the four seasons, celebratory lines, songs of parting and of travel, love poems, and so forth.

Court Poetry

Writing and reciting poetry was a favorite pastime of the ancient Japanese nobility, particularly between the 8th and 12th centuries when the capital was located in *Kyouto*(Kyoto). Formally judged poetry contests were held frequently, court lords and ladies* communicated in poetry, and poetry was an integral part of court life in every way.

Not everyone was satisfied with the rarified poetry of the court, however. The 12th-century poet-priest *Saigyou* preferred to walk the countryside, immersing himself in nature. *Sanka-shuu* (The Mountain Hermitage) is one product of his wanderings.

Contemporary *Tanka*

Tanka are loved a literary art in which anyone can participate. Not long ago, *Tawara Machi* pioneered a new style using everyday language to describe everyday events, and there is a movement of sorts in experimental *tanka* using modern language and unfettered by restrictions of rhythm. For the most part the classical 31-syllable form with its clearly defined word devices and ethereal quality remains the most popular. There is much to be admired in the durability and timeless appeal of the ancient *tanka* poetry.

連歌の発生

平安時代のころから盛んに行われた歌合わせは，それぞれが詠んだ歌の優劣を競うものであったが，14世紀ごろから一つの歌の上の句（5・7・5音）と下の句（7・7音）を別の人が詠む，いわゆる「付け句」のゲームがもてはやされるようになった。その上の句を「発句」，下の句を「挙げ句」と呼ぶ。しかしそれだけでは単純なので，次々に歌をつないでいく形式も行われ，こうした座の文学を「連歌」と呼び，取りもつ役を「連歌師」と言った。連歌師は「宗匠」「連歌会所奉行」などと言われ，これを職業とする人さえ現れた。特に15世紀，室町時代に活躍した宗祇やその門人の宗長などはよく知られている。また連歌作者の二条良基が著した歌論書『近来風体抄』（1387年），これも良基の撰に成る連歌集『菟玖波集』（1356年），宗祇など3人の連歌を集めた『水無瀬三吟百韻』（1488年）などは，今日でもよく読まれている。

俳句の発生

伴吟者を必要とする不便さからか，今日では連歌を読み興ずることはほとんど行われなくなったが，俳句のほうは単独でもできる文芸としてたいへん盛んである。俳句は，連歌の上の句，つまり「発句」を詠む形式が独立したもので「荒海や（5音），佐渡に横たふ（7音），天の河（5音）」（松尾芭蕉の句）のように，世界にも例を見ない17音で構成する短詩型文学である。

短い形式だけに，詠まれる内容はむだのない，それでいて豊かなイメージであることが要求される。そのために春夏秋冬いずれかの季節を表す用語，「季語」を詠み込むことが原則として考えられている。また，それらの「季語」を分類整理した「歳時記」が広く用いられている。

俳句は当初「俳諧」と呼ばれ，滑稽の意味をもっていたが，いつしかそうした要素はもっぱら「川柳」という分野に引き継がれ，俳句はしだいに芸術性を高めるべく練磨される。17世紀に活躍した松尾芭蕉とその門人たち，18世紀の与謝蕪村・小林一茶などは特記すべき俳人たちである。特に西行の足跡を慕って各地を旅した芭蕉の『奥の細道』の自筆本が1996年に発見されて大きな話題を呼んだが，多くの紀行俳文集も今日よく読まれている。現代の俳句はさまざまな改革運動が進められたりしたが，大きな変化は望めないというのが現状である。

Renga

In the poetry contests of the *Heian* period poets vied to compose the best poem. In the 14th century, however, a new form of entertainment evolved of linked verse in which one poet would compose the first three lines (5-7-5 syllables) of a poem and another would complete it with two more lines (7-7 syllables). The first three lines are called the *hokku* and the remaining two the *ageku*. To include more people and make it more interesting, this pattern was repeated in long *renga* or linked-verse compositions. Poets who excelled in this kind of work were called *renga* masters, and there even emerged a professional class of *renga* poets. Particularly famous *renga* masters include the 15th-century *Sougi* and his disciple *Souchou, Nijou Yoshimoto*'s authoritative work *Kinrai Fuutai Shou* (Notes on Poetic Styles of the Recent Past) written in 1387, his *Tsukuba-shuu* collection of *renga* compiled in 1356, and the 1488 *Minase Sangin Hyakuin* sequence by the *renga* master *Sougi* and two other poets are still widely read.

Haiku

Because they require several participants, *renga* are seldom composed today, but *haiku*, in other words the *hokku* portion of a *renga*, remain popular as an independent form. Only 17 syllables, the *haiku* is one of the most succinct poetic verse types in the world. A good example is *Matsuo Bashou*'s verse:

A-ra-u-mi ya	How rough a sea
Sa-do ni yo-ko-ta-u	and, stretching over *Sado* Isle,
A-ma-no-ga-wa	the Galaxy

(Tr. Harold B. Henderson)

Its concise form mandates that the *haiku* convey a rich imagery with no superfluous words. Seasons are often indicated by fixed words or phrases, and these seasonal indicators are such a common device in *haiku* that several glossaries have been compiled solely for the convenience of the *haiku* poet.

Originally *haiku* (or *hokku*) were often humorous or burlesque in nature, but over time rediculous or satirical verse evolved as an independent genre known as *senryuu*, while the *haiku* was refined into a highly sophisticated form of serious poetry. Some of the most famous *haiku* poets are the 17th-century *Matsuo Bashou* and his disciples, and *Yosa Buson* and *Kobayashi Issa* in the 18th century. Many of these poets wrote *haiku* travelogues still enjoyed today, the most well-known probably being *Bashou*'s *Oku no Hosomichi* (The Narrow Road to the Deep North) written to commemorate his retracing of the northern route traveled by the *waka* poet-priest *Saigyou*, and the discovery of a copy of this collection in *Bashou*'s own hand created a considerable stir in 1996. Still a popular medium, *haiku* continue to be written today and there is little prospect for any drastic changes in the genre, although new *haiku* forms have been experimented with.

新聞漫画

日本の新聞には必ず漫画(多くは4コマ)が載っている。時に世相を風刺し，時に庶民の哀歓を描き，一服の清涼剤として，多数の読者の共感を得ている。

新聞漫画の代表としては，まず長谷川町子の「サザエさん」がある。戦後間もなく始まり，ほぼ4半世紀にわたり，1974年まで『朝日新聞』に長期連載された。主婦であるサザエさんを中心に，一家7人を巡る，明るくユーモラスな生活描写は，そのまま日本人の庶民の暮らしの反映でもあった。何と言っても主人公サザエさんの，明るく，お人好しで，少々慌てん坊のパーソナリティーが人気の秘密で，新聞連載が終わった後も，テレビのアニメで放映されている。また「サザエさん」には時々の世相，流行も巧みに取り入れられ，世相史的役割も果たした。

これを例えば，アメリカの長寿新聞漫画「ブロンディー」と比べると，「ブロンディー」はブロンディーと夫ダグウッドが中心で，話題も夫婦の間柄に重点が置かれているのに対し，「サザエさん」は，夫よりもむしろ弟，妹，母親といった家族に多く題材を求めており，日米社会の違いがおのずと反映している。現実には「サザエさん」とは逆に，日本の社会は核家族化が進んでおり，一面，大家族への憧憬(どうけい)の裏返しであったかもしれない。80年代には「サザエさん」と同様な家族漫画で，70年代を舞台にして，小学生の女の子，まる子の日常を描いた「*ちびまる子ちゃん」がテレビアニメの人気を独占した。

劇画

今日，出版界を席捲(せっけん)しているのは，上に述べた4コマ漫画ではなく，より物語性のある漫画，すなわち，劇画と呼ばれるものである。従来は漫画と言えば(新聞漫画を除き)子供の読み物であったが，1970年前後から始まった劇画ブームの主体はむしろ青年層で，漫画週刊誌は何誌にも及び，膨大な発行部数を誇っている。一般に，笑いよりストーリー性が強く，時代物，闘魂物，人情物，評伝等々バラエティーに富む。しかし売らんかなのあまり，エロ・グロ・ナンセンスも横溢(おういつ)し，問題も抱えている。

人気劇画の多くは，テレビのアニメとして放送されるばかりでなく，今日ではテレビドラマにも多数脚色されて放送されている。

Newspaper Strips

Just about all of Japan's many daily newspapers carry comic strips, mostly of the four-frame format. These comic strips, with themes ranging from pointed social satire to poignant renderings of everyday joys and sorrows, provide light interludes of relaxation for millions of Japanese readers.

The classic newspaper comic is *Hasegawa Machiko*'s *Sazae-san*. This comic strip started in the *Asahi* soon after the war and did not end until 1974. Centered on the fictional housewife *Sazae-san*, it depicts the problems of the typical Japanese three-generational household. The key to *Sazae-san*'s success has been the cheerful, good-natured, and slightly befuddled personalities of its main character. Even after the *Sazae-san* newspaper strip had ended, the series was continued on television. At times *Sazae-san* has included social commentary and current fads, making it a chronicle of its times.

Compared to the Blondie comic strip in the United States, which centers on the relationship between Blondie and her husband Dagwood, *Sazae-san* embraces the whole family and is, if anything, more concerned with *Sazae*'s relations with her brother, sister, and mother, and this difference may be indicative of the differences between Japanese and American societies. In fact, however, postwar Japanese society has been shifting toward the nuclear family, and in this sense *Sazae-san* may actually represent the extended family of the past. In the late 1980s, another cartoon series dominated—this one *Chibi Maruko-chan** (Little *Maruko*) depicting the daily life of grade-schooler *Maruko* and her family in the 1970s.

Comic Books

Yet the most successful comics in print today are not the four-frame strips but the longer comic-book stories called *geki-ga*. With the exception of newspaper comics, virtually all comics up until the late 1960s were for children, but since then there has been a phenomenal boom in *geki-ga* for teenagers and young adult readers, and all manner of comic-filled weeklies have won huge followings. Generally, they are more serious than comical, and the rich variety of themes includes historical drama, warfare, melodrama, and biography. However, many include an alarming amount of erotic, brutal, and bizarre material.

Not only are the more popular comics animated and serialized on television as *anime*, a number have been made into television dramas and movies with real actors.

仏教の歴史

仏教が日本に公式に伝えられたのは538年，朝鮮の百済(くだら)からとされているが，すでに5世紀には大陸からの渡来人によってもち込まれ，信仰されていたと言われている。インドから中国という中央集権国家を経て日本に伝わったことと，そのとき，日本が中央集権国家確立の時期であったことから，鎮護国家の色彩の濃い仏教となった。

6世紀末から奈良時代を通じ，仏教は天皇家をはじめ，有力氏族に支持され，国教的存在となり，聖徳太子の建立(こんりゅう)した法隆寺をはじめ，興福寺，東大寺，薬師寺，唐招提寺など当時の遺構は世界最古の木造建築として1200〜1300年後の今日にまで伝わっている。

仏教は，日本に初めてもち込まれた系統的な思想体系であったため，それ以後の日本に計り知れない影響を与えた。思想，文化ばかりでなく，仏教は建築，金属工芸，さらに医学，農業技術に至るまでの文明の代名詞でもあった。中国からもたらされる仏教文化・文明は，これ以後，平安時代，室町時代，さらに江戸時代に至るまで，日本にとっては常に学ぶべき新文化，新技術であった。

平安時代中期に起こった，一種の終末思想である*末法思想は，政治や社会の乱れ，その後の，武士の台頭による戦乱に裏付けられて急速に広まり，鎌倉時代の新仏教を生む下地を作った。鎌倉仏教と呼ばれる*日蓮宗，浄土宗，*浄土真宗，禅宗など，今日の日本の仏教の主流を成す宗派は皆この時代に生まれたものである。いずれも，奈良時代以来の仏教の貴族的，学問的な色彩とは異なり，一心に「南無妙法蓮華経(なむみょうほうれんげきょう)」の題目や「南無阿弥陀仏(なむあみだぶつ)」の念仏を唱えたり，座禅に打ち込むことだけで救われるという個人的，庶民的なものであり，それゆえに爆発的に信徒を増やしていった。江戸時代にはキリスト教禁圧のため，すべての人々に地域の寺への登録を強制し，檀家(だんか)制度が作られ，寺は幕府の末端管理機構として檀家の冠婚葬祭をつかさどるようになった。

現代の仏教

現代では仏教信徒は約6200万人(1996年末)とされており，伝統仏教が地方で根強い力をもっているのに対し，大都会では日蓮宗系の創価学会(約800万世帯と言われている)，立正佼成会(614万人)，霊友会(189万人)など，第二次世界大戦の少し前に作られた在家仏教団体が大きな力をもっている。近年では伝統仏教も新仏教も，互いに宗教協力によって共存共栄し，平和や難民救済などに協力している。

Buddhism

History

Buddhism is said to have been officially introduced into Japan in 538 from the Paekche kingdom (Korea). But visitors actually introduced it much earlier, and there were Japanese adherents already by the 5th century. Buddhism made its way to Japan from India through centralized China just when Japan was itself consolidating into a centralized state, and the newly unified Japanese nation quickly adapted Buddhism's teachings to its own mores and needs.

From the end of the 6th century, Buddhism was the main faith of the imperial and other ruling clans—virtually a national religion, at least as far as the nobility was concerned. Prince *Shoutoku* (574-622), one of Buddhism's strongest adherents, commissioned the building of the *Houryuuji,* today the oldest wooden building in the world, and this was followed by the construction of other temples which exist to this day: *Koufukuji*, *Toudaiji*, *Yakushiji*, and *Toushoudaiji*.

The first systematic religious philosophy to be introduced into Japan, Buddhism had a profound cultural and philosophical impact. Architecture, metallurgy, medicine, and even agricultural techniques, were strongly influenced by Buddhist concepts. Further waves of new Buddhist teachings from China continued to add to Japanese culture in succeeding periods, from the *Heian* period all the way through the *Edo* period.

Political and social unrest and the rise of the warrior class in the mid-*Heian* period gave credence to an apocalyptic Buddhism* that laid the foundation for a new Buddhism in the *Kamakura* period. This new Buddhism emerged as the *Nichiren*,* *Joudo*, *Joudo Shinshuu*,* and *Zen* sects—still the leading Buddhist sects—teaching a salvation through grace that was quite different from the intellectual Buddhist philosophy of the *Nara*-period nobility. These sects taught that simple repetition of "*Namu myou houren gekyou*" (I place my faith in the Lotus Sutra) or "*Namu amida butsu*" (I place my faith in *Amida* Buddha), or meditation in the case of *Zen*, were sufficient to save one's soul. With its much broader popular appeal, the new Buddhism spread rapidly, and this was reinforced in the *Edo* period by the shogunate's *danka* system requiring all families to be registered with one of the country's many Buddhist temples. Instituted as an instrument for repressing Christianity, this system also helped the government keep tabs on the people.

Buddhism Today

As of 1996, there were 62.0 million registered Buddhists. The traditional sects are still strong in the rural areas, but new *Nichiren*-based sects founded just before World War II have won many urban adherents—including *Souka Gakkai* (claiming about 8 million households), *Risshou Kouseikai* (6.14 million adherents), and *Reiyuukai* (1.89 million adherents). Old and new Buddhist sects coexist today in ecumenical harmony, actively promoting peace and aiding refugees.

禅の根本目標は，菩提(悟り)を求めて参禅生活に励み，すべての衆生(人類と全生物)が救われるのを待って，自分もまた救われようと願うことである。

禅の歴史

仏教では悟りを得る方法の一つとして古くから座禅を行ってきたが，中国に起こった禅宗では座禅に徹することを要求し，日常生活すべてを座禅の修行の一環であるとしている。

日本には12世紀末に栄西によって臨済宗が，鎌倉時代初めに道元によって曹洞宗がもたらされた。臨済宗は座禅をしながら，師匠から次々に出される「公案」と呼ぶ問題を考え，それを解決することによって悟りを開こうという派。公案の一例に「隻手の音声」がある。「両手を打てば音がするが，片手だけではどんな音がするか」と問うて，哲学的な考察を重ねさせる。主に貴族や上級武士に支持された。京都の大徳寺，南禅寺，鎌倉の建長寺，円覚寺などがこの派に属する。

曹洞宗の特徴は道元が言っているように「只管打坐」である。つまり，ひたすら座禅をすることによって悟りを開こうとするもの。権力と虚栄を嫌った道元は福井県の山中に永平寺を開いて，だれでもが悟りを開けるのだと，下級武士や一般の人々に座禅を勧めた。

江戸時代初期には，中国から来朝した隠元によって黄檗宗が開かれた。経文や動作，飾りなどすべて中国風そのままであることを特徴とした。

禅と日本文化

禅が日本文化に与えた影響は大きい。特に室町時代，中国との交流が盛んで，その先端に立った臨済宗の僧侶が，貴族や上級武士の間に中国文化を紹介した。文学では，禅僧を中心にした漢文学が「五山文学」の名で呼ばれた。五山とは，最も格式の高い5つの禅寺のことである。絵画では水墨画が中国からもたらされると同時に，雪舟ら多くの禅僧が山水画や頂相と呼ばれる僧侶の肖像画を描いている。また庭園では禅の精神にのっとった飾り気のない石庭，枯山水の庭などが作られた。さらに茶も，栄西により抹茶による喫茶法が伝えられ，安土・桃山時代には千利休をはじめとする多数の茶の宗匠が禅を学び，その精神を生かしたわび茶を生み出した。

現在，禅宗の信徒は約327万人(1996年末)で，仏教の5.3%であるが，仏教寺院約7万5000のうち2万1000が禅宗系で，特に曹洞宗は約1万4700と，全寺院の2割を占めている。これらの寺院では一般の信徒を含めた参禅会などを開いている。海外へは鈴木大拙が積極的に紹介し，曹洞宗では弟子丸泰仙がヨーロッパへの布教に力を入れた。

Zen

The *Zen* practitioner seeks enlightenment through discipline and meditation and awaits salvation for himself and for all sentient beings.

History

The *zazen** meditative posture has long been a Buddhist technique for attaining enlightenment. It was the *Zen* sect, originating in China, however, which first taught that all of life, every act of eating, sleeping, walking, and sitting, could be applied to meditative purposes.

The monk *Eisai* introduced the *Rinzai* sect of Buddhism from China in the late 12th century and the monk *Dougen* introduced what is now the *Soutou* school of Buddhism soon afterward in the early *Kamakura* period. Stressing the combination of *zazen* with *kouan*, paradoxical riddles put by a master to provide the substance for meditation, the *Rinzai* sect was especially popular among upper-class *samurai* and nobility. *Daitokuji* and *Nanzenji* in *Kyouto* (Kyoto), and *Kenchouji* and *Engakuji* in *Kamakura* are *Rinzai* temples. Perhaps the most famous of these *kouan* is to ask, "What is the sound of one hand clapping?"

The *Soutou* sect stresses meditation, claiming that single-minded devotion to *zazen* is sufficient to attain enlightenment. *Dougen* had little interest in power or fame and established his monastery in the mountains of *Fukui* prefecture far from the capital. Teaching that anyone can attain enlightenment, he drew many followers from the lower *samurai* classes and the common people.

Another *Zen* sect, the *Oubaku* school, was introduced from China by *Ingen* in the early *Edo* period. Its sutras are read in Chinese, and its rituals and decor retain a strong Chinese flavor.

Culture

Zen has had a profound influence on Japanese culture. *Rinzai* monks were important in introducing Chinese culture to the *Muromachi* establishment. *Gozan* literature, the writings of monks at the five major *Zen* temples, contributed much to literature. The *Zen* influence was strong in painting as well, and *Sesshuu* and others produced outstanding ink paintings and religious portraits.* The rock and sand gardens considered so typical of Japan are also *Zen* creations. Likewise, the tea ceremony traces its origins back to the first powdered tea brought back from China by *Eisai*, and a number of tea masters, including *Sen no Rikyuu*, learned about *Zen* and suffused the tea ceremony with the *Zen* spirit.

Today, there are about 3.27 million registered *Zen* followers, or 5.3% of all Japanese Buddhists. Of the roughly 75,000 Buddhist temples in the country, 21,000 are *Zen* temples (14,700 of them *Soutou* sect). These temples sponsor a variety of activities to propagate their teachings including short *Zen* "training camps" for their followers. *Suzuki Daisetsu** introduced *Zen* to the West, *Deshimaru Taisen** of the *Soutou* sect did much to popularize it in Europe.

30 神道

神道が果たして宗教であるのか否か，これまでも論議が絶えなかった。神道には，宗教の要件である教義，聖典，宗団，布教などの明確なものがないからだ。一般に「神道」と言った場合，「日本民族に固有の神，神霊に基づいて発生し，展開してきた宗教の総称」であるとされているが，神や神霊についての信念や伝統的な祭祀(さいし)ばかりでなく，広く生活習俗や伝承されている考え方などもその中に含まれる。

現代の日本人は，日常はまったく神道と無関係だと言えるが，正月の初もうで，神社の祭り，受験のときの合格祈願，七五三などのときには神社に参拝し，結婚式は神式でやることが多い。

古来の神道は，日本の原始信仰である農耕神，土地神，祖先神崇拝に基づくものであり，氏神などとも呼ばれ，氏族集団によって祭られたものである。祭神は八百万(やおよろず)の神と言われるように多種多様である。原始神道においては，3，4世紀に至るまで神殿も作らなかった。4世紀に大和(やまと)政権がほぼ日本を統一し，古代国家が成立すると，原始神道は天つ神と国つ神(天神地祇(ちぎ))を祭る古代神道に発展した。天つ神は大和政権の神で，天皇が最高の祭司となり，地方神の国つ神の上に置かれた。また大和政権系神話に各地の氏族神話を取り入れ，記紀神話を作り上げた。最初の神道の教義が現れるのは平安時代中期になってからで，仏教の天台宗，真言宗の教理と結び付いた本地垂迹(ほんじすいじゃく)説がそれである。これはインドの仏・*菩薩(ぼさつ)（本地）が日本でさまざまな神となって現れる(垂迹)という，奈良時代からある神仏習合を主仏従神として理論化したものである。中世・近世に至り，伊勢神道，吉田神道，復古神道など，神道の独自性を説く理論が作られ，明治になると，皇室の祭祀を基準に，神社の祭祀・教義を統一して，神職は祭祀だけを行い，国民すべてを氏子とする国家神道を作り上げた。

戦後は，神社個々が宗教法人となり，文化庁の統計では神社の申告によって信徒9595万人（1996年）となっているが，NHKの調査（81年）では「神道を信仰している」という人は3％にすぎない。

教派神道には金光(こんこう)教，大本(おおもと)教，禊(みそぎ)教などの数百の教団があるが，国家神道中心の戦前にはしばしば迫害を受けた。信徒数は約715万人。

民俗神道は田の神，かまど神，道祖神などを家庭や個人で祭るもので，生活習慣と結び付き，今も地方に残っている。

Shintou

Because it lacks the usual teachings of religion, there is still some question whether *Shintou* should be classified as a religion. Basically, *Shintou* is the name generally given to Japan's indigenous beliefs, rituals to native spirits, daily practices, and traditional ways of thinking.

Though Japanese are not consciously *Shintou*, many *Shintou* customs are still practiced, including visiting a shrine during the New Year's holidays, taking part in local *Shintou* shrine festivals, praying to the *Shintou* gods for success in school exams, and taking children to be blessed by shrine deities at *Shichi-go-san*. Most weddings are *Shintou*.

Shintou originated in the Japanese worship of agrarian, earthly, and ancestral gods. Every *uji* or clan had a tutelary god known as an *uji-gami*, and the *Shintou* gods are collectively known as *yaoyorozu no kami* (lit. the eight million deities). Ancient *Shintou* did not bother to erect shrines until the 3rd or 4th century. Not until the country was unified under the *Yamato* in the 4th century did *Shintou* begin to acquire a clear hierarchical structure with the *Yamato* gods and high-priest emperor at top, and local gods at bottom. The first known Japanese histories were efforts to legitimize the imperial line by merging myths and legends concerning local *uji-gami* with the *Yamato* mythology. No *Shintou* doctrine as such, however, was postulated until the mid-*Heian Honjisuijaku* doctrine stipulating that the *Shintou* gods were really manifestations of Buddhist deities,* thereby linking indigenous beliefs to Buddhist teachings.* In the feudal and early-modern periods, a number of sects emerged professing an independent and pure Shintoism. These included *Ise*, *Yoshida*, and *Fukkou Shintou*. In the *Meiji* era the government made a determined effort to promote emperor worship and all the trappings of *Shintou*. Local shrine teachings and festivals were brought into line with the national doctrine, and local priests lost the authority to do much but conduct ceremonies.

When state and religion were separated after the war, *Shintou* became just one more of the many Japanese religions. While 1996 statistics volunteered by *Shintou* shrines show 95.95 million *Shintou* followers, a 1981 NHK survey showed only 3% of the people identifying as *Shintou*.

There are numerous *Shintou* sects, including *Konkoukyou*, *Oomotokyou*, and *Misogikyou*, though many of them were prosecuted in the zeal to establish State *Shintou* prior to World War II. Today these more-than-500 sects claim 7.15 million believers.

Folk *Shintou* is closely tied to local and family religious practices. Its worship of the gods of the fields, the hearth, and all things close to home remains an integral part of local customs in many regions today.

伝来から現在まで

日本にキリスト教が最初に伝来したのは，1549年，カトリック・イエズス会の宣教師フランシスコ・ザビエルの来日によってであった。宣教師たちとともにもたらされる南蛮貿易の利益に大いに関心のあった大名たちが布教を歓迎したため，たちまち多数の信徒を獲得した。1590年前後で信徒20万人は，ピーク時には40万人に達したと言われている。当時の人口から言えばたいへんな比率である。しかし，蜜月時代は短く，豊臣秀吉の禁教令(1587年)で突如終わる。江戸幕府はさらに弾圧を強化して，多くの殉教者を生み，悲劇は1637年の*島原の乱で頂点に達する。こうして日本が再びキリスト教の信仰の自由を認めるのは1873年，明治新政府になってからであった。その間，一部の信者は“隠れキリシタン”として細々と信仰の火を守った。

現在，キリスト教信者は約91万6000人(1996年末)。うち，カトリックは44万8000人，プロテスタントは各宗派を合わせて46万人。このほか，キリスト教系を名乗る新宗教の信者が約55万人いる。ザビエルに始まる初期布教時代と比べ，この数字はあまりにも少ない。しかも，ほぼ横ばいである。結婚式は神式で，葬式は仏式でと，宗教に対してよく言えば寛容，悪く言えば無頓着(とんちゃく)な日本人にとって，キリスト教はしょせん根付かぬものなのだろうか。元来，多神教的であった神道の影響が根底にあるのだろうか。同じアジアにある隣国・韓国では，仏教と比べてもキリスト教が大きな影響力を有しているのを考えると，これはきわめて興味深い現象である。

日本文化の中のキリスト教

とはいえ，日本のキリスト教の問題は単に量に還元できないのも事実である。信者の数こそ少ないが，明治以降の日本の近代化に，キリスト教およびその文化が及ぼした影響は計り知れない。それは時にライフスタイルとして，道徳として，倫理として，日本人の生活に入り込んでいる。

教育，特に女子教育や中等教育に果たした役割も大きい。今日でもミッションスクールは約800校(中高校)を数え，他のどの宗教学校よりも多い。新島襄(にいじまじょう)，内村鑑三，植村正久など，優れた思想家を輩出し，また，社会事業の分野でもキリスト教は大きな力を果たした。その人道主義は社会主義運動にも関連し，いわゆる，キリスト教社会主義の流れを作った。今日，キリスト教信者には作家の故遠藤周作，曽野綾子，評論家の犬養(いぬかい)道子，故大平正芳元首相など著名人も少なくない。

Historical Development

Christianity was brought to Japan by a group of Jesuit missionaries led by Francis Xavier in 1549. Christianity spread rapidly, thanks to the open-arms policy of feudal lords who appreciated that the missionaries brought not only a new religion but also new trade opportunities. However, this proved to be a brief honeymoon for Christianity in Japan, for in 1587 *Toyotomi Hideyoshi* suddenly banned the new religion. By one count, there were about 200,000 Japanese Christians a few years later—a significant portion of the population at that time but still only half of the suspected peak figure. Suppression of Christianity became stricter under the *Tokugawa* regime, coming to a tragic climax in 1637 when a Christian rebellion in *Shimabara** was crushed. Japan continued to ban Christianity until 1873, when freedom of religion was reinstated by the *Meiji* government, yet throughout this period the flame of Christian belief was surreptitiously maintained by small groups of "closet Christians."

Including Catholics (448,000) and Protestants (460,000), Japanese Christians now number about 916,000. There are also a number of new religions flying the Christianity banner and claiming about 550,000 adherents. As a percentage of the total population, this is fewer than there were in the 16th century. With Shintoist weddings and Buddhist funerals, Japanese may be termed tolerant or even indifferent to religion, and they are not very receptive to Christian conversion. Perhaps this is because of Japan's polytheistic *Shintou* roots, but Japan presents a striking contrast to the situation in such neighboring Asian countries as South Korea where Christianity ranks right alongside Buddhism in popularity.

Christianity in Japanese Culture

However, Christianity's impact on Japanese culture cannot be measured by numbers alone. Although only a small percentage of Japanese are Christians, Christian thought has had a major impact on Japan during its modernization beginning in the late 19th century. Christian lifestyles, moral codes, and ethics have become interwoven into Japanese life.

Christianity has also come to play a major role in education, especially for girls' schools and secondary schools. There are currently some 800 mission schools at the secondary level, far more than there are non-Christian religious schools. Many of Japan's great modern thinkers have been Christian, including *Niijima Jou*, *Uchimura Kanzou*, and *Uemura Masahisa*, and Christians have also figured prominently in social work. Along the way, many of these humanists developed ties with socialism, resulting in a Christian current that forms part of Japan's socialist movement. Among the famous Japanese Christians of recent years are the novelists *Endou Shuusaku* and *Sono Ayako*, social commentator *Inukai Michiko*, and former Prime Minister *Oohira Masayoshi*.

日本の神話は，『古事記』(712年)と『日本書紀』(720年)の最初の部分に出ている神々の物語を指すのが普通である。

記紀の神話は，その舞台によって，高天原(たかまがはら)，出雲(いずも)，日向(ひゅうが)の3つに分けられる。天皇の祖神で，神々の王者である太陽神*アマテラスが支配する高天原つまり天上の国であり，まずそこで天地開びゃく，イザナギ・イザナミの国生み・神生みや，天岩屋(あめのいわや)などの物語が展開する。次いで出雲神話では出雲地方(今の島根県東部)を主要な舞台として，スサノオとオオクニヌシが主神として活躍する。天孫降臨の前提として，オオクニヌシが高天原から派遣された神々に，国土を献上するいわゆる国譲りをする。日向神話は日向地方(今の宮崎県)が舞台で，アマテラスの命により，その孫ニニギが日向の高千穂の峰に降りる天孫降臨によって，日本を創始する。

各神話は，天地の開びゃくから国生みへ，国生みから国譲りへ，国譲りから天孫降臨へと，互いに因果関係をもって時間的に結び付けられ，究極的には，神の子孫である天皇の国土統治を合理化する物語になっている。このように高度な国家的・政治的配慮をもってつくられている点が，他民族に見られない日本神話の特色である。

『古事記』によって，よく知られた神話を3つ紹介する。

- **国生み**　イザナギ，イザナミの男女2神は天神から矛(ほこ)を与えられ，海上を流れ動く大地を固めるよう命じられる。そこで2神は矛を海に入れてかき回し，それを引き上げると，そのしずくが固まって島になった。そこに降りて柱を立て，2神は柱を右と左から回り，出会った所で結婚し，次々と島を生んでいった。
- **天岩屋**　弟スサノオの暴状を怒ったアマテラスが天岩屋に隠れたため，天下が暗やみになった。神々が相談して，物を飾り，祝詞(のりと)をあげ，アメノウズメに半裸で踊らせた。外の笑い声につられてアマテラスが岩戸を少し開いたので，タヂカラオが手をとって引き出し，世が再び明るくなった。同種の話は広く太平洋周辺民族にも見られる。
- **八岐大蛇(やまたのおろち)**　出雲国簸川(ひのかわ)の上流に，頭と尾がそれぞれ8つに分かれた大蛇がすみ，娘を次々に食べるので，スサノオが酒を飲ませて退治し，助けた娘と結婚する。三種の神器の一つである剣を大蛇の尾から得た。

Japanese mythology is based on stories in the 712 *Kojiki* (Record of Ancient Matters) and the 720 *Nihon Shoki* (Chronicle of Japan). Broadly divided according to its three principal scenes of action—*Takamagahara* (the High Plain of Heaven), *Izumo*, and *Hyuuga*—Japanese mythology tells of Japan's creation and the adventures of its numerous gods.

Takamagahara is eventually ruled by the sun goddess *Amaterasu*,* ancestor of the emperor. The earliest *Takamagahara* myths deal with the separation of heaven and earth, the creation of land by the gods *Izanami* and *Izanagi*, the many other gods to which they give birth (including *Amaterasu*), and *Amaterasu*'s flight to a heavenly cave. The *Izumo* myths center in the *Izumo* district (eastern *Shimane* prefecture) and deal primarily with the adventures of *Amaterasu*'s brother, *Susanoo*, and his descendant, *Ookuninushi*.

Taking place in what is now *Miyazaki* prefecture, the *Hyuuga* tales deal primarily with the god *Ninigi* who descends to Mt. *Takachiho* under orders from *Amaterasu* to subdue and rule the land, in the process establishing the imperial line and the Japanese nation.

From the separation of heaven and earth to the establishment of the imperial line, this mythology marshals divine descent to buttress imperial authority in a blatantly nationalistic and political mythology.

Kojiki Myths

Three myths from the *Kojiki* are especially well known. The first tells of *Izanagi* and *Izanami*, male and female deities, who are given a spear and told to solidify the drifting land. They thrust the spear into the sea and stir the churning brine. When they lift the spear, drops of brine harden to form an island. *Izanagi* and *Izanami* descend to the island and erect a pillar around which they walk from opposite directions. They unite upon meeting, giving birth to the Japanese islands.

The *Amenoiwaya* myth concerns *Amaterasu* and *Susanoo*. Angered by his violent behavior, she sulks in the heavenly cave and, deprived of her light, all is plunged into darkness. The other gods try to entice her out. Finally, the goddess *Amenouzume* dances half naked, much to the delight of all, and *Amaterasu*, lured by the unexpected sound of laughter, moves the great rock blocking the cave entrance to see what is going on. The god *Tajikarao* pulls her out and the world is once again blessed with her light. Similar myths are found throughout the Pacific.

One of the best-known *Susanoo* myths is about the great eight-headed, eight-tailed serpent of the *Hino* River in *Izumo*. *Susanoo* tricks the dreaded devourer of sacrificial maidens into drinking *sake* and kills it while it lies in a stupor. In one of the serpent's eight tails, *Susanoo* discovers a sword which later (along with a mirror and a curved jewel) becomes one of the three imperial regalia.

昔話は，語り初めが「昔，昔」，語り納めが「…であったとさ」のような一定の形式をもったものを言う。出てくる時代・場所・人物を特定せず，空想的である点が伝説と異なる。

日本の昔話の研究は，まだ数十年にしかならないが，昔話への関心は強く，すでに何万という昔話が収集され，民俗学，文学など各分野からの研究が進められている。最近では，ユング派分析家の河合隼雄（かわいはやお）が，日本の昔話の深層を分析して，西洋人の自我は「男性の意識」であるのに対し，日本人の自我は「女性の意識」とする説を発表して注目された。

五大昔話

室町時代末期ごろに成立し，江戸時代から明治にかけて有名昔話として定着した五大昔話が日本人によく知られている。

- ***かちかち山**　爺（じじい）は畑からいたずらタヌキを捕らえて帰る。タヌキは爺の留守に婆（ばば）をだまして殺し，婆に化けて爺に婆汁を飲ませる。悲しむ爺のために，ウサギがタヌキに大やけどをさせ，とうがらしを塗り付ける。最後にタヌキをどろの舟に乗せて沈め，殺す。
- **猿かに合戦**　ずるい猿は自分の拾ったカキの種をカニの拾った握り飯と交換する。カニがまいたカキの種が大きな木になり，実を結ぶと，猿はカニをだまして熟した実を食べ，青い実をカニに投げつけて殺す。カニの子は，うす，きね，ハチ，クリの助けで親のあだを討つ。
- **舌切りすずめ**　のりをなめたスズメを意地悪な婆は舌を切って追い出す。優しい爺がスズメの宿を訪ね，*つづらをもらう。小さいつづらを選ぶと，中に*大判・小判や宝が入っていた。婆はそれをまねてスズメの宿を訪ね，大きいつづらをもらうと，中から蛇・ムカデや化け物が出てくる。決まり文句→「舌切りすずめ，お宿はどこだ」
- **花さか爺**　正直者の爺がかわいがっていた犬に教えられて木の下から宝を掘り出す。死んだ犬を埋めた場所に大きな木が生え，爺がそれでうすを作ってもちをつくと，大判・小判が出てくる。うすの灰で枯れ木に花を咲かせて爺は殿様に褒められる。それをまねた隣の爺はことごとく失敗する。決まり文句→「ここ掘れワンワン」
- ***桃太郎**　川で洗濯をしていた婆が拾った桃から子供が生まれる。桃太郎と名づけられたその子は，大きくなって日本一の*きびだんごを持って，犬，猿，キジを連れて鬼が島へ鬼退治に行き，宝物を持って帰る。決まり文句→「大きな桃がどんぶらこどんぶらこと流れてきた」

Folk Tales

Japanese folk tales, like folk tales everywhere, have set patterns starting with "Once upon a time" and ending with "and that's the way it was." Unlike legends, all the elements of the folk tale are imaginary.

It is only in the last few decades that scholars have begun to study Japanese folk tales, but interest is strong and specialists have already collected tens of thousands of stories. The Jungian analyst *Kawai Hayao* did a celebrated psychological study of Japanese folk tales that found that, in comparison to the masculine ego revealed by Western folk tales, Japanese folk tales suggest a feminine ego.

Five *Muromachi* folk tales have remained especially popular.

- ***Kachikachi-yama**** (*Kachikachi* Mountain) An old man captures a *tanuki*, a kind of badger, and takes it home. While the old man is out, the *tanuki* tricks his wife and kills her. He then transforms himself into the old woman and, when her husband returns serves him soup containing her flesh. To avenge the old man, a rabbit burns the *tanuki*, rubs hot peppers into its charred skin, and sets it adrift on a boat of mud, finally drowning it.
- ***Saru Kani Kassen*** (Battle Between the Monkey and the Crab) A bad monkey tricks a crab into trading his rice ball for the monkey's persimmon seed. Yet the crab plants the seed and it sprouts into a tree laden with fruit. The monkey tricks the crab again and eats the fruit, throwing unripe fruit at the crab and killing it. The crab's children eventually get revenge with the help of a mortar and pestle, a bee, and a chestnut.
- ***Shitakiri Suzume*** (Tongue-cut Sparrow) Finding a sparrow eating her laundry starch, a mean old woman cuts its tongue out. Her gentle husband visits the sparrow's home and is given a choice of gifts. He takes the smaller box,* only to find it full of money* and treasure. Hearing this, the old man's greedy wife also visits the sparrow and takes the bigger box home, only to find it full of snakes, bugs, and goblins.
- ***Hanasaka Jijii*** (Ash Scatterer) An honest old man's dog leads him to buried treasure. When the dog dies, a great tree sprouts from its grave. The old man cuts down the tree and makes a mortar in which he pounds rice. To his astonishment, gold coins come out of the mortar. After his jealous neighbor burns the mortar, the old man scatters its ashes onto a withered tree, making it bloom and pleasing the local lord. Each time, the neighbor's attempts to mimic his feats end in disaster.
- ***Momotarou**** (Peach Boy) A child is born from a great peach an old woman discovers floating down a stream. Named the Peach Boy, he grows into a sturdy youth and sets out on a journey to Devil Island carrying the best millet dumplings* in Japan and accompanied by a dog, a monkey, and a pheasant. He and his companions defeat the devils in battle and return home laden with treasure.

34 伝説

伝説は，具体的な事物と結び付いていて，真実と信じられている言い伝えである。昔話のように，決まった形式や空想性・娯楽性をもたない。日本には，昔話と同じく，伝説も豊富である。出てくる主役によって，ふつう次のように分類する。

自然伝説……動植物，鉱物，天体，気象，地形，火，水など
歴史伝説……神仏，聖地，長者，偉業，事件，地名など
信仰伝説……各種の神(田の神・山の神ほか)，各種の霊(樹・岩石ほか)，幽霊，妖怪(ようかい)など

有名伝説

• **浦島伝説**　若い漁夫の浦島太郎は，釣ったカメを助けたお礼に竜宮城に招かれ，乙姫(おとひめ)と3年間楽しく暮らす。故郷に帰るとすでに700年たっている。心細さのあまり乙姫との約束を破って，みやげの玉手箱を開くと紫の煙が上がり，たちまち老人となる。これは丹後国(今の京都府北部)水の江の「浦島の子」という漁夫の伝説に基づく，「浦島太郎」の物語で，伝説は『万葉集』『日本書紀』『丹後国風土記(ふどき)』その他に見え，室町時代には『*御伽草子(おとぎぞうし)』や能の「浦島」になった。世界に広がる仙郷滞留譚(たん)，竜宮伝説の一つである。

• **羽衣(はごろも)伝説**　駿河国(するがのくに)(今の静岡県)三保の松原で天女が水浴びをしているところへ漁夫が通りかかり，天女の羽衣をとってしまう。天に帰れなくなった天女は男の妻になり，子供が生まれる。天女は後に羽衣を取り戻して天に帰る。原形は『駿河国風土記』『近江国(おうみのくに)風土記』『丹後国風土記』に出ており，能に「羽衣」がある。異種婚姻譚の一つ。

• **弘法(こうぼう)伝説**　弘法大師(空海)が諸国を遍歴した際に生まれた伝説。弘法大師がサトイモを所望したのを断ると，サトイモが石になったというたぐいの話が各地にたくさん残っている。このほか実在の人物に関する伝説は，*小野小町，源義経(よしつね)，*弁慶，徳川光圀(みつくに)(水戸黄門)など数多い。

• ***金太郎**　金太郎は相模国(さがみのくに)(今の神奈川県)の足柄山(あしがらやま)で，山うばに育てられ，クマ・シカ・猿などを友とした。怪力で全身赤く，まさかりを持ち，腹掛けをした子供の姿で描かれる。成人して*源頼光(よりみつ)に仕えて坂田金時と名乗り，大江山の*酒呑童子(しゅてんどうじ)を退治して*四天王の一人となった。今でも金太郎にあやかって強くなるようにと，5月5日の端午(たんご)の節句には，金太郎の像を飾る風習がある。

Legends

Legends are stories linked to historical persons and events believed to have once existed or happened. Not purely imaginary amusement, they lack folk tales' set formula. Japan's numerous legends are usually classified into nature legends of animals, plants, metals and minerals, heavenly bodies, weather, geography, fire, water, and so on; historical legends of gods, sacred sites, wealthy merchants, heroic deeds, events, and place names, etc.; and religious legends of gods (e.g., fields and mountains), spirits (of trees and rocks), ghosts, and goblins.

• ***Urashima Tarou*** A young fisherman, *Urashima Tarou*, saves a turtle, and the grateful turtle takes him to *Ryuuguujou*, the Palace of the Dragon King, where he spends three happy years with the king's daughter, *Otohime*. He gets homesick, however, and returns home only to find that 700 years have passed. Alone and at a loss what to do, he opens the magic box, even though *Otohime* had given him with strict instructions not to open it. In that very instant he ages. This story is based on a legend of *Mizunoe* in the ancient province of *Tango* (now part of *Kyouto* [Kyoto] prefecture) about a fisherman named *Urashima no Ko*. The legend appears in several ancient compilations including the *Man'youshuu*, *Nihon Shoki*, and the *Tango Fudoki*. In the *Muromachi* period it was retold in *otogi-zoushi** short stories and made into the *nou* (noh) play *Urashima*. Such tales about visits to enchanted lands are common worldwide.

• ***Hagoromo*** (Feathered Robe) In *Miho no Matsubara* in *Suruga* province (now *Shizuoka* prefecture), a fisherman comes upon an angel bathing in the sea. He takes away her beautiful feathered robe and, unable to return to heaven without the robe, the angel marries the fisherman and has his child. Finally she retrieves her robe and flies off to heaven. A tale of marriage between a celestial being and a human, *Hagoromo* appears in the *Suruga*, *Oumi*, and *Tango Fudoki*. It is also the basis for a well-known *nou* (noh) play.

• ***Koubou* Legends** Legends about the monk *Koubou Daishi* (a.k.a. *Kuukai*) and his travels abound. In one story *Koubou Daishi* is refused some sweet potatoes and turns them to stone. There are many other legends concerning historical figures such as *Ono no Komachi*,* *Minamoto no Yoshitsune*, *Benkei*,* and *Tokugawa Mitsukuni* (a.k.a. *Mito Koumon*).

• ***Kintarou**** Raised on Mt *Ashigara* in *Sagami* province (*Kanagawa* prefecture) by a mountain ogress, *Kintarou* is a child of superhuman strength. Friends with the mountain animals, he is commonly depicted as bright red, wearing a bib, and carrying a hatchet. As an adult *Kintarou* becomes *Sakata no Kintoki*, a trusted follower of *Minamoto no Yorimitsu*.* After capturing *Shutendouji*,* who had been terrorizing the Mt *Ooe* area, *Kintarou* becomes one of the four trusted followers* of *Minamoto no Yorimitsu*. It is customary to display a *Kintarou* doll on May 5, Boy's Day, to symbolize the hope that sons will be as strong and brave as *Kintarou*.

Notes

■1. Architecture

Houryuuji（法隆寺）Said to have been built in 607. Some of this temple's structures are known as the oldest wooden buildings in the world.

***Ise* Shrine**（伊勢神宮） Located in the city of *Ise* in *Mie* prefecture, the *Ise* Shrine is dedicated to *Amaterasu*, sun goddess and legendary ancestor of the imperial house.

tokonoma（床の間） An alcove with a slightly raised floor, usually in a traditional-style Japanese guest room. The *tokonoma* is used to hang scrolls and as a setting for ornaments and flower arrangements.

△*Houryuuji*

***Katsura* Detached Palace**（桂離宮） Located in the south-western section of *Kyouto* (Kyoto).

△*Ise* Shrine

△*Katsura* Detached Palace

△*Himeji* Castle

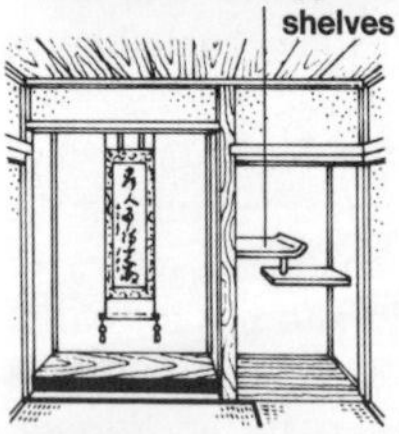

△*Tokonoma*

***Himeji* Castle**（姫路城） Also known as *Shirasagi-jou*, *Himeji* Castle was completed in 1609 and is located in the city of *Himeji* in *Hyougo* prefecture.

Rokumeikan（鹿鳴館） Built in 1883 in *Hibiya*, *Toukyou* (Tokyo), this was a social club for the elite and state guests. The *Rokumeikan* came to symbolize cultural achievement at a time when it was deemed important to adopt all things Western.

■2. Gardens

artificial hills（築山） Mounds of dirt or sand made to look like mountains.

kondou（金堂） Building enshrining an image of a temple's principal object of worship. Called the *kondou* or golden hall, because either the image or the interior of the building, or both, were gilded with gold.

△*Ryouanji*

■3. Music

min'you（民謡） In a broad sense, folk songs are also a part of traditional Japanese music. Songs which were once very much a part of daily life, *min'you* are today primarily sung only for parties, *bon-odori* dances, and on other special occasions. Every region has its own unique folk songs.

■4. Traditional Japanese Music

wandering Buddhist monks（虚無僧） The *komusou* did not wear monk's robes or shave their heads, but instead wore cylindrical straw hats that completely hid their faces, and played the *shakuhachi*. This costume was popularized by

△*Komusou* with *shakuhachi*

△*Biwa*

△*Shamisen*

△*Koto*

the *Fukeshuu* sect, and disappeared when the sect was banned in the *Meiji* era.

puppet theater drama (人形浄瑠璃) *Ningyou-joururi* are puppet plays performed to the accompaniment of *joururi* narration. Today, *ningyou-joururi* is most commonly referred to as *bunraku*, the name of the only surviving puppet theater troupe.

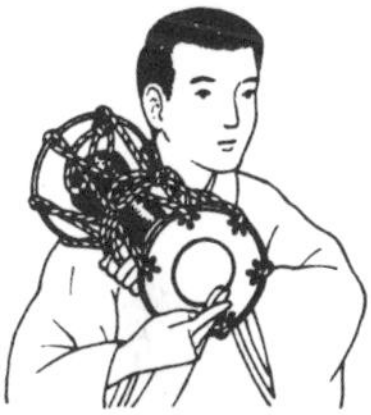

△small hand drum

■5. *Nou* (Noh)

See picture.

■6. *Kabuki*

shrine maiden (巫女) A *miko* is unmarried woman at a *Shintou* shrine who performs dances and recites incantations to the gods.

Okuni (阿国) (?-1607?) The supposed founder of *kabuki*, also known as *Izumo no Okuni*.

yagou (屋号) A *kabuki* actor's stage name.

△*Kabuki-za*

■7. *Bunraku* and *Buyou*

ballad-reciting chanter (太夫) *Tayuu* is an informal title bestowed upon performers of the highest rank in several traditional performing arts. A *joururi* singer is very often called a *tayuu*, as is the case in *gidayuu-joururi*, a type of *joururi* ballad chanting first developed by *Takemoto Gidayuu* I, and marked by its powerful delivery and accompaniment by a large, deep-toned *shamisen*.

Important Intangible Cultural Asset (重要無形文化財) Men and women who have been designated Bearers of Important Intangible Cultural Assets because they preserve

△*nou*

△*kabuki*

△*Bunraku*

△*Rakugo*

important techniques in traditional crafts and arts and the performing arts.

Living Cultural Treasures（人間国宝） A more popular name for Bearers of Important Intangible Cultural Assets.

■8. Popular Entertainment

rakugo（落語） See picture.

■9. Flower Arrangement

water trays（水盤） A shallow, ceramic or metal dish with a flat bottom used in flower arranging.

△*Rikka*

△*Seika*

△*Moribana*

△*Nageire*

■10. The Tea Ceremony

Okakura Tenshin（岡倉天心）(1862-1913) More popularly known by his pen name, *Tenshin*, *Okakura Kakuzou* was a prominent art critic and philosopher. He studied under Earnest Fenollosa and was an ardent promoter of Japanese arts.

matcha（抹茶） A high-quality tea ground into a fine powder. *Matcha* is dissolved in hot water and whipped to a froth with a bamboo whisk.

whisk（茶筅） A bamboo whisk used in preparing *matcha*.

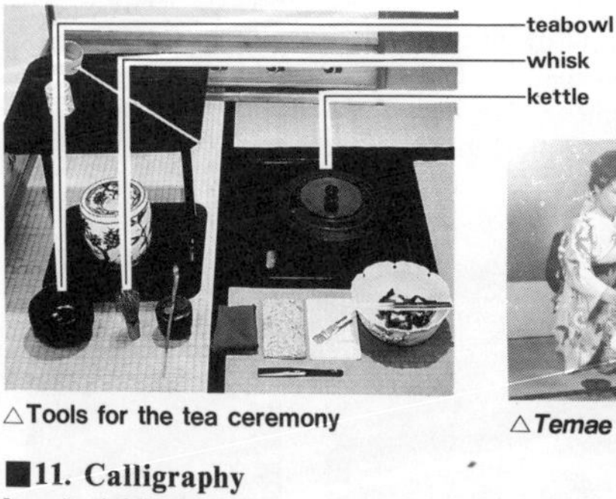

△Tools for the tea ceremony

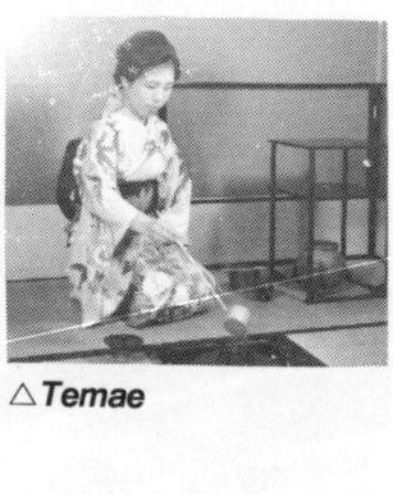

△*Temae*

△Brushes and black ink

■11. Calligraphy

brush（毛筆） A brush made of sheep, *tanuki*, rabbit, or other animal hair inserted into a thin bamboo tube or wooden handle.

black ink (墨) A block of ink rubbed on a wet stone to produce the ink used in calligraphy and painting. Made of the oily ash residue of burned vegetable oil and pine roots mixed with various fragrances, combined with natural glue, and formed into solid blocks.

△*Kaisho*

△*Gyousho*

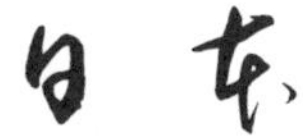

△*Sousho*

■12. Painting

liquid glue (にかわ水) Liquid glue made from boiled animal and fish skins, tendons, and bones. Liquid glue is also used to treat paper and silk in *nihon-ga* because it facilitates the application of the chalk-like white undercoating.

***Kanou* School** (狩野派) The *Kanou* School dominated Japanese painting from the end of the *Muromachi* period through the *Edo* period. Founded by *Kanou Masanobu*, this school flourished under the patronage of successive shoguns and produced many masters such as *Motonobu*, *Eitoku*, *Sanraku*, and *Tan'yuu*.

folding screens (屏風) Folding screens used as room dividers and protective screens, *byoubu* also served a decorative purpose. Made of paper or cloth stretched on wooden frames, *byoubu* consist of two, four, six, or more panels that fold together accordion-fashion.

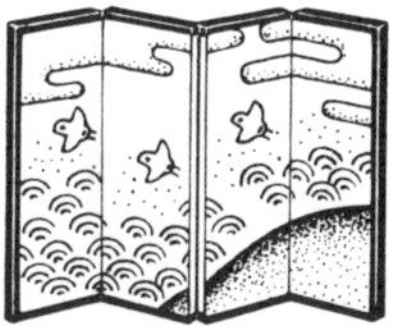

△*Byoubu*

■13. *Ukiyo-e*

△*Harunobu*

△*Utamaro*

△*Sharaku*

△*Hokusai*

△*Hiroshige*

■14. Ceramics

Shousouin (正倉院) A *Nara*-period repository of imperial treasures located in the *Toudaiji* compound in *Nara*. Famous for its collection of Tang China and *Nara*-period art objects.

Imari (伊万里) A port city in northern *Saga* prefecture in *Kyuushuu*.

△*Imari*

■15. Lacquer Ware

■16. The Japanese Sword

△Lacquer ware

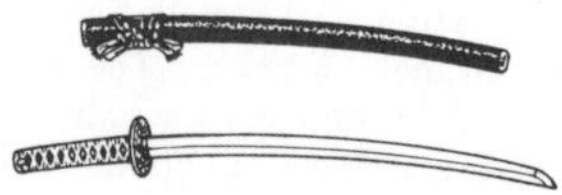

△Japanese sword

■17. Japanese Dolls

haniwa (埴輪) Low-fired earthenware figures found in and around *Kofun* period tombs.

△*Haniwa*

△*Hina* dolls

△Warrior dolls

△*Hakata* doll

△*Kokeshi* doll

△Standard doll

△*Saga* doll

△*Gosho* doll

△*Kimekomi* doll

■18. Japanese Literature (1) (Beginnings)

Emperor *Jinmu* (神武天皇) Legendary first emperor to appear in the earliest records of ancient Japan.

Hieda no Are (稗田阿礼) (?-?) A person of prodigious memory, *Hieda no Are* is said to have memorized the contents of the *Teiki* and *Kyuuji*. *Oono Yasumaro* recorded *Hieda no Are*'s account of these records in the *Kojiki*.

Oono Yasumaro (太安万呂) (?-723) A court noble and man of letters.

Toneri Shinnou (舎人親王) (676-735) The fifth son of Emperor *Tenmu*.

Ootomo no Yakamochi (大伴家持) (718?-785) Court official and poet.

4,500 poems Though the *Man'youshuu* contains two types of *waka* poetry, *chouka* and *tanka*, the *tanka* are by far the most numerous. The *chouka* has three or more alternating lines of five and seven syllables and always ends with a seven-syllable line. The *tanka* has 31 syllables arranged in a 5-7-5-7-7-syllable pattern.

■19. Japanese Literature (2) (Court Literature)

Ariwara no Narihira (在原業平) (825-880) Poet.

Murasaki Shikibu (紫式部) (?-?) A mid-*Heian* period court lady, poet and writer who wrote the world's first novel, the *Tale of Genji*.

Sei Shounagon (清少納言) (?-?) A mid-*Heian* period court lady, poet, and writer. Though her real name and dates of birth and death are not known, she was a sensitive and eloquent writer noted for her essays compiled in *Makura no Soushi* (Pillow Book).

■20. Japanese Literature (3) (Medieval)

***Hougen* Disturbance** (保元の乱) A military disturbance in *Kyouto* (Kyoto) in 1156 sparked by rivalries within the imperial household.

Heike (平家) Another name for the *Taira* clan.

Genji (源氏) Another name for the *Minamoto* clan.

***Heiji* Disturbance** (平治の乱) A clash between *Minamoto* and *Taira* forces in 1159 which forced the *Minamoto* out of the court and placed the *Taira* in a position of power.

biwa-houshi (琵琶法師) Blind, minstrel monks who played the *biwa*. The term *houshi* is another name for monk.

△*Biwa-houshi*

■21. Japanese Literature (4) (Town Pleasures)

shop owner(飛脚問屋) The *hikyaku* were swift-footed couriers supplied by a *hikyaku-don'ya*, a business establishment specializing in courier services.

San'yuutei Enchou (三遊亭円朝) (1839-1900) A highly talented *rakugo* storyteller. His many original stories contributed to the great popularity of *rakugo* in the *Meiji* era.

■23. Japanese Literature (6) (Early Twentieth Century)

Great *Kantou* Earthquake (関東大震災) This massive

earthquake on September 1, 1923, extended from Tokyo and the *Kantou* region out to *Shizuoka* and *Yamanashi* prefectures. The earthquake and the fires that followed left 140,000 dead or missing.

■25. *Waka*

court ladies (女房)　*Nyoubou* were originally ladies-in-waiting of high rank within the imperial palace and in the homes of the nobility.

■27. *Manga* (Comics)

▽*Chibi Maruko-chan*

■28. Buddhism

apocalyptic Buddhism (末法思想)　*Mappou* is a concept of the end of the world expressed in Buddhist terms. According to this concept, there are three periods after the attainment of *nirvana* by Sakya (the historical Buddha). The *shoubou*, a thousand years of "true law," the *zoubou*, a thousand years of "imitative law," and finally the *mappou*, the "latter day of the law" when people fail to live by Buddhist law and are unable to attain enlightenment. This last stage was believed to have begun in 1052 in the mid-*Heian* period when the military's rise to ascendency plunged Japan into internal turmoil. The people of this period were very much concerned with the after-world and many sought the saving grace of the *Amida* Buddha.

***Nichiren* sect** (日蓮宗)　A Buddhist sect founded by the priest *Nichiren*. See p. 21.

Joudo Shinshuu (浄土真宗)　A Buddhist sect established by *Shinran*. See p. 21.

■29. *Zen*

△*Zazen*

portraits (頂相)　*Chinzou* (or *chinsou*) are full- or half-size portraits of eminent *Zen* monks. Their extreme realism is unusual in Japan given the lack of a portraiture tradition.

Suzuki Daisetsu (鈴木大拙) (1870-1966)　A prominent Buddhist scholar who introduced *Zen* to the West.

Deshimaru Taisen (弟子丸泰仙) (1914-82)　*Deshimaru* became a *Zen* monk in 1965 after turning fifty and traveled extensively overseas, establishing 60 *Zen* meditation halls in Europe and northern Africa.

■30. *Shintou*

Buddhist deities (菩薩)　*Bosatsu* or bodhisattvas are holy beings on the threshold of enlightenment who vow not to become Buddhas until they have helped all other beings to attain the same state.

Buddhist teachings　Two Buddhist sects that *Shintou* developed close ties with were the *Tendai* and *Shingon* sects. *Tendai* is a Buddhist sect introduced from China in the *Heian* period by the priest *Saichou* who established the sect's headquarters at *Enryakuji* on Mt *Hiei* near *Kyouto* (Kyoto). The founders of the *Joudo*, *Nichiren*, and *Zen* sects in the *Kamakura* period were all *Tendai* monks. *Shingon* was a Buddhist sect based on the esoteric Buddhist teachings introduced from China in the early *Heian* period by the priest *Kuukai* (a.k.a. *Koubou Daishi*).

■31. Christianity

Christian rebellion in *Shimabara* （島原の乱） A 1637 rebellion by Catholic Christians of *Kyuushuu* against the suppression of their faith. Instigated by the farmers and merchants of the *Amakusa* Islands off the *Shimabara* peninsula, the rebellion only served to make the shogunate step up its suppression of Christianity and close Japan to the rest of the world.

■32. Mythology

Amaterasu （アマテラス） *Amaterasu Oo-mikami*, child of the gods *Izanagi* and *Izanami*, and the ancestral god of the imperial family. *Ise* Shrine in *Mie* prefecture is dedicated to *Amaterasu*. An important deity for an agricultural society, the sun goddess was probably gradually incorporated into the imperial lineage as the imperial power grew.

■33. Folk Tales

Kachikachi-yama （かちかち山） In this tale the rabbit burns the *tanuki* by creeping up behind it and setting fire to the straw it is carrying on its back. The word *kachikachi* is an onomatopoeia for the clicking sound of the flint the rabbit uses.

box （つづら） The *tsuzura* box woven of strong *tsuzura* vines was used to store clothes.

money （大判，小判） *Oo-ban*, *ko-ban* were oval gold and silver pieces used as currency mainly in the *Edo* period.

Momotarou （桃太郎） The peach is a symbol of long life and the tale of *Momotarou* probably originated in the story of an old couple who were rejuvenated by eating peaches and then had a child. The peach was also believed to be effective in warding off devils and other evil creatures.

millet dumplings （きびだんご） Dumplings made of millet were thought to bestow great strength upon a person. Hence, the ability of *Momotarou* and his companions, a dog, monkey, and pheasant, to vanquish the devils.

△*Momotarou*

■34. Legends

otogi-zoushi （御伽草子） Anonymously written fiction, moralistic stories, and legends.

Ono no Komachi （小野小町） An early *Heian* period poet. Though little is actually known about *Ono no Komachi*, she is believed to have been a great beauty, and there are

△*Tsuzura*

△*Benkei*

△*Kintarou*

many legends about her which have been employed as themes in *nou* (noh) chants and *joururi* narration.

Benkei (弁慶) (?-1189) A monk, *Benkei* died protecting his master *Minamoto no Yoshitsune*, younger brother and rival of *Minamoto no Yoritomo*. *Benkei* is a popular hero figuring prominently in *otogi-zoushi* and *kabuki* and *nou* (noh) dramas.

Minamoto no Yorimitsu (源頼光) (948-1021) A warrior of the mid-*Heian* period renowned for his courage.

Shutendouji (酒呑童子) A legendary bandit said to have preyed on women and children. He appears in *otogi-zoushi* and *kabuki* and *nou* (noh) plays.

four trusted followers (四天王) Originally the four Buddhist guardian deities, *shitennou* is also used in reference to particularly faithful retainers and followers of historical and legendary heroes. The term is still used today.

PART・5

超自然・動植物のイメージ
AFFINITIES WITH NATURE

犬

［イメージ］ 英語の表現と同じように，日本語の表現でも犬のイメージはよくない。「犬死にする」は「むだに死ぬ」の意味だし，単に「イヌ」と言えば，「スパイ，回し者」のことで侮辱語である。

［昔話］ 犬は縄文(じょうもん)時代から家畜として飼われていた。昔話の「桃太郎」や「花さか爺(じじい)」にも，犬は重要な役割で出てくる。白い犬は霊犬とされていたので，昔話の犬はしばしば白い犬として語られる。

［故事］ 江戸幕府の5代将軍徳川綱吉は，仏教を信じるあまり生類憐(しょうるいあわ)れみの令を出して犬や鳥獣の保護を命じ，それを厳しく励行したため，庶民の反感を買い，「犬公方(いぬくぼう)」と言われた。

現代では，昭和初期の「*忠犬ハチ公」の話が有名である。ハチは毎日，主人を東京・渋谷駅に見送り，出迎える習慣があったが，主人の死んだ後10年間も駅で主人の帰りを待ったという。ハチは当時の小学校の教科書に取り上げられ，日本中の人気者になった。死後はく製にされて博物館に保存され，渋谷駅前には銅像がある。

かつて，自動車事故に遭った主人をかばって，左前足を切断した盲導犬に，人間並みの保険金が下りて話題をまいたことがあった。

［風習］ 日本では，欧米のようにしつけを厳しくしない。また愛犬は死ぬまでかわいがるが，不要な犬は簡単に捨てる風習がある。

日本では犬に「太郎」「ジョン」といった人名や，「クロ」「ポチ」といった犬専用の愛称をつける。犬の鳴き声は「ワン，ワン」。

猫

［イメージ］ 猫のイメージは悪く，「猫を殺せば七代たたる」とか「化け猫」などと言う。日本には魔女の手先という迷信はない。

日本で猫といえば，*夏目漱石の猫を主人公にした小説『吾輩(わがはい)は猫である』を思い出す人が多い。

［風習］ 昔から猫が飼われたのは，ネズミを退治してもらうため。

飲食店など客商売の家で「*招き猫」という置き物を飾る。後足で身を立て，一方の前足を挙げて人を招いている猫の像で，顧客，財宝を招く縁起物とされている。

［表現］ 仲が悪いのは，欧米では猫と犬だが，日本では猿と犬で，「犬猿の仲」と言う。猫の好物は，英米ではミルク，日本ではかつおぶしである。そこから「猫にかつおぶし」という表現が生まれた。猫の鳴き声は「ニャン，ニャン」「ニャー，ニャー」。

Dogs and Cats

Dogs

Derogatory phrases referring to dogs are common in Japan as they are in the West. Thus to die like a dog is to die meaninglessly, and to call someone a dog is to accuse him/her of being a spy or dupe.

Dogs are believed to have been domesticated in Japan as early as the *Joumon* period. White dogs, thought to be especially auspicious, often appear in such folk tales as *Momotarou* and *Hanasaka Jijii*.

Tokugawa Tsunayoshi, the fifth *Tokugawa shougun* and an ardent Buddhist, ordered the protection of all animals, especially dogs. So extreme were his regulations concerning dogs that he was ridiculed by the common people as the Dog *Shougun*. A more recent story is the 1920's tale of the faithful dog, *Hachikou** who met his master at *Toukyou*'s(Tokyo's) *Shibuya* station at the end of every workday. Even after his master died one day at work, *Hachikou* continued to wait at the station for 10 years. *Hachikou*'s story was in elementary school texts and he became a popular symbol of devotion. After his death, *Hachikou*'s body was put in a museum, and there is a bronze statue of him in front of *Shibuya* station. Many years ago, the story of a seeing-eye dog who protected his master in a car accident caused quite a stir, both for the dog's bravery and because the dog was covered by as much insurance as a human.

Dogs are not usually trained as rigorously in Japan as they are in the West. While pets are generally well taken care of, unwanted dogs are often abandoned. Dogs may be given such human names as *Tarou* and John or such strictly dog names as *Kuro* and *Pochi*. The onomatopoeia for a dog's bark is *wan-wan*.

Cats

Cats do not have a very savory reputation in Japan, as evidenced by the saying "Kill a cat and you will be cursed for seven generations" and the many tales about *bake-neko* or monster cats, but there are no superstitions such as those of the West which portray the cat as the minion of witches. Perhaps the most famous cat in Japan is the hero of *Natsume Souseki*'s* *I Am a Cat*.

Traditionally, cats were kept to kill rats. In restaurants and other businesses in which customer turnover is important, it is customary to display a figure of a *maneki-neko** or beckoning cat. Sitting upright with one paw raised in a beckoning motion, the *maneki-neko* is thought to invite customers and riches.

In the West, animosity between cats and dogs is assumed, but in Japan this animosity is thought to exist between dogs and monkeys, such that two people who cannot get along are said have a dog-and-monkey relationship, *ken'en no naka*. In Japan a cat's favorite dish is *katsuo-bushi* (dried bonito flakes) rather than cream or milk, and the expression *neko ni katsuo-bushi* is a warning not to put temptation in people's way. A cat's meow in Japanese is *nyan-nyan* or *nyaa-nyaa*.

馬

［イメージ］ 昔，馬は神霊の乗り物として神聖視された。「神馬(しんめ)」として神社に奉納されたり，白馬，葦毛馬(あしげ)は神の召すものとして，常人が乗ることを禁じられたりしたこともある。

その一方で，馬は「馬鹿(ばか)」と書くように，頭が悪いと考えられていたらしい。「馬の耳に念仏」とか「馬耳東風」という表現は，いくら言ってもなんの反応もないことだし，「どこの馬の骨かわからない」と言えば，素性のわからない人を軽べつした言い方である。

馬を精力的と見るのは欧米と同じである。「馬力(ばりき)」と言えば，英語のhorsepowerのほかに，活力，体力を意味する。

［伝説］ 神が馬に乗って来臨した跡とか，英雄が乗っていた愛馬の足跡と称する「馬蹄石(ばていせき)」が各地に残っている。武将や貴人が馬をつないだという「駒(こま)つなぎ松」「駒つなぎ桜」も多い。

［表現］ 日本人は馬から長い顔を想像し，「馬面(うまづら)」というのは長い顔のたとえ。「馬が合う」は気が合うこと。馬の鳴き声は「ヒヒン」。

［利用］ 馬は昔から農耕・軍事・輸送用などに広く使われてきた。東日本に馬の産地が多い。

日本でも競馬(けいば)は人気があるが，欧米のように上流階級から下層階級までが熱狂するというようなことはない。

一部で馬肉を食べる習慣があり，肉が桜色なので「さくら肉」または「さくら」と言う。

牛

［イメージ］ 牛には遅鈍，忍耐のイメージがある。しかし，イギリスのジョン・ブルがもつ，男性的力強さと忍耐力のイメージとは異なる。

のろいものの代表とされ，遅いことを「牛の歩み」と言う。国会では「牛歩戦術」という投票の引き延ばし作戦がよく採られる。

［表現］ 牛がごろっと横になっているようすからの連想で，食後横になることを「牛になる」と言って嫌う。大いに飲んで食べるのは「牛飲馬食」である。牛の鳴き声は「モー」。

［利用］ 牛も昔から農耕・輸送用に使われてきた。日本人が牛乳を飲み，牛肉を食べるようになったのは明治中期以降で，牛肉を使った独特の料理にすきやき，*しゃぶしゃぶ，*牛丼(ぎゅうどん)がある。

Horses and Cows

Horses

The horse has traditionally been treated as a sacred creature and *shinme* or divine horses were once commonly kept at *Shintou* shrines. Also in the past, commoners were forbidden to ride white or dappled horses, considered to be servants of the gods. Still, the horse is thought of as a rather stupid creature as epitomized in the word *baka*, written with the characters for horse and deer, and such expressions as *uma no mimi ni nenbutsu* (prayers to a horse's ears) and *baji toufuu* (the east wind in a horse's ear) referring to someone who never listens. Another expression, *doko no uma no hone ka wakaranai*, is used to describe a person of questionable character, someone whose antecedents are completely unknown. The horse is a symbol of power in Japan as in the West. *Bariki* is like its literal translation "horsepower" but also has connotations of vitality and stamina.

There are many legends of gods descending to earth on horses and of heroes and their steeds. Rocks called *batei-seki*, thought to be the hoofprints of these horses, are to be found throughout Japan. Pine trees and cherry trees to which famous warriors and nobility are believed to have tied their horses also abound.

A person with a long face is described as *uma-zura* or horsefaced. To get along well with someone is expressed as *uma ga au*. A horse's neigh in Japanese is *hihin*.

Horses have traditionally been employed in agriculture and transport and as military steeds. Horse breeding and raising is most prevalent in eastern Japan today, but racing, although popular, does not have the wide appeal it does in the United Sates and Europe. Some Japanese eat horse meat, and it is often referred to by the euphemism *sakura-niku* or simply *sakura* because of its pink, cherry blossom color.

Cows

The cow has a plodding persevering image and, unlike John Bull's masculinity and fortitude, is often used to represent dullards and slowpokes. To walk like a cow, *ushi no ayumi*, is to be extremely slow. In the Diet, opposition legislators sometimes try to delay passage of controversial legislation by walking to the ballot box at a snail's pace in what is called *gyuuho-senjutsu* or "cow-walk tactics."

A person who lies down immediately after eating is warned that s/he will turn into a cow—a reference to the ungainly sight of a reclining cow. To eat and drink in excess is called *gyuuin bashoku* (drinking like a cow and eating like a horse). A cow's mooing sound in Japanese is pronounced like "mow."

As with horses, cows have been traditional beasts of burden for transport and agriculture. Japanese did not drink milk or eat beef in appreciable amounts until the 20th century, but today there are many popular beef dishes including *sukiyaki, shabu-shabu*,* and *gyuudon*.*

タヌキ

［イメージ］ 日本人はタヌキに俳味と禅味と，特有の飄逸(ひょういつ)さを与えた。大きな腹を張り出し，小笠(こがさ)を首にかけ，酒どくりと通帳を下げた*信楽(しがらき)焼の像にそれがよく出ている。昔話の「かちかち山」では，タヌキは悪役だが，どこか間が抜け，憎めないところがある。

　昔からタヌキは化けて人をだますとされる。いろいろなものに化けるほか，音をまねるのが得意で，走る汽車やひづめの音などを出す。

［昔話・伝説］ 昔話や伝説には欠かせない動物。「文福茶がま」は命を助けられたタヌキが恩返しに茶がまに化けて福をもたらす話である。「*証城寺のたぬきばやし」は伝説に基づくよく知られた童謡。

［表現］ 「たぬきそば」は，天ぷらの揚げかすを入れたそば。「たぬきおやじ」は，ずるい，年取った男の人を言う。「たぬき寝入り」は，眠っているふりをすることで，タヌキを急に驚かすと仮死状態になることからきている。「たぬきばやし」は，タヌキの腹鼓による囃子(はやし)のこと。夜どこからともなく聞こえてくる祭ばやしを，タヌキが腹鼓を打っていると考えたことから。

キツネ

［イメージ］ キツネもタヌキ同様，化けて人をだますと考えられてきた。タヌキが「*大入道」や「高僧」など男に化けるのに対し，キツネは「女」に化ける。火と関係が深く，夜，山野に見える怪火を「きつね火」と言う。きつね火が連なって嫁入り行列のちょうちんのように見えるのが「きつねの嫁入り」である。「きつねの嫁入り」はまた，日が照っているのに雨が降ることも指す。

　性質は陰性でずる賢いとされる。この点は欧米と同じである。

［俗信］ キツネは稲荷(いなり)神社の神の使いとされ，一般に「いなり」と言うと，稲荷神社，キツネ，いなりずしなどを指す。

　ある種の精神錯乱の症状を「きつねつき」とする俗信がある。ついたキツネは，専門の祈禱(きとう)師に頼んで落としてもらう。

［昔話・伝説］ 女に化けて人間の男と結婚する「きつね女房」をはじめ，キツネも昔話・伝説によく登場する。

［表現］ 「きつねうどん」は，キツネの好物である油揚げを入れたうどん。「いなりずし」は，甘く煮た油揚げに酢飯を詰めたもの。

Tanuki and Kitsune

Tanuki

The *tanuki*, sometimes translated into English as raccoon dog, holds a special place in Japanese folklore. Both loved and feared, the *tanuki* is often depicted in ceramic statues* with a large protruding stomach, a small straw hat around its neck, a flagon of *sake* in one hand, and its account book strapped to its waist. In the folk tale *Kachikachi-yama* (*Kachikachi* Mountain), the *tanuki* is cast as the villain, but he is more often a playful villain with a certain innocence that makes him impossible to hate.

From ancient times, *tanuki* have been thought to have the power to trick people by changing their appearance. Not only could they change their appearance, they were also supposed to be very good at imitating sounds such as of a locomotive or hoofbeats.

The *tanuki* figures prominently in many legends and folk tales. *Bunbuku Chagama* (The Miraculous Tea Kettle) is the story of a *tanuki* who turned into a tea kettle and brought good fortune to someone who had saved its life. There is also a well-known children's song based upon the legend of *Shoujouji no Tanuki Bayashi** (The Song of the *Tanuki* of *Shoujouji* Temple).

Tanuki-soba is noodles with *tenpura* crumbs in the broth. A *tanuki oyaji* is a crafty old man. *Tanuki-neiri* is playing possum and comes from the *tanuki*'s habit, when surprised, of pretending to be dead or asleep. *Tanuki-bayashi* is the sound of drums heard distantly in the night and comes from the fact that the *tanuki* is supposed to enjoy beating his drum-like belly.

Kitsune

Like the *tanuki*, the *kitsune* or fox is thought to be able to change its appearance. While the *tanuki* usually changes into a man, be it a huge monster* or a great priest, the fox usually changes into a woman. This pattern of changing into a woman also shows up, for example, in *Kitsune Nyoubou* (Fox Wife), a tale of a fox who changed into a woman and married a man. Foxes are also associated with fire, and the distant fires sometimes seen at night are referred to as foxfire. Because it looks like a line of foxfire, having a long line of lanterns in a bridal procession is referred to as *kitsune no yomeiri* or the fox's bridal procession. The same term also refers to when it rains even though the sun is shining.

In both East and West, the fox is a crafty animal with a secretive personality.

In Japan, it is also the guardian deity of the *Inari* shrines, and hence *inari* can be used to refer to *inari-zushi*—rice stuffed deep-fried *toufu* (*abura-age*). People who are slightly deranged are thought to be possessed by a fox, and special priests might be employed to exorcise the fox.

The fox's fondness for *abura-age* also explains its use as a main ingredient in *kitsune-udon* noodles.

タイ

［イメージ］　タイは「めでたい」に通じるところから，縁起物とされ，結婚式をはじめとする祝儀の席に欠かせないものである。「腐ってもタイ」という表現は，もともと優れた価値のあるものは落ちぶれてもそれなりの価値があるという意味で，日本人のタイへの愛着ぶりをよく表している。

［伝説］　日本は古代からタイを食べてきたので，いろいろ伝説が残っている。タイの産地瀬戸内海には，その昔，*神功（じんぐう）皇后の船にタイが寄ってきたので，祝いの酒樽（さかだる）を投げ入れたところ，たくさんのタイが酒に酔って浮き上がってきたという伝説がある。今でもその場所では，毎年，春先にタイが浮くが，これは実は強い潮流でタイが浮袋の調節機能を失うためである。

［利用］　タイは数種類がよく知られているが，その中で最も珍重され，味がよいのはマダイである。瀬戸内海では，４～６月ごろ産卵のために外海から入ってきたマダイを桜ダイと言って賞味する。これは性ホルモンの関係で，体色が濃い赤色，つまり婚姻色を帯びるところから名づけられたものである。ただ，味は産卵期よりも，冬から早春にかけての旬（しゅん）のほうが勝る。刺し身，塩焼きその他，マダイの料理法は多い。タイの眼球はビタミンB_1に富むことで知られている。

コイ

［イメージ］　欧米では薄汚い魚，大食いで貪欲（どんよく），ばか者といった，あまりよくないイメージをもたれているが，日本と中国では，勇気・忍耐・努力の象徴であり，男子の意気を表す。コイは滝を上って竜になるという中国の伝説に由来する，「こいの滝登り」という表現は，立身出世を意味する。古くは中国の伝説に従って，魚の王とされたが，江戸時代以降はタイがコイに取って代わった。

［行事］　男の子がコイにあやかって立身出世するようにという願いから，５月５日の端午（たんご）の節句に，戸外に「こいのぼり」（紙または布でコイの形に作った吹き流し）を立てる風習がある。

［表現］　「まないたのこい」は，運命を他人に握られ，逃げ場のない状態を言う。

［利用］　日本のニシキゴイは，観賞用として世界的に有名。

Sea Bream and Carp

Sea Bream

Because the Japanese name for sea bream, *tai*, suggests the word *medetai* (auspicious), it is considered a celebratory food often gracing the table at weddings and other happy occasions. "Even a rotten *tai* is worthwhile," a saying to indicate that something of great value always retains some of its worth no matter how low it falls, expresses the high esteem the Japanese people have for the sea bream.

Sea bream figures prominently in Japanese legends. A tale from the Inland Sea area where sea bream abound tells how the legendary Empress *Jinguu** ordered a barrel of *sake* thrown overboard when a school of sea bream appeared by her ship. Made drunk by the *sake*, the sea bream floated to the surface ready for the taking. This tale is actually based on a natural phenomenon in which strong seasonal currents deprive the sea bream of its ability to regulate its depth with its swimming bladder, forcing it to the surface.

While a wide range of fish are called *tai*, the *madai* or sea bream is the most highly valued. In the Inland Sea, sea bream come in from the outer ocean to breed in the spring between April and June. These fish are called *sakura-dai* and are especially prized for their deep pink color resembling the color of cherry blossoms. The sea bream is considered to be most delicious in the cold winter months and the early spring. It is eaten in many ways, the most popular being as *sashimi*, or salted and grilled. The eyes of the sea bream are especially rich in vitamin B_1.

Carp

The carp tends to be considered a dirty, foolish glutton in the West. In Japan and China, however, the carp is a masculine symbol of valor, endurance, and tenacity. The carp's annual upstream fight to get to its spawning grounds—in Chinese legends its climb up waterfalls to turn into a dragon—symbolizes a male child's healthy and vigorous growth and acceptance into society. In keeping with Chinese tradition, the carp was long considered the king of fish in Japan, until it was usurped by the sea bream in the *Edo* period.

The *koi-nobori*, flying carp made of paper or cloth and attached to a tall flagpole, which are part of the May 5 Children's Day's ornamentation, symbolize every parent's wish that sons will grow to be strong and brave like the carp.

A carp on the chopping board, *manaita no koi*, refers to someone whose fate is in the hands of another and who has no way of escape.

The colorful *nishiki-goi* are ornamental carp bred over centuries, and Japanese *nishiki-goi* are today known the world over.

ツル

［イメージ］「つるは千年，かめは万年」と言われ，ツルは長寿でめでたい鳥とされている。そのため，「*折りづる」を糸でたくさんつないだ「千羽づる」を病気見舞いにもっていったりする。祝儀用の風呂敷などにもよくツルの文様が描かれている。

白い美しい姿から，ツルには清純なイメージもある。昔話の「鶴(つる)女房」には，清純な魂をもつツルの化身とそれを取り巻く醜い人間の世界とが対照的に描かれている。また，権威者，優れた者のイメージもあり，「つるの一声」は，権威者，有力者などが多くの人の意見や議論を押さえつける一声を指す。「はきだめにつる」は，つまらない所に不似合いに優れたものが入ってくることのたとえである。

［伝説］ツルは小枝や羽をくわえて運ぶ習性があるので，ツルが稲穂を運んできて稲作が始まったとする，「穂落とし伝説」がある。豊臣秀吉が糸の間にツルの羽を織り込んで，「つる毛の陣羽織」を作ったという話もある。

［種類］日本ではタンチョウ・ナベヅル・マナヅルが見られる。山口県ではナベヅルが県の鳥，北海道ではタンチョウが道の鳥になっている。

カラス

［イメージ］カラスのイメージは悪い。黒い姿，雑食性，耳ざわりな鳴き声などから，昔から不吉なことの象徴とされている。この点は，洋の東西を問わず同じである。

［俗信・信仰］カラスの異常な鳴き方を死の前兆としたり，ふんがかかるのを凶兆とする人は，今でもいる。

カラスを神のお使いとする神社は全国各地にあり，「からす祭り」が行われる。カラスに食物を与え，その食べ方で神意を占ったり，農作の豊凶を占ったりもする。

［表現］黒いもののたとえに用い，「髪はからすの濡(ぬ)れ羽色」のように言う。「からすの行水」は，カラスが水浴びするときのように，入浴時間の短いことのたとえ。「からすの雌雄」は，カラスは雌，雄ともに黒くて区別しにくいので，二つのものがよく似ていて区別しにくいことを言う。カラスの鳴き声は「カーカー」。

［種類］ハシボソガラスとハシブトガラスの2種が普通。

Cranes and Crows

Cranes

As in the old saying that a crane lives for 1,000 years and a tortoise 10,000, the crane is a symbol of longevity. Drawing upon this, *origami* paper cranes* are often strung in strings of 1,000 and presented to patients recovering from an accident or illness. The crane is also a common motif on *furoshiki* used at weddings and other auspicious occasions.

Because of its beautiful white form, the crane is also symbolic of purity. The folk tale of *Tsuru Nyoubou* (Crane Wife), for example, is a story of the conflict between the pure-hearted crane and the despicable world of man. The crane also carries connotations of authority and excellence, and the term *tsuru no hitokoe* refers to the way a word from a person of authority or learning can overcome the objections of the masses. *Hakidame ni tsuru* (lit. crane in the trash) refers to a person of quality who is unaccountably in a lowly state.

Because the crane often flies with a twig or feather in its beak, legend has it that the crane brought the first ear of rice to begin Japan's tradition of rice cultivation. Another story tells how *Toyotomi Hideyoshi* wove crane feathers into a fabric to create a great coat.

The three most common cranes in Japan are the Japanese crane (*Hokkaidou*'s prefectural bird), hooded crane (*Yamaguchi*'s prefectural bird), and white-naped crane.

Crows

Crows have an unsavory reputation. Garbed in black, these scavengers with their ear-grating caw have traditionally been seen as harbingers of ill fortune in Japan as in the West.

An abnormal cawing of crows is said to portend a death, and many people believe even today that getting hit with crow droppings brands a person as marked for disaster.

Yet there are also numerous shrines which celebrate the crow as messenger of the gods and hold Crow Festivals. Fortune-tellers in some areas claim to be able to tell if the harvest will be good or poor by the way a crow eats its prey.

The crow is symbolic of blackness, as in the expression that someone's hair is as black as crow's feathers slick with water. *Karasu no gyouzui* (a crow's dip) refers to a very quick bath. Finally, since both male and female crows are black and it is very difficult for non-crows to tell them apart, *karasu no shi-yuu* (crow male and female) is equivalent to the English six of one, half a dozen of the other to describe two things that are virtually indistinguishable. A crow's caw is *kaa-kaa* in Japanese.

The two most common species of crow in Japan are the carrion crow and the jungle crow.

6 松

[イメージ]　松は常緑樹で，樹齢が長く，巨木となるところから，長寿や節操を表すめでたい木とされる。正月や祝いの席に松の生け花や*盆栽を飾るのはこのためである。めでたく縁起のよいものなので，松は*家紋にも選ばれ，その種類が100以上もある。

[由来]　「神が天降(あまくだ)るのを待つ」とする語源説があるように，松は古くから神木とされてきた。正月に立てる門松も神を招き寄せるというのが起源である。

[故事・伝説]　全国各地に，文学作品，伝説，神社仏閣の縁起，有名な武将・高僧の故事や伝説と結びついた老樹・名木が1500以上もあり，*天然記念物に指定されているものもある。『万葉集』には松に関する歌が約80種，能にも「高砂(たかさご)」「老松」など松にちなんだ名作がある。「高砂」は祝いの席で今でも謡われる。

[表現]　「松の内」は，正月の松飾りのある間のことを言い，現在は1月7日までである。

[利用]　松は日本の山野のいたるところに自生し，観賞・実用の両面で日本人の生活と切っても切れないものとなっている。岩手・群馬・福井・岡山・山口・島根・愛媛(えひめ)・沖縄の各県が県の木に指定しているのを見てもそれはわかる。日本に自生するのは，クロマツ・アカマツ・ゴヨウマツなど7種。植林・庭園樹・盆栽のほか，材は土木・建築・器具・パルプ用として広く用いられる。

日本の風景に松は欠かせない。白砂青松の舞子の浜(兵庫県)，羽衣伝説の三保の松原(静岡県)，虹(にじ)の松原(佐賀県)の三大松原をはじめ，松の名所・歌枕(うたまくら)は多い。ただ最近は開発や松食い虫の被害によって，昔の面影をとどめている所が少なくなった。

「松竹梅」はめでたいものとして，正月や慶事に生け花や盆栽として飾る。起源は中国で，中国では寒さに耐えて美しい姿を見せるところから画題とされていたのが，日本へ来てめでたいものとなった。飲食店などで料理の品質，価格を示すとき，上・中・下としないで松・竹・梅とする習慣がある。露骨さを避けるためであろう。

[マツタケ]　マツタケは，秋にアカマツ林に自生する。日本人は昔からこの芳香をもったキノコを好み，マツタケ狩りなどをして楽しんできたが，最近はあまりとれなくなり，きわめて高価なものとなった。

Pine Trees

Because pines are majestic evergreens that grow into towering trees, they are taken as symbolic of longevity and steadfastness. Pine decorations or *bonsai** are set out at New Year's and on other auspicious occasions. Thought to portend good things, the pine has been incorporated in over 100 family heraldic designs.*

As seen in the theory that says the pine stand "pining" for the day the gods descend to earth, the pine has long been accorded a certain reverence. Even the *kadomatsu* set out at New Year's are there to invite the gods in.

Pine trees abound throughout Japan as venerated figures in literature, historical legends, founding fables for shrines and temples, and other folklore, and there are over 1,500 famous old trees throughout Japan, some of which have been designated for protection as natural monuments.* There are about 80 poems about pine trees in the *Man'youshuu*, and many of the famous *nou* (noh) plays have pine themes, including *Takasago* (performed even today on festive occasions) and *Oimatsu* (Ancient Pine).

The term *matsu no uchi* refers to the time the New Year's *kadomatsu* decorations are left out, today until January 7.

Indigenous to Japan's hills and plains, pine trees have long been valued for both scenic and practical purposes. The pine has been designated the official prefectural tree by *Iwate*, *Gunma*, *Fukui*, *Okayama*, *Yamaguchi*, *Shimane*, *Ehime*, and *Okinawa*. There are seven species native to Japan, including the *Kuromatsu* black pine, *akamatsu* red pine, and *goyoumatsu* five-needled pine. In addition to being used for decorative purposes, in gardens, and in *bonsai*, pine are favored for construction material, furniture, pulp, and other industrial uses.

Pine is an essential part of any Japanese landscape, and there are many famous trees including those along white-sanded *Maiko* Beach (*Hyougo* Pref), *Hagoromo*'s pined plain at *Miho (Shizuoka* Pref), and *Niji no Matsubara (Saga* Pref). However, even these scenic sites are losing their splendor to the encroachments of development and the pine weevil.

The *shou-chiku-bai* (pine, bamboo, plum) combination signifies good fortune and is used in flower arrangements or *bonsai* on festive occasions. Originating in China as a trio able to withstand the cold and still appear beautiful, this combination took on connotations of good fortune when transplanted to Japan. Very often this same threesome is used in restaurants as names for the three levels of quality (and price) of its offerings.

Matsutake is a mushroom that grows naturally near red pine in the fall and is savored for its fragrant odor. People used to go *matsutake*-gathering, but it has become scarce in recent years and turned into an expensive gourmet item.

[イメージ]　竹は強い萌芽力，まっすぐにすくすく伸びる生長力，常緑のすがすがしい姿，地下茎の豊かな広がり，などから繁栄の象徴とされる。竹はまた神霊を招くとされ，正月の門松に添える。

中国では竹を，梅・ラン・菊とともに四君子と言い，君子のように節操の正しい植物とみなしている。さっぱりした性格を「竹を割ったような」と言うように，竹は淡白さ，純粋さをも表す。

[伝説・昔話]　竹にちなむ伝説は中国，日本ともに多い。「竹林の七賢」は，中国の西晋時代に，世俗を避けて竹林にこもり清談に時を費やした7人を言う。昔話では日本の『竹取物語』(9世紀ごろ)が有名。竹から生まれたかぐや姫が，5人の貴族と帝の求婚を退け，8月15日の満月の夜に月の世界に帰っていくという物語。最古の仮名による物語文学である。

[行事]　年中行事にも魔よけとして竹，笹が取り入れられている。関西では1月10日の*初えびすに，商売の神恵比寿さまに参って商売繁盛を祈り，笹に札・大判・小判・*俵・*槌などを結び付けた縁起物の「福笹」を買う。6月20日，京都の北郊鞍馬寺では，大蛇を退治した故事にちなみ，雄蛇になぞらえた青竹を切る竹切式を行う。7月7日の七夕には，笹竹に5色の短冊に願いごとなどを書いて飾る。

[表現]　「竹に木を接ぐ」は不調和なことをするたとえ。「破竹の勢い」は，竹を割るときのように，とどまることを知らない猛烈な勢いのこと。「やぶ医者」は下手な医者のこと。竹やぶの葉は少しの風でもザワザワするところから，ちょっとした風邪でも大騒ぎをする医者という意味だが，真偽のほどはわからない。「やぶ蛇」は，やぶをつついて蛇を出す，つまりしなくてもよいことをして，自分の不利を招くたとえ。

[利用]　日本の温暖多湿の気候が適しているため，日本の竹は美しく，日本画の重要な題材となっている。「竹にすずめ」，「竹にとら」は図柄の組み合わせの妙を言う。

竹は日常生活の中でも重要で，植栽用のほか，建築や生活調度品の材料になる。*尺八，*能管も竹が材料である。地震のとき竹やぶへ逃げると安全と言う。竹やぶは地下茎が網のように広がり，ちょうどハンモックに乗ったような状態になるからである。

Bamboo

Bamboo is a very strong plant that grows very straight, very tall, and very quickly. With a sturdy root structure, it is symbolic of prosperity. Bamboo is also used in the New Year's *kadomatsu* decorations for its attraction to the gods.

In China, bamboo is grouped with *ume*, orchid, and chrysanthemum as one of the four gentlemanly plants because it is supposed to be as straight-arrow as a true gentleman. Simple and unadorned, the bamboo is symbolic of purity and innocence, as in the adjectival phrase "*take o watta you na*" (like fresh-split bamboo).

Bamboo figures in many ancient tales from both China and Japan. *Chikurin no Shichi-ken* (Seven Sages of the Bamboo Grove), for instance, is a Chinese tale of seven scholars who fled the vulgar life of the Western Chin dynasty and lived pure lives in a bamboo grove. Among the best-known Japanese tales is *Taketori Monogatari* about a beautiful maiden who was born of bamboo and, rejecting numerous suitors, ascended to the heavens on a moon-lit night in mid-August. This is, in fact, the oldest known narrative literature in *kana* script.

Bamboo and bamboo-like *sasa* are used in many festivals to ward off evil. In the *Kansai* area, for example, merchants pray to the god of commerce (*Ebisu*) and purchase lucky *sasa* branches decorated with replicas of coins, straw rice bundles,* and mallets* at *Hatsu Ebisu** on January 10. On June 20, the festival at *Kyouto*'s(Kyoto's) *Kuramadera* Temple, celebrating the death of the great serpent, features the cutting of green bamboo symbolizing the serpent. *Tanabatu*, on July 7, includes writing one's aspirations on five-color paper streamers and hanging them on bamboo branches for the gods to see.

Putting bamboo and wood together is synonymous with disharmony *Hachiku no ikioi* indicates the powerful momentum needed to break bamboo. *Yabu-isha* refers to a quack doctor, perhaps because, just as leaves in a bamboo grove (*yabu*) rustle in the slightest breeze. an incompetent doctor makes a great to-do about even the slightest ailment. Finally, *yabu-hebi* comes from the likelihood that poking a clump of bamboo may well flush a snake. It is reaping ill fortune from an unnecessary act, a little like not letting sleeping dogs lie.

Because Japan's warm, humid climate is well-suited to bamboo cultivation, bamboo is very pretty and is a popular motif in traditional Japanese paintings of sparrows or tigers in bamboo groves. Bamboo is also an integral part of Japanese life, as a decorative plant, building material, and numerous kinds of utensils for daily use. Many wind instruments* are also made of bamboo. For years, people were told to run into the bamboo groves in the event of an earthquake because the bamboo's strong root structure would hold the earth together.

[イメージ]　桜は日本の国花である。日本人にとって，桜は花の中の花であり，「花」と言えば桜を考える。欧米人のように，桜からサクランボのなる桜の木を思い浮かべるようなことはない。

一般に桜はめでたいものとされる。桜の咲く4月に入学し，入社する習慣のある日本では，希望に満ちた第一歩，明るい未来といったイメージが桜と強く結び付いている。また花びらの塩漬けに熱湯を注いだ桜湯は，めでたいものとして結婚式など祝いの席に出される。

めでたさとは逆に，日本人は桜の花に滅亡，死も見る。昔の武士や第二次世界大戦以前の軍人は，戦場で桜のように潔（いさぎよ）く散るのを本領としたし，歌舞伎で桜の出る場面は怪異が跳梁（ちょうりょう）し，悲運が起こることが多い。「桜は七日」という言い方があるように，花の盛りがきわめて短く，一夜の風に誘われて散ってしまうから，桜に潔さ，はかなさを感じたためであろう。

[名歌]　梅の奈良時代を経て，国風文化の隆盛とともに，平安時代には桜が最も愛好されるようになる。『古今和歌集』にも桜の歌が断然多い。以来1000年有余，その伝統は続き，桜を取り入れた文学作品や故事・伝説は枚挙にいとまがない。

日本人の心情をよくとらえた名歌2首を挙げる。

▷願はくは花の下にて春死なむそのきさらぎのもちづきのころ

平安時代末期から鎌倉時代初期に活躍し，桜の詩人と言われた西行（さいぎょう）の歌の一つ。彼は歌のとおり2月に死に，希望に従って桜のある塚に眠っている。西行の歌で構成した夢幻能「西行桜」がある。

▷敷島の大和（やまと）心を人問はば朝日ににほふ山桜花

江戸時代中期の国学者本居宣長の作。清楚な山桜を大和心の表象と見た名歌である。

[表現]　「花より団子」は，風流より実利を取ること。「さくら」は売り手となれ合いで買ってみせ，他の客の購買心をあおる者を言う。元は芝居の無料の見物人を言い，桜の花見が無料でできることからきている。「花にあらし」は，好事には障害の多いことのたとえ。

[種類]　現在多く見られるのは美しい園芸種で，明治初年から広まったソメイヨシノである。それ以前に日本に自生し，ひかえ目な花をつけるヤマザクラに取ってかわった。日本では，花見の時期になると，天気予報といっしょに桜前線（ソメイヨシノの開花前線）の北上予想が発表される。

Sakura

The cherry blossom is Japan's national flower—the flower of flowers, the first flower that comes to mind. Japanese love the cherry tree, not for its juicy red fruit, but for its delicate pink blossoms.

The cherry blossom is a felicitous symbol. For children just starting school and graduates starting new jobs alike, April's cherry blossoms suggest a bright future. *Sakura-yu*, a tea-like drink of salted cherry petals, is served at weddings and other auspicious times.

Yet there is also a dark side. For *samurai* of old, there was no greater glory than to die on the battlefield like scattered cherry blossoms. In *kabuki* dramas, cherry blossoms often portend a villain's rampage or imminent disaster. Resplendent in full bloom, cherry blossoms seldom last more than a week, and they are easily swept away with one strong wind, a fleeting beauty that suggests purity and transience.

Plum (*ume*) blossoms were favored in the *Nara* period, but gave way to the cherry with the emergence of *Heian* culture. *Kokin Wakashuu* (Collection of Ancient and Modern Poetry) has numerous poems on cherry blossoms, a tradition which has continued for over 1,000 years. There seems no end to cherry blossom literature and legends.

Two poems capture the Japanese fondness for the cherry blossom.

Ne-ga-wa-ku wa	I would die in the spring,
ha-na no shi-ta ni te	under the blossoms,
ha-ru shi-na-mu	in the second month
so-no ki-sa-ra-gi no	at the time of
mo-chi-zu-ki no ko-ro	the full moon.

Written by *Saigyou*, a poet of the late *Heian* and early *Kamakura* period noted for his verses on cherry blossoms, these lines proved prophetic, for *Saigyou* did indeed die in the second month of the lunar calendar and cherry trees shade his grave. *Saigyou Zakura* is a *nou* (noh) performance based on *Saigyou*'s poetry.

The second is by *Motoori Norinaga*, a mid-*Edo* Japanese scholar.

Shi-ki-shi-ma no	If one should ask,
Ya-ma-to-go-ko-ro o	what is the spirit of Japan—
hi-to to-wa ba	Shining in the morning sun,
a-sa-hi ni ni-o-u	these blossoms of the
ya-ma-za-ku-ra ba-na	mountain cherry.

The phrase *hana yori dango* (dumplings over flowers) refers to a preference for tangible goods rather than elegance. A *sakura* is a shill who raves about his mock purchase. Originally referring to people who were admitted to plays free, the term arose because cherry blossoms are free for the viewing. *Hana ni arashi* (flowers before the storm) suggests the bad likely to follow good fortune.

Most cherry trees today are a lovely cultivated variety (*somei-yoshino*), which supplanted the naturally growing but less spectacular mountain cherry in the early *Meiji* period. Spring weather forecasts include reports on the "*sakura* front" as the blossoms sweep north.

梅

[イメージ] 梅は清楚(せいそ), 清雅, 気品, 忍耐などのイメージをもつ。早春, 百花にさきがけ, 高い香気を放って咲く梅の花の愛好者は多い。

[故事・伝説] 梅は奈良時代に中国から渡来した。当時は万事が中国風であったから, 中国に倣(なら)って梅が好まれ, 『万葉集』では萩(はぎ)に次いで118首が詠まれている(桜は第5位で40首)。

平安時代, *菅原道真が九州の*大宰府(だざいふ)に流されるとき, 「東風(こち)吹かば匂(にほ)ひおこせよ梅の花あるじなしとて春な忘れそ」と自邸の庭で梅の木に詠みかけた別離の歌は有名。これがもとで, その梅の枝が大宰府まで飛んで行って根づいたという飛び梅伝説が生まれた。

[表現] 「梅にウグイス」は取り合わせのよいこと。「梅に桜」は美しい物やよい物が並んでいることのたとえ。

[利用] 花は白色, 淡紅色, 紅色など。花木用は庭木, 盆栽として観賞する。各地に名木があり, 天然記念物に指定されたものもある。果樹用は6月ごろ熟した果実を*梅干し・梅酒・梅酢などにする。

水戸の偕楽園(かいらくえん), 九州の太宰府天満宮など梅の名所が各地にある。茨城(いばらき)・福岡・大分県では郷土の花, 茨城・大分では県の木になっている。

桃

[イメージ] 『古事記』に, 桃を投げて神の窮地を救ったという神話があるように, 悪魔を払う魔よけの木とされる。桃は中国原産で, 中国でも, 古来, 邪気を払う仙果とされ, 桃源郷を彩る花であった。

[故事] 平安時代, 清少納言は紅梅を花木の第一としたのに対し, 紫式部は近くで眺める桃が勝るとした。

[風習] 3月3日のひな祭りは桃の節句と呼ばれ, ひな人形といっしょに桃の花を飾る。

[昔話] 桃は五大昔話の一つ「桃太郎」を連想させる。

[表現] 「桃栗3年柿8年」は芽ばえてから実がなるまでの年数を言う。桃は生長も早いが寿命も短い。

[利用] 桃は梅の後, 桜の前に, 淡紅色または白色の豪華な花をつける。観賞用のハナモモは採果用とは別品種。

Plum and Peach

Plum

The plum, *ume*, is neatness, purity, dignity, and patience. Blossoming in early spring, its sweet fragrance has won it many admirers.

Introduced from China in the *Nara* period when everything Chinese was in vogue, the plum figures in 118 *Man'youshuu* poems, second only to the Japanese bush clover (*hagi*) in popularity as a motif. (The cherry ranks fifth with only 40 poems.)

One of the most famous poems the *Heian* scholar-statesman *Sugawara no Michizane** wrote before being exiled to *Dazaifu** in *Kyuushuu* is a poignant ode to the plum in his *Kyouto* (Kyoto) garden. Legend has it that *Michizane*'s plum tree flew to *Dazaifu* and took root there in response to this poem:

Ko-chi fu-ka ba	When the east wind blows
ni-o-i o-ko-se-yo	release your fragrance,
u-me no ha-na	flower of the plum.
a-ru-ji na-shi to-te	Even without your master there
ha-ru na wa-su-re so	forget not the spring.

Ume ni uguisu (warbler in a plum) refers to a perfect match, and *ume ni sakura* (plum plus cherry) means a pairing of beautiful objects.

Blossoming white, pink, or red, plums are planted as ornamental trees and make exquisite *bonsai*. There are famous plum trees throughout Japan, some protected under the Cultural Properties Law. The plum is picked in June to be salted* or used for plum wine or vinegar.

Mito's *Kairakuen* Park and *Dazaifu*'s *Tenmanguu* Shrine are noted for their plum blossoms. The plum is the *Ibaraki* and *Ooita* prefectural flower and tree and the *Fukuoka* prefectural flower.

Peach

The peach is considered good for warding off evil. It is mentioned in the *Kojiki* (Record of Ancient Matters) as an instrument of salvation used to rescue a god from a predicament. In China, where it originated, the peach tree was believed to keep away ills of all kinds while its flowers were symbols of the earthly paradise of Shangri-La.

In the *Heian* period, *Sei Shounagon* declared the red plum supreme among all flowers while *Murasaki Shikibu* claimed the peach was best.

The *momo no sekku* on March 3 is also celebrated as the Doll Festival, and sprigs of peach blossoms are commonly displayed with the ornamental *hina-ningyou* dolls.

Momotarou, one of the best-known Japanese folk stories, is about a heroic youth born from a peach.

The peach grows quickly but has a short life span. Peach and chestnut trees are said to take three years to mature, and the persimmon eight.

White or pale pink, the peach blossoms after the plum and before the cherry. The ornamental peach is a different variety from the trees cultivated for their fruit.

［イメージ］ 幽霊は，うっとうしい雨の夜，草木も眠る丑(うし)三つ時(午前２時～２時半)に，川端や井戸の柳の下で，生前のままの姿で現れる。幽霊は怨恨(えんこん)によって出るのであるから，まず「恨めしや」と言う。それから，こまごまと恨みを述べていく。これが中世から近世にかけて，文学的，演劇的に手が加えられてでき上がった幽霊の型である。幽霊はふつう死霊(しりょう)（死者の霊)で，亡霊と言うこともある。

幽霊には足がないとされ，幽霊が出るとまず足の有無を見るというのが日本の常識(ただし，歌舞伎や能には足のある幽霊が出る)。また，幽霊の話は夏のものと考えられていて，夏になると歌舞伎・落語・テレビなどがいっせいに怪談の特集を組む。この風習はすでに江戸時代からあって，当時は明かりを一つずつ消しながら怪談を次々に話し合い，真っ暗になったとき幽霊が出るとした百物語の会が開かれた。

［妖怪(ようかい)との違い］ 幽霊が妖怪・お化けと異なる点は，現れる時と場所が一定しない，縁故ある人の前に生前の姿のままで出る，関係のある特定個人にしか認められない，など。

［怪談］ 『日本霊異記(りょういき)』（９世紀)や『今昔(こんじゃく)物語』（12世紀)のころから日本に怪談は多い。中でも知られるのは，怪異短編小説集の『雨月物語』(18世紀)である。これをもとにした映画「雨月物語」は，1953年のベニス映画祭でグランプリを受賞した。

「耳なし芳一(ほういち)」は，芳一という琵琶(びわ)法師が滅亡した*平氏一門の亡霊の前で琵琶を弾唱し，それを他言したため両耳をもぎとられる話。*小泉八雲が『怪談』(1904年)に書いて広く知られるようになった。

1825年に初演された歌舞伎『東海道四谷怪談』は通称『四谷怪談』として知られる。浪人民谷(たみや)伊右衛門が，女房のお岩を殺し後妻の縁で出世しようとするが，お岩の亡霊に悩まされるという筋。実説・風説を取り混ぜて四世鶴屋南北(つるやなんぼく)が作った，怪談物・生世話(きぜわ)物の傑作である。

落語の『怪談牡丹灯籠(ぼたんどうろう)』は，1861～64年に成立した人情話。艶麗(えんれい)な怪談話として有名である。中国の怪奇小説や実話を参考にして，落語家三遊亭円朝が作った。お露という娘が浪人萩原(はぎわら)新三郎を恋い慕って亡くなり，盆の13日の夜，女中お米が下げる*牡丹灯籠をもって，足のないとされている幽霊がカランコロンと*げたの音を響かせて新三郎を訪れるという設定で，複雑な話がからみ合い，結局悪人が滅び，善人が栄える話になっている。

Ghosts*

Japanese ghosts are said to appear on dreary, drizzly nights in the third hour of the cow (2:00-2:30 a.m.) when even the trees and grasses sleep. Most often materializing under willow trees beside rivers or wells, they are nearly always the spirits of people who have died unhappy deaths and bear grudges. A ghost's first words are "*urameshiya*" (a curse upon you) followed by a long recital of its grievances. This is the ghost depicted in the literature and drama of the middle ages and early modern Japanese history. Such specters are also called *shiryou* or *bourei*.

The Japanese ghost is distinguished by its lack of feet, something that is always checked for in confrontations with such spirits. (As exceptions, *kabuki* and *nou* (noh) ghosts are expected to have feet.) Ghosts are assumed to be summer creatures, and ghost stories are standard fare on summer *kabuki* drama, *rakugo* stories, and television programs. A popular pastime in the *Edo* period was to take turns telling ghost stories, blowing out a lamp with the end of each story until everything was plunged into darkness and all was right for the ghosts to appear.

Unlike *youkai* apparitions and *bakemono* goblins, ghosts can appear anywhere anytime, generally taking the same form as they had before dying, and can often be seen only by the people they are appearing to.

Ghost stories are to be found in such ancient compilations as the *Nihon Ryouiki* (9th century) and the *Konjaku Monogatari* (12th century). An especially well known compilation of short ghost stories is the *Ugetsu Monogatari* (18th century), and a film based on this work won the Grand Prix at the 1953 Venice Film Festival.

Miminashi Houichi (Earless *Houichi*) was popularized by Lafcadio Hearn* in his 1904 book *Kaidan*. In it, an itinerant *biwa* player, *Houichi*, chances upon the spirits of the *Taira** clan which had been wiped out by the rival *Minamoto* clan. He plays his *biwa* for them, but the spirits tear his ears off when he recounts his strange experience to others.

First performed in 1825, *Toukaidou Yotsuya Kaidan* (often called simply *Yotsuya Kaidan*) is the most famous *kabuki* ghost play. A masterless *samurai* kills his wife so that he may make a more advantageous match with another woman, but she comes back as a revengeful ghost to haunt him. A mixture of real and imaginary events, this play written by *Tsuruya Nanboku* IV is a good example of the realistic ghost story genre of *kabuki* drama.

*Botan-dourou** is a popular *rakugo* ghost story combining elements of Chinese ghost stories and true incidents. Written by the *rakugo* master *San'-yuutei Enchou* about a young maiden named *Otsuyu* and a masterless *samurai* named *Hagiwara Shinzaburou*, it has all of the trappings of the traditional story, including love, death, the clip-clopping of wooden *geta*,* and justice triumphant in the end.

鬼

［イメージ］ 人に似て，牛の角とトラのきばがあり，口は耳まで裂け，裸でトラの皮のふんどしを締めている。人を捕らえて食うと言われる。非情・怪力，勇猛の象徴である。風神・雷神など荒々しい神を鬼の姿で表す。

［行事］ 節分(立春の前日)の夕暮れ，悪鬼を払い，疫病を除くために，ヒイラギの枝にイワシの頭を刺したものを戸口に立て，いった大豆を，「福は内，鬼は外」と言いながらまく風習がある。

［伝説］ 平安時代，平城京の羅生門(らしょうもん)に住む鬼は，毛深くて爪(つめ)が長く，刀のような歯をもっていて，人を捕まえた。渡辺綱がその鬼の片腕を切り落としたという。また，丹波国大江山に住む酒呑童子(しゅてんどうじ)という鬼(盗賊)は，財をかすめ，婦女子を略奪するので，源頼光(よりみつ)やその四天王の渡辺綱・坂田金時たちによって退治された。この話は絵巻・御伽草子(おとぎぞうし)・草双紙(くさぞうし)・浄瑠璃(じょうるり)・歌舞伎などの題材となっている。

［昔話］ 昔話の「桃太郎」や「一寸法師」などに，鬼は重要な敵役として登場する。

［表現］ 「鬼に金棒」は，ますます強さが増すたとえ。「鬼のいぬ間に洗濯」は，怖い人の留守中に楽をすること。「鬼の首をとったよう」は，大成功を喜ぶようすの表現。

天狗(てんぐ)

［イメージ］ 天狗は深山に住み，神通力(りき)があって空中を自由に飛行できる。大天狗は赤顔で鼻が高く，羽(は)うちわを持つ。その部下に烏(からす)天狗，木葉(このは)天狗がいるとされる。

天狗は山伏が祭った山の神の像なので，山伏の姿をしている。

［世間話］ 天狗の思想は中国伝来。平安時代，天狗は流星やトビとみられ，人についたり，未来を予言した。鎌倉時代には天狗による「神隠し」(人が突然行方不明になること)が，しばしばあったという。 天狗のしわざとされる話は多い。「天狗倒し」は理由がないのに突然暴風のような激しい音がして物が倒れること。「天狗笑い」は深山で高笑いする声や多数の人の声が聞こえること。

［表現］ 「天狗になる」は，天狗のように鼻を高くすること，つまり自分について自慢することを言う。

Oni*

Resembling humans but having the horns of a cow and the fangs of a tiger, the *oni* has a mouth running from ear to ear and wears a tigerskin loincloth. *Oni* are said to eat people, and they represent ruthlessness, prodigious strength, and daring. Strong and virile gods, such as the gods of wind and thunder, are depicted as *oni*.

At *setsubun* (the day before the first day of spring on the lunar calendar), it is customary to tack a sardine head pierced with a holly branch over the door and scatter roasted soybeans from the entrance, chanting, "*Fuku wa uchi, oni wa soto*!"("In with good luck, out with demons!") to drive away evil spirits and disease.

There is an ancient tale from the *Heian* period about a hairy *oni* with long claws and saber-like teeth who lived in the capital city's *Rashoumon** gate and captured people passing through. The warrior *Watanabe no Tsuna* is said to have cut off one of this creature's arms. Another *oni*, a thief named *Shutendouji* who lived on Mt *Ooe* in *Tanba*, preyed upon women and young girls until he was captured by *Minamoto no Yorimitsu* and his warriors *Watanabe no Tsuna* and *Sakata no Kintoki*. This tale of daring has inspired many of the short stories of feudal Japan, the popular literature of the *Edo* period, the *joururi* puppet theater, and *kabuki*.

Folk tales in which *oni* appear include *Momotarou* (Peach Boy) and *Issun-boushi** (One Inch Boy).

Oni ni kanabou refers to making one invincible (by giving an *oni* an iron pike), while *oni no inu ma ni sentaku* expresses the relief one feels when someone one fears is away. To achieve a major success is likened to beheading an *oni* as in *oni no kubi o totta you*.

Tengu*

A mythical mountain creature, the *tengu* has supernatural powers that allow him to fly about. The *Oo-tengu* or Great *Tengu* has a red face and immensely long nose, and carries a feathered fan. Under him are *karasu tengu* (crow *tengu*) and *konoha tengu* (leaf *tengu*). *Tengu* are worshipped by *yamabushi*,* mountain ascetics, and are usually depicted wearing the *yamabushi*'s distinctive clothing.

The *tengu* idea is of Chinese origin, and in the *Heian* period falling stars and kites were thought to be *tengu* capable of possessing people's spirits and predicting the future. In the *Kamakura* period, sudden disappearances were attributed to kidnapping by *tengu*.

Many natural phenomena were thought to have been the doings of *tengu*. When an object falls over with a crash for no apparent reason, a *tengu* is said to have pushed it over. *Tengu warai* refers to distant sounds heard in the mountains of shrill laughter or of many people speaking.

To become a *tengu* is to grow a long nose, in other words to become conceited.

河童

［イメージ］ 河童は川や池，沼など淡水に生息する水陸両生の動物である。身長は1m内外，4，5歳の子供のようで，目が丸く，口がとがり，手足に水かきをもつ。肌は赤黒または青黒，全体がぬめぬめし，鱗甲（りんこう）がある。頭髪が少なく，中に皿が隠れ，その皿に水があれば活動力があると言われる。相撲が好きで人によく挑戦する。また，人や牛馬を水に引き込んで，肛門（こうもん）から肝をとる。

河童は人に害を与えるけれども，人に捕らえられてわび証文を書いた，秘伝の妙薬をくれた，田植えを手伝ってくれた，田の水を引いてくれた，といった話が各地に残されているように，どこか憎めない，愛嬌のある一面がある。よく漫画の題材にされるのはそのせいである。

［由来］ 妖怪は，神が落ちぶれたものと言われ，河童も水底に住む小童神が変化したものとされてきたが，最近では，妖怪と神とは別で，人々によって祭られる超自然が神，祭られない超自然が妖怪という説が出されている。

［伝説］ 河童の伝説は，北海道を除く全国に分布する。地方によって形態・習性が異なり，川太郎，ガタロなど異名も多い。

［表現］ すし屋でキュウリを「かっぱ」と言うのは，キュウリが河童の好物とされているから。キュウリを食べながら川を渡ると，河童に川に引き入れられると言われる。「おかっぱ」という髪型は，河童の髪型からきた。「河童の川流れ」は，達人でも時には失敗することのたとえ。「河童の屁」または「屁の河童」は，全く容易でなんでもないこと。

一つ目小僧

［イメージ］ 一つ目小僧は，その名のとおり目が一つの妖怪である。ふつう，口が耳まで裂け，人を脅かすとき舌を出す。一本足で飛び飛びに歩くとか，小僧でなく大入道であるとか，地方によって形態はさまざまである。

［由来］ 昔，神の名代（みょうだい）である神主を普通の人と区別するため，片目を傷つけた。その神主の霊が妖怪に落ちぶれたというのが従来の見方である。

［風習］ 関東地方では，旧暦の2月8日（事初め），12月8日（事納め）の夜に，一つ目が来るとされ，門口に目かごを掲げ，ヒイラギの枝を挿して，静かに家に引きこもる風習があった。長野県や奈良県でも，一つ目が出て人を食うとされている日があり，その日は山に入らなかった。

Kappa*

The *kappa* is a supernatural amphibious creature residing in rivers, lakes, and swamps. Around a meter tall, about the size of a four-or-five-year old child, the *kappa* has large round eyes, a protruding mouth, and webbed hands and feet. Its skin is either dark red or green, slimy, and covered with scales. The *kappa* has very little hair on the top of its head which is shaped like a saucer. As long as this saucer is full of water, the *kappa* retains its supernatural powers. A great *sumou* (sumo) lover, the *kappa* will often challenge people to wrestle with it. Another, more gruesome, favorite pastime is dragging people, horses, and cows into the water and pulling out their livers through the anus.

Although the *kappa* does harm people sometimes, there are many tales of contrite *kappa* asking forgiveness for their mischief, giving people magical potions, or helping with farm chores. Cartoons have contributed to the *kappa*'s lovable but mischievous image.

These spirits are said to be fallen water gods, but the trend recently has been to distinguish between gods (supernatural forces that are worshipped) and spirits (supernatural forces that are not worshipped).

Tales of *kappa* are to be found throughout Japan, except *Hokkaidou*. The *kappa*'s appearance and characteristics vary somewhat by region, and it has many other names such as *kawatarou* and *gataro*.

Cucumbers are called *kappa* in *sushi* shops because they are thought to be a *kappa* favorite. To cross a river while eating cucumbers is to tempt a *kappa* to pull you into the water. Bobbed hairstyles are called *okappa* because they resemble the *kappa*'s coiffure. The unexpected failure of someone who is expected to excel is said to be *kappa no kawa nagare* (a drowning *kappa*). *Kappa no he* and *he no kappa* (a *kappa*'s breaking wind) refers to something that is very easy to do—a breeze.

Hitotsume-kozou*

Characterized by its single eye, the *hitotsume-kozou* has a mouth that goes from ear to ear and sticks out its tongue to scare people. Some stories depict it hopping about on a single leg, while in others it takes the form of a giant ogre rather than a young boy.

The *hitotsume-kozou* are said to come from the ancient messengers of the gods, who were half-blinded to distinguish them from mere mortals.

In the *Kantou* region, *hitotsume* were thought to appear on the nights of the eighth days of the second and twelfth lunar months, the days marking the beginning and the end of the year. It was customary to remain indoors on these nights and to place openwork baskets pierced with holly branches against the entrance of the home to ward away the evil apparition. In *Nagano* and *Nara* prefectures there were certain days on which *hitotsume* were thought to eat people, and people did not venture into the mountains on these days.

Notes

■**1. Dogs and Cats**

Natsume Souseki (夏目漱石) (1867-1916) Novelist and English literature scholar. With *Mori Ougai* (1862-1922), one of Japan's most important modern writers. *Wagahai wa Neko de Aru*(I Am a Cat) was his first novel.

■**2. Horses and Cows**

shabu-shabu (しゃぶしゃぶ) A dish of thinly sliced meat dipped in boiling water and eaten with a sauce and various condiments.

gyuudon (牛丼) Slices of cooked beef and onion atop a bowl of rice.

△*Hachikou*

△*Manekineko*

△*Gyuudon*

△Ceramic *tanuki*

△*Oo-nyuudou* (huge monster)

■**3. *Tanuki* and *Kitsune***

ceramic statues (信楽焼の像) The most popular ceramic *tanuki* are those made in the town of *Shigaraki* in southern *Shiga* prefecture.

Shoujouji no Tanuki Bayashi (証城寺のたぬきばやし) A legend about many large and small *tanuki* who sing and beat their round bellies, frolicking in a *bon-odori*. These *tanuki* were alleged to appear in the yard of a temple in *Kisarazu* in *Chiba* prefecture on the night of the harvest moon.

■**4. Sea Bream and Carp**

Empress *Jinguu* (神功皇后) A legendary figure who appears in the *Kojiki* and the *Nihon Shoki*, consort of the Emperor *Chuai*. She is said to have mustered an army and sailed to conquer the kingdom of Silla on the Korean peninsula.

■**5. Cranes and Crows**

***origami* paper cranes** (折りづる) See picture.

■**6. Pine Trees**

△*Origami* paper cranes

△*Bonsai*

natural monuments (天然記念物)　Animals, plants, natural formations, and the regions in which they exist that have been designated as important natural monuments by the Minister of Education.

●**Some heraldic designs**

■**7. Bamboo**

mallets (槌)　By shaking one of these magical mallets and repeating the name of whatever one desires, one will be granted every wish.

Hatsu Ebisu (初えびす)　Festivals honoring the god *Ebisu* are held on January 10 and 20 and October 20 in many regions as well as on the twentieth day of the eleventh month by the lunar calendar. The first, held on January 10, is called *Hatsu Ebisu*.

wind instruments (尺八, 能管)　The five-hole *shakuhachi* is the more commonly played flute. The *noukan* has seven holes and is used in *nou* (noh) accompaniment.

△**Straw rice bundle**

△**Mallet**

■**9. Plum and Peach**

Sugawara no Michizane (菅原道真)(845-903)　A court official exiled to *Dazaifu* in *Kyuushuu*. A scholar and master calligrapher, *Sugawara* is celebrated today as *Tenjin-sama*, god of letters.

Dazaifu (大宰府)　A regional administrative post during the era of the *ritsuryou* government located in what is now *Fukuoka* prefecture.

salted (梅干し)　*Ume-boshi* are plums pickled in salt and purple perilla leaves and dried in the sun.

■**10. Ghosts**

Lafcadio Hearn (小泉八雲)(1850-1904)　Author and translator, Lafcadio Hearn was born in Greece, raised in Dublin, and arrived in Japan in 1890. He wrote many works introducing Japan to the world, among them *Glimpses of Unfamiliar Japan*(1894) and *Kokoro*(1896). He is known in Japan by his Japanese name, *Koizumi Yakumo*.

△***Ghost*** **(by *Maruyama Oukyo*, 18th century)**

△*Botan-dourou*

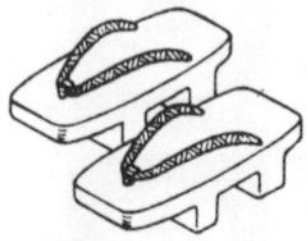

△*Geta*

Taira (平) Beginning with *Takamochiou*, the *Taira* clan dominated court politics near the end of the *Heian* period. The clan was annihilated in the Battle of *Dannoura*, fought against their arch-rival the *Minamoto* clan, only 20 years after they had first risen to power. The *Heike Monogatari* telling of the rise and fall of the *Taira* clan is colored by the Buddhist concept of transiency.

botan-dourou (牡丹灯籠) A lantern made of silk crepe with a *botan* (peony) motif.

■11. Monsters and Apparitions (1)

Issun-boushi (一寸法師) The story of a boy only one *sun* (approximately three centimeters) tall. With a needle as a sword and a bowl and chopstick as boat and oar, *Issun-boushi* makes his way to *Kyouto* (Kyoto) where he becomes a retainer to a princess. On his way to make an offering to *Kannon* for the princess, *Issun-boushi* is accosted by two *oni* whom he quickly defeats. He uses the *oni*'s magical mallet, called *uchide-no-kozuchi*, to make himself tall and becomes a brave warrior.

●Monsters and apparitions

△*Rashoumon*

△*Yamabushi*

APPENDIX & INDICES

Chronology of Japanese History
日本史年表

◇Cultural events
◆Political events

Period	Year	Events
Diluvial (洪積世)	BC 30,000	◇First human occupation of central Japan (exact date uncertain) ◇Old Stone Age; chipped stone tools; no pottery
Joumon (縄文時代)	10,000	◇New Stone Age; *Joumon* pottery; chipped and polished stone and bone tools 〈縄文文化時代〉
Yayoi (弥生時代)	c.200	◇Rice cultivation, bronze, and iron introduced from the continent 〈弥生文化時代〉 ◇*Yayoi* pottery is produced and metal and stone tools used 〈弥生土器〉
	AD 57	◆The local chieftain of "*Wa no Na*" is given a gold seal reading "*Kan no wa no na no kokuou*" after offering tribute to the emperor 〈倭の奴国王，後漢に入貢，「漢委奴国王」の金印を受ける〉
	239	◆*Himiko* of the *Yamatai* kingdom sends tribute to Wei 〈邪馬台国女王卑弥呼，魏に献使〉
Kofun (古墳時代)	AD c.300	◇Large tomb mounds built marking advent of the Tomb Culture 〈古墳文化の発生〉
	c.360	◆Most of Japan united under the *Yamato* court 〈大和朝廷全国統一〉 ◇Korean immigrants from the Paekche kingdom introduce continental culture to Japan 〈大陸文化伝来〉
	c.538	◇Buddhism introduced into Japan when the king of Paekche sends envoys with Buddhist images and sutras (one theory dates this 552) 〈仏教伝来〉
	593	◆Prince *Shoutoku* becomes regent for Empress *Suiko* 〈聖徳太子摂政〉
	603	◆12-cap rank system established within *Yamato* court 〈冠位十二階制定〉
	604	◆Seventeen-Article Constitution is drafted legitimizing centralized *Yamato* state and emperor's supreme authority 〈憲法十七条制定〉
	607	◆*Ono no Imoko* sent as court emissary to Sui China 〈遣隋使派遣〉 ◇*Houryuuji* constructed and *Asuka* culture flourishes 〈法隆寺建立・飛鳥文化〉
	630	◆*Inugami no Mitasuki* sent as imperial emissary to Tang court in China 〈遣唐使派遣〉
	645	◆*Taika* Reforms instituted after *Soga* family's dominance of imperial court ends with assassination of *Soga no Iruka* by Prince *Naka no Ooe* and others. Emperor *Koutoku* ascends the throne using the reign name of *Taika* 〈大化の改新〉
	672	◆*Jinshin no Ran* (civil war over succession) 〈壬申の乱〉
	701	◆*Taihou* Code of laws completed establishing a single code for the whole nation 〈大宝律令完成〉
	708	◇*Wadou Kaichin*, first Japanese coins, minted 〈和同開珎〉
	710	◆Capital moved to *Heijoukyou* (now *Nara*), city modeled on the Chinese capital of Chang-an 〈平城京遷都〉

Period	Year	Events
Nara (奈良時代)	712	◇ *Kojiki*, Japan's first official history, compiled by *Oo no Yasumaro* and *Hieda no Are* 〈『古事記』〉
	713	◇ Provincial governments ordered to compile regional records known as *fudoki* 〈『風土記』〉
	720	◇ *Nihon Shoki*, first of Six National Histories, compiled by Prince *Toneri* and *Oo no Yasumaro* 〈『日本書紀』〉
	751	◇ *Kaifuusou*, first anthology of Chinese poetry written by Japanese, is compiled 〈『懐風藻』〉
	752	◇ Ceremonies held at *Toudaiji* to commemorate completion of Great Buddha 〈東大寺大仏開眼供養〉
	754	◇ Chinese monk *Ganjin* introduces *Ritsu* Buddhism 〈律宗伝わる〉
	?	◇ *Man'youshuu*, first anthology of *waka* poetry and written with *man'you-gana*, compiled 〈『万葉集』〉
Heian (平安時代)	794	◆ Capital moved to *Heiankyou* (now *Kyouto*) to escape the dominance of *Nara*'s Buddhist temples and to right corruption in imperial court 〈平安京遷都〉
	805	◇ *Saichou* establishes *Tendai* sect of Buddhism 〈天台宗の開宗〉
	806	◇ *Kuukai* establishes *Shingon* sect of Buddhism 〈真言宗の開宗〉
	807	◇ *Inbe no Hironari* compiles the *Kogo Shuui*, a collection of myths and legends not found in the *Kojiki* or *Nihon Shoki* 〈『古語拾遺』〉
	c.822	◇ Buddhist monk *Kyoukai* writes *Nihon Ryouiki* (Miraculous Stories of Japan), the earliest Japanese example of Buddhist fables 〈『日本霊異記』〉
	884	◆ *Fujiwara no Mototsune* appointed *kanpaku*, thereby cementing *Fujiwara* control over imperial court 〈藤原基経関白〉
	894	◆ *Sugawara no Michizane* halts missions to Tang China 〈遣唐使中止〉
	901	◆ *Sugawara no Michizane* exiled to *Dazaifu* in *Kyuushuu* 〈菅原道真大宰府に左遷〉
	905	◇ *Kokin Wakashuu*, first imperial anthology of waka poetry, compiled by *Ki no Tsurayuki*, *Ki no Tomonori*, and others 〈『古今和歌集』〉
	c.935	◇ *Ki no Tsurayuki* writes *Tosa Nikki*, first diary written in *kana* 〈『土佐日記』〉
		◇ *Kuuya* promulgates Buddhist teachings of *Amida* Buddha and Pure Land paradise and recitation of *nenbutsu*, *Amida*'s name 〈空也念仏を広める〉
	c.974	◇ *Fujiwara no Michitsuna*'s mother writes *Kagerou Nikki* (The Gossamer Years), the first diary of literary consequence written by a woman 〈『蜻蛉日記』〉
	985	◇ *Genshin* (a.k.a. *Eshin Souzu*) writes *Oujouyoushuu* (Essentials of Pure Land Rebirth), a major influence on development of Pure Land Buddhism 〈『往生要集』〉
	c.1001	◇ *Sei Shounagon*'s *Makura no Soushi* (Pillow Book) written 〈『枕草子』〉
	c.1007	◇ *Izumi Shikibu*'s *Izumi Shikibu Nikki* written 〈『和泉式部日記』〉
	c.1010	◇ *Murasaki Shikibu*'s *Murasaki Shikibu Nikki* and *Genji Monogatari* (Tale of *Genji*) written 〈『紫式部日記』『源氏物語』〉

Period	Year	Events
Heian (平安時代)	1053	◇ *Byoudouin*'s Phoenix Hall constructed 〈平等院鳳凰堂建立〉
	c.1058	◇ *Sugawara no Takasue*'s daughter writes *Sarashina Nikki* 〈『更級日記』〉
	1086	◆ Emperor *Shirakawa* retires to become first of the cloistered emperors 〈白河上皇院政開始〉
	c.1101	◇ Historical narrative *Eiga Monogatari* (A tale of flowering Fortunes) written 〈『栄華物語』〉
	c.1107	◇ *Konjaku Monogatari* written 〈『今昔物語』〉
	c.1131	◇ *Oo Kagami* (The Great Mirror), first critical history, appears, followed by three more *kagami* texts, *Ima Kagami* (1170), *Mizu Kagami* (late 12th c), and *Masu Kagami* (c.1376) 〈『大鏡』『今鏡』『水鏡』『増鏡』〉
	1156	◆ *Hougen* Disturbance marks ascendency of warrior class 〈保元の乱〉
	1159	◆ *Heiji* Disturbance leads to rise of *Taira* clan 〈平治の乱〉
	1175	◇ *Hounen* founds *Joudo* sect of Buddhism, inaugurating new era in Japanese Buddhism 〈浄土宗の開宗〉
	1185	◆ *Taira* clan annihilated by *Minamoto* clan in Battle of *Dan no Ura* 〈平氏滅亡〉
	1191	◇ *Eisai* (a.k.a. *Yousai*) returns from China and promulgates *Rinzai* sect of *Zen* Buddhism 〈臨済宗広まる〉
Kamakura (鎌倉時代)	1192	◆ *Minamoto no Yoritomo* acquires the title of *shougun*, marking establishment of *Kamakura bakufu* government 〈源頼朝征夷大将軍〉
	1203	◆ *Houjou Tokimasa* becomes first regent of *Kamakura* shogunate, establishing *Houjou* clan's authority 〈北条時政執権〉
		◇ Buddhist sculptors *Unkei* and *Kaikei* complete statue of *Kongou Rikishi* for *Toudaiji's* south gate 〈東大寺南大門の金剛力士像〉
	1205	◇ *Shin Kokin Wakashuu* anthology of poetry compiled by *Fujiwara no Sadaie* and others 〈『新古今和歌集』〉
	1212	◇ *Kamo no Choumei* writes *Houjouki* (Ten-foot Square Hut) 〈『方丈記』〉
	1213	◇ *Shogun Minamoto no Sanetomo* compiles *Kinkai Wakashuu* poetry anthology 〈『金槐和歌集』〉
	c.1220	◇ Monk *Jien* writes his critical history *Gukanshou*, revising it after the *Joukyuu* Disturbance 〈『愚管抄』〉
	c.1221	◇ *Shinran* founds *Joudo Shinshuu* sect of Buddhism 〈浄土真宗の開宗〉
	1227	◇ *Dougen* returns from China and establishes *Soutou* sect of Buddhist teachings 〈曹洞宗の開宗〉
	?	◇ *Heike Monogatari* becomes one of most popular war tales 〈『平家物語』〉
	1253	◇ *Nichiren* promulgates *Nichiren* sect of Buddhism 〈日蓮宗広まる〉
	1274	◆ The first assault of the Mongolian force on northern *Kyuushuu* (*Bun'ei no Eki*) 〈文永の役〉
	1281	◆ Mongols attempt second invasion with force of 140,000 but fail (*Kouan no Eki*) 〈弘安の役〉
	c.1300	◇ *Azuma Kagami* written 〈『吾妻鏡』〉
	c.1330	◇ *Yoshida Kenkou* writes *Tsurezuregusa* 〈『徒然草』〉

Period	Year	Events
Muromachi (室町時代)	1333	◆ Fall of *Kamakura bakufu* 〈鎌倉幕府滅亡〉
	1336	◆ Conflict between the Northern and Southern Dynasties (unified in 1392) 〈南北朝の対立(〜1392合一)〉
	1338	◆ *Ashikaga Takauji* acquires the title of *shougun*, marking beginning of *Muromachi bakufu* 〈足利尊氏征夷大将軍〉
	1356	◇ *Nijou Yoshimoto* compiles *Tsukuba-shuu*, first collection of *renga* poetry 〈『菟玖波集』〉
	c.1370	◇ *Taiheiki* chronicle of northern and southern courts written 〈『太平記』〉
	1397	◇ *Ashikaga Yoshimitsu* builds *Kinkaku* at *Kitayama* in *Kyouto*, marking flowering of *Kitayama* culture 〈金閣，北山文化〉
	c.1400	◇ *Zeami* writes *Fuushi Kaden* (The Transmission of the Flower of Acting Style) 〈『花伝書』〉
	1401	◆ *Ashikaga Yoshimitsu* sends Japan's first emissary to Ming China 〈第1回遣明船派遣〉
	1467	◆ *Ounin* Civil War starting a long period of civil strife 〈応仁の乱・戦国時代始まる〉
	1489	◇ *Ashikaga Yoshimasa* builds *Ginkaku* at *Higashiyama* in *Kyouto*, marking flowering of *Higashiyama* culture 〈銀閣，東山文化〉
	1543	◇ Portuguese traders land at *Tanegashima*, introducing guns to Japan 〈鉄砲伝来〉
	1549	◇ Francisco Xavier arrives in *Kagoshima* as Christian missionary 〈キリスト教伝来〉
	1559	◆ *Oda Nobunaga*'s forces enter *Kyouto* 〈織田信長京都に入る〉
	1573	◆ *Oda Nobunaga* exiles *Ashikaga Yoshiaki*, 15th *Ashikaga shougun*, ending *Muromachi* period 〈室町幕府滅亡〉
Azuchi-Momoyama (安土・桃山時代)	1583	◇ *Toyotomi Hideyoshi* builds *Oosaka* Castle, symbolic of *Azuchi-Momoyama* culture 〈大坂城築城〉
	1590	◆ *Toyotomi Hideyoshi* succeeds in uniting country 〈豊臣秀吉全国統一〉
	1592	◆ *Hideyoshi* launches four-year attempt to invade Korean peninsula (*Bunroku no Eki*) 〈文禄の役〉
	1597	◆ *Hideyoshi* launches second attempt to invade Korean peninsula (*Keichou no Eki*) 〈慶長の役〉
	1600	◆ *Tokugawa Ieyasu* emerges victorious at *Sekigahara* 〈関ケ原の戦い〉
Edo (江戸時代)	1603	◆ *Tokugawa Ieyasu* acquires title of *shougun, officially* establishing *Edo bakufu* government 〈徳川家康征夷大将軍〉
	1612	◇ *Tokugawa Ieyasu* issues edict prohibiting Christianity 〈キリスト教禁止令〉
	c.1624	◇ *Katsura* Detached Palace, famous for its *shoin* style architecture and *kaiyuu* gardens, completed 〈桂離宮造営〉
	1635	◆ Codes of conduct are issued by *Tokugawa* shogunate to control *daimyou*, including *sankin-koutai* system requiring *daimyou* to spend alternate years in *Edo* and leave families as hostages when returning to their fiefs 〈参勤交代の法制化〉
	1637	◆ *Shimabara* Uprising 〈島原の乱〉
	1641	◆ Japan closed to foreign commerce 〈鎖国の完成〉
	1654	◇ Chinese monk *Ingen* promulgates *Oubaku* sect of *Zen* Buddhism 〈黄檗宗伝わる〉

Period	Year	Events
Edo (江戸時代)	1682	◇ *Ihara Saikaku* writes *Koushoku Ichidai Otoko* (The Life of an Amorous Man) 〈『好色一代男』〉
	c.1694	◇ *Haiku* poet *Matsuo Bashou* writes *Oku no Hosomichi* (The Narrow Road to the Deep North) 〈『奥の細道』〉
	1703	◇ *Chikamatsu Monzaemon*'s drama *Sonezaki Shinjuu* (The Love Suicides at *Sonezaki*) performed at *Takemoto-za joururi* puppet theater 〈『曽根崎心中』〉
	1776	◇ *Ueda Akinari* publishes *Ugetsu Monogatari* (Tales of Moon-light and Rain) series 〈『雨月物語』〉
	1798	◇ *Kokugaku* scholar *Motoori Norinaga* completes *Kojiki Den*, study of *Kojiki* 〈『古事記伝』〉
	1802	◇ *Jippensha Ikku* published first book in *Toukaidouchuu Hizakurige* (Shank's Mare) series 〈『東海道中膝栗毛』〉
	1814	◇ *Takizawa Bakin* began to publish 98 volumes of *Nansou Satomi Hakken-den* (*Satomi* and the Eight Dogs), and completed them in 1842 〈『南総里見八犬伝』〉
	1829	◇ *Katsushika Hokusai* creates "Thirty-six Views of Mt *Fuji*" 〈『富嶽三十六景』〉
	1853	◆ Commodore Perry arrives 〈ペリー来航〉
	1858	◆ Unequal commercial treaty with United States signed, followed by similar treaties with the Netherlands, Russia, Britain, and France 〈日米修好通商条約調印〉
Meiji (明治)	1868	◆ *Meiji* Restoration and *Boshin* Civil War 〈明治維新・戊辰戦争〉
	1871	◆ Abolition of the *han* system 〈廃藩置県〉
	1877	◆ *Satsuma* Rebellion, last major rebellion against *Meiji* government reforms 〈西南の役〉
	1889	◆ The Constitution of the Empire of Japan is promulgated 〈大日本帝国憲法発布〉
	1890	◆ First session of Imperial Diet is held 〈帝国議会開設〉 ◇ *Mori Ougai* writes *Maihime* (The Dancing Girl) 〈『舞姫』〉
	1894	◆ Anglo-Japanese Commercial Treaty providing for abolishment of extraterritoriality signed, the first revision of unequal treaties 〈第 1 次条約改正〉 ◆ Outbreak of Sino-Japanese War 〈日清戦争〉
	1904	◆ Outbreak of Russo-Japanese War 〈日露戦争〉
	1905	◇ *Natsume Souseki* writes *Wagahai wa Neko de Aru* (I am a Cat) 〈『吾輩は猫である』〉
	1910	◇ *Mushanokouji Saneatsu*, *Shiga Naoya*, and others establish *Shirakaba* (White Birch) school of writing 〈『白樺』創刊〉
	1911	◆ Second revision of unequal treaties, recognizing Japan's right to set own tariffs 〈第 2 次条約改正〉
Taishou (大正)	1914	◆ First World War 〈第一次世界大戦〉
	1915	◇ *Akutagawa Ryuunosuke* writes *Rashoumon* 〈『羅生門』〉
	1923	◆ Great *Kantou* Earthquake leaves 140,000 dead or missing 〈関東大震災〉
	1925	◆ Peace Preservation Law enacted to quell communists and anarchists prior to enactment of universal (manhood) suffrage 〈治安維持法発布〉
	1931	◆ Manchurian Incident 〈満州事変〉

Period	Year	Events
Shouwa (昭和)	1937	◆ Sino-Japanese incident 〈日華事変〉
	1939	◆ Start of Second World War (Germany invades Poland) 〈第二次世界大戦〉
	1941	◆ Japanese attack on Pearl Harbor triggers Pacific War 〈太平洋戦争〉
	1945	◆ Atomic bombs dropped on *Hiroshima* and *Nagasaki* 〈原爆投下〉
		◆ Japan accepts terms of Potsdam Declaration and surrenders unconditionally 〈ポツダム宣言受諾〉
		◆ *Zaibatsu* business combines broken up in effort to democratize economy 〈財閥解体〉
	1946	◆ Agrarian land reforms instituted 〈農地改革〉
		◆ *Toukyou* Tribunal convened 〈極東国際軍事裁判〉
		◆ Postwar Constitution promulgated 〈日本国憲法公布〉
	1950	◆ Outbreak of Korean War 〈朝鮮戦争〉
	1951	◆ San Francisco Peace Treaty signed with 48 nations. Prime Minister *Yoshida Shigeru* signs Mutual Security Treaty with United States 〈平和条約・日米安保条約調印〉
	1953	◇ NHK begins television broadcasting 〈NHKテレビ放送開始〉
	1954	◆ Police Law and Self-Defense Forces Law enacted and Defense Agency established 〈自衛隊発足〉
	1960	◆ U.S.-Japan Security Treaty revised 〈日米新安保条約調印〉
	1964	◇ *Toukaidou shinkansen* goes into operation 〈東海道新幹線開通〉
		◇ 20th Olympics held in *Toukyou* 〈東京オリンピック開催〉
	1970	◇ Expo '70 in *Oosaka* held 〈大阪万国博〉
	1972	◆ Joint communique issued by Prime Minister *Tanaka Kakuei* and Chinese Premier Zhou Enlai marks normalization of Japan's relations with People's Republic of China 〈日中国交回復〉
	1973	◆ Prices skyrocket with first oil crisis 〈石油ショックによる狂乱物価〉
	1976	◆ Former Prime Minister *Tanaka* arrested in connection with the Lockheed scandal 〈ロッキード事件で田中元首相逮捕〉
	1988	◇ World's longest underwater tunnel (approx. 54km) opened between *Aomori* and *Hakodate* 〈世界最長(約54km)の青函海底トンネル開通〉
Heisei (平成)	1989	◇ Consumption Tax introduced 〈消費税導入〉
	1995	◆ Great *Hanshin-Awaji* Earthquake 〈阪神・淡路大震災〉
	1995	◆ Sarin terrorist incident 〈オウム真理教徒によるサリン事件〉
	1998	◇ Japanese Big Bang finance reform 〈日本版ビッグバン開始〉
	1999	◆ Accident at the uranium refining plant in *Toukaimura* 〈東海村のウラン加工施設で臨界事故〉
	2001	◇ Home Electricity Recycling Law 〈家電リサイクル法施行〉

Japanese Index
日本語索引

お，オ

か，カ

さ，サ

し，シ

す，ス

せ，セ

そ，ソ

た，タ

ち，チ

つ，ツ

て，テ

と，ト

な，ナ

に，ニ

ぬ，ヌ

ね，ネ

の，ノ

は，ハ

ひ, ヒ

ふ, フ

へ, ヘ

ほ, ホ

English Index
英語索引

N, n

O, o

P, p

R, r

U, u

V, v

W, w

Y, y

Z, z

日本タテヨコ
(JAPAN AS IT IS)
〈改訂第4版〉

1985年11月16日　初版発行
1990年4月2日　第2版発行
1997年4月25日　第3版発行
2002年1月8日　第4版発行
2004年4月1日　第4版第5刷発行

発行人　東樹正明
印刷所　株式会社 廣済堂

発行所　株式会社　学習研究社
〒145-8502 東京都大田区上池台4-40-5

★この本に関するお問い合わせは，次のところへ
お願いします。
●電話の場合は――
a. 編集内容について：編集部直通　03-3726-8373
b. 在庫・不良品について：出版営業部　03-3726-8154
c. その他：学研お客様センター　03-3726-8124
●文書の場合は――
〒146-8502 東京都大田区仲池上1-17-15
学研お客様センター「日本タテヨコ」係
学研の辞典に関する情報は――
http://www.gakken.co.jp/jiten/

140°
142°
144°
146°
オホーツク海
SEA OF OKHOTSK
44°
0 100km
北海道
Hokkaido
札幌
Sapporo
42°
中国地方
Chugoku District
34°
島根
Shimane
鳥取
Tottori
山口
Yamaguchi
広島
Hiroshima
岡山
Okayama
福岡
Fukuoka
佐賀
Saga
福岡
Fukuoka
香川
Kagawa
長崎
Nagasaki
大分
Oita
愛媛
Ehime
徳島
Tokushima
32°
熊本
Kumamoto
高知
Kochi
四国地方
Shikoku District
宮崎
Miyazaki
鹿児島
Kagoshima
九州地方
Kyushu District
130°
0 100 200km
132°

MAP OF JAPAN

136°
138°
140°
142°
40°
38°
36°
27°
26°
128°
日　本　海
SEA OF JAPAN
太　平　洋
PACIFIC OCEAN
青森
Aomori
秋田
Akita
岩手
Iwate
東北地方
Tohoku District
山形
Yamagata
宮城
Miyagi
仙台
Sendai
石川
Ishikawa
新潟
Niigata
福島
Fukushima
富山
Toyama
福井
Fukui
岐阜
Gifu
長野
Nagano
群馬
Gunma
栃木
Tochigi
関東地方
Kanto District
中部地方
Chubu District
埼玉
Saitama
茨城
Ibaraki
滋賀
Shiga
名古屋
Nagoya
東京
Tokyo
三重
Mie
静岡
Shizuoka
千葉
Chiba
横浜
Yokohama
愛知
Aichi
神奈川
Kanagawa
近畿地方
Kinki District
山梨
Yamanashi
沖縄
Okinawa
0
50km